KU-431-812

Diana Preston is an Oxford-trained historian, writer and broadcaster who lives in London. She is the author of *The Road to Culloden Moor: Bonnie Prince Charlie and the '45 Rebellion*; *A First Rate Tragedy: Robert Falcon Scott and the Race to the South Pole*; *Besieged in Peking: The Story of the 1900 Boxer Rising* and *Wilful Murder: The Sinking of the Lusitania*. Michael Preston, Diana Preston's husband, read English at Oxford University and is now an historian and traveller.

WITHDRAWN

A PIRATE
OF EXQUISITE MIND

The Life of William Dampier:
Explorer, Naturalist and Buccaneer

DIANA & MICHAEL PRESTON

CORGI BOOKS

CONTENTS

Acknowledgements 7

Prologue 15

PART I. THE ADVENTURER

I   'A Self-Conceited Young Man' 41

II   'A Great Prospect of Getting Money Here' 56

III   'To Seek a Subsistence' 73

IV   'A Door to the South Seas' 84

PART II. THE BUCCANEER

V   'That Sacred Hunger of Gold' 99

VI   'Two Fat Monkeys' 120

VII   The *Bachelor's Delight* 141

VIII   The Enchanted Islands 158

IX   'We Ran for It' 175

PART III. THE TRAVELLER

X   'You Would Have Poisoned Them' 197

XI   'As White as Milk and as Soft as Cream' 210

XII   'This Mad Crew' 227

XIII   'New-Gotten Liberty' 244

XIV   'Our Little Ark' 257

XV   Gut Rot and Gunpowder 268

XVI   The Painted Prince 286

PART IV. THE CELEBRITY

XVII   The Rover's Return 303
XVIII   'Good Copy' 322
XIX   'Dampier's *Voyage* Takes so Wonderfully' 339
XX   Kiss My Arse 350
XXI   Shark's Bay 370
XXII   'A Flame of Fire' 383
XXIII   'Not a Fit Person' 395

PART V. THE ANCIENT MARINER

XXIV   'Brandy Enough' 415
XXV   The Manila Galleon at Last 427
        Epilogue 448

Notes and Sources 463
Bibliography 483
Picture Credits 491
Index 493

ACKNOWLEDGEMENTS

We are indebted to several individuals and organizations in the United Kingdom for their help and expertise: Peter Allmond, Bodleian Library, Oxford, who traced some rare publications; Dr Serena Marner of the Fielding-Druce Herbarium, Oxford University, for showing us the botanical specimens Dampier brought back from New Holland, New Guinea and Brazil; Mike Dorling, Collections Manager, the Sedgwick Museum of Earth Sciences, Cambridge, for access to the stone axe and slingshot Dampier brought back from his voyages. Dr James Kelly, Worcester College, Oxford, for his guidance on the story of the buccaneers and, in particular, for sharing his knowledge of Captain Sharp and of the parallels between Dampier's and Defoe's writings; Professor Glyndwr Williams for his insight into the early history of Europeans in New Holland; Tim Severin for guidance on visiting the Darien; Patric Dickinson, Richmond Herald, College of Arms, for help with sources; and Richard Timmis for his kindness in allowing us to visit Hymerford House, and Pat Switzer, who gave us a fascinating tour. Our thanks also to the staff and archivists of the Bodleian Library, the British Library, the London Library, the Royal Society, the Public Record Office, the Guild Hall Library, the Bristol Central Library, the Bristol Record Office, the Somerset Record Office, and the Bury St Edmunds branch of the Suffolk Record Office.

In Australia, we greatly appreciated the help of Dr Mike

McCarthy, of the Western Australia Maritime Museum, who advised us on our Australian research and travel, as well as sharing his experiences of his discovery of the wreck of the *Roebuck* off Ascension Island. We are also grateful to the Aboriginal communities of One Arm Point, especially Irene Davey, and of Bidyadanga, especially Edna Hopiga, Lenny Hopiga, Norman Munroe and Gordon Marshall, for allowing us to visit Dampier's landing sites at Karrakatta and Lagrange Bays. Both communities generously shared their people's memories with us. We also appreciated the advice and expertise of Alex George and Roberta Cowan about Dampier and the flora and fauna of Western Australia, and the help of Hugh Edwards and Les Moss, who shared their knowledge of the history of Western Australia and Shark Bay in particular. The State Library of New South Wales gave us useful advice on sources. In addition, we thank Daniel Balint and Geoff Parker in Broome, who facilitated our visits to Karrakatta and Legrange Bays; Heath and Travis Francis, who took us in their boat to Dirk Hartog Island; Quoin Sellenger and Lini Ironfield of the Monkey Mia Dolphin Resort; Alex Dent, who led us into the bush; and Qantas, Skywest Airlines, and the Western Australia Tourist Commission, which helped make our visits possible.

In the United States, we are grateful in particular to Dr Joel Baer of Macalester College, who generously shared some of his own research with us and pointed us to other potential sources of information; Dr Susan Solomon for advice about the history of meteorology; and Lily Bardi-Ullmann, who once again tirelessly tracked down rare publications. We would also like to thank Jean Merritt Mihalyka for her advice about the Accomack County Records and the staffs of the Virginia Record Office, the Mariners' Museum, Newport News, the Jamestown Museum, the College of William and Mary, Williamsburg, and the Peabody Essex Museum, Salem, for their helpful responses to our requests for information.

In Panama, our thanks go to Marco Gandasegui of Ancon Expeditions, who arranged for us to see as much of the Darien associated with Dampier as was possible, given armed activity in some places, and to our guide, naturalist Alvaro Perez, who not only saved us from snakes but opened our eyes to the beauty of the rainforest. In Jamaica, Colin MacDonald's insights, as he took us around Spanish Town and to the site of Bybrook, were invaluable. In Hong Kong, we appreciated the advice of the Hong Kong Geographical Society, in particular Jacs Taylor-Smith, Catherine Hui, and Ron Clibborn-Dyer, about St. John's Island. For our trip to the Galapagos, we are grateful to David Howells of Galapagos Adventure Tours, to our guide, Juan Talapia, and to the crew of the sailing yacht *Sulidae*. In Southeast Asia, we are grateful to Robert Scoble for his advice on the history of the region and for helping us arrange our travel. Our grateful thanks also to the crew of the brigantine *Soren Larsen* for sharing their knowledge of the sea and sailing ships and for tolerating our landlubberly attempts at rope hauling, steering and sail-setting with kindness and good humour.

The advice of our agents, Bill Hamilton in London and Michael Carlisle in New York, has, as usual, been invaluable. So has the support and encouragement of George Gibson and his excellent team at Walker & Company in the United States and of Marianne Velmans at Transworld/Doubleday in the United Kingdom. Family and friends have as ever been generous with their support and encouragement. We especially want to thank St John Brown, Clinton Leeks, Kim and Sharon Lewison and Neil Munro for their insightful comments on the draft, Lydia Lewison for help with Spanish translation, and Donald and Ingrid Wallace for their medical advice, in particular on reasons why livers go black and dry.

A PIRATE OF EXQUISITE MIND

PROLOGUE

One day, in September 1683 in the Cape Verde Islands off the west coast of Africa, William Dampier lay 'obscured' among the scrubby vegetation to do some bird-watching. He was excited. He had just caught his first sight of flamingos. The detail and delicacy of his descriptions would gladden any modern ornithologist. The flamingos were 'much like a heron in shape', though 'bigger and of a reddish colour', and in such numbers that from a distance they appeared like 'a brick wall, their feathers being of the colour of new red brick'. They nested in shallow ponds 'where there is much mud which they scrape together making little hillocks like small islands . . . where they leave a small, hollow pit to lay their eggs . . . They never lay more than two eggs . . . The young ones are at first of a light grey.'

Then, as a practical and hungry seventeenth-century sailor, and to the probable revulsion of an ornithologist, Dampier noted the birds' culinary qualities: 'The flesh is lean and black yet very good meat' . . . their tongues have 'a large knob of fat at the root which is an excellent bit, a dish of flamingoes' tongues being fit for a prince's table'.

Dampier also observed the movements of the tides, currents and winds around the islands, meticulously recording them in his journal. He would later use such data to draw far-reaching conclusions about their behaviour and

*Engraving of William Dampier
from a portrait by Thomas Murray.*

the relationships between them. However, he would fail to mention that while he was deep in these worthy scientific observations, his companions were otherwise engaged in plotting to seize a better ship for the piratical voyage to the South Seas on which they and Dampier were bound.

These scenes highlight the contradictions in the career

and character of William Dampier. His portrait in London's National Portrait Gallery shows a lean, strong-featured man with a thoughtful expression, brown shoulder-length hair and a plain coat, holding a book in his hand. He is styled 'Pirate and Hydrographer', but even that tells only part of his story. He was a pioneering navigator, naturalist, travel writer and explorer as well as hydrographer who was, indeed, quite happy to seek his fortune as a pirate.

In his early years Dampier was an adventurer, fighting with the buccaneers preying on Spanish ships and the towns and villages of the Spanish Main. He marched with a buccaneer army through dense, humid, snake- and spider-infested jungles and over the Isthmus of Panama in search of Spanish gold. He might well have been hanged at London's Execution Dock and his tarred corpse exhibited as a warning like that of Captain Kidd. Instead he became the first man to voyage three times around the world, recording nature with passion, even obsession. The books he wrote based on his observations brought him from obscurity to celebrity, changed scientific perceptions and altered the literary landscape.

Dampier's best-selling, rollicking accounts of his voyages (*A New Voyage Round the World* in 1697, *Voyages and Descriptions* in 1699, and *A Voyage to New Holland* published in two parts in 1703 and 1709) aroused an enthusiasm for travel writing which made it the most popular form of secular literature for the next quarter of a century and beyond. His books fuelled the imaginations of Jonathan Swift and Daniel Defoe.

Dampier's understanding and mapping of winds and currents were pioneering. James Cook and Horatio Nelson studied his methods and used his maps. He, not Cook, was the first Englishman to lead an expedition to Australia and to document its wildlife. His work as a naturalist influenced Alexander von Humboldt and Charles Darwin, who used his acute observations and detailed descriptions as building blocks for their theories. Humboldt admired 'the remarkable English buccaneer' to whose works he thought 'the subsequent studies of great European scholars, naturalists and travellers had added little'. Although born nearly a century after Dampier's death, Darwin found his work 'a mine' of information and felt so familiar with him that he referred affectionately to 'old Dampier' in his diary.

Dampier lived at a time of physical and intellectual curiosity, when enquiry was fashionable and ingenuity admired. The seventeenth century saw a revolution in the approach to natural philosophy, as science was then usually known. In Britain, Francis Bacon, who died in 1626, was the pioneer. He saw clear parallels between geographic and the expansion of scientific knowledge. He advocated setting aside reliance on ancient texts and artificial divisions imposed by ancient philosophers in favour of experiments: 'Whether or no anything can be known can be settled not by arguing but by trying.' Bacon thought that science was a single body of knowledge capable of continuous and unlimited development by the ingenious and curious based on data they had collected from around the world. It was not an end in itself but a means of improving the human condition. Bacon thought 'there is much ground for hoping that there are still laid up in the womb of nature many secrets of excellent use'.

The Royal Society, given its royal charter by Charles II in 1662, put Bacon's philosophy into practice. In this 'learned and inquisitive age' its goal was 'to overcome the mysteries of all the works of nature . . . for the benefit of human life' and to undertake 'an universal constant and impartial survey of the whole of creation'. In its work the society emphasized building up a large body of observations, not only of unusual phenomena but also of the normal and commonplace, which it rightly considered the more helpful to understanding.

Fellows included scientists, writers such as John Evelyn and John Dryden, aristocrats and men-about-town. Sometimes their discussions were erudite and highly significant, as when they debated the work of the chemist Robert Boyle, the astronomer Edmund Halley and the physicist Isaac Newton. This emphasized the mechanical nature of the world, in which identified cause produced observed effect and study brought understanding of the order and symmetry governing Creation. Sometimes the discussions were more speculative – for example, when they considered 'the scheme of a cart with legs instead of wheels' or whether two pigs with 'human faces' had been engendered by a man copulating with a sow. At other times, casual conversations have an uncanny prescience. They talked of spectacles for seeing in the dark (or night-vision goggles). The minutes recorded the following exchange: 'Mr Boyle mentioned, that he had been informed, that the much drinking of coffee did breed the palsy. The Bishop of Exeter seconded him and said that himself had found it to dispose to paralytical effects . . . Dr Whistler suggested that it might be enquired whether the same persons did take much tobacco.'

Guided by a desire to study subjects with practical applications, the society instigated research into marine topics to improve knowledge of the sea and hence the reliability of sea travel. To aid them, they drew up and regularly updated *Directions for Seamen Bound for Far Voyages*. These directions asked seamen to 'study nature rather than books and from the observations made to compose such a history of her, as may, hereinafter, serve to build a solid and useful philosophy upon'. Dampier was the only 'far voyager' to respond. He went further than providing new, accurate and comprehensible observations by advancing theories about how his data should be interpreted. The society summarized his work in its *Transactions* as soon as it was published and invited him to address its fellows – both rare accolades.

Dampier's 'A Discourse of Trade-Winds, Breezes, Storms, Seasons of the Year, Tides, and Currents', included in his second book, established his reputation as a hydrographer beyond challenge. A classic of its era, it has been quoted ever since by scientists and meteorologists. The 'Discourse' differentiated between the various types of winds, such as the steady trade winds and the seasonal monsoons. Dampier distinguished for the first time between tidal streams, which flowed near the shore and regularly reversed their directions, and ocean currents, which flowed farther out, usually in the same direction. He established that the region of equatorial currents coincided with that of the trade winds and was the first to deduce correctly from these observations that the winds were the cause of the currents.

At this time Edmund Halley was also investigating wind patterns. Both Dampier and Halley produced maps that became landmarks in the early history of scientific knowledge of prevailing winds, but Dampier's were the more accurate and complete. Dampier alone and for the first time created a wind map of the Pacific, a region of which Halley was ignorant, and Dampier's maps, not Halley's, became the prototype for the many maps and globes picturing the trade winds that appeared throughout the eighteenth century.

Dampier's lack of prejudice and inextinguishable curiosity made him an instinctive, intuitive naturalist. He pioneered what is today known as descriptive botany and zoology, later developed by Joseph Banks, the naturalist who sailed with Captain James Cook – the careful, detailed, and objective recording of the world's living things. New sights, sounds and smells consumed Dampier. He was one of the first Englishmen to document the effects of marijuana, recording: 'Some it keeps sleepy, some merry, some putting them into a laughing fit, and others it makes mad.'

The first naturalist to visit all five continents and to travel widely in areas largely unknown to Europeans, Dampier was able to compare and contrast animals, birds, reptiles and plants across the globe. He was among the first party of Britons to visit the Galapagos Islands. Here, his scientific observations of marine green turtles led him to write that they were 'bastard' green turtles compared with those in the Caribbean, thus suggesting location-dependent differences within species and prefiguring Darwin. Dampier's continuing deep interest in such relationships later led him, in a study of Brazilian water-fowl, to introduce *sub-species*, both as a word and as a concept. Darwin later regularly referred to Dampier's works during the voyage of the *Beagle*. The famous red notebook in which Darwin first formulated his theory of natural selection quotes observations from Dampier.

Dampier was the only major British maritime explorer between Francis Drake and his fellow adventurers of the sixteenth and early seventeenth centuries and James Cook and his fellow naval expeditioners in the mid- to late eighteenth century. He uniquely bridged those two eras, fusing the piratical plundering and derring-do of the former with the scientific inquiry and meticulous chart and record keeping of the latter.

An inspired navigator, Dampier during his three circumnavigations pioneered sea passages for those who came after him, measuring distances more precisely than his predecessors. He pinpointed the location of islands, while giving practical tips on the best approaches through reefs, tidal races and shoals. He did not have the sophisticated navigational instruments that would appear during the eighteenth century. But even with them, the British navy still used Dampier's 'Discourse' – well into the twentieth century in fact – because of its accuracy and attention to detail.

Dampier was among the first recorded party of Britons to set foot on Australia, eighty years or so before Cook. He returned there in command of the English Admiralty's *Roebuck* expedition, the first specifically planned voyage of scientific and geographic exploration and hence the forerunner of the expeditions of Cook and Darwin. The artist he took with him drew the earliest known images of Australian flora and fauna. Despite shipwreck, Dampier brought home the first collection of botanical specimens from that unknown land. Cook took Dampier's books on all his voyages, and his journals and those of his officers often refer to them as sources of 'accurate' and authoritative information.

But perhaps Dampier's greatest gift was to convey in words to his fellow countrymen the frontiers opening up around them. His were the first modern travel books. *The Works of the Learned*, the first literary magazine in English, recommended his books to the 'sedentary' traveller for the 'variety of descriptions and surprisingness of the incidents'. Like a modern backpacker, he travelled out of curiosity for its own sake, not merely in hope of commercial and political gain. As well as being a sound recorder of facts, he was sufficiently skilled to infuse and enthuse his readers with the excitement he felt. More than a century later Alexander von Humboldt still called him 'the finest of all travel writers', and the poet Samuel Taylor Coleridge advised contemporary travel writers 'to read and imitate him'.

Dampier's writings inspired a 'rational wonder' at what he had seen, and his simple English and homely similes connected the lives of his readers to a new and broader world. A hummingbird was 'a pretty little feathered creature, no bigger than a great, over-grown wasp'. An armadillo had 'a small head' with 'a nose like a pig'. A poison blow-dart was 'like a knitting needle', and St Elmo's Fire like a glowworm. Dampier was the first to compare the vast expanse of the flat ocean to the surface of the millpond so familiar to English country dwellers. His occasional whimsical asides are reminiscent of Tristram Shandy, for example, when he gave personality to clouds gathering before a storm, describing them as 'pressing forwards as if all strove for precedency'.

Dampier can claim more than 1,000 entries in the *Oxford English Dictionary*. To take only the first three letters of the alphabet, he gave to the English language such words as *avocado*, *barbecue*, *breadfruit*, *cashew* and *chopsticks*. He was the first to write in English about Southeast Asia, describing the taste and manufacture of soy sauce and of what we now know as Thai fish sauce. He described government structures and the social practices of peoples and rulers he encountered. Anyone researching the places Dampier visited (such as the Chinese coast, the Pacific islands, and the logwood settlements on the Caribbean coast of Mexico) often finds him cited as the earliest and frequently the only authority for his period.

The literary world embraced him. The diarist John Evelyn wrote, 'I dined with Mr Pepys, where was Captain Dampier, who had been a famous buccaneer.' Dampier opened other writers' eyes to new possibilities in human experience and primed their imaginations. Without Dampier there might have been no Yahoos, no Robinson Crusoe, no Man Friday. Daniel Defoe studied Dampier's voyages, including his accounts of his shipwreck on the uninhabited Ascension Island, of his tattooed companion, the painted prince, and of a Moskito Indian named William, marooned for three years on the Pacific island of Juan Fernandez – as well as the testimony of Scottish sailor Alexander Selkirk, abandoned on that same island on one of the voyages on which Dampier sailed and rescued on another. Dampier's adventures also strongly influenced Jonathan Swift's *Gulliver's Travels*, published in 1726, eleven years after Dampier's death. Gulliver actually refers in the opening passages to 'my cousin Dampier'. A leading biographer of Swift wrote that Dampier's books began the process of replacing fantasy with fact. Swift's fantasies were given a framework of verisimilitude by laconic passages of practical seamanship, coolly lifted from those books.

Like the age in which he lived, Dampier was full of contradiction, contrast and moral ambiguity. He was an opportunist but also a patriot. He wanted desperately to make his fortune but was seduced by the quest for knowledge. He lived a large part of his life with pirates yet managed to preserve what Coleridge called his 'exquisite mind'. He believed that cruelty was the hallmark of the coward, yet while briefly a naval officer was court-martialled

Samuel Taylor Coleridge.

for putting one of his officers in irons and assaulting him. Although he often acted as a peacemaker and an adviser among the pirates who respected him, he was a poor leader. He was a loner who found it difficult to commit himself fully to either people or projects. Neither responsibility nor relationships came easily. He married yet immediately left his wife for twelve years, never wrote of her, and, unlike many of his time, seldom discussed sex in his narratives. His sensuality was expressed through his feelings for nature. He wrote not of carnal delights but of lying on shore, waiting 'to receive the pleasure' of softly wafting sea-breezes.

William Dampier has been largely forgotten.* We knew nothing of him when we found his portrait in a book on

*Except, we later discovered, in Western Australia.

pirates. The juxtaposition of *pirate* and *hydrographer* in the picture title intrigued us. The portrait is not normally on view in London's National Portrait Gallery, but when a helpful curator brought it up for us from the basement, what struck us most was Dampier's sardonic expression, his knowing, watchful eyes. By the time this portrait was painted, we learned, Dampier had confounded the expectations of those who despised him for his background and his buccaneer associations. He had seen much of the world, and his rational brain had analysed what he had observed. His first book had brought his findings to an avid and appreciative public.

We also learned that almost everything known about Dampier comes from his published books. What authors choose, or their publishers think it prudent to allow them to reveal in print, is often far from the whole story. We therefore made determined efforts to trace other documents or artefacts relating to him. None of his original journals have survived. Neither have the drafts of his books except for an early version of his first book, *A New Voyage Round the World*, written by a copyist but annotated in Dampier's spiky hand. Reading this manuscript in the British Library and comparing it with the published version, we tried to recapture Dampier's thought processes as he crossed out, amended and crossed out yet again such tricky passages as the abandoning of his captain on a Philippine island, or debated how best to present his credentials as an author. We pondered why he had added so much natural history material at a later stage than this manuscript draft.

In the Public Record Office we found a mixed bunch of papers referring to Dampier – many documenting legal disputes. Some are neat, official Court of Admiralty records. The copperplate writing looks too prim for the rambunctious events it records, like the argument aboard the royal naval vessel *Roebuck*, when Dampier's second-in-command shrieked that he could 'kiss his arse'. Some still retain the sand used to blot them; some, like the log of HMS *Roebuck*, on which Dampier was shipwrecked off Ascension Island, are water-stained. Yet others are large, yellowing, cracked sheets, folded many times as writers crammed in as much information as possible, because the newly introduced penny-post charged by the sheet. Compared with Dampier's own style, some documents are in stilted lawyers' English; others are ungrammatical, with frequent crossings out; some sailors' depositions are in a clerk's hand, simply signed with a cross as the sailor's mark. Many, including Dampier's own writings, are not easy to read. As we struggled, we were struck by the unchanging nature of bureaucracy and of legal jargon.

Papers in the local record office in Somerset – the county where Dampier was born – are more revealing of Dampier, the man. Letters, including one in Dampier's own hand, lay bare his thoughts and aspirations as a young man working in Jamaica on a sugar plantation. They show his anger at how he had been 'nipped in [his] bud' and his high hopes disappointed. Yet, after more than 300 years, such personal records are tantalizingly sparse. To flesh Dampier out, to get closer to him and understand him better, we decided to track his path across the world.

We began in the village of East Coker, Dampier's birthplace and where his passionate interest in nature first flared. It looks surprisingly unchanged. Thatched stone cottages hemmed by water meadows exude a mellow glow in the afternoon light. Dampier's childhood home still stands – a large, weathered, barn of a building with high

Gothic arches and stone tracery. A carved coat of arms gives it a baronial feel. The arms are not the Dampier family's, but his origins were clearly less humble than sometimes suggested. His determination 'not to slave it', but to see the world on his own terms was perhaps rooted in this substantial, prosperous dwelling.

A network of paths encircles the village. It led us across fields, through woods and along age-old byways edged with oak trees. The grass was a rich, glossy green from recent rain. Here and there the path had dissolved into mud, and the loudest sound was the squelching of our feet and birdsong. We came unexpectedly upon a medieval priory with high-Gothic façade and towering chimneys and were face to face with the past – sharing sights entirely familiar to Dampier in his boyhood. The hedge and field patterns are just as they would have been in the seventeenth century. So are the village ponds with their bulrushes and placidly swimming ducks. The rich, slightly

Dampier's birthplace.

acrid scent of wood smoke was rising from ancient chimneys – the very essence of home but, as events proved, not world enough for Dampier.

We walked over the gentle swell of a hill to medieval St Michael's Church. The afternoon light was ebbing as we entered the dark interior to search for Dampier's memorial brass. The proposal to erect it caused a great ruckus in 1907. A local worthy objected, calling Dampier 'a pirate ruffian that ought to have been hung'. There was just enough light to read the inscription, which begins:

TO THE MEMORY OF
WILLIAM DAMPIER
BUCCANEER EXPLORER HYDROGRAPHER
and sometime Captain of the Ship Roebuck
in the Royal Navy of King William the Third.
Thrice he circumnavigated the Globe
and first of all Englishmen
explored and described the coast of Australia.
An exact observer
of all things in Earth, Sea and Air
he recorded the knowledge won by years of
danger and hardship in Books of Voyages
and a Discourse of Winds, Tides and Currents
which Nelson bade his midshipmen to study
and Humboldt praised for Scientific worth.

As we were taking notes, another visitor slipped inside. He was seeking the memorial of T. S. Eliot. The poet's ancestor, Andrew Eliot, emigrated to America from East Coker in 1660, when Dampier was nine years old. They must have known each other.*

---

*T. S. Eliot himself visited the village only once, but his ashes were buried in 1965 in the church's northwest corner.

From East Coker we, like Dampier, went to sea. Our short experience of life aboard a sailing ship added to our admiration for him. Like Dampier, we preferred 'a warm voyage' and signed on as 'voyage crew' on the brigantine *Soren Larsen* in the Pacific. We learned at first hand how sailors' clothes never get dry. The salt attracts moisture, and shirts and trousers turn stiff as cardboard. The winds rose and the ocean became much rougher than we had expected. As Dampier often did, our captain abandoned our island anchorage for the greater safety of the open sea. We stood legs braced, hauling on the ropes as waves broke over the rocking, rolling decks and foaming water poured through the scuppers. We thought of Dampier leaping squirrel-like into the bow rigging at the height of a storm to spread his coat to catch the wind and angle the ship around.

We also thought of him at 4 a.m. in the moonless rain-forests of Darien on the Isthmus of Panama and wondered whether we had been entirely wise to follow in his foot-steps. Dampier had put his faith in the Kuna Indians; we were trusting in the eyes, ears and snakecraft of our Panamanian guide, Alvaro. 'Shine your torches well ahead of you, not by your feet. Snakes attack the circle of light,' he muttered. Soon he halted abruptly at the sound of rustling. He flicked his torch over tangled leaves, creepers and tree roots. A poisonous four-foot-long brown snake – a 'monstrous adder' just as the buccaneers described – was advancing, spitting. Alvaro grabbed a length of tough, tagua palm we had cut as a walking stick. Sweeping it to and fro in front of his body like a blind man with his cane, he held the snake at bay, shouting to us to run by. We stumbled shakily past, sweating more than either the humidity or lack of fitness justified.

But as the pale dawn light penetrated the canopy, we saw the wild, dappled beauty that had captivated Dampier. Oversized versions of every houseplant we had ever owned, from rubber plants to monsteras, abounded. Monkey ladder vines, up to a mile in length when unravelled, looped crazily across our path. Broad leaves from branches 100 feet above spiralled slowly to the ground. The fine webs of golden spiders – reputedly of greater tensile strength than spun steel – shone in the patchy sunlight. The pervasive sweet almond smell of the rotting fruit of the dipterix tree lingered in our nostrils. Flocks of acid-green parrots flew screeching overhead as we finally emerged into the cleared savannah.

The reason for our dash through the darkness was to reach El Real de Santa Maria de Darien – known in Dampier's day simply as Santa Maria – in time to catch the tide and a canoe downriver. The rivers and their huge tidal rises and falls still govern travel in the roadless western Darien. Our skin prickled as we tramped into the town so often attacked by the buccaneers and the focus of Dampier's 'golden dreams'. Today, nothing remains of the wooden fort, which the Spanish fought futilely to defend. Ironically, though, the town was full of soldiers – weary, wary, combat-hardened Panamanian troops returning from counterguerrilla operations on the nearby Colombian border. Only their commander looked spruce in spotless green fatigues with a black T-shirt hugging his peerless pecs, gleaming jungle boots, designer shades, and drenched in cologne – the epitome of Dampier's chauvinistic vision of the decadent, perfumed don.

The steep riverbanks scaled by the attacking buccaneers

and their Kuna allies remain. We slithered clumsily down them through glossy brown mud just in time to meet our canoe. We did not have to paddle like Dampier. Instead an outboard motor powered us through the liver-coloured waters of the Pirre River. The canoe bucked slightly as we shot out into the wider, fast-flowing Tuira River, leading down to the Gulf of San Miguel on the Pacific coast. Black mangroves with tangled roots crowded the water's edge. Creeks large enough to hide a buccaneer party opened and disappeared within an instant. We asked for the motor to be switched off and, like the buccaneers 300 years before us, bobbed with the ebbing tide out into the clear, blue waters of the gulf. We shared the buccaneers' delight at the sight and tang of the sea after the oppressive humidity of the jungle.

We also felt their vulnerability, as we tossed on the lengthening swells. We landed on a nearby island where the remains of a Spanish fortress, built to keep watch for the enemy, poke through the dense vegetation. We clawed up a steep, gritty slope through spiny bushes and dry leaves, cursing as we snagged our hands and clothes and slipping back two feet for every three we climbed. How, we wondered, could marauders ever have crept unawares on the defenders? Our descent became an involuntary slide on our backsides. As we gingerly picked grit, thorns and crushed insects from our skin and doused our grazes in stinging antiseptic, we realized Dampier's strength of will and his courage.

Our days in Darien had been not unlike his. We had followed Indian guides through the rainforest, watching them make poultices from the leaves of monsteras to treat cuts, just as they had done in the seventeenth century. We had almost collapsed with heat exhaustion. We had waded chest-high across fast-flowing rivers and learned at first hand the difficulties of protecting our notes. Our notebooks were torn and spattered with mud, blood and mosquito repellent. Though our time in the jungle was limited and precious, we had sometimes felt too tired to take notes. We were all the more impressed that, while dodging Spanish patrols, Dampier had found time and energy to mix ink, scratch entries in his journal and painstakingly preserve his papers from water in a stoppered, hollow bamboo tube.

As we continued our journey through Panama, it was equally humbling to discover how accurate Dampier had been. Everything from his depiction of ants 'with a sting like a spark of fire' to the quam – 'a large bird as big as a turkey' – was true. And so it continued everywhere, as we pieced his life together. In Jamaica we followed Dampier's route from Spanish Town through the dramatic limestone gorge of the milky-sage Cobre River to the sugar plantation at Bybrook where he worked. Just as in Dampier's time, a dense mist cloaks it from midnight until dawn. We took slow boats along lotus-choked rivers to Hanoi (in Dampier's time known as Cachao), made the buffeting voyage around Cape Horn, and sampled exotic food from barbecued locusts to prickly pear and durian. The sights, tastes and experiences could have come straight from Dampier's books.

Some of Dampier's most important observations were of the Galapagos Islands. Like him, we arrived in a sailing ship, cruising past islands still clothed with incense trees. On Santiago, we crunched across Buccaneer Cove – the wide, gently shelving beach where the buccaneers careened their ships and where shards of their broken pots have been found. The islands still evoke Dampier's startled wonder. Giant land iguanas, with psychedelic skins of orange, ochre and green, browse bushes of yellow flowers. Round-eyed male boobies lift their great blue feet in their solemn but ludicrous mating dance.

As dusk fell, the sunset coloured the sea and sky pink. Beyond the breaking surf small dark heads popped up like tiny periscopes – turtles preparing to come ashore by night and lay their eggs. Sadly, though, the fabled armies of giant tortoises so relished by Dampier are gone, plundered by successive generations of human predators. The sole survivor of one subspecies is confined to a conservation park. Huge and craggy as a chunk of rock, he munches slowly in the shade of tall candelabra cacti. A bleak and emblematic notice reads 'George, the last of his race'.

Dampier's books prepared us well for Western Australia. We flew up the northwest coast over improbably clear blue seas laced with white surf. We thought of small wooden ships, sails teased by the wind, of Dampier cautiously probing the reefs and dropping the lead line to check the depth. Our first destination was Karrakatta Bay in King Sound, north of Broome, the point where in January 1688 Dampier and the men of the *Cygnet* probably landed. Today, the bay belongs to the One Arm Point Aboriginal community, members of the same Bardi people whom Dampier encountered. The red-soiled landscape looks as arid and unforgiving as Dampier described, but our guide, community leader Irene Davey, explained that 'bush tucker' was all around if you only knew where to look. She showed us vitamin-rich fig, vinegar plum and crab apple trees and pandanus palms, a sure sign that fresh water is near, all of which Dampier and his shipmates missed.

Shark Bay, where Dampier landed in HMS Roebuck in 1699,
eleven years after his first landing in Karrakatta Bay.

Irene described the treacherous whirlpools and strong currents at the entrance to King Sound, remarking 'how skilful – and lucky' the men of the *Cygnet* had been to get through. From sandy cliffs crisscrossed with dingo tracks we looked down on scallop-shaped Karrakatta Bay. We imagined sweating men hauling the worm-riddled *Cygnet* up above the waterline and blows from the carpenters' hammers cracking and echoing out – the first mechanical, metal sounds in an otherwise quiet natural world. This still remote and lovely stretch of coast was probably where white and Aboriginal people first tried to understand each other's worlds and each other's motives. As we wandered, Irene spoke movingly of the impact of Dampier's arrival on her people. She suggested that the Europeans must have looked to the Bardi like the devils from their ancestral stories of the dream time. Perhaps, she wondered, the

guttural words that Dampier heard and recorded were not
gurry, gurry but *narri, narri, devil, devil*.

Next we went south to Shark Bay, where, in 1699, eleven
years after his first visit, Dampier arrived commanding a
royal naval expedition aboard HMS *Roebuck*. We chartered
a boat from the mainland to Dirk Hartog Island, where
Dampier first landed. As we scanned the shimmering,
glinting bay, a great gush of fishy-smelling water exploded
near us, and a dark, forked tail smacked the sea. We were
in the heart of a pod of humpback whales blowing and
breaching. It was exhilarating, though we recalled how
nervous Dampier's men had been, off this same coast,
hearing the 'very dismal noise' of whales 'blowing and
dashing of the sea' all around them in the darkness of the
night.

Once again, Dampier proved an utterly reliable guide.
His map, which we had brought, was so accurate that the
young skipper of our boat, who had never been there
before, used it to pinpoint where we should land. We
splashed ashore on the same arc of blindingly white sand as
Dampier and scrambled into the high-domed dunes
beyond. Today, in a small depression in dunes strewn with
white coral and cuttlefish bone, a plaque commemorates
Dampier's visit. All around, thrusting out of the powdery
sand, we found the same unique, 'sweet and beautiful'
plants that Dampier had gathered for the Royal Society,
and which we had seen preserved in Oxford University.

Like Dampier and the *Roebuck*, we finally headed north
from Shark Bay to Lagrange Bay – a massive safe, sandy
beach. Today, the area belongs to the Aboriginal community of Bidyadanga. Our guide here was an elderly,
gentle-voiced lady, Edna Hopiga, who led us down to the
beach. The tide was out, and the distant sea was just a thin

blue ribbon; the still-wet, rippled sand looked pewter-colored under a heavy sky. A strong, salty wind blew in off the sea as Edna spoke of a story handed down through the generations. It told of a ship that long ago had sailed into Lagrange Bay – the first vessel her people had ever seen.

As Dampier's was the first ship to enter the bay, we were tempted to suspend our disbelief and romantically to believe the ship must have been his, ignoring the reality that the story was probably a fusion of events captured in folk memory. But as we sat with Edna on this peaceful shore, we sensed an additional presence, quiet but determined. That rational, meticulous and objective observer William Dampier was warning us not to be so fanciful.

PART I

PART I

The Adventurer

I

'A SELF-CONCEITED YOUNG MAN'

On 6 April 1674 the merchant ship *Content* sailed down the Thames, bound for the fast-growing colony of Jamaica. Onboard was a nervous, thin-faced young man on his way to work on a sugar plantation. Twenty-two-year-old William Dampier had balked at the last moment. He feared being sold as an indentured servant when the ship berthed in Jamaica. As wind filled the sails and the small vessel began to creak and roll, it was too late to change his mind. However, he had sensibly agreed with the ship's captain, John Kent, that he would work his passage as an able seaman. As such, the law required Kent to discharge him as a free man on his arrival.

Dampier had good reason to be suspicious. The colonies had a ferocious appetite for cheap labour for their burgeoning tobacco and sugar plantations. Agents determinedly roamed London's streets and taverns searching for people to cajole and bully into signing indentures, thereby selling themselves into periods of servitude. Sometimes they simply befuddled them with drink before bundling them up the gangplank; then they took their commission and hastily departed. Their victims sobered up to find themselves at sea. Seaman Edward Barlow often watched such servants going under the hammer in Jamaica and knew the going rate: 'for country men and such as have no trades ten, twelve or thirteen pounds . . . but they that have any trades, they sell for sixteen, twenty, and sometimes for twenty-five pound'.* On the slightest and most dubious pretexts, employers arbitrarily extended the period of indentures without recompense. It was little better than slavery.

William Dampier's position was, he realized, somewhat ambiguous. He had accepted 'a seasonable offer' to go to Jamaica from Colonel William Helyar, squire of East Coker in Somerset, and his late father's erstwhile landlord. Helyar was on the lookout for young men willing to work on his sugar plantation, Bybrook. As a boy, Dampier had impressed the squire with his knowledge of the crops grown by Helyar's tenants. Dampier wrote proudly, '[I] came acquainted with them all, and knew what each sort would produce . . . in all which I had a more than usual knowledge for one so young, taking a particular delight in observing.'

Helyar had provided Dampier with some supplies on the understanding that he would work for a period in return, but there was no formal agreement between them specifying for how long or on what terms. This perplexed Helyar's London agents, Rex Rock and Thomas Hillyard, particularly when Dampier began to demand further items before the voyage: paper, ink and quills, a pair of shoes and a pound of soap. He also insisted on a grater, a nutmeg and two pounds of sugar – essential ingredients for making punch. The two men complained to Helyar 'that William Dampier has been very extravagant'.

Dampier rightly suspected that Rock and Hillyard

---

*Comparisons of money values are notoriously difficult, but to reach modern sterling values, sums should be multiplied by at least 100.

intended to recoup the outlay by indenturing him on their own account, if not that of Squire Helyar, but they had waited too long. They tried to make Dampier sign indentures aboard the *Content* before she sailed, but he protested angrily. He was supported by fellow passengers also on their way to Bybrook – a doctor, carpenter, mason, and the doctor's boy, Charles Wentworth. The carpenter and mason in particular became 'very quarrelsome', fearing they too would be compelled to sign indentures. Customs officials, alerted by the angry shouting on deck, began to ask awkward questions about kidnapping. Helyar's exasperated agents gave up, pacifying the vociferous Bybrook group with shoes, pipes, 'more brandy and a joint of fresh meat'.

The situation degenerated further into farce. An embarrassed Hillyard later confessed to Squire Helyar that 'the person that went by the name of Charles Wentworth that was supposed to be the doctor's boy was discovered to be a young woman'. 'Charles Wentworth' was, in fact, the doctor's mistress. She insisted vehemently that she was a boy until an intimate body search in the captain's cabin 'found her otherwise'. One of the officials suggested that she might even be a murderess escaping in disguise, and she was taken ashore to explain herself. She claimed that, knowing Squire Helyar opposed sending women to his plantation, she had disguised herself 'for the love of her husband'. Rex Rock, determined to see the last of the doctor and his paramour, hastily forged a marriage certificate, perfunctorily ageing it by rubbing it on an old shoe. He also dredged up a witness prepared to swear he had seen the couple married. The stratagem worked: 'The searchers seeing the evidence so plain' caved in and said '"What love is this! . . . God forbid that we should part man and wife." ' Yet further expenditure followed. 'Mrs Wentworth' needed suitable clothes, and Squire Helyar received a bill for shoes, stockings, blue aprons, and a becoming velvet cap, as well as for yet more brandy.

By 11 April the *Content*, with her expensive passengers was out into the Atlantic beyond Land's End. Dampier observed with a practised eye how the favourable winds drove the *Content* 'merrily along'. He was no novice at sea. Born in East Coker the second son of a tenant farmer in 1651, he was lucky to receive a good education, including a grounding in Latin and arithmetic.* A sharp intelligence and a driving curiosity prompted a desire 'of seeing the world'. His father, George, had died at the age of forty when Dampier was seven and his mother, Anne, seven years later during the Great Plague. Orphaned, Dampier persuaded his guardians to apprentice him to a shipmaster in Weymouth. A short voyage to France was followed by a longer one to Newfoundland. The latter left him 'pinched' with cold and with a lifelong distaste of cold climates.

Nevertheless, the sea, and what it seemed to promise, nagged at him. Before long, he was in London, drawn by the densely massed ships anchored in the River Thames whose swaying masts resembled a forest stripped of leaves. Here, at the end of 1670, he was offered the 'warm voyage and a long one' which he had 'always desired'. He sailed downriver on the East Indiaman *John and Martha*, gazing on a city still partly wrecked by the Great Fire four years earlier. The shattered fabric of St Paul's Cathedral lay untouched, awaiting the gunpowder and battering rams

---

* Dampier's elder brother was named George. Two younger children, Thomasina and Josias, survived infancy. Dampier's birthday is not known but would have been shortly before his christening in St Michael's Church, East Coker, recorded on 5 September 1651.

that would clear the way for Christopher Wren's grand new design.

That earlier voyage took Dampier around the Cape of Good Hope to Java in the East Indies. He began to learn the art of 'conning', or navigating the ship. In those days, navigation was indeed such an art that the ship's navigator was often known as the ship's 'artist'. As part of his education, Dampier began to observe the patterns of the winds and weather, how they varied, and how best to use them to secure a safe passage. He found out about the difficulties of navigation the hard way. On the return voyage, poor weather and the consequent inability to navigate by the sun and stars meant that they sailed past St Helena, 'where [they] thought to water and to refresh'. Water was strictly rationed. For 'the first time', lamented Dampier, 'I began to know the value of fresh water for we took in none all our way home from the East Indies'.

Returning to England, he quickly wearied 'of staying ashore'. The outbreak in 1672 of the Third Dutch War provided an opportunity to return to sea. The war was the continuation of an intermittent and bitter trade conflict between the English and the Dutch that had first flared twenty years earlier, and which had, among other matters, resulted in the ceding in 1667 of New Amsterdam to England to become New York. At the age of twenty-one, Dampier enlisted in the Royal Navy, where he served on the *Royal Prince* under the ebullient, hard-living Sir Edward Spragge. His shipmates reputedly included the future pirate William Kidd. Dampier fought in two engagements, experiencing for the first but not the last time the acrid smell of smoke from the guns, shot crashing through oak timbers, the crack of musketry and the screams of the injured. However, he fell ill and in August 1673 witnessed the final engagement of the war from the deck of a hospital ship. Dampier 'languished a great while' in a hospital in Harwich, but as his health returned, so too did his 'old inclination for the sea' and his hunger to travel. Squire Helyar's offer came at just the right time.

The *Content* finally sighted Jamaica towards the end of June 1674. The island had been in English hands since 1655, when Oliver Cromwell's Puritan forces – under Admiral William Penn (father of the founder of Pennsylvania) and General Robert Venables – had seized it from the Spanish. Many soldiers and sailors from among 'the strict Saints', as the Puritan forces liked to be known, had settled on the fertile island. They took over the cattle ranches and cocoa walks abandoned by the Spanish and benefited from generous duty and tax concessions. After Charles II's Restoration in 1660, new waves of royalist settlers arrived with promises of rewards for their loyalty.

Jamaica was an excellent base from which to harass the Spanish Main – as the British called the mainland of Central and South America bordering the Caribbean. Also, the great Spanish treasure galleons carrying silver and gold from Cartagena to Havana lumbered temptingly past within 300 miles. Unsurprisingly, Jamaica soon attracted pirates and privateers anxious to raid Spanish wealth. The Jamaican authorities, first Puritan and later royalist, connived with them, and they had some spectacular successes.

In April 1671, Welshman Henry Morgan sailed triumphantly into Jamaica's Port Royal with loot from Panama, one of the New World's wealthiest settlements. Morgan had sacked the city after crossing the Isthmus of Panama with 1,200 men in less than nine days. As they

Henry Morgan.

retreated, the Spaniards had scorched the country behind them, and Morgan and his men were compelled to chew leather bags to quell their hunger. In a pitched battle before the walls of Panama, Morgan outflanked his enemy and took the city. Morgan's zeal led to an orgy of drunken rape and pillage. In their zest for profit Morgan and his men reportedly used torture, including suspending unfortunate Spaniards by their testicles, to make the citizens reveal their treasure. It took 175 pack animals to carry the booty back over the isthmus to the Caribbean.

Three years later, Dampier stepped ashore into a thriving town of 6,000 inhabitants. It stood on the natural breakwater of a jutting, cactus-covered sand-spit and was already one of the busiest ports of the New World. The deep, wide harbour could accommodate 500 ships, many bringing ever-increasing numbers of slaves direct from West Africa to work the plantations. Others carried anything from lace to grindstones, flints for muskets, and white clay pipes. Warehouses crowded the waterfront. Departing vessels were loaded with sugar, hides, tortoiseshell, ebony, cotton and dyes. The nostril-twitching scent of ginger and cinnamon spiced the dockside air.

Close to the water's edge was the first building thrown up by the English: a small fort with a round tower hurriedly constructed to repel Spanish attempts to retake the island. At the Restoration it was judiciously christened Fort Charles by the ruling Puritans, and the surrounding town, previously known by the English as Cagway, renamed Port Royal in nervous tribute to the new monarch. Some of the 800 or so houses lining the narrow, sandy streets were imposing four-storey buildings, built from the red brick brought out by ships as ballast. They were handsomely furnished with oak tables, chairs and chests, some inlaid with ivory and tortoiseshell, much of it looted from the Spanish and cheerfully sold in the shops of Port Royal. Most citizens ate and drank off Spanish pewter. The wealthy supped off Spanish silver. The thriving population of tradesmen earned twice or thrice what they would have made in England.

Residents had plenty to spend their money on, from bullbaiting and cockfights to alcohol. Port Royal had no

Port Royal in the seventeenth century, drawn by Dampier's contemporary, seaman Edward Barlow.

fresh water of its own. Canoes brought supplies from the site of modern Kingston across the bay, and a high wind could easily mean a day without water. Perhaps in compensation, Port Royal's superabundance of imported alcohol struck contemporaries as remarkable. Given the amount of sugar grown, there was also a huge quantity of cheap local rum, originally called 'rumbullion' and nicknamed 'Kill devil'. Not everyone liked it. One visitor dismissed it shudderingly as 'hot, hellish and terrible'.

All the favourite foods from home were available, but care was needed to prevent meat from spoiling. 'They cannot keep beef past some few days and [even] that [when it is] salted. Otherwise in three–four hours tis ready to corrupt.' But menus provided additional 'very good victuals', in particular the meat of the green turtle – so named from the colour of its fat. Forty sloops were involved at any one time in hunting them in the Cayman Islands and bringing them to Port Royal, where they were kept in pens till needed. They fetched the high price of 'fifteen shillings a piece'. A rather cheaper delicacy was sold by the dozen: rats. One observer rather doubtfully recorded, 'when they have been bred among the sugar canes [they] are thought by some discerning people very delicious victuals'.

Port Royal was famous for sexual excess. Brothels abounded, filled with 'such a crew of vile strumpets, and common prostitutes, that tis almost impossible to civilize' the town, since they were 'its walking plague, against which neither cage, whip nor ducking-stool would prevail'. Men paid 500 pieces of eight just to see 'a common strumpet' naked. These 'hot Amazons' congregated in taverns like Betty Ware's, where seamen duelled with cutlasses in a mad hubbub of 'obscene masculine talk and behaviour' from these women. Their numbers included No-Conscience Nan, Salt-Beef Peg and Buttock-de-Clink Jenny. The most famous of them, Mary Carleton, had recently departed. Of her, a contemporary said: 'A stout frigate she was or else she never could have endured so many batteries and assaults . . . she was as common as a barber's chair: no sooner was one out, but another was in'. Even Jamaica's governor admitted that formerly 'strict puritan Saints' were now among the colony's 'most debauched devils'. The sights so disgusted one cleric that he left by the same ship that had brought him, declaring: 'This town is the Sodom of the New World' and 'the majority of its population pirates, cut-throats, whores and some of the vilest persons in the whole of the world'.

* * *

Dampier and his companions travelled inland from Port Royal to the more sober and respectable Spanish Town, as the old Spanish capital of St Jago de la Vega was known. Here they were given a cordial welcome by William Whaley, the manager of Bybrook and Squire Helyar's godson. The friendly reception left Dampier buoyant. He was convinced his 'critical years' lay behind him and 'future fortune' beckoned. He confidently anticipated a prominent role in running the estate, including keeping the accounts, and enjoying a status similar to Whaley's. The party rode on the ten miles to Bybrook at Sixteen Mile Walk in the parish of St Katherine's.

Encircled by densely wooded hills, Bybrook was sited a few miles below the mountains dividing Jamaica's well-populated south from the wilder northern side. It lay near the southern end of a valley where swift-flowing streams converged to flow into the Cobre River. The soil was coarse, red and fertile. In the evenings a thick mist arose over the valley, growing ever denser until it evaporated with the dawn. It was a dramatic and beautiful setting, despite the fact that one disaffected member of the Helyar family had dismissed it as a 'pisspot'. Dampier was most struck by the beauty of ripe sugar canes as 'yellow as gold'.

Dampier, the doctor and his wife moved into the plantation house with Whaley. The doctor was to be responsible for the health of the dozen indentured white servants who superintended the plantation mill, the boiling house, the sugarcane fields and the stables. Jamaica was not a healthy place. In 1672, a resident lamented, 'The diseases generally are here, at first coming, the flux, which turns to the bloody flux and a violent fever, which

seldom keeps any one above 4 days, for in that space of
time they either recover or die.' Gangrene quickly
invaded the smallest wound. No one then knew that
mosquitoes carried malaria and yellow fever.

The universal remedy was bleeding. Despite some
recent pioneering experimental work – such as that of
William Harvey on the circulation of the blood – surgeons
and physicians still based their practice on the theory of
humours propounded by the Greek Galen 1,500 years
earlier. They believed there were four humours, or bodily
fluids: blood, phlegm, yellow bile and black bile. These
humours corresponded to the four elements – earth, fire,
air and water – whose qualities were, respectively, dry-
ness, heat, cold and wet, with their origins in the liver,
kidneys, gallbladder and spleen. Disease was caused by the
humours getting out of balance. Therefore the doctor's
skill was to identify which humour was in excess and then
to draw off that excess, usually by letting blood –
phlebotomy.

In tropical climates like Jamaica, ill humours were often
blamed on the cool night air. Europeans were warned:
'Your stomach is ever to be kept warm, either with a cotton
or woollen stomacher, and never go unbuttoned after
sweating, for the wind is cold.' Care with diet could also
help balance the humours: 'For digestion and to avoid the
flux . . . use pepper in all your broths . . . Eat not much flesh,
fruit or saltmeats. Oatmeal, pease, rice, wheat, flour, butter
and Holland cheese [are] your best diet of all.' Of course,
few paid attention, eating and drinking copiously.
Overindulgence in the heat aggravated the bacillary
dysentery to which newcomers were particularly vulnerable. Cures for this often fatal 'bloody flux' – and other
forms of acute diarrhoea – ranged from taking quinces,

grated nutmeg, or opium to those involving warming the rear end – for example, squatting on a heated brick, or proceeding as follows: 'Take a hard egg and peel off the shell, and put the smaller end of it into the fundament or arsehole, and when that is cold take another such hot, fresh, hard, and peeled egg and apply it as aforesaid.'

But if the doctor had enough to occupy him, Dampier soon found he did not. His relationship with Whaley, initially so promising, was falling apart. Dampier believed he had been sent to Bybrook not just as an assistant but to send home firsthand accounts of how the plantation was faring, and bluntly told Whaley so. The plantation manager needed little more convincing that the tactless, self-important Dampier had been sent to spy, and froze him out.

Whaley's position was difficult. He owed his loyalty to Squire Helyar but had his own interests to protect. He had inherited a half share in the estate in 1672 on the death of Cary Helyar, Squire Helyar's younger brother and the founder of Bybrook. Young, impecunious and inexperienced – his previous occupation had been as a purveyor of silk stockings – Whaley had lacked the necessary capital to invest and had yielded his entitlement to Squire Helyar in return for a half share in the profits, which at this stage were modest at best.

Whaley had no intention of allowing an assertive, argumentative, and ambitious young man to report on his progress. He insisted that he 'needed none to keep accounts but himself'. A dismayed Dampier realized that the 'fair promises' made to him by Squire Helyar, more than 4,000 miles away in England, counted for nothing. Worse still, Whaley suggested that the new arrival might care to learn the trade of sugar boiling – provided, of course, he was prepared to indenture himself by the year. When Dampier refused, Whaley reported to the squire that the young man 'thought it an under valuing of him to handle either skimmer or ladle' and refused to pay him any wages.

The impasse lasted four months, during which there was no word from Squire Helyar. There was little enough amusement locally other than to drink. One neighbour, Dr Foster, had grown so bored that he 'had tamed a great snake and kept it about him within his shirt'. It would wind itself 'fast about his arm and drink out of his mouth'. Dampier, left in a vacuum, simply roistered with the doctor and his wife, whom Whaley dismissed furiously as 'the nastiest wasting slut as ever came into a House and one . . . fit to do nothing at all'. He disapproved of her extravagance. Returning after a week's absence, Whaley was shocked to discover that the three of them had gone through fifty pounds of pork. He also doubted the doctor's wife's morals, telling Dampier that she had clearly 'been some whore or other' and that he thought 'she had had the pox [syphilis] by reason of several blotches which she had about her', judgements Dampier had no hesitation in relaying to the doctor, with whom he was 'great cronies'. The indiscretion hardly endeared him to Whaley, who thought it 'a dirty trick'.

Unsurprisingly, the verbal sparring grew more bitter. Soon it turned physical. At the height of yet another heated argument, Whaley gave Dampier 'a good box or two', to which Dampier 'returned the like'. But Dampier had even less money than Whaley and in November 1674 reluctantly signed on for a year's service in return for twelve pounds. It was harvest time, and Whaley ordered him to go to Spanish Town and fill empty hogsheads with the sugar arriving there from Bybrook. Whaley followed in December, only for Dampier to tell him that he 'could not be subject' to anyone and had 'not come hither to slave it, neither would he'. Whaley released Dampier with six weeks' wages – thirty shillings – all he had to show for the nine months since leaving England. He spent most of it getting drunk with the doctor.

Destitute and disillusioned, in January 1675 Dampier wrote to Colonel Helyar that Whaley had been jealous – seeing him 'so diligent', and that consequently he had been 'nipped in [his] bud' and was 'like one led by an ignis fatuus [will-o'-the-wisp]' to disaster. Whaley spitefully discouraged other plantation owners from giving him work, informing them Dampier was too 'lofty' to be useful and – quite incorrectly – that he was illiterate to boot. He also said patronizingly that had Dampier 'been anything ingenious he might have been a good boiler'. Instead he was 'a self-conceited young man and one that understands little or nothing'.

Whaley was far closer to the mark when he wrote to Squire Helyar that Dampier had been 'given to rambling and could not settle himself to stay long in any place' because he still hankered for the sea.

II

'A GREAT PROSPECT OF
GETTING MONEY HERE'

*W*ithin six months of his dismissal by Whaley, Dampier was aboard a small ketch captained by a sailor named Hudsel outward bound from Port Royal to the wild, largely unsettled Bay of Campeachy. This 'deep bending of the land', as Dampier described it, formed part of the southern Gulf of Mexico. Hudsel planned to load a cargo of logwood, a timber prized by European textile manufacturers and makers of ink and furniture for the rich, dark dye extracted from its heart.

By Dampier's time, logwood fetched an astonishing £110 per ton in London, but the trade-minded English had been uncharacteristically slow to grasp its value. After the capture of Jamaica, when English ships began to probe the Bay of Campeachy, they had seized barks piled high with it. Ignorant of its true worth and annoyed not to have found silver, they tossed it into the water or burned it as fuel. Eyes were finally opened when one Captain James, 'having captured a great ship laden with logwood, sailed it back to England', where he found he could sell it at a fat profit. He brought the glad tidings back to Jamaica, prompting eager merchants to despatch vessels to scour the bay for logwood. They discovered caches where the Spanish were leaving it ready-cut, waiting to be shipped. Jamaican seamen helped themselves until the furious

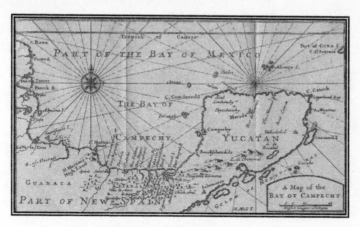

From the original edition of William Dampier's Voyages and Descriptions, *1699.*

Spaniards sent soldiers to end their depredations. After much searching, the English finally came upon the lonely creeks of Terminos Lagoon, lined by mangrove swamps and flourishing logwood trees. It was to this isolated corner of the Bay of Campeachy with its colony of logwooders that Dampier and Hudsel were bound.

Two weeks after leaving Jamaica, Hudsel's shallow-drafted ketch sailed into the lagoon. They anchored off One-Bush-Key – a landing place half-hidden under piles of oyster shells and named for the single crooked little tree that grew there. Years later, in one of the books that were to make him famous, Dampier remembered how the oysters clung in clusters to the roots of the mangroves along the edges of the creeks.*

Soon the logwooders began to arrive, elbowing their way on board the swaying vessel. They were a curious

---

*It was, perhaps, such sights that had sparked stories in Elizabethan times, believed by Sir Walter Raleigh and others, that oysters literally grew on trees.

fraternity leading a tough life, even by seventeenth-century standards. Logwood trees grow in low-lying marshy ground and mangrove swamps – perfect breeding grounds for mosquitoes. During the rainy season in July and August, the men laboured thigh-high in water, their arms stained red from the dye and their skin and hair reeking with the sweet, cloying scent of the yellow log-wood flower. Their main relaxations were shooting wild cattle, drinking binges lasting for days, and occasional skirmishes with raiding parties from Spanish Mexico.

Many were former pirates and buccaneers who had fought with Morgan. They had turned to logwooding because the political fallout from the sacking of Panama in 1671 had forced them from Jamaica. Morgan's expedition had been commissioned by Sir Thomas Modyford, the governor of Jamaica. However, unknown to him, in July 1670 England and Spain had signed the Treaty of Madrid under which Spain acknowledged England's right to hold American colonies, including Jamaica, while England pledged no longer to attack Spanish possessions. The sacking of Panama aroused such an international howl of protest that a new lieutenant governor, the gouty Sir Thomas Lynch, was despatched to Jamaica with orders to arrest Modyford and send him home. A few months later Morgan was also shipped to London, for a time in disgrace, and Lynch began rooting out the pirates operating from Jamaica. The result, as Dampier recalled, was that 'the privateers who had hitherto lived upon plundering the Spaniards were put to their shifts; for they had prodigally spent whatever they got'. Forced to find other ways of subsisting, 'the more industrious sort' had turned to logwooding.

It was a precarious life. Although a clause in the Treaty of Madrid had legitimized those loggers already settled in the Bay of Campeachy, Spain resented them and the growing number of new arrivals. Unable to police the vast territories it claimed to control, Spain could not stamp out the trade, but it harassed the loggers, carrying off captured men as slaves. Dampier's second book, *Voyages and Descriptions*, contains the only detailed, firsthand account of the logwooders to survive. He thought the Spanish attitude towards the trade foolish and illogical: 'It is not my business to determine how far we might have a right of cutting wood there, but this I can say, that the Spaniards never received less damage from the persons who generally follow that trade than when they are employed upon that work.' In other words, they were less nuisance to the Spanish logging wood than being pirates.

The logwooders were eager to trade with Captain Hudsel. No money changed hands. The currency was rum and sugar. Traders dispensed rum by the gallon or firkin in return for logwood priced at five pounds a ton. They also offered their visitors free rum punch to drink. Logwooders had a way of dealing with traders who were niggardly with their hospitality. Those who failed to 'treat all that come the first day with punch' were repaid with the 'worst wood'. The logwooders filled hollow logs with dirt, plugged the ends with a piece of proper wood driven in hard, and then sawed it off so neatly 'that [it was] hard to find out the deceit'.

Hudsel was clearly generous, and the logwooders 'grew frolicsome'. It was traditional to fire off the ship's guns as the party got into full swing, but, as Dampier wrote, 'we had none but small arms to fire at their drinking healths, and therefore the noise was not very great at a distance; but on board the vessel we were loud enough till all our liquor was spent'.*

The freedom and independence of the logwooders attracted Dampier. They lived in small companies of three to ten. They had drawn up a 'Short Compendium of Rules', a code defining a species of democracy that banned capital punishment. Their huts were thickly thatched with palm leaves to keep out the hot, heavy rains. For sleeping, they had a 'barbecue', or wooden frame, raised three and a half feet above the ground and placed against one side of the hut. 'Pavilions', rudimentary mosquito nets fashioned from sailcloth – 'out of which here is no sleeping [because of] moskitoes' – were stretched over the frame and fastened to wooden stakes at each corner. Another barbecue frame covered with earth formed a cooking place,† while a third served as a seat. During the rainy season men stepped 'from their beds into the water perhaps two feet deep, and continue standing in the wet all day, till they go to bed again'. Dampier saw 'a great prospect of getting money here, if men would be but diligent and frugal'.

Hudsel sailed for Jamaica in late September 1675. The return voyage gave Dampier time to reflect on his experiences but also brought home the dangers of trespassing in a region patrolled by the Spanish. Only forty miles into their journey, the crew spied two ships making directly for them. Hudsel thought they must be from Jamaica. Hungry for news and hoping 'to get some liquor from them', since there was now none on board except a few bottles he had 'reserved for his own drinking', he decided to wait for

*He did not mention whether they were downing it in the traditional way, mixed with gunpowder for extra kick.

†Hence the modern term *barbecue,* which Dampier first used in his book.

them. He and his men were only saved from disaster by a seaman from Jamaica named William Wooders whom they had fortuitously taken aboard a few days earlier. Wooders had just escaped from imprisonment on a Spanish ship moored at the town of Campeachy. While awaiting his chance to flee, he had noticed two Spanish vessels preparing to sail for the Tobasco River. He was convinced they were the same as the pair bearing down on them.

Although sceptical, Hudsel ordered his deeply laden ship to alter course. The two vessels immediately followed suit. Hudsel's horrified crew 'were now assured they were Spaniards'. They made frantic efforts to escape what had become a close pursuit, but the ketch 'even when light was but a dull sailor'. For a while they believed themselves 'but a degree from prisoners' when, by good fortune, the wind died. This gave them the chance to alter their sails to take advantage of the sea breeze that soon arose. Hudsel's ship ran before it, just managing to keep ahead of their Spanish pursuers. Then 'the wind freshening on by the coming of a tornado' gave them a chance to make a dash for it. The Spaniards, caught by surprise, fired at them but then abandoned the chase. By nightfall the Spaniards were beyond the horizon.

Danger over, the ketch made tedious, sluggish progress. They drifted among remote islands well colonized by birds. Landing on one, they found quantities of boobies with large, ungainly feet 'flat like ducks'. Unlike most birds, they had round eyes that were pointed directly forward, giving them a comical look.* They were 'very tame' and so thickly packed in their breeding colony that Dampier and

---

*Their name derives from the Spanish word *bobo*, meaning 'clown' or 'stupid'.

A booby.

the others could not 'pass through their quarters without coming within reach of their bills with which they continually pecked [them]'. Dampier was amused by the tactics of some 'old and lame men-of-war-birds' living in an adjacent colony. Like pirates, they preyed on others, invading the booby colony 'to seek for booty'. Finding a young booby unguarded, they assaulted it by giving it 'a good poult on the back' with their bill to make it disgorge what it had eaten. The muggers' victim swiftly regurgitated 'a fish or two as big as a man's wrist'.

The man-of-war bird has the largest wingspan-to-body-weight ratio of any bird, making them highly manoeuvrable and acrobatic fliers. These abilities, as Dampier observed, allowed them to steal from other birds when both were in flight: 'I have seen a Man-of-War fly directly at a booby and give it one blow which has caused it to cast up a large fish and the Man-of-War flying directly

*Man-of-war bird, now more commonly
known as the frigate bird.*

down after it, has taken [the fish] in the air before it reached the water.'

In following days, though, Dampier's delight in new experiences faded. He was by this time thoroughly convinced of Captain Hudsel's incompetence as seaman and navigator. They were also running short of food because, as he wrote years later, his colleagues had not taken his advice to kill and salt fresh food – fish, seabirds, and alligators – 'which we might easily have done'. The increasingly hungry crew anchored off an island near Cuba, and all but the cook and cabin boy went ashore to hunt for beef and hogs in the woods and savannahs. The prospects were not good since they had only 'two bad fowling pieces' between them.

They landed in a sandy and, as they thought, uninhabited bay but were alarmed to discover footprints in the wet sand, probably left by Spanish hunters. On closer inspection they were relieved to see that they looked at least a week old, but they kept a wary eye for ambushers. Dampier tried to catch some of the large, white land crabs that lived in 'swampy, dirty ground' near the sea, but succeeded only in getting his fingers nipped. Their hunting was equally unsuccessful. The captain managed to wound a hog, and he and Dampier followed the trail of blood for a while but lost their quarry in the woods. 'Weary and vext', they returned onboard. Worryingly, there was no sign of two other crew members who had also set off hunting. The most likely explanation seemed that they had been captured by Spaniards from the garrison on the nearby southwest coast of Cuba. 'Thoughts about their danger and our own kept me waking all night,' confessed Dampier. The following morning, he was relieved to hear a gun fired as a signal by the missing crewmen, who had simply got lost. Even better, the men had killed a hog, and, although they had eaten much of it themselves, there was enough for the others to feast upon.

It was a temporary respite. They set sail again, and soon there was nothing left to eat but the rotting contents of two barrels of beef, which they had intended to sell to the logwooders 'but twas so bad that none would buy it'. Every day the crew boiled some six or seven pounds of it in the copper kettle in the galley, then cut it into small pieces and stewed it up again in water thickened with a little flour. 'It did not stink, yet it was', Dampier wrote, 'very unsavoury and black, without the least sign of fat in it.' Water was also running low. The anxious captain, uncertain how long it would take to reach Jamaica given the wind conditions, asked his crew whether they should try to get there or 'bear away before the wind for the South Keys'. Everyone except Dampier was for sailing to the South

Keys, but he insisted this was folly, arguing that they had as little chance of finding food on the keys as on the previous island and that, by the time they reached them, they would anyway be too weak to hunt for it. He urged them to risk a slightly longer voyage and make it back to Jamaica, where they could send in their boat for provisions. Several of the crew were swayed, but the majority voted for the South Keys. For the first but not the last time Dampier, clear-sighted and logical, was overruled. He told his comrades 'we should all be starved', and retired to his berth in a sulk to brood on their stupidity and the days of fasting ahead.

Much to his relief, not long afterward the cry went up, 'Land! Land!' They had been closer to Jamaica than they had realized, and its mountains were in sight. They were home after a thirteen-week meander from the Bay of Campeachy. As soon as they anchored they despatched a boat to buy provisions. They were about to celebrate with a bowl of punch when, unexpectedly, the captain of a New England vessel came aboard with a logwooder, Mr Hooker. The two men were invited into the cabin for a drink. The punch bowl, as yet untasted, sat invitingly on the table. Dampier described with commendable restraint how Mr Hooker announced that 'he was under an oath to drink but three draughts of strong liquor a day, and putting the bowl to his head, turn'd it off at one draught, and so, making himself drunk, disappointed us of our expectations, till we made another bowl'.

The next day they sailed into Port Royal, probably suffering a hangover, and so ended 'this troublesome voyage'. Despite the blundering around, Dampier still found some satisfaction: 'in all these rambles we got as much experience as if we had been sent out on a design'.

* * *

The voyage suggested a new path to Dampier: He would return to the Bay of Campeachy and 'spend some time at the logwood trade'. He purchased hatchets, axes, machetes, saws, 'a pavilion to sleep in', a gun, powder and shot, and took passage back to Terminos Lagoon. Dampier again recorded prominent features – the location of fresh-water, water depth and the approaches to anchorages – which would later appear in his books in sufficient detail to guide future navigators. He described how the Indians had learned from experience to be wary of both Spanish and English ships: 'When they are out at sea if they see a sail they [immediately] sink their canoes even with the edge of the water; for the canoes when they are full of water will sink no lower and they themselves lie just with their heads above water, till the ship which they saw is passed by . . . I have seen them under sail and they have thus vanished on a sudden.'

Dampier arrived in Terminos Lagoon in February 1676 and settled himself in a creek with 'some old logwood-cutters', determined to learn the trade. At this time, about 270 men were living on the lagoon and neighbouring Beef and Trist Islands. Among them was said to be a man who, one day, would be the most successful pirate of all: Henry Avery.

Dampier adapted quickly, observing everything around him from the coco-plum bushes of Trist Island with their plump black, white and red fruits to the grape trees whose wood burned with 'a clear, strong fire' and was used by the men 'to harden the steels of their guns'. One of the keys in the lagoon was named after Captain Serles, who had fought with Morgan at Panama and been murdered by one of his company 'as they were cutting logwood together' – a reminder that violence flared quickly, sparked by the awesome binges in which some logwooders indulged. Dampier witnessed 'many sober men' debauched by such 'careless rioting'.

There were also sexual tensions. Some men lived with Indian women, while the richer loggers might have European women, purchased at Port Royal for thirty pounds apiece. Some had formed homosexual attachments. The Navy Articles passed by Parliament in 1661 stipulated that sodomy in the navy should be punished by 'death without mercy', but no such strictures applied in the lagoon.

When the logwooders became bored, finding it 'a dry business to toil at cutting wood', they went hunting. They were good marksmen and their favourite quarry was the wild cattle. Upon killing one, they hacked the carcass into four quarters. After removing the bones, each man made a hole in the middle of his quarter, just big enough for his head to go through, and then put it on 'like a frock' and trudged home. 'If he chances to tire he cuts off some of it, and flings it away.' Sometimes they hunted swimming cattle from canoes, taking care that an injured beast, plunging about in the water, did not overturn their craft.

As a newcomer, Dampier was paid a ton of wood for a month's work helping to carry 100 tons of ready-cut timber to the creek where a New England ship was expected. The men worked systematically: 'Some fell the trees, others saw and cut them into convenient logs, and one chips off the sap; and when a tree is so thick, that after it is logg'd, it remains still too great a burthen for one man, we blow it up with gun-powder.' The logwooders were 'generally sturdy strong fellows' who could carry some 300 or 400 pounds, but, as Dampier wrote approvingly, 'every man is left to his choice to carry what he pleaseth, and commonly they agree very well about it: For they are contented to work very hard.'

Dampier's main aim was to make money, but his main pleasure was in his new surroundings. When not logging, he went for long walks through the 'pleasant grassy savannahs' and up to the high forested ridges beyond. He observed bears, porcupines, land turtles, legions of lizards and 'four-footed, hairy, sad-coloured' sloths that, he later wrote, could be 'neither frightened nor pushed to move faster'. He was struck by the regiments of aggressive spider monkeys – 'the ugliest I ever saw'. They had 'coarse, long, black, staring hair' and leathery black skin and roamed in groups of twenty or thirty. He was alone the first time he encountered them. They began 'chattering and making a terrible noise; and a great many grim faces, and shewing antic gestures'. Enraged to find Dampier on their turf, they 'scattered their urine and dung about [his] ears' and followed him, screaming. He once shot one and broke its limb, but immediately regretted it as he watched 'the poor creature . . . handle the wounded limb and turn it side to side'. Jonathan Swift would later draw on Dampier's description for his portrayal of the Yahoos.

Dampier picked his way through wet 'mangrovy' land, slithering on the soft yellowish clay covered with a crust of black mould in which the logwood trees thrived. He examined the trees' small, pale green leaves and learned to tell which would be easiest to fell. He noticed how the experienced logwooders selected 'the old black-rinded trees', which required 'but little pains to chip or cut'. The treasured wood at the heart of the tree – the source of the dye – was a vivid red.

Dampier must have kept copious notes, because his portrayal of the armadillo in his book is a model of the descriptive zoology he pioneered:

> The armadillo, (so-called from its suit of armour), is as big as a small sucking pig. The body of it pretty long, this creature is enclosed in a thick shell, which guards all its back, and comes down on both sides and meets under the belly leaving room for the four legs. The head is small with a nose like a pig, a pretty long neck, and can put out its head before its body when it walks; but on any danger, she puts it under the shell, and drawing in her feet she lies stock-still like a land-turtle [tortoise]. And though you toss her about she will not move herself. The shell is jointed in the middle of the back so that she can turn the fore-part of her body about which way she pleases. The feet are like those of a land-turtle, and it has strong claws wherewith it digs holes in the ground like a coney.

As a man who often had to live off the land, he added for others' culinary guidance that 'the flesh is very sweet and tastes much like a land-turtle'.

Dampier became familiar with the 'great, many poisonous creatures in this country'. He learned to watch out for alligators with dusky, yellow bellies lurking in the creeks. The logwooders would always 'keep sentinels out to watch for these ravenous creatures, as duly as they do in other places for fear of enemies, especially in the night, for fear of being devoured in their sleep'. One day, desperate for water, Dampier was forced to drink from a pond within two yards of a group of alligators whose cold eyes were 'looking on me all the while'.

He also watched swarms of ants of all sizes and colours: 'great, small, black, yellow'. The black ants marched in

military-type formation behind their leaders – 'through
our huts, over our beds, or into our pavilions, nay sometimes into our chests and there ransack every part'.
Sometimes there were so many it took two or three hours
for them to troop by. Snakes too were everywhere. Ever
curious about what was edible, he chewed a segment of
yellow snake but could 'not commend it'. He reported that
the yellow snake was commonly as thick as a man's calf but
was sceptical of some logwooders' claims that some grew
as thick as 'a man's waist', writing, 'I never saw such'. The
'spiders of a prodigious size' and 'near as big as a man's fist'
with their dark, yellowish down, 'soft as velvet', amazed
him. Some men used what he called their 'teeth or horns'
as toothpicks or to clean their pipes.

The birds charmed him, especially the hummingbird.
He described how the 'pretty little feather'd creature, no
bigger than a great, over-grown wasp, with a black bill
no bigger than a small needle' haunted the fruits and
flowers. He went on, 'This creature does not wave his
wings like other birds when it flies but keeps them in a continued quick motion like bees or other insects, and like
them makes a continuous humming noise as it flies'.

When Dampier's month was up, some of his group
went off to Beef Island to kill bullocks for their hides.
Dampier described without enthusiasm the process of
stretching the skins on pegs and beating them with sticks
'to strike off the worms that breed in the hair'. Not that he
was squeamish. At one stage a hard, red, angry swelling
like a boil on his right leg became so painful he could
hardly stand. His comrades recommended that he apply
the roasted roots of white lilies to the boil to bring it to a
head. He followed this advice for several days, but nothing
happened. Then he noticed two white specks in the middle

of the boil. He squeezed vigorously until 'two small white worms spurted out'. They were three-quarters of an inch long, 'about the bigness of a hen's quill', and, he noted interestedly, had three rows of black, short, stiff hairs.

Dampier joined a team with three members of his former group, all Scots, but they were not hardworking enough for him. One in particular had already accumulated a good stock of logwood and had little interest in labouring on. Dampier decided that the well-bred 'were generally most careful' to be industrious and frugal, whereas those inured to hard labour who suddenly acquired wealth 'would extravagantly squander away their time and money in drinking and making a bluster'. Dampier clearly identified himself with the 'better-bred'. Characteristically, he also decided he would be better off working alone.

Yet his labours would be for nothing. In June 1676 a hurricane hit the bay. Meteorologists value Dampier's account as the first accurate description of this phenomenon. He was cutting logwood when he noticed how 'the wind whiffled about to the south, and back again to the east, and blew very faintly'. Although the weather seemed set fair, unusually large numbers of man-of-war birds were hovering inland. He dismissed his comrades' view that this heralded the arrival of a fleet of ships. Even more strangely, the water in the creek where Dampier was living began to ebb away. Instead of the seven or eight feet usual at low tide, it became 'almost dry'. Then at about four o'clock in the afternoon the sky turned black, the wind began to blow, and the storm burst over them. In less than two hours, it had flattened all the men's huts but one. Dampier and his companions struggled to shore up the surviving structure with wooden posts. They threw ropes over the roof and tied the ends to tree stumps and huddled apprehensively inside.

The hut was no refuge. A vicious, unceasing rain began to flood the creek. The men secured their canoe to a tree, realizing it would be their only means of escape. There was no prospect of walking to safety. The water was too high, and 'besides, the trees were torn up by the roots, and tumbled down so strangely a-cross each other, that it was almost impossible to pass through them'. They managed to embark and rowed for the sanctuary of One-Bush-Key, only to find that it had caught the full fury of the storm. Three of the four ships there had been torn from their anchors. The remaining vessel could offer only 'cold entertainment', with neither bread, nor punch, nor rum. Dampier and his friends rowed over to Beef Island to find a vessel blown into the woods, flag still fluttering amid the treetops. Dead fish floated in multitudes on the lagoon or lay in gaudy piles on the shore.

In the days that followed the men salvaged goods from the damaged ships. They also went hunting for 'a beef', but a weary Dampier tripped over an alligator, stumbling three times before he got away. It must have seemed the final straw.

III

'TO SEEK A SUBSISTENCE'

After the hurricane Dampier and his destitute companions made their base on Beef Island. They shared it with a small population of Indians who had fled there from the Spanish. Dampier respected the Indians. All his books portray them with sympathetic insight as 'a very harmless sort of people; kind to any strangers; and even to the Spaniards, by whom they are so much kept under, that they are worse than slaves . . . This makes them very melancholy and thoughtful . . . sometimes when they are imposed on [by the Spanish] beyond their ability [to bear], they will march off whole towns, men, women and children'. The Indians who lived in their own villages were 'like gentlemen' in comparison with those who lived degraded lives on the edge of Spanish towns, forced to work by the Spanish for little or no wages.

Dampier's pressing problem was how to preserve his own highly prized independence. Months of hard work in the sweltering, mosquito-infested creeks among screaming monkeys and musky-scented alligators had yielded nothing. He had no reserves of logwood to sell, and his equipment had been washed away. In his account of his life among the logwooders he would write that his dire circumstances 'forced' him to 'to seek a subsistence in company of some privateers' in the Bay of Campeachy. He implied that he was 'with them' but not 'of them' – a fellow traveller observing on the fringes. The reality was different. Physically toughened by months of logwooding and determinedly ambitious, Dampier knew exactly into what kind of company he was getting. The chance to rove appealed to his burgeoning intellectual curiosity, but loot was also a powerful incentive.

Although Dampier described his new companions as 'privateers', they were not. Privateers were 'legalized' maritime raiders given official letters of marque in wartime by their governments to attack enemy shipping, usually in return for a cut of the proceeds, which also had to be shared with the ship's owners. The men with whom Dampier threw in his lot were 'buccaneers' – adventurers whose activities often had no legal sanction and crossed the boundary into out-and-out piracy, when all ships were fair game, and the loot had to be shared with no one. Buccaneering had a long history in the Caribbean, or the 'North Sea', as it was known in Dampier's time. Early buccaneers were runaway indentured servants and slaves, many from French possessions. They settled first along the shores of northwestern Hispaniola and later on the nearby island of Tortuga. Some were white and some black, the latter known as 'cimarrons' or 'maroons'. Over time, a motley and cosmopolitan collection of felons, religious and political refugees and social outcasts joined them. Some were sailors put ashore for mutinous behaviour, idleness, or incompetence.*

Hispaniola's savannahs and dense forests teemed with pigs and cattle left behind by early Spanish settlers. The new

---

*The act of abandoning them to live among the maroons gave rise to the word *marooning*.

arrivals survived by hunting the vast herds. They learned the art of preserving the meat from the Carib Indians.* They sold it in bundles of 100 strips for six pieces of eight, together with tallow and hides, to any visiting foreign ships that defied Spain's ban on foreign trade to its possessions. The dried meat was ideal for long voyages, keeping for weeks until the cook softened it in salt water to make it edible.

Over time the buccaneers developed a code of living. They hunted in small groups of six to eight, and no one was allowed to eat until as many beasts had been killed as there were members in the company. They lived in two-man units in an arrangement called *matelotage*, a kind of single-sex marriage. The two men shared everything, including their dogs and – as not all were homosexual – their women when they could get them. Like logwooders, they sometimes went on massive binges. Alexander Exquemelin – who famously chronicled the buccaneers – landed on Hispaniola around 1666. He reported primly that the 'service of Venus is not forgotten' and that they drank brandy like water. They also had their own indentured servants. When a young man complained that God had ordained the seventh day of the week as a day of rest, he was mercilessly thrashed by his master, who shouted, 'Get on, you bugger; my commands are these – six days shalt thou collect hides, and the seventh shalt thou bring them to the beach'.

Exquemelin described the buccaneers' distinctive clothing: a peaked hat to keep the sun out of their eyes, trousers and boots of untreated hide, and coarse tunics and

---

*The term *buccaneer* derived from the French *boucanier*, meaning people who smoked or cured strips of meat on a frame of green sticks, or *boucan*, over a slow fire fed by animal bones and pieces of hide.

A buccaneer.

shirts. Their garments were encrusted with blood from all
the skinning and butchering and stained with the marrow,
which they called their brandy and sucked from the bones
as they worked. They coated their exposed skin with
lard as protection against the innumerable insects that bit
and sucked the blood from bare flesh.

The Spanish made determined efforts to drive them
out, slaughtering the animals on which they subsisted. The
buccaneers, in turn, went on the offensive, driving their
large, fast dugout canoes, or *periagos*, through the surf in
pursuit of Spanish ships. They graduated to quick, one-
masted sloops that could be rowed as well as sailed. Armed
with muskets, the buccaneers were excellent marksmen,
even from a rocking boat. Their technique was to pick off
the Spanish helmsman and any man working aloft. Then,

lowering their own mast and braving the fire of any Spaniard who dared to raise his head over the rail, they rowed close in under the stern of the enemy ship to jam her rudder and thus disable her.

By Dampier's time the term *buccaneer* had broadened to embrace any adventurer such as himself in the Caribbean bent on assaulting Spanish towns and shipping. Sometimes they attacked on land, sometimes by sea. Dampier's book, however, made the twelve months he spent with them sound more like a nature ramble than a pirate venture. As he and his eighty or so companions ranged in their two boats up and down the tumbling, fast-flowing rivers of the bay, he kept vivid and meticulous notes about everything from the coasts, currents and cocoa walks to ducks and dunghill fowls. Once again, the Indians he saw particularly fascinated him. Modern ethnologists and anthropologists still prize Dampier's books for the clarity and objectivity of his descriptions of indigenous peoples, many portrayed for the first time in English.

He described the Indians' practice of subsistence farming, making 'use of no more land than to maintain their families in maize' and thus leaving much land uncultivated. Dampier noticed how, when hunting, the Indians were careful to kill only the older wild cattle and to leave the young to breed, 'by which means they always preserve their stock entire'. He praised this sound policy of conservation, which contrasted with the 'folly of the English and French who kill[ed] without distinction' and soon had no animals left to hunt.

Indians slept in hammocks made with 'small cords like a net, fastened at each end to a post'. Their homes

contained little furniture, only earthen pots and calabashes
to cook their maize in. In appearance they were

> generally well-shaped, of a middle size, straight and clean-
> limbed. The men more spare, the women plump and fat, their
> faces are round and flat, their foreheads low, their eyes little,
> their noses of a middle size, somewhat flatish, full lips, pretty full
> but little mouths, white teeth and their colour of a dark tawny.
> The men wear only a short jacket and breeches. These with a
> palmeto-leaf hat is their Sunday dress; for they have neither
> stockings nor shoes; neither do they wear their jackets on week-
> days. The women have a cotton-petticoat and a large frock down
> to their knees; with sleeves to their wrists but not gathered. The
> bosom is open to the breast and embroidered with black or red
> silk two inches broad on each side the breast and clear round the
> neck. In this garb, with their hair tied up in a knot behind, they
> think themselves extreme fine.

Dampier recorded the wares of Indian traders, trudging
from settlement to settlement with their miscellany of
knives, scissors, silken thread, faux gold and silver rings
gaudily set with glass stones, and portraits of pale-faced
saints. He was struck by the surprisingly high prices fetched
by 'old hats new dress'd'. With the entrepreneurial streak that
was so much a part of him, he wondered whether there
might be money to be made from importing them.

Dampier's book reveals an increasingly seasoned
traveller but does not dwell on the fact that he was also
becoming a hardened adventurer. He described only one
attack in detail: the taking of a Spanish fort at the town of
Alvarado, near Vera Cruz. It was difficult and bloody. Sixty
buccaneers in two boats attacked the fort. Only after a
protracted assault, in which they lost ten or eleven men,

did they finally capture it. The local inhabitants had meanwhile fled by river with their valuables. The disappointment was intense. No rich pickings, no chests of silver. Yet Dampier still delighted in the discovery of large numbers of tame parrots with yellow and red plumage who could 'prate very prettily'. The buccaneers sent so many of these squawking cageloads on board that there was scarcely room to manoeuvre between them and the sea chests, hen coops and barrels of salt beef.* Sailing out of the Alvarado River, the buccaneers were immediately attacked by seven Spanish ships sent from Vera Cruz to deal with them. Heaving 'all the lumber' overboard, the buccaneers made a successful run for it.

Perhaps it was this close call, together with the arrival of a new logwooding season, that convinced Dampier to go back to Terminos Lagoon. However, by April 1678 he had had enough. He returned to Jamaica, where, with some reluctance, he took passage for England. He regretted leaving behind the freedom of life in the Bay of Campeachy and planned 'to return hither after I had been in England'. Yet he was shrewd and clear-sighted enough to realize that the casually bibulous logwooders would ultimately be no match for the Spanish. In April 1680, the Spanish raided Beef Island and broke up the logwooders' camps. Dampier later wrote with real sadness, 'It is most certain that the logwood-cutters, that were in the Bay when I was there, were all routed or taken; a thing I ever feared, and that was the reason that moved me at last to come away, although a place where a man might have gotten an estate'.

---

*Dampier's account of the buccaneers' love of talking parrots validates later fictional stories of Long John Silver and other pirates with parrots on their shoulders.

* * *

After an absence of four and a half years, William Dampier
landed in England in early August 1678. His experiences
had matured him and confirmed his love of nature and
adventure. He would also have made some money from his
logwooding and buccaneering. Perhaps this was what
prompted him to marry. Also, he was in his late twenties,
an age when men of his time commonly settled down.
Dampier chose as his wife a woman named Judith, who
belonged to the household of Isabella, duchess of Grafton.
She may have been a lady-in-waiting to the duchess, but
very little is known of Judith and no record of the marriage
seems to have survived.

The late seventeenth century was a time of confusion
over what was or was not a legally binding marriage. Some
believed a couple were married in the eyes of God provided that they exchanged simple vows before a witness
and then consummated the relationship. While this was
indeed acceptable under ecclesiastical law, common law
would only confer property rights on those who had
undergone a 'public' ceremony, but the definition of *public*
was elastic. There were many places where marriages
could take place. The least salubrious included the cellar of
London's oldest prison, the Fleet, where ceremonies were
conducted by 'degraded clergymen' for under a guinea, as
well as the forty or so 'marrying houses' in the taverns in
the noisome maze of alleys near the Fleet River.

Dampier and his bride probably had a respectable public
ceremony, given the official recognition later accorded to
Judith. Brides of the time wore brightly coloured silk robes
with red, white or blue garters. After drinking, dancing and
munching on bride cakes, the bridal couple were escorted

to bed. On the way attendant gallants pulled off the bride's garters to fasten on their hats. If she was wise, she had already loosened them to prevent too many wandering hands. (Women wore no drawers and were naked under their skirts.) Her bridesmaids then carried her to the bed-chamber, stripped off her clothes and laid her in the bed, taking care to find and dispose of every single pin to avoid bad luck. Sometimes the bride would wear gloves to bed. Their removal symbolized the coming loss of virginity. The bridegroom was undressed in an adjacent room and led in by his friends.

Departing guests joked about the sexual exploits to follow. Physical pleasures were joyously and frankly acknowledged. Unlike future generations, Dampier's age recognized that sex should be a pleasure for the woman as well as the man. Sex guides informed couples that male and female genitalia were essentially the same, explaining that 'the use and action of the clitoris in women is like that of the penis or yard in men, that is, erection'. It made women 'lustful and take delight in copulation'. Not only were women capable of multiple orgasms, it was desirable for them to have them. Furthermore, young women needed regular injections of semen to cure them of adolescent anemia – the 'green sickness'.

Judith and William Dampier are not known to have had any children, even though there was little by way of contraception in the seventeenth century. Condoms made of sheeps' intestines, nine inches long, three inches wide, and fastened on with a ribbon, were imported from France. They were used to protect against venereal disease, particularly 'the great pox', as syphilis was then known, rather than against conception. A contemporary described them as 'an armour against enjoyment and a cobweb against danger'. But any protection was welcome against syphilis, which began with an ulcerated penis, rashes, open sores, and could ultimately lead to paralysis and insanity. The treatment was gruesome, involving parboiling in mercury vapour and mercury-based ointments, enemas and tablets. The mercury sent the patient into insanity, caused his hair and teeth to drop out, and destroyed the soft tissues of palate and nose. Silversmiths made a good living hammering out false silver noses to conceal where nostrils had once been.

Despite the backdrop of a libertarian age, marriage was above all a financial arrangement. Women outnumbered men by thirteen to ten because so many males were leaving for the colonies, and marriage was a buyer's market for men. A London marriage broker advertised 'a catalogue of women wanting marriage, some young, some not, all tame as a city cuckold chid by his wife'. Many sought wives precisely because they needed capital to set themselves up in business. It is unknown how much money Judith brought Dampier, but unless it was an out-and-out love match, she must have provided some dowry.

Dampier did not have the temperament to expend very much of it on the extravagance and display characteristic of newlyweds at the time. England's commerce and that of its capital city in particular were expanding fast.* Instead of spending Judith's dowry on fripperies, Dampier doubtless invested some of the money in the goods he was soon planning to take out from England to Port Royal to sell. There he intended to buy 'such commodities as I knew I would sell among the Campeachy logwood cutters'.

---

*So fast that Samuel Lee had found it worthwhile to publish the world's first trade directory, *A Collection of Names of Merchants Living in and about the City of London*. It contained 1,953 entries.

In the spring of 1679, only a few months after their marriage, he left his new wife to make what was supposed to be a short trading trip to Jamaica. Instead it would turn into his epic twelve-year journey around the world and make him famous.

IV

'A DOOR TO THE SOUTH SEAS'

Once he arrived in Jamaica, Dampier's plans quickly changed. He sold his goods successfully, but then, 'upon some maturer considerations', decided against returning to the Bay of Campeachy. Perhaps the old spectre of being captured by the Spanish deterred him. Instead he lingered in Jamaica 'in expectation of some other business'. Part of that 'business' was the purchase of a small estate in the rolling Dorset countryside back in England, where his brother George had settled. Clearly, he had made enough money to set himself and Judith up in what would have been a new, but for Dampier familiar, life. His youth in Somerset had prepared him, except this time he would be the landowner, his own man, not 'in thralldom which [he] always hated'. It would be a tranquil, rural, land-bound existence. His cropland would be washed by a soft rain, not ripped by violent tropical storms. Wasps and bees, not mosquitoes and hummingbirds, would buzz among the flowers in his gardens and the fruit in his orchards. Above all, he would be trading his 'rambling kind of life' amid the swaggering male brio of logwooders and buccaneers for a settled domestic life with a woman and, very likely, children.

These latter attractions were not so immediately enticing that they prevented Dampier from accepting a last-minute offer from a trader named Hobby. He invited Dampier to join him on a short voyage to trade with the Moskito Indians along what is now Nicaragua's eastern coast. It was an opportunity to make some money, but Dampier's motivation for accepting went deeper, for he seldom resisted the chance to indulge his curiosity and to see something new. Perhaps, too, it offered an escape from responsibility.

Dampier sent home the deeds for the Dorset estate and set sail from Port Royal, the warm wind in his face. At Negril Bay, on Jamaica's western tip, he and Hobby encountered a buccaneer fleet of nearly a dozen ships. Most of the 500 men aboard were English, but there were also a number from the North American colonies. Their experienced leaders included two of the best-known buccaneers of the day, Bartholomew Sharp and John Coxon, who had both served under Morgan. Although they carried commissions from the governor of Jamaica to cut logwood in the Bay of Honduras, they were instead busily recruiting for a raid against the Spanish. All Hobby's men decided without a moment's reflection to join the expedition. 'Being thus left alone', Dampier later wrote, 'I was the more easily persuaded to go with them too'. It was clearly not a difficult decision. Dampier probably knew in advance whom he would meet at Negril Bay – a favourite buccaneer haunt – even if he did not admit this in his book.

In early January 1680, driven by a 'fresh gale of wind', the buccaneers set course for the Isle of Pines off the Panamanian coast after electing John Coxon as their commander in chief. Almost at once, things went wrong. Most of their vessels were old and leaky, causing one captain to resort to the desperate measure of lashing his ship together with hawsers and cables to keep her afloat.

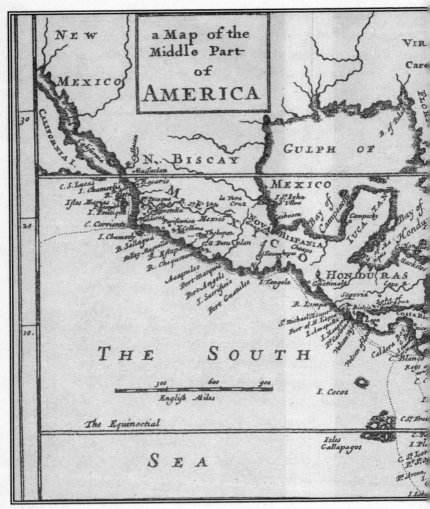

From the original edition of William Dampier's A New Voyage, *1697.*

Dampier, who had joined Captain Sharp's ship, watched as
high winds and strong currents pulled the ships in different
directions. As the weather grew yet wilder, Sharp lost his
bowsprit. Coxon – whose sixty-ton ship mounting eight
guns and carrying ninety-seven men was 'the best sailor' –

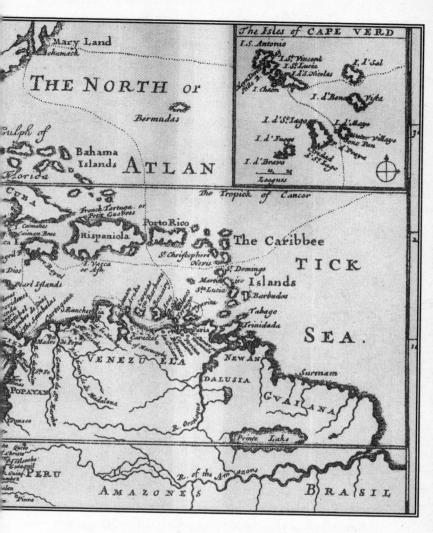

managed to reach the Isle of Pines, where he waited impatiently for news of the others. After a nervous few days some vessels came limping in. There were enough men to make an attack on the Spanish viable, but the question was where. Indians living nearby who had 'a great antipathy towards the Spanish' urged the buccaneers to trek over the isthmus to the Pacific coast. They offered to act as guides and promised rich plunder. Instead, the small army decided to assault Portobello on the north coast of the Isthmus of Darien, as Henry Morgan had done eleven years earlier, three years before his attack on Panama.

The splendid if notoriously unhealthy Portobello – the 'beautiful port' where Columbus had anchored – was an entrepôt where gold and silver were brought to be loaded aboard the Spanish treasure fleet. Spain's economy depended on regular imports of these precious metals. The quantities were enormous. At Potosi, in present-day Bolivia, the Spanish had discovered a 15,381-foot-high 'silver mountain'. By Dampier's time, Potosi was the wealthiest city of the Spanish empire, with a population of 160,000. The Spanish lived in elegant houses, their courtyards bright with flowers and cooled by fountains. They paid high prices for imported goods – four to six times higher than those in Panama – but they could afford it thanks to relays of Indians slaving and dying in a honeycomb of mines, hacking out the ore and converting it into coins in the mills.

Mules carried the Potosi silver through the sage-green Andes and around the reed-fringed shores of Lake Titicaca to the port of Arica. From here it was shipped up the Pacific coast to the city of Panama, built by the Spanish as a staging post on the large bay on the Pacific side of the isthmus. The treasure was carried from the ships, carefully counted and registered, and then loaded on mules and horses. Staggering under the weight of their heavy panniers, the strongly guarded lines of swaying, sweating, snorting beasts wound through the dense jungle and up over the mountains to Portobello.

Each year 'the armada from old Spain' sailed into the

harbour to collect the treasure and was greeted by a gun salute from the fort. The arrival sparked a tremendous nocturnal torchlight fair lasting several weeks. In the flickering light merchants bartered and bickered over everything from spices to silk stockings in their booths made from the sails of ships. There was not a room to be had in the crowded inns or a servant to be hired. Oppressive heat and clouds of mosquitoes and sticky black flies did not diminish the gaiety of the fiesta.

Neither did an average death toll of 300 to 400 people during the course of the fair. For all its wealth and luxury, Portobello was a breeding ground for disease. When the tide went out, it exposed black, stinking mud, which gave off 'noisome vapours, through the heat of the climate'. Their best-known victim was the most famous – or to the Spanish most infamous – of all privateers. In the small hours of 28 January 1596, Sir Francis Drake, suffering from acute dysentery, asked a servant to help him into his armour so that he might die like a fighting man. An hour later he did so. He was buried in a lead coffin at sea outside the harbour 'as the trumpets in doleful manner echo[ed] . . . [his men's] lamentation for so great a loss'.

Coxon was anxious not to lose the advantage of surprise. Although the town had been rebuilt and was again a handsome place, many inhabitants had vivid memories of Henry Morgan's raid. They would have recalled stories, which lost nothing in the telling, of how he had compelled stumbling, terrified friars and nuns to act as human shields to force the garrison to surrender. If news of the buccaneers' presence reached their intended victims, Coxon knew they would hide their riches and flee.

Coxon embarked 250 men in canoes, Dampier among them, leaving sufficient crew behind to sail the ships nearer to Portobello to pick up the raiders and their booty. As Coxon's men paddled through the San Blas Islands toward the mainland, they encountered a ship with eighty French privateers, who, learning their plans, decided to join them. The raiders landed sixty miles from Portobello and began a six-day march, intending to creep up on the undefended rear of the town. They made slow progress over difficult, thickly forested terrain. By the third day many were weak from hunger, with feet badly 'cut with the rocks for want of shoes'.

Nevertheless, they kept the element of surprise. Only on 7 February, as they were finally approaching with muskets primed, did a cry of 'Ladrones! [robbers!]' go up. A young boy shouted, 'To arms, Christians, the English are coming'. Many townspeople 'refused to believe him' until they saw 'five or six Englishmen coming towards them at a quick pace pointing their guns which was sufficient to send them fleeing'.

The buccaneers surged into Portobello. To their surprise, they took the town in just a few hours with only five or six men wounded, although official Spanish accounts would claim that thirty were slain. They held it two days, during which, as one buccaneer recounted, they 'plundered what [they] could', piling the best of the loot, including bales of glistening cloth of silver, into periagos. One was so heavily loaded it sank. The buccaneers then sent a boat to summon their fleet to meet them at a small cay some ten miles to the northeast. They set out for the rendezvous, some paddling their canoes downriver, dodging musket fire from the small forts along the bank. Others marched overland with more plunder and prisoners for ransom. They reached the cay and waited. A few Spaniards fired at them from the shore, but their ships swept in and bore the triumphant buccaneers 'out of their reaches'. They were lucky. A punitive force of 700 Spanish soldiers arrived at Portobello the day after they quit the city. Failing to catch the buccaneers, the Spanish burned an Indian village in reprisal, killing twenty men.

The buccaneers lingered offshore, sharing out their plunder, or 'purchase'. Dampier, like the other ordinary buccaneers, received 100 pieces of eight. The commanders received an extra share, and there were additional payments to the wounded, as well as to surgeons and carpenters whose skills were so important to the well-being of the crew and ship respectively.*

As the buccaneers withdrew from the waters off Portobello, they were joined by Edmund Cook, a privateer from Jamaica. His crew included the young surgeon Lionel Wafer, bringing the number of surgeons on the expedition to five. Wafer, who would become Dampier's friend and eventually publish his own book, was originally a chemist's assistant. He had first gone to sea as a surgeon's mate on an East Indiaman bound for Java to load pepper. Within a month of returning home, he again signed on, this time for a voyage to the West Indies. Arriving in Jamaica, he opted to leave the ship and practise as a surgeon in Port Royal. Wafer's decision to stay in Jamaica was fortunate. On her onward voyage to the logwood settlements, the merchant ship on which he had sailed out was captured by the Spanish and her captain enslaved and transported to

*Like modern health insurance companies, the buccaneers had a recognized scale of compensation payments, so much for a lost limb, so much for an eye, and so on. One surviving scale shows the highest payment was 600 pieces of eight for the loss of a right arm, with 500 for the left arm or right leg but only 400 for the left leg and 100 each for the loss of an eye or finger. There is no record that payments varied if the victim was left-handed.

Mexico City, where he was seen with a log chained to his leg and a basket on his back 'crying bread around the streets for a baker, his master'. Nevertheless, Wafer clearly shared Dampier's wanderlust: when he heard that Captain Cook was recruiting and needed a surgeon, he eagerly applied. Like Dampier, he proved reticent about why he joined the buccaneers. In his book, he wrote simply, '[Cook] took me along', and left it at that.

Plunder divided, the buccaneers sailed in convoy to Boca del Toro, the 'bull's mouth', near the Isla de Colon, keeping a careful eye on the horizon for the arrival of a vengeful Spanish fleet. Here they refitted their ships and hunted sweet-fleshed turtle, manatee and fish in the clear, warm waters and were joined by yet another group. Its leader was Captain Richard Sawkins, another of Morgan's former men and a quick-witted and impulsive adventurer 'whom nothing could terrify'. He was swiftly followed by Captain Peter Harris, whose ship, at 150 tons and mounting twenty-five guns, was the largest in the assembled fleet.

Dampier related with irony that letters discovered aboard Spanish ships intercepted on their way from Cartagena to Portobello suggested where the buccaneers should go next. Their contents were 'very surprising'. Written by merchants in Spain and gloomy and anxious in tone, they warned of 'a certain prophecy' sweeping the country that English privateers in the West Indies were about to 'open a door to the South Seas', which the Spanish supposed 'was fastest shut'. The merchants cautioned their comrades in the New World to be 'very watchful and careful of their coasts'. The buccaneers guessed that the letters were referring to 'the passage over land through the country of the Indians of Darien' who had been urging them to 'pass through their country, and fall upon the Spaniards in the South Seas'.

The Spanish were right to be concerned. The South Seas – also known then, as now, as the Pacific Ocean – had long fascinated successive English governments and generations of freebooters. They were depicted in literature as the possible home of a terrestrial paradise. On a more worldly level the Pacific coast of South America was seen as a portal to 'El Dorado', a shimmering land of unimaginable wealth whose gilded ruler was ritually anointed with gold dust. The late-sixteenth-century Pacific voyages of Francis Drake and Thomas Cavendish had given substance to the dream. Drake seized bullion worth 447,000 pesos off the coast of Peru. Cavendish captured pearls, spices, silks, satins and damasks in such quantities and with such ease off Peru and Mexico that Queen Elizabeth observed, 'The King of Spain barks a great deal but he does not bite. We care nothing for Spaniards'.

After the Restoration, the English hoped to open a new trade route into the South Seas. In 1669 John Narborough sailed from London in HMS *Sweepstakes*. His ambitious task was to explore south and assess the possibilities for trade but not to upset the Spanish. He was accompanied by a shadowy figure named Don Carlos who claimed to know the South Seas. However, as they approached the Strait of Magellan, he confessed that he did not. Late in 1670 Narborough finally reached Valdivia, in the Pacific, where the Spanish appeared friendly. The tiresome Don Carlos went ashore and was arrested. Narborough's angry threats failed to secure his colleague's release, and he sailed home. In 1680, while Dampier and the buccaneers contemplated their next move, Don Carlos was still imprisoned, being

rigorously and regularly interrogated. He was nearing the
end of more than a decade spent spinning his captors a web
of amazing stories, including that he was an illegitimate
member of the English royal family. The Spaniards finally
tired of all this and garroted him, but one of his earliest
'confessions' had made a deep impression. He claimed that
the English intended to establish a settlement to control
the Strait of Magellan, to occupy Valdivia, and then to 'sack
and destroy the port of Callao and swallow up shipping in
the South Sea'.

After Narborough's incursion, the Spanish colonists in
South America had reflected nervously that they had
allowed their coastal defences in the Pacific to fall into
ruins. The once thickly buttressed walls around Callao, the
port of Lima, were full of holes. An attack on the Pacific
coast had indeed come, but it was not an official English
expedition rounding the Horn. It was Morgan marching
purposefully over the Panamanian isthmus from the
Caribbean in 1671. Ever since, the Spanish had known that
they were vulnerable by land as well as by sea. However,
they could comfort themselves that the land crossing was
dangerous and difficult. Since Morgan's march there had
been only two attempts, both made by French buccaneers.
Both had failed.

Coxon's men understood the risks but decided nevertheless to take the Indians' advice and seek 'new adventures
in the South Seas'. As Dampier noted, they shrewdly
believed they would have a psychological edge if they 'took
advantage of the fears the Spaniards were in from that
prophecy'. They cunningly resealed the letters and sent
them ashore, hoping the Spanish would not realize they
had been tampered with. Then the fleet of nine vessels
made for the San Blas Islands, off the Panamanian coast,

where Indians had, as agreed, been waiting for them 'for three moons'. Canoe-loads of men and women paddled out to them, bringing plantains, fruits and venison to exchange for beads, needles, knives, and what they coveted above all else: axes and hatchets to cut timber.

Dampier watched all this with fascination. So did Basil Ringrose, a civilized, educated young man born in Kent who spoke fluent Latin. Apprenticed to a planter in Jamaica, he had run away and somehow drifted into the company of the buccaneers. Like Dampier, Wafer, Sharp, a New Englander named John Cox, and at least two other sailors, Ringrose kept a journal which would one day be published.*

The appearance of the local Kuna Indians particularly struck Ringrose. They differed considerably from those Dampier had seen around Campeachy. The men, whose bodies were painted with streaks of black, went 'almost naked, as having only a sharp and hollow tip, made either of gold, silver, or bark, into which they thrust their privy members'. They wore in their noses gold or silver plates, shaped like half-moons, which they lifted out of the way when they drank. The women decorated their bodies with a red pigment and wore gold or silver nose rings. For clothing they draped themselves with a blanket. Ringrose admired these 'well-featured women': 'Among them I saw several fairer than the fairest of Europe, with hair like the finest flax. Of these it is reported they can see far better in the dark than in the light'.† Batholomew Sharp gloated that the women were not only 'very beautiful' but also

---

*One of the most remarkable aspects of this remarkable adventure is how well documented it was and how many accounts would survive.

†Even now the Kuna have a greater proportion of albinos among them than other races.

'very loving and free to dispose of themselves to Englishmen answering them in all respects according to their desires'.

The thought of what lay ahead was too much for the main party of Frenchmen, who decided to remain in the Caribbean. On 23 March the expectant buccaneers made for Golden Island, another of the San Blas group, and anchored in a small cove 'out of sight of any Spaniard'. The Indians suggested they cross the Darien mountains and attack the settlement of Santa Maria, inland and eastward from Panama. On a river leading down to Panama Bay, Santa Maria was a collecting station for 'much gold' from the mines in the mountains. If that attack failed, they would be within easy striking distance of Panama.

The buccaneers readily agreed and made their final plans. A party of seamen and two captains were ordered to stay behind to protect the ships. At 6 a.m. on 5 April 1680, some 330 men rowed ashore and formed up into companies on the hard, wet sand. With them was an Indian chief, Andreas, who would act as their head guide. William Dampier and Basil Ringrose were in Sharp's troop, the first to march. They carried a red flag festooned with green and white ribbons. Sharp himself was feeling faint and weak from 'a great fit of sickness'. Sawkins's men followed with their banner of red striped with yellow. Next came two companies under Peter Harris, bearing green flags aloft, then John Coxon's two companies with vivid red colours, and, bringing up the rear, Captain Edmund Cook's company with colours of 'red, striped with yellow, with a hand and sword for his device'.

To the screaming of birds and the humming of insects and led by six Indian guides, the buccaneers marched into the humid rainforest to try their luck.

PART II

The Buccaneer

V

'THAT SACRED HUNGER OF GOLD'

The sweating column wound its way under the high forest canopy, their Kuna guides treading with light, certain steps. After marching all day, the buccaneers reached a riverbank towards nightfall, where they prepared to camp. 'Sparks of gold' flashing from stones on the riverbed caught their eye. The men forgot their fatigue as they excitedly splashed about in the clear water, smashing the rocks open. Meanwhile, their Kuna escorts gathered plantains. One of the Kuna leaders warned the buccaneers not to lie in the long grass 'for fear of monstrous adders'.

Dampier and his colleagues bedded down with care, with 'the cold ground for our bedding and the spangled firmament for our covering'. As they slapped at persistent mosquitoes and listened to the sounds of the night, they must have wondered what awaited them. As one buccaneer candidly wrote: 'Gold was the bait that tempted a pack of merry boys of us ... That which often spurs men on to the undertaking of the most difficult adventure is that sacred hunger of gold'.

They rose early, wiping the dew from their long-muzzled muskets and gathering up their heavy knapsacks in the pale, grey light. As well as a small amount of food and their weapons, the buccaneers were each carrying twenty-one pounds of powder and shot. During the night four men had decided to return to the safety of the ships, but the rest moved quietly off. Soon they were climbing high into the heavily wooded Darien hills. It was exhausting work, tripping over roots and creepers, 'almost famished' for lack of water in temperatures of over ninety degrees. Before long another man decided to turn back. The remainder stumbled at last to a stream, where the men flung themselves full-length on the banks and drank deeply. The path grew even steeper, 'the mountain being so perpendicular and the path so narrow that but one man at a time could pass'.

Around noon the next day, they reached a Kuna settlement. The sight of tidy huts built of cabbage trees, with roofs of wild canes thatched with palm leaves, was reassuring in this strange, hazardous terrain. Ringrose wrote admiringly that the houses were 'far neater than ours at Jamaica'. The local 'king' came to look them over. He was an elderly man wearing an ankle-length, fringed, thin, white cotton coat. The buccaneers were more interested in his crown, which was 'made of small white reeds which were curiously woven, having no other top than its lining which was of red silk'. A wide fillet of gold encircled it, adorned with a row of golden beads 'bigger than ordinary peas'. In his nose was a large gold plate shaped like a half-moon, and in each ear great golden rings nearly four inches across. The buccaneers called him 'the Emperor of Darien'. He gave his visitors 'a very kind reception' with plantains, cassava, and an intoxicating corn beer. There was something of a party. The Kuna enjoyed hearing the buccaneers' drums beat and watching their colours fly, though they were frightened by gunfire. The king's comely young daughters 'fancied much' to be in the buccaneers' company and paid them frequent visits. Their faces were painted with streaks of red, their necks and arms laden with brightly colored beads. The buccaneers learned that the king's eldest daughter had been carried off by one of the garrison from Santa Maria, 'which rape had hugely incensed him against the Spaniards'.

The Kuna were determined to recover her and exact revenge. The buccaneers soon had an escort of 250 Indians, all armed with bows and arrows. The farther they went into the jungle, the more deeply the buccaneers were placing themselves in the power of these people. They had traditionally had 'dreadful apprehensions' of the Indians' 'numbers and fierceness'. Dampier attributed the 'late friendship' with the Indians to a Kuna boy captured some years earlier by an English captain who had nicknamed him 'John Gret'. The boy later returned to his people, singing the praises of the 'English, who had used him very kindly' and 'were not enemies to them, but to the Spaniards'. As a result, the Kuna had 'invited the English through their country into the South Seas'. Dampier noted with relief that the subsequent fate of John Gret had not yet come to the ears of the Kuna. He had disappeared, and the Indians assumed that the Spanish had seized him. In fact, as Dampier knew, Gret had been murdered by Englishmen trying to kidnap him to sell as a slave.

Trusting in the Kuna's detestation of the Spanish, the buccaneers set out again. As they passed Kuna dwellings, the owners courteously presented each man with 'either a ripe plantain or some sweet cassava-root'. So that they knew how many buccaneers they had to provide for, the Kuna counted them by dropping a grain of corn for each man that went by because they could 'count no farther than twenty'. The terrain became 'something bad', and the column was forced to cross and recross rivers fifty or sixty times in a day. Struggling to stay upright in the surging currents, the buccaneers tried to keep their guns, ammunition and knapsacks of provisions dry.

Despite the hardships and dangers, Dampier still found time to record the wind patterns of the isthmus. The land wind blew all night until 10 or 11 a.m., when 'the flying of the clouds' heralded a rising sea breeze. Dampier had heard tales of a strange and dangerous phenomenon when 'ships sailing in the Bay of Panama are toss'd to and fro at a prodigious rate: Sometimes (they say) they are by the boiling of the water, dash'd against islands; and in a moment left dry there, or staved in pieces; at other times they are drawn or suck'd up, as t'were, in a whirl-pool and ready to be carried under ground into the north-seas, with all sails standing'. As he trudged and waded, he pondered the common belief that the isthmus was 'like an arched bridge [between the Caribbean and the Pacific] under which the tides make their constant courses, as duly they do under London-Bridge'. He listened for the allegedly 'continual and strange noises made by those subterranean fluxes and refluxes'. He heard nothing of the kind. In his celebrated 'Discourse of Trade Winds', part of his second book, he later correctly dismissed all these beliefs as false. The loudest sounds around him were probably the chattering of cicadas and the curses of his hungry, mud-spattered, increasingly discouraged companions. Made edgy by heat and fatigue, Coxon and Harris began exchanging angry words. The discussion became so animated that Coxon fired his gun – whether directly at Harris or into the air is not clear – and threatened to turn back with his men. Dampier's commander, Sharp, later claimed that he, Sharp, was the peacemaker who persuaded Coxon 'to the contrary'.

They marched on, but many were clearly suffering from heat exhaustion. Foreseeing such problems, the Kuna had gathered canoes so that some of the buccaneers could use the river network. Captains Sharp, Coxon and Cook with around ninety of 'those that were most tired' embarked, including Ringrose. Dampier probably remained with the land party, stumbling along the riverbank and soon losing sight of their waterborne companions. The Kuna guided the canoes expertly with their long poles, negotiating rivers where 'the current runs like an arrow out of a bow' and the merest brush against a rock or tree stump was enough to flip them over. Grimly, the passengers focused their minds on reaching 'that fair South Sea', as Sharp called it.

At last the canoes emerged into a fast-flowing river, which carried them quickly down to the agreed rendezvous point, but there was no sign of those on foot. The Kuna sent a canoe to reconnoitre up a tributary while the buccaneers waited anxiously. One wondered if their friends had been captured by the Spanish or, indeed, murdered by the Kuna, whose purpose in dividing the group had been 'to bring [them] all to destruction'. They were all 'hugely glad' when, at last, the exhausted land party came into view.

The buccaneers were just a day and a night away from Santa Maria. They prepared carefully for the coming attack on the settlement, cleaning guns, checking flints and drying powder to avoid the misfire, or 'flash in the pan', which could cost them their lives in combat. The Kuna had assembled a larger fleet of canoes, and the buccaneers chopped down trees, from whose wood they hewed rough oars and paddles.

They set out, accompanied by fifty Kuna, including one of the king's sons, nicknamed 'King Golden Cap' by the buccaneers on account of his 'cap or hat of beaten gold'. The men paddled hard all day. By midnight they were within half a mile of the town. They struggled ashore, grabbing hold of the tangled branches of the trees that overhung the water and using their makeshift paddles as bridges to stop themselves from sinking into the deep, oozing, malodorous mud at the water's edge. Ashore at last, they hacked their way into the jungle, where they 'lay still' until daybreak.

The sound of a small gun being fired from the direction of Santa Maria awoke the buccaneers. Leaping to their feet, they grabbed their arms, formed up, and emerged from the woods to find themselves under fire from the Spanish, 'who had received intelligence beforehand of [their] coming'. Most Spaniards had withdrawn into a fort with palisades about twelve feet high. Fifty buccaneers made a determined rush, pushing and pulling down the palisades and pouring in. The Spanish soon surrendered. The buccaneers found that they had 260 prisoners, but the governor, priest and other grandees, for whom the buccaneers might have expected a handsome ransom, had already fled. The buccaneers were further dismayed to learn from their prisoners that they had missed by just three days a consignment of 300 pounds of gold sent by boat to Panama. The town itself, 'a small pitiful place', was barely worth plundering.

At least the king's daughter had been 'found and redeemed', but she was pregnant. The vengeful Kuna began dragging the Spaniards into the adjoining woods and 'stabbing them to death with their lances'. The buccaneers put a stop to this 'barbarous cruelty', but to salve the king's feelings they burned down the fort, the church and the town.

*King Golden Cap of the Kuna Indians,
from Bartholomew Sharp's manuscript.*

This did not relieve their own frustration. Their 'great expectations of taking a huge booty of gold being totally vanished', they had to decide what to do. Some, including Coxon, were nervous at being so far from their familiar haunts, with so little means of subsisting. Others were unwilling to have travelled 'so far for nothing' and were convinced that 'vast riches were to be had at no great distance'. The buccaneers placated Coxon by confirming him as overall commander. He agreed to lead an attack on Panama.* It was, as Ringrose acknowledged, a 'dangerous enterprise'. However, they were encouraged by José

---

*The city of Panama was about 120 miles away down the Tuira River and then northwest up the Pacific coast.

Gabriel, the Spaniard who had ravished the king's daughter. Terrified that he would be left to the mercy of the Kuna, he grovellingly 'promised to lead [the buccaneers] not only into the town but even to the very bedchamber door of the governor of Panama' and that the city and its wealth would fall into their hands like a ripe fruit.

On 17 April 1680, the buccaneer force took to their canoes again with a small party of Kuna, including Golden Cap, who was determined to go with them. Some Spanish prisoners had been despatched back over the isthmus with the paltry booty from Santa Maria. Others, desperate not to be left behind to be massacred by the Indians, begged to be taken along with the main raiding party to Panama. The buccaneers took as many as they 'possibly could', but as they pushed off from the shore they heard 'a miserable cry' as the Kuna killed 'all the poor souls that were left'.

As the canoes 'sailed or rather rowed down the river in quest of the South Sea', the men battled a vicious on-coming tide.* Eventually, the flotilla bobbed safely out into the ocean, but the buccaneers were still 'in an enemy's country and unknown seas' and potentially in great peril. Desperately thirsty, they landed on an island where they gulped brackish water from 'stinking holes of rocks'.

The next essential was to acquire larger vessels. Among the Pacific swells, the canoes felt no safer than being

---

*Unlike the comparatively tideless North Sea (Caribbean), the South Sea (Pacific) at Panama had a rise and fall of twenty feet. Ships that floated happily at high tide could at low tide sometimes find themselves sitting helplessly in the silty mud of Panama's shallow harbour.

A seventeenth-century Spanish barque.

'confined to an egg-shell'. The raiders seized two Spanish barques. While Sharp sailed off westward in one to search for food and water among the islands, probably taking Dampier with him, Coxon, Sawkins and the remaining men sailed for Panama. Before sunrise on 23 April they gazed on it. A new city of stone and brick was rising some four miles west of the remains of the old town, whose airy villas of carved and fragrant cedar had been burned down by Morgan.

There was little time for reflection. Five large Spanish ships were riding at anchor, while the Spaniards had despatched three armed barques to patrol the waters of the bay. On sighting the buccaneers, the Spanish barques made straight for them. According to one of the buccaneers, John Cox, rather than 'perish in the sea or be taken', the buccaneers decided to make a fight of it. A fierce, bloody battle began shortly after sunrise. It lasted three hours, during which both sides were 'giving and receiving death unto each other as fast as they could charge'. Using one of their favourite manoeuvres, the buccaneers eventually used their small canoes to get in close under the stern of the leading Spanish vessel and jam her rudder. Discharging volley after volley of musket shot, they slaughtered two-thirds of the crew and seized the vessel. Meanwhile, a yelling Sawkins succeeded on his fourth attempt in boarding and capturing the second ship, exploiting the mayhem caused aboard her by exploding barrels of powder. 'Sadly burnt', shrieking men ran about in pain and confusion amid the smoke. The third Spanish barque had fled, taking advantage of a freshening wind, so the buccaneers next attacked the five larger vessels at anchor, surging aboard the 400-ton *La Santissima Trinidad*, whose crew soon surrendered. Of the remaining four Spanish ships, the buccaneers burned two and commandeered the others.

Eighteen buccaneers had been killed and twenty-two wounded. Captain Harris was a casualty. Shot through both legs as he tried to board a Spanish ship, he died two days later: 'the doctors cutting off one leg, it festered, so that it pleased God he died, so we lost that valiant, brave soldier'. Sharp and his men rejoined the main group, and arguments soon broke out over what to do next and who should lead them. Coxon, piqued by charges of cowardice in the recent battle, decided irrevocably to return over the isthmus with seventy of his men and the Kuna leaders, including Golden Cap. His colleagues were incensed that he departed not only with his surgeon but, according to John Cox, with 'the best of our medicines unknown to the majority of us'. The buccaneers elected Sawkins, who had fought valiantly, as leader in Coxon's place. He declared his intention to seek gold in the Pacific and then 'to go home round about America, through the Strait of Magellan'. He took command of the biggest prize, *La Santissima Trinidad*, which, renamed *Trinity*, became their flagship.

The buccaneers lingered in Panama Bay. They captured a barque with 50,000 pieces of eight – the wages of the Panama garrison – 1,400 jars of wine and brandy, and a large amount of powder and shot. This was lucky, for, as Sharp wrote, 'we had almost spent our ammunition'.

The governor of Panama and Sawkins engaged in verbal Ping-Pong. The governor enquired what the buccaneers thought they were doing, since England and Spain were supposed to be at peace. Sawkins replied silkily that he and his men had come to assist 'the King of Darien', who was 'the true lord of Panama', and demanded, as the price of their peaceful departure, 500 pieces of eight per man, 1,000 for each commander, and a promise that the Spaniards would not 'annoy the Darien Indians' any further. The governor, determined not to pay protection money, and knowing that the buccaneers carried no letters of marque to justify their incursion into the South Sea, shrewdly asked to see Sawkins's privateers' commission. The reply, signed by 'the Commanders of the Whole South Seas', proclaimed that, unless paid off, the buccaneers would visit him at Panama, bringing '[their] commissions on the muzzles of [their] guns, at which time he could read them as plain as the flame of gunpowder could make them'.

The governor refused to be intimidated by these 'commanders', who soon realized that they had to seek easier prey. Once the defenders were alerted, Panama was too strong to attack. Instead, they raided the coastal town of Pueblo Nuevo in quest of fresh meat, but the attack backfired. Sawkins, with his usual daredevilry, was the first man ashore but was shot down as he stormed at the head of his men towards a breastwork hastily thrown up by the Spanish. His death caused a crisis, provoking, according to a buccaneer named William Dick, 'a mutiny amongst our men; for our [remaining] commanders were not thought to be leaders fit for such great and hard enterprises'. Sharp made a passionate address to the assembled buccaneers, promising to abide by Sawkins's plan to stay in the South Seas, and to make every man who remained with him worth £1,000. He was elected and took command of the *Trinity*, but sixty-three dissenters sailed back to the isthmus. Dampier, ever eager for new sights and experiences, remained. So did Wafer and Ringrose, though the latter would have loved to quit these 'hazardous adventures' but, as he wrote wistfully, he was too afraid 'to trust [himself] among wild Indians any farther'. His malaise was probably exacerbated a few days later when he was caught in a shower of rain under a mançanilla tree, which leaks a corrosive white milk, causing the skin to erupt in painful red blotches.

A few weeks later, near the Isla de Plata,* they sighted a small ship and captured her after a fight. Aboard they found some 3,276 pieces of eight and 'a parcel of merry blades, gentlemen, who drinking in a tavern made a vow to come to sea with that vessel and thirty men, and take us'. Two days later the buccaneers shot the Spanish ship's

*The island is near the Ecuadorean coast just below the equator and was famous among buccaneers as 'where Sir Francis Drake shared his money'.

chaplain and threw him overboard 'before he was dead' in an act of casual brutality to which Dampier did not refer. A shocked Ringrose wrote that he condemned 'such cruelties' but felt unable to speak out.*

The frightened evidence of the remaining prisoners convinced the buccaneers that Guayaquil and Lima would be too well prepared to attack. They were deeply disappointed when the same proved true of the port of Arica, in the very north of Chile. They had been at sea many weeks and were desperately short of provisions, with each man rationed to just five ounces of flour and a pint of water a day. Some, half crazed by thirst, were trading thirty pieces of eight for an extra pint 'and right glad they were to get it'. Landing along this well-defended coast seemed impossible until, at last, on 28 October they sent in canoes and seized the small town of Ilo.† Their first priority was to find fresh water, flour, and fruit, and they were particularly delighted to discover a small amount of 'good chocolate'. Some of the men who were 'very much troubled and diseased' from scurvy found that 'a dish of that pleasant liquor' was an effective remedy.

---

*Buccaneers and pirates had a reputation for cruelty. Some were psychopathic like the Frenchman Montbars of Languedoc, known as 'the exterminator', who claimed to be taking vengeance on the Spanish on behalf of the ill-treated Indians. One of his favourite tortures was to rip open his victim's abdomen and to pull out the intestines, which he nailed to a post. Then he applied a burning brand to the victim's buttocks to make him dance and die, unreeling his intestines as he went. Another Frenchman, Francois L'Ollonois, routinely roasted prisoners alive. Once in a rage he was said to have sliced open a man's chest, pulled out his heart, and bitten into it, still pulsating, warm and dripping. One English pirate, Dirk Chivers, took up a sail needle and sewed up the lips of a captured merchant captain who irritated him with his complaints. Many such stories were exaggerated in the telling by pirate chroniclers such as Daniel Defoe to boost sales. But it was an age when cruelty was commonplace ashore and at sea.

†About 100 miles north of Arica.

The symptoms of scurvy – the biggest killer at sea –
were at first unpleasant and soon disgusting. Sufferers
became listless, lethargic and depressed. Their slackening
gums drooped down their teeth, then began to drip blood
and pus. Soon their teeth began to drop out. Their bodies
became swollen and blotched blue-black. Old wounds
reopened, and men began to putrefy alive. In 1617, John
Woodall, surgeon-general to the East India Company, had
published *The Surgeon's Mate*, a manual that had become
the bible of ships' surgeons. Woodall recommended that
scurvy sufferers eat citrus fruit. By Dampier's time, it was
generally accepted that fresh fruit and vegetables cured the
disease – sufferers craved the chance to suck a lemon or
gorge on fistfuls of green leaves – but no one had yet made
the logical deduction that eating such things in advance
would ward it off. Other remedies included doses of
vinegar, drenching in hot steam, or even bathing in
animals' blood. The buccaneers hurried on board with
'great plenty of all sorts of garden herbs, roots, and most
excellent fruit' and then destroyed the town's sugar works
when its Spanish citizens failed to come up with a suitable
ransom.

Strength recovered, on 3 December the buccaneers
steered for the pretty town of La Serena, some 600 miles
farther south in Coquimbo Bay. Extraordinary sights
punctuated the voyage. A patch of shimmering white
water, a mile wide, proved not to be sandbanks but 'great
shoals of anchovies'. On another occasion, buccaneers
hanging over the side saw great sea snakes undulating
through the clear water. Arrived off La Serena, the
buccaneers quickly disembarked, attacked, and took
the town, but once again there was no real booty. The
Spaniards had been warned of their approach and had fled

into the hills with their treasure after cold-bloodedly slaughtering most of their slaves in case they aided the invaders. The Spanish claimed to wish to ransom their lovely town, and the buccaneers spent several days ashore in fruitless haggling until the Spanish opened the irrigation sluices to try and flood them out. The angry raiders set the town ablaze in revenge and, repelling a halfhearted ambush, decamped to their ships with 500 pounds of silver plate and a few jewels.

Despite their own wanton vandalism, they were outraged to discover that, in their absence, the Spanish had made an ingenious attempt to set fire to their largest ship. 'Some fellow of a Spaniard' had inflated a horse's hide like a bladder to serve as a raft and floated out from the shore to beneath the ship's stern, where he packed oakum, brimstone and other combustible material around the rudder before igniting it. The men on watch caught the acrid smell. It was only by prompt action 'and good fortune' that they saved the ship by jumping into their boats and pushing the raft away. Even so, those returning found 'all the ship in a smoke'. An aggrieved Cox decried 'the Spaniard whose mercy to the English is more barbarous than any heathen's cruelty'. Suspecting that their Spanish prisoners might have colluded in the attack, they sent them ashore. One buccaneer candidly wrote, 'We were glad to be rid of them but they much more glad to be clear of us'.

The buccaneers sailed on, pausing to bury at sea one of their number, who apparently expired of high fever exacerbated by hiccups brought on by a drinking bout at La Serena. On Christmas Eve 1680, Dampier caught his first glimpse of the brooding, mountainous Juan Fernandez Islands with their wild goats, high, windswept valleys, and tumbling rivers and streams.* This was to be their farthest point south. They landed on a beach colonized by so many seals they were 'forced to kill' some to make a path ashore.

Quarrels again broke out over the direction of the voyage and who should be leader. Sharp had accumulated a personal fortune of some 3,000 pesos, much of it from gambling with his men, and was contemplating rounding the Horn and returning to the Caribbean. Others who had fared less well were determined to have gold and silver first.

Nearly all buccaneering voyages and many privateering ones were covered by a code of conduct that was highly democratic, particularly for the seventeenth century. On a buccaneer ship, the crew elected the captain on a one-man, one-vote basis. They looked for a man 'superior for knowledge and boldness, pistol proof they call it', as Daniel Defoe wrote in his *General History of the Pirates*, and he could be deposed if the majority turned against him. The captain had absolute authority in battle, and 'when chasing or being chased'. However, a council of war of every man on board made all other decisions, such as the destination of a voyage, again on the basis of one man, one vote.

At the beginning of an expedition, or upon a change of captain, each member of the crew was required to sign or make his mark on a set of articles to govern the conduct of the voyage. Though the *Trinity*'s articles have not survived, they would have typically included agreement about compensation for injury and the division of the spoils, and set

---

*These then-uninhabited islands are more than 400 miles off the coast of Chile, due west of Valparaiso. They were named after the Spanish captain who first visited them in 1574, and claimed by Spain, but became a frequent rendezvous and provisioning place for buccaneers.

out the punishments for desertion, cowardice, and for those trying to conceal plunder for their own benefit rather than pooling it for communal distribution. These punishments could range from death or marooning to having nose and ears slit. The articles also provided for food to be shared equally without distinction of rank and often detailed other such mundane matters as the 'lights out' time belowdecks and the performance hours of the musicians.

The buccaneers called a council of war to resolve the leadership question. To his fury, their vote deposed Sharp, and they locked him up. Dampier wrote that the company was not happy with 'his courage or behaviour'. Sharp himself blamed the coup on John Cox, 'that dissembling New England man . . . whom merely for old acquaintance sake, I had taken from before the mast and made my vice-admiral; not from any valour or knowledge he was possessed of; for of that his share was but small'. However, Sharp knew that he 'could not help himself' and had to abide by the buccaneer code.

The men elected Captain John Watling, 'an old privateer' and 'stout seaman', in Sharp's place. One of his first tasks was to sort out an accusation of sodomy and treachery. 'This day William Cook servant to Captain Edmund Cook confessed that his master had often buggered him in England, leaving his wife and coming to bed to the said William, once in Jamaica and also in these seas before Panama'. William Cook also alleged that he had found among his master's papers a list with all their names, which he had been intending to give the Spaniards. The exasperated Watling ordered Edmund Cook to be placed in irons. Perhaps to improve the morals of his crew, he also revived a rule of Captain Sawkins that the Sabbath must be observed.

On 12 January a group of keen-sighted buccaneers,

returning in their canoes from a hunting expedition ashore on the main island of Juan Fernandez, spotted sails on the horizon and fired their guns to raise the alarm. The ships were one of several squadrons sent out by the governor of Chile to hunt them down. Men rushed aboard the *Trinity* and hauled up her anchors. In the confusion, a Moskito Indian named William, who had gone inland to hunt wild goats high in the pungent forests of sandalwood trees and shiny-leaved pimento, was left behind. Intending to return for him if they could, the buccaneers sailed out of reach of the approaching, vengeful Spanish ships and 'gave them handsomely the slip'.

Ten days later, somewhat at a loss as to how to proceed, Watling decided to make another attempt on Arica. First, though, he needed 'intelligence of the posture of affairs' there. He despatched canoes to snatch some prisoners. They returned with two unfortunate elderly men, whom Watling quizzed and no doubt threatened. One warned that Arica was strongly defended, but Watling refused to believe him and had him shot for lying. Ninety buccaneers, not including Dampier, then landed on a beach some distance from the town on 30 January 1681. They picked their way for several miles over the many boulders obstructing the narrow beach, which was overshadowed by high cliffs. When they reached the town, they stormed into it. Even a Spanish account spoke admiringly of their 'daring and ferocity' and their 'super-human effort', but they failed to take Arica's heavily defended fort. The Spanish militia counterattacked several times, forcing the buccaneers' withdrawal.

The retreat was long and disorganized, back along the beach in the heat. Although the boulders hindered the buccaneers' flight, they also prevented the Spanish from charging them on horseback. Instead, the Spanish pushed rocks down onto the retreating buccaneers from the cliffs above while firing at those who broke cover. Some buccaneers became so choked for water in their hiding places that they drank their own urine. Only half the force that had set out made it back to the re-embarkation point. Watling and the two quartermasters were among the dead. The Spaniards gleefully hacked off Watling's head and paraded it around the town on a pole. The surviving buccaneers licked their wounds both physical and mental. They had suffered 'great loss', as Dampier described bleakly. More serious even than the casualties was the fact that three of the buccaneers' surgeons – who, according to conflicting accounts, either had become hopelessly drunk during the attack or were busy in the hastily established hospital 'dressing of [their] wounded men' – had been abandoned in the hasty withdrawal. Their loss, coming on top of Coxon's defection with his surgeon, was serious. There was no question of being able to ransom them. The surgeons were as valuable to the Spanish as they were to the buccaneers, and the loss of so many seemed a fatal blow.*

Leaderless, nearly doctorless, and with little water, the

---

*The surgeon's chest, often among the first things to be seized on captured vessels, held a formidable array of syrups, ointments and elixirs such as the mercurial compounds for treating syphilis and ferric chloride, known as 'soldier's ointment', for wounds, but most important were the instruments. There was a large metal syringe used for colonic irrigation of those suffering from the chronic shipboard complaint of constipation. If this did not produce the desired effect, the surgeons warmed spatulas, dipped them in oil, and simply scooped the dried turds from the men's rectums. In addition, there were specula for holding wounds open so they could be investigated, forceps for plucking out bullets, knives for carving through flesh, saws for cutting through bone, irons for cauterizing wounds, and needle and thread for sewing wounds together. The most usual painkiller was opium, though many a seaman underwent the torture of a shipboard operation with only rum to deaden his senses.

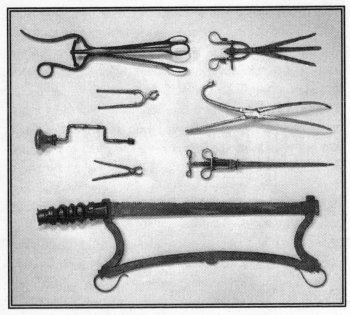

Surgical instruments of the seventeenth century.

disheartened buccaneers headed north and anchored off
the Isla de Plata. At a council of war, Sharp 'thrust himself
captain again'. In a vote he was supported by 'a great
number of the meaner sort', as Dampier disparagingly dismissed them. The abler and more experienced men, he
added, would not accept Sharp at any price. Consequently,
it was agreed that the party should split, and whichever
was the largest should keep the *Trinity*. The vote took
place, and Sharp's party won. Ringrose and Cox elected to
sail on with him. Dampier declared himself 'on the side of
those that were out-voted'. He added that he had never
been impressed with Sharp – 'though I had hitherto kept
my mind to myself'. Dampier thus threw in his lot with a
small group that intended to sail north and trudge back

over the isthmus. It included Lionel Wafer, who later wrote, 'I was of Mr Dampier's side in that matter', and that he considered Sharp a coward. Dampier respected the young surgeon's intelligence and must have been pleased to have a doctor in his party.*

At 10 a.m. on 17 April 1681 Dampier, Wafer and forty-two other buccaneers climbed down into a longboat and two canoes. Their elected leader was another man named Cook, Captain John Cook. Dampier described him as a 'very intelligent person' and 'a sensible man', a rare and high accolade from him. They had spent the previous three days sifting and packing up as much flour as they could carry. They had also 'rubb'd up 20 or 30 pound[s] of chocolate with sugar to sweeten it'. They were accompanied by two Moskito Indians and five slaves, the latter to carry on their backs the provisions and a large kettle to cook them in over the tortuous mountain tracks of the isthmus.

The buccaneers knew the 600-mile voyage in small boats back to Panama Bay would be hazardous. Even if they reached the mainland safely, they faced the 'toilsome' march back over the isthmus. Dampier recorded their agreement that if any man faltered, 'he must expect to be shot to death', for if the Spanish caught him, they would force him to reveal the 'strength and condition' of the others.

---

*Sharp eventually brought his men safely back round the Horn, after capturing a Spanish ship, the *Rosario*, carrying a complete set of maps of the Pacific coast of South America. On his return to England, an indignant Spanish ambassador insisted Sharp be tried for piracy, but he won a pardon from King Charles II by presenting a beautifully illuminated copy of the charts to the king. He was further rewarded for this piece of mercantile espionage with a commission in the Royal Navy but soon reverted to piracy. He was last heard of in 1698, imprisoned on the Danish Caribbean island of St Thomas, partially paralysed by a stroke.

VI

'TWO FAT MONKEYS'

The sea was calm, with barely a whisper of wind. The buccaneers' improvised sails hung limp. Then a sharp, salty sea breeze began to blow, churning up the water until it was 'like to founder' them. They hacked up an old hide and lined the longboat with it to stop her leaking, then braced themselves. For ten anxious hours the reinforced boat and the two accompanying canoes tossed about on the foaming water until finally the weather calmed and the buccaneers drew closer to the coast. The drenched, exhausted party knew they would never survive the voyage in their fragile craft. On the evening of 18 April, in desperation, they crept up on a small barque that they had spotted riding at anchor. It was risky because of their small numbers and inadequate arms. Dampier wrote they had not intended to 'have meddled' with any ships 'nor to have seen any if [they] could have helped it'. Nevertheless, they boarded and captured the barque, which had been carrying timber to Guayaquil, and gained a seaworthy craft.

They sailed furtively northwards, ever alert for the sight of Spanish sails angling over the horizon. Six days later, they approached the island of Gorgona, off the Colombian coast. The buccaneers waited until nightfall before landing, fearful that the Spaniards might be lying concealed in the dense vegetation, weapons primed. When they at last came cautiously ashore, they discovered that the Spanish had indeed been on the island but had left again. Before doing so, they had built a shelter, large enough to accommodate 100 men, and left a large cross before the doors. To Dampier, it was ominous proof that 'the Spaniards did expect [them] this way again'.

The buccaneers boiled up a restoring 'kettle of chocolate', but 'very violent' rains, which Dampier noted were a characteristic of the island, poured down from a lowering sky. They tried to drink the chocolate from their calabashes but 'could not sup it up so fast as it rained in'. Dampier finally tossed the watery liquid away in disgust. After less than a day spent doing essential maintenance to the barque, the buccaneers hastily put to sea again, where 'excessive showers of rain' pounded the decks of the little ship. When the weather cleared, the tired, sodden men saw through watery sunlight 'two great ships' to the west. They recognized them as Spanish patrol vessels, and so, furling sails still heavy with water, they slunk in close to the shore again. Before long, the rain returned. The warm, fat drops veiled them as they slipped past. They were nearing the Isthmus of Panama and made thankfully for 'the place where [they] first came into the South Seas, and the way by which [they] designed to return'.

Despite all the hardships and disappointments, Dampier was leaving the Pacific with some regret. He tried to persuade his companions to attempt to capture a Spanish ship carrying treasure from the mines. His 'sacred hunger' for gold was undiminished, but he 'found them all tired without life or soul to undertake anything'.

Anchoring off one of the many small and thickly wooded islands in the Gulf of San Miguel, they came cautiously ashore to dry their sodden clothing in the

baking sun, clean their guns and check their ammunition.
They kept a careful lookout, expecting at any moment to
be challenged or attacked, but the only sounds were the
lapping of the water, the rasping cries of circling birds and
the thick drone of insects. The next day, however, they
were dismayed to find their entry to the river mouth
blocked by a ship and a large tent by it, and realized it
would be a hard task to escape them. The ship was waiting
like a cat by a mouse hole. Some of the men were 'a little
disheartened', but Dampier was philosophical, writing, '[It
was] no more than I ever expected'.

The buccaneers landed on a nearby island to keep
watch. Before long, they spotted a small canoe paddling
towards the shore. Dampier and his colleagues lay low
until the canoe was 'within pistol-shot', then leaped up,
brandishing their muskets, and seized the occupants – a
white man and two Indians. Their frightened prisoners told
them that the Spanish ship had been lying in wait for
returning buccaneers for some six months. She was carrying twelve guns and was manned by 150 soldiers and
sailors. They also told of other troops in the vicinity and of
two armed ships cruising among the islands. But the 'worst
news of all' was that 'the Indians on this side of the
country were our enemies'. Nevertheless, the buccaneers
knew they had to cross the isthmus. If they delayed, the
Spanish would surely catch them. They hoped to placate
the Indians 'by such toys as we had purposely brought
with us', since 'we very well knew the hearts of the
Indians', or else – and this unrealistic proposition
was a mark of their desperation – to 'force our way
through [the Indians'] country, in spite of all their
opposition'.

Nature would also be against them. The dry season was

ending, and violent, relentless rains would make the tangled jungle very hard going on foot. Dampier tried to persuade the others to sail up the Congo River nine miles away, remembering that it could carry them deep into the interior. But because 'there was not a man but myself that ever heard of this river', his arguments failed to work on 'their stubborn nature'. It galled him. Impatient of others' ignorance, he could not hide his irritation that his companions were determined to land somewhere although 'they neither did know how, where, nor when'.

On 1 May 1681, having 'rowed and towed against the wind all night', the buccaneers sailed up a small creek and disembarked warily. After unloading their remaining provisions, they sank the barque to conceal the evidence of their landing. While they prepared for the march ahead, their 'ingenious' Moskito Indians, 'coveted by all privateers' for their extraordinary skill at spearing fish, turtles and manatee, went hunting. Dampier wrote admiringly of these 'tall, well-made, raw-boned, lusty, strong [men]', whose sharp eyes could 'descry a sail at sea farther, and see any thing better than [the buccaneers]'.

The party feasted on fish brought back by the Moskitos. At around 3 p.m. they began their hazardous journey. They slept that night in rough bivouacs, built from branches, listening to heavy rain falling outside. The next day they followed a narrow, muddy Indian track up a steep hill into the dense rainforest. Fearing the path was leading them off course, some scrambled up trees to scan the horizon. They spied Indian huts in the distance and made for them, hoping their owners would be friendly. They were. The people could speak no Spanish but gave each buccaneer a calabash brimming with the highly intoxicating corn-drink *chichah*.*

Dampier and his companions purchased fowls, wild pig, yams, potatoes, and plantains and 'supped plentifully'. They had agreed that provisions should be held in common in deference to their rule that 'none should live better than others'. That night one of the Indians agreed in sign language that, in return for a hatchet, he would guide the buccaneers to the house of a Spanish-speaking Indian, who would take them farther on their way. The next day, after walking eight miles, they reached the house safely, although one of the buccaneers 'being tired gave us the slip'.

Their reception, though, was cool, even hostile. This Indian told them in excellent Spanish that it was impossible to find a path north. The buccaneers, biting back anger and disappointment, humoured the man. As Dampier later observed, 'It was neither time nor place to be angry with the Indians; all our lives lying in their hands'. They tried every inducement they could think of, offering beads, money, hatchets, machetes and knives. Nothing was of any use until one of the buccaneers in desperation pulled 'a sky-coloured petticoat out of his bag' and gave it to the Indian's wife. She was delighted and 'immediately began to

---

*Had they known how it was made, they might have drunk it less joyfully. According to Lionel Wafer, a large quantity of bruised maize was first steeped in a trough of water until the liquid began to turn 'sour'. Then 'the women, usually some old women, who have little else to do, come together, and chew grains of maize in their mouths, which they spit out each into a gourd or calabash'. Once they had a sufficient quantity of 'this spittle and maize' in the calabashes, they emptied them back into the trough of water to serve as a yeast to 'set all the trough of liquor in a small ferment'. When the liquor was ready, they decanted it into another trough, leaving the sediment behind, and then it was ready for drinking. It caused the drinker to 'belch very much'.

chatter to her husband and soon brought him into a better humour'. The man admitted to the relieved buccaneers that he did know a path north. He could not accompany them himself because his foot was injured, but he would arrange for the Indian who had brought them to him to guide them for two more days in return for another hatchet.

In thunderous rain they set out again. Deep in the interior of the rainforest the Indians had no paths – they guided themselves by rivers. Conditions were atrocious as the group struggled across swollen torrents. At night the buccaneers clustered miserably around fires too small to dry their soaking clothes and with little food 'for the belly . . . which made it very hard' for them. Even the ascetic Dampier confessed that 'these hardships quite expelled the thoughts of an enemy'. For once, he was oblivious to the sights and sounds around him as they forced their way through 'wild pathless woods' that seemed to wrap around them like a suffocating shroud.

On the fifth day, the starving, ragged group stumbled to the doors of a young Indian. He responded to their plight with kindness and generosity, offering them yams and potatoes from his plantation. He had no meat, so Dampier and some other buccaneers shot 'two fat monkeys'. They were an acquired taste since, in the words of one sailor, 'they looked so like young children broiled'. Nevertheless, they cooked and fed the grey-furred animals to those who were 'weak and sickly'. The buccaneers rested for an afternoon, drying out their clothes, cleaning their guns, and trying to prepare mentally and physically before continuing their punishing trek.

At this critical moment Lionel Wafer suffered a 'sad disaster'. The young surgeon later reported, '[As I was]

sitting on the ground near one of our men, who was drying of gun powder in a silver plate, but not managing it as
he should, it blew up, and scorched my knee to that degree,
that the bone was left bare, the flesh being torn away, and
my thigh burnt for a great way above it'. He rummaged
through his rucksack for 'such remedies' as he had so that
he could treat the wound and continue. Although in
terrible pain, he 'was unwilling to be left behind'. His dismayed companions allocated him a slave to carry his things
and watched as he 'made hard shift to jog on'. As Dampier
candidly admitted, the buccaneers were all the more concerned because they themselves were liable 'every moment
to misfortune' but had 'none to look after us but him'.

On the sixth day the weary band set out again, having
hired another guide. Dampier reflected sourly that they
were trudging along the banks of the very river they could
have paddled up by canoe if he 'could have persuaded them
to it'. They forded rivers by standing the tallest men in the
deepest places to help the 'sick, weak and short men'. Ever
fearful of capture and putting their lives in the hands of
people they did not necessarily trust, the buccaneers found
the mental as well as the physical pressures draining.

It is a mark of Dampier's preoccupation with preserving
his papers that he had foreseen such difficulties. Even
before the march began, '[I had taken care] to provide
myself a large joint of bamboo, which I stopped at both
ends, closing it with wax, so as to keep out any water. In
this I preserved my journal and other writings from being
wet, though I was often forced to swim'. On one occasion,
Wafer, dizzy with pain, was carried downstream by the
violent current to a bend in the river, where he managed to
catch hold of something and drag himself ashore. Two
stragglers, Robert Spratlin and William Bowman by name,

watched him threshing in the water and, too afraid to attempt a crossing themselves, were left stranded.

One night, flash floods forced the exhausted men from their makeshift shelters on a riverbank. On the next, they cowered under the trees as a terrific storm burst over them. Lightning patterned the sky, and 'terrible claps of thunder' echoed and rolled under the jungle canopy. Indifferent to everything but survival, they forgot to place any men on watch. As a result, all but one of their slaves slipped away into the forest, taking Lionel Wafer's gun, his money and, worst of all, most of his remaining medicines, depriving him of 'wherewithal to dress [his] sore'.

Disheartened, the buccaneers gathered their sodden belongings from beneath the dripping branches and trailed after their guide. Another swollen river confronted them. They tried to set up a rope line to help their invalids over safely, but a man called George Gainy, attempting to take it across the rushing, muddy water, became entangled with the rope, which flipped him on his back. Gainy had kept on his knapsack, which contained 300 pieces of eight, rather than leaving it to bring over later when the line was rigged. The pack weighed him down. He struggled to right himself but could not. Dampier watched aghast as the swift current ripped away his flailing body. The buccaneers found his corpse but were too demoralized to consider stripping it of his fatal pieces of eight.

Eventually, the buccaneers crossed the river by felling a tree to make a makeshift bridge and reached a plantation where their guide put them in the care of 'an old Indian'. The buccaneers followed this new guide across yet another river but then into a fertile valley. It was a relief to be out of the dense jungle. Dampier wrote of pleasant country with 'the fattest land I did ever take notice of'. The paths were crisscrossed by the trotting hooves of wild hogs. The men rested at the old man's hunting quarters, drying their clothes and ammunition, munching potatoes and yams.

The next day, their ninth on the march, brought them to a hilltop settlement. The sight of 'many wooden crosses' as they approached caused a few moments of panic that 'here were some Spaniards'. The buccaneers primed their guns and readied themselves 'for an enemy'. Advancing cautiously, they met only Indians. The latter had little food since their plantations were young and the corn not yet ready for harvesting, but Dampier noted, 'they made us welcome to such as they had'. The Indians tried to persuade them to remain, but the buccaneers were anxious to be off. When the Indians showed no enthusiasm for taking them farther, they decided to 'go without a guide'. It was all too much for Wafer, who had 'marched in great pain ever since his knee was burned with powder' and was 'not able to trudge it further through rivers and woods'. He asked to be left, as did two others: Richard Gopson, a scholarly man, carrying a copy of the Testament in Greek, from which he loved to read aloud, and John Hingson, a mariner. Both preferred the uncertainty of remaining with the Kuna to the leeches, oozing mud and stinging rains of the jungle. Their fellow buccaneers agreed to their remaining. There was no question of enforcing the agreement to shoot any men who lagged behind. As Wafer later remembered, it had only been intended 'to terrify any from loitering'.

The remaining buccaneers set out. At the last moment some Indians agreed to go with them and guided them downhill and eastwards. The buccaneers wondered why they were not going north and anxiously showed their pocket compasses to their guides, who dismissed them as 'pretty things but not convenient'. They led the buccaneers down into a valley and along a river, which, according to Dampier, who must have been keeping careful count, they crossed precisely 'thirty-two times', covering nine miles in all before they made camp. The men had no provisions, so Dampier shot a quam, 'a large bird as big as a turkey', which they shared with their guides. The next night, the eleventh of the odyssey, they were not so lucky and after a ten-mile march 'went supperless to bed'. The passing days condensed into a blur of 'deep rivers', 'low swampy ground' and increasing starvation. They were at a very low ebb. Dampier wrote feelingly, 'Not a man of us but wished the journey at an end; our feet being blistered, and our thighs stript with wading through so many rivers; the way being almost continually through rivers, or pathless woods'. Yet for the first time they began to have 'fair weather'. The oppressive, brooding humidity was yielding to fresher breezes and clearer skies.

At last, struggling breathlessly over high hills, they saw to their 'great comfort' the glint of the North Sea – the Caribbean. On the twenty-third day of their journey they found canoes to carry them down the Concepcion River to the sea. Dampier calculated that they had travelled 110 miles. It had taken them over 'very high mountains' and across 'deep and dangerous rivers', yet he did not glorify their achievement. In his book he recalled that they had not taken the best route. If they had canoed up the Cheapo or Santa Maria Rivers, they could have saved themselves fifty miles and reached places from where 'a man may pass from sea to sea in three days time with ease', and where the Indians could do it in one and a half days. He acknow-ledged the buccaneers' overwhelming debt to the Indians: 'I must confess the Indians did assist us very much, and I question whether ever we had got over without their assistance'.

On 24 May the buccaneers went aboard a 'privateering' vessel, which they found lying at La Sounds Key in the San Blas Islands, and immediately bought whatever they could 'to gratify our Indian guides, for we were resolved to reward them to their hearts content'. They presented them with beads, scissors and looking-glasses and 'half a dollar a man' from each member of their party. The Indians, Dampier wrote, were delighted, returning 'with joy' to their friends.

The ship sailed off with Dampier and his comrades to join a buccaneer fleet anchored off nearby Springer's Key. There they were reunited with Coxon, who had survived his own trip across the isthmus the previous year and was apparently 'delighted' to learn that Dampier and his companions had been rescued. Quite unabashed, he and his men rushed to greet them and bombard them with questions: 'How we lived? how far we had been? and what discoveries we made in those seas?' The embarrassing fact that Coxon had decamped back over the isthmus, taking most of the expedition's medical supplies, was, it seems, tactfully ignored.

Jollity and carousing over, the buccaneers spent days debating what to do next. Dampier wisely advised against a further venture across the isthmus, painting a bleak picture of 'the fatigue of our march'. Instead they embarked on a series of raids against Spanish ships and settlements in the Caribbean. Dampier was asked to transfer to a French privateer ship that was undermanned. The behaviour of his new Gallic shipmates did not accord with Dampier's principles of hard work and enterprise. He dismissed them in disgust: '[They were] the saddest creatures that ever I was among; for though we had bad weather that required many hands aloft, yet the biggest part of them never stirred out of their hammocks but to eat or ease themselves'. He packed up his clothes and his journal and insisted on transferring again. Dampier knew he was within his rights since 'privateers are not obliged to any ship, but free to go ashore where they please, or to go into any other ship that will entertain them, only paying for their provision'. An English captain named Wright agreed to take him under his command.

Dampier had become a full-fledged rover, still keen to make his fortune but increasingly hooked on new experiences of the natural world. While he and the other buccaneers searched for prey and dodged Spanish patrols, Dampier found time to marvel at the manatee, a mammal that lives in the brackish water of river estuaries and creeks. Sailors who were sex-starved, myopic, drunk, or a combination of all three, often mistook these creatures with their smooth, pale bellies, dolphinlike tails, and elongated nipples, when pregnant or suckling, for mermaids. The reality of nature was wonder enough for Dampier. His description was accurate and used comparisons his readers sixteen years later would readily understand. The manatee was 'about the bigness of a horse' and ten to twelve feet long, with a mouth like that 'of a cow, having great, thick lips', eyes 'no bigger than a small pea', and ears just 'two small holes on each side of the head'.

Dampier sniffed the scent of bushes of pungent vanilla 'with which chocolate is perfumed' and walked through groves of mançanilla trees, the tree whose caustic sap had burned Ringrose's skin. Its yellow-green fruit was, Dampier noted, so poisonous that men even fell ill after feasting on crabs that had eaten it. He had previously noticed that birds never touched mançanilla and other poisonous fruits and therefore wisely resolved only to eat fruits he had seen pecked by birds.

He wrote with pity of the plight of some 'poor, naked, Indians' who had been plundered so often they had almost nothing left. He noted how they wore pieces of tortoise-shell through their pierced lips and how 'they have likewise holes bored in their ears both men and women when young and by continual stretching them with great pegs they grow to be as big as five shilling pieces'.

In late August 1681, Dampier and some of his companions from the isthmus expedition returned to La Sounds Key, anxious for news of their five men whom they had 'left in the heart of the country among the Indians'. They fired two guns as a signal to the Indians, and soon canoes came skimming out from the shore. As one approached, the buccaneers excitedly recognized four men sitting among a group of Indians as Spratlin and Bowman, who had been cut off by the rising river water, and Hingson and Gopson, who had stayed with Wafer. They climbed aboard amid much rejoicing and backslapping, followed by their Indian escorts who squatted down in a group on the deck. One of the Indians was taller than the others, but as lean, painted and tanned, and with the same silver ornament in his nose. It was Wafer.

He had allowed the women to paint intricate patterns on his face and body with bright red, yellow and blue vegetable dyes. '[As I sat] cringing upon my hams . . . all naked but only about the waist, and with my nose-piece . . . hanging over my mouth', he later wrote with amusement, ''twas the better part of an hour before one of the crew, looking more narrowly upon me, cry'd out, here's our doctor; and immediately they all congratulated my arrival among them'. Perhaps the observant crewman was Dampier. He admitted that it was 'some time' before he recognized the muscular, painted figure clad in just a loin-cloth. He took Wafer's appearance as a sign of how the Indians had taken him to their hearts. Exhibiting his usual disregard for hardship and his dedication to 'curiosity', Dampier wrote a little enviously that Wafer 'not only got more of their language but was in a capacity to make better observations' than the rest of them.

Wafer had an extraordinary story to tell. At first the Kuna had been wary of him and his companions, Gopson and Hingson, who were soon joined by Spratlin and Bowman. The Indians treated Wafer's wound by chewing herbs to make a paste, which they smeared on plantain leaves and applied daily to his knee. The poultice was so effective that after twenty days he was completely cured except for a numbing weakness that remained with him through his life. Yet, in everything else, the Indians 'were not altogether so kind'. They looked 'very scurvily' on the party of 'cringing and shivering' Englishmen, throwing green plantains at them 'as you would bones to a dog'.

Gradually, Wafer and his companions learned the reasons for the hostility of the Kuna, whom, like Dampier, he lauded as 'generally a kind and free-hearted people'. They believed Dampier and the other buccaneers who had gone on to the coast had forced their Indian guides to go with them 'very much against their wills' because 'the severity of the rainy season being then so great even the Indians had no mind for travelling'. Even though the Kuna were still tending Wafer's wound, as the days passed and there was no sign of the guides, they began seriously to consider killing the lot of them. The Indians set a time limit of ten days for the guides' safe return, 'reckoning it up to us on their fingers'. On the tenth day they 'prepared a great pile of wood' to burn them.

The men were reprieved by a chief named Lacenta, who 'passing that way dissuaded them from that cruelty' and wisely suggested sending the buccaneers north with an Indian escort to enquire of other Kuna living near the coast into the fate of the guides. The journey turned into a terrifying odyssey through viscous swamps and across 'roaring' rivers. They endured storms when it 'fell a raining as if heaven and earth would meet', accompanied by 'horrid claps of thunder and such flashes of lightening, of a sulphurous smell, that we were almost stifled in the open air'. At one stage they were forced to shin up trees to save themselves from a great onrush of floodwater. At length, famished, barely alive, and having lost touch with their guides, the five men came to an Indian house. Wafer was deputed to approach the house alone, to test the reception he would get, while the others hid in the forest. Wafer tottered up, not much caring whether the occupants killed him, and as he entered he fell 'into a swoon'. The settlement was, in fact, the one they had started out from so many days before.

This time, though, he was warmly received, and he revived. The 'long expected guides' had returned, jubilantly displaying the beads and baubles given them by Dampier and his companions, so that 'all the Indians were become now again [their] very good friends'. The Indians took Wafer and his four colleagues to Lacenta's dwelling in a grove of huge, silken-barked cotton trees protected by hedges of prickly pears. The chief insisted that, as the rainy season was at its height, they had to remain.

Wafer soon learned that one of the chief's wives had

*Bloodletting the Kuna way, from the original
1699 edition of Lionel Wafer's book.*

fallen ill. The young surgeon watched her being bled and
was appalled by the process. The woman, who was
running a high fever, was placed naked on a stone in the
river, while an Indian using a small bow shot tiny arrows
into her body as fast as he could, 'not missing any part'.
When one of the arrows struck a vein and blood spurted
out, the Indians leaped about in 'rejoicing and triumph'.
Wafer offered to show them 'a better way' of bloodletting
'without putting the patient to so much torment'.
Although he had lost most of his remaining medicines
when the slaves had run off, he still had a few instruments
and medicaments wrapped up in an oilcloth in his pocket.
He took out his lancet and cut carefully into a vein in the
woman's arm. Her blood began 'to issue out in a stream'.

Lacenta panicked. He seized his lance and threatened that if any harm came to his beloved wife he would have Wafer's 'heart's blood'. Wafer kept calm, drew off twelve ounces, and bound up the woman's arm. By the next day her fever had abated, and Wafer was in high favour.

The Indians carried Wafer aloft in a hammock from plantation to plantation, where he administered 'both physic and phlebotomy to those that wanted'. He had become a sort of demigod and admitted in his own book, 'The heathen did in a manner worship me'. He cast aside his cotton trousers and jacket for a loincloth and silver penis-sheath and allowed the women to paint his body. He watched the Indians pan for gold washed down from the mountains by the violent rains. He drank *quecha* and lay among the drunken Indians as solicitous women sponged their hot, comatose bodies.

As the weeks passed, Wafer began to suspect that the chief meant to keep him in the isthmus 'all the days of my life'. He even offered him one of his daughters in marriage as soon as she was old enough – a serious gesture from the Kuna, who believed in preserving their bloodline. At his wit's end over how to escape, Wafer was on a hunting trip with Lacenta when the chief complained about his hunting dogs. Scenting an opportunity, Wafer cunningly offered to fetch him mastiffs from England if the chief would allow him to go there for a short while. At first the chief refused, and then, reluctantly, gave way, making the surgeon swear to return. Wafer and his four companions set out with an escort of armed Indians, following almost the identical route taken by Dampier to the mouth of the Concepcion River, where the reunion took place. Wafer and his comrades – with the exception of Greek-loving Gopson, who died three days after coming aboard – joined Dampier on Captain Wright's ship.

* * *

The buccaneer fleet continued to dodge about, preying on small vessels. This further meandering gave Dampier more opportunities to chart the pattern of winds, tornadoes and 'thunder-showers' and to observe his surroundings. He described how the Indians in their attacks on the Spanish blew poison darts 'about the bigness and length of a knitting needle' out of hollow wooden tubes about eight feet long. The darts were barbed to make them difficult to extract from the wounds, while the Indians, 'so silent in their attacks . . . retreat so nimbly again that the Spaniards never find them'.

Dampier watched the parasitical sucking-fish, remora, pursue the ship through the clear blue waters to feast on 'such filth as is daily thrown over-board or on mere excrements'. The ship's sanitary arrangements provided an ample supply of the latter. Toilets at this time were usually in the bows of the ship, at what was known as the 'beakhead' or 'head'. Here the carpenter constructed an overhanging wooden frame on which were two or three 'seats of easement', simple wooden boxes with holes cut into them on which the sailors sat to defecate into the water below. To urinate, they simply climbed out onto the platforms along the side of the ship, used mainly for the spreading of the rigging, taking care to check the wind direction to avoid soaking themselves or others.

To supplement their diet, the buccaneers sent parties ashore to gather bags of cocoa nuts, which kept for a long time in the hold without rotting in the slopping bilgewater. Cocoa had long been in use among the Maya, with the addition of chilli to give the drink added bite. They particularly valued it as a celebratory drink and often gave it to sacrificial victims to heighten their courage during the ceremonies. Montezuma is said to have had a warehouse big enough to contain nearly a billion cocoa beans. The Spanish brought cocoa to Spain, and by the first half of the seventeenth century it had become a popular drink at the Spanish court. When English privateers and pirates first captured Spanish ships with cocoa beans on board, they dismissed them as 'sheep's droppings'. However, chocolate drinking boomed in England after Charles II's Restoration, helped no doubt by the contemporary belief that it was an aphrodisiac.*

Dampier would devote several pages of his first book to describing the cocoa tree and its cropping patterns, drawing on his memory and journals: 'The cacao tree hath a body about a foot and a half thick and seven or eight feet high to the branches, which are large, and spreading like an oak, with a pretty thick, smooth, dark-green leaf, shaped like that of a plum tree, but larger. The nuts are enclosed in cods as big as both a man's fists put together'. Some varieties of nut were 'better and fatter'. Instead of drying this type, the Spaniards 'do in a manner burn them to dry up the oil; for else, they say, it would fill them too full of blood, drinking chocolate as they do, five or six times a day'.

When the buccaneers slunk past the heavily defended port of Cartagena, Dampier had the chance to see the fabled nunnery of La Popa, perched atop a hill overlooking

---

*Dr Henry Stubbes, England's great expert on chocolate, who often brewed Charles II's cocoa for him, taking care to use twice as much cocoa kernel as he did for ordinary mortals, commended 'the great use of chocolate in venery and for supplying the testicles with a balsam or a sap'. Perhaps the number of Charles II's illegitimate children owed something to the double-strength doses of chocolate fed to him by Stubbes.

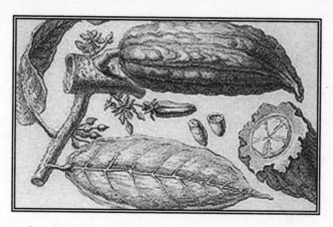

An early eighteenth-century drawing of the leaves and fruit of the cocoa plant.

Cartagena's great fortified harbours. It was dedicated to the Virgin Mary and contained a famous statue of her, and 'any misfortune that befalls the privateers' was, he noted, 'attributed to this lady's doing'. One of the greatest triumphs claimed for her was the sinking of Morgan's flagship, the *Oxford*, in 1669. Dampier wrote with Protestant irony of how the Spaniards believed that the Virgin went physically to battle with the buccaneers, returning home from sinking the *Oxford* 'all wet', with her 'clothes dirty and torn with passing through wood', and that she doubtless deserved 'a new suit for such eminent pieces of service'.

Despite the pleasure he took in observing, by the summer of 1682 Dampier had grown weary of his companions. Although he had turned down an offer to join a French man-of-war – '[because] I ever designed to continue with those of my own nation' – he was exasperated that many among the buccaneer fleet were 'drunk and quarrelling'. He felt their voyage lacked purpose. Captain

Wright agreed. They exercised their right to leave the fleet and, with a group of about twenty men, sailed northwards to Virginia – fast becoming a favoured hideaway and resting place for buccaneers.

VII

THE *BACHELOR'S DELIGHT*

By the time Dampier arrived in July 1682, Virginia was prospering with 43,000 inhabitants spread throughout the colony. The focus was Chesapeake Bay, a massive estuary 10 to 20 miles wide and 200 miles long, dividing what were known as the Western and Eastern Shores. The bay was fed by four major rivers – the James, York, Rappahannock and Potomac – which, with numerous smaller rivers, produced a series of peninsulas. The rivers drew from settlers favourable comparisons to English waterways. The Potomac was 'the sweetest and greatest river I have seen, so that the Thames is but a little finger to it', wrote one. Another thought that the James River contained 'great plenty of fish of all kinds, as for sturgeon all the world cannot be compared to it'. The rivers' green and sedge-grey waters were fringed with tall, swaying bulrushes. Cedars and pines on the banks swept upwards, nourished by the sandy soil. One early visitor thought that the shore looked from the sea 'like a forest standing in water'. The bay seemed a garden of Eden, offering plenty 'as in the first creation without toil or labour'.

But the early days of the colony had not been easy. Jamestown, on the James River, was the first permanent settlement in 1607, and the settlers had huddled inside its triangular-shaped palisade. They suffered terrible

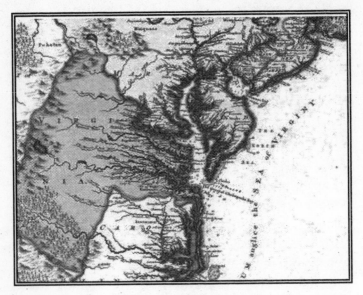

Early map of Virginia.

malnutrition. In the winter of 1609–10, 440 out of 500 starved to death. Malaria, typhoid, dysentery and influenza ravaged the skeletal settlers, and disputes with Powhatan Indians led to periodic but savage fighting. The colonists spoke philosophically of a seasoning time during which people either became inured to the hardships or perished.

The colony had been founded as a profit-making enterprise, but at first this seemed a pipe dream. The settlers' hopes of finding gold were soon disappointed. Attempts to grow 'exportable' crops such as pineapples and olives failed. However, tobacco saved the struggling colony and turned the pipe dream into pipe-smoking reality.

By Dampier's day, 20 to 30 million pounds of tobacco annually were being rolled down in great hogsheads from bulging warehouses to waiting English merchantmen.

Virginia's plantations were growing so fast that they were unable to secure enough indentured labourers from Britain and were turning to the import of slaves from West Africa, who, within just ten years, would make up about one in five of the population.

Virginia was popular with seamen of all sorts because the cost of living was low. Five pounds bought as convivial a life as thirty pounds in London, and spirits were cheeringly cheap. Dampier and his fellows arrived in high anticipation of disposing handsomely of their booty and relaxing in congenial surroundings. Initially, they lived quietly on the Eastern Shore, but unfortunately their arrival was quickly followed by one of the first pirate raids on Virginia itself, which shocked the authorities and soured the atmosphere. It is therefore unsurprising that Dampier encountered what he called 'troubles' in Virginia. The word *troubles* in buccaneer chronicles was nearly always a euphemism for a brush with the law. He was almost certainly questioned about his recent activities, although there is no evidence in surviving records that any charges were brought against him. In his book Dampier would gloss over his time in Virginia, writing simply, 'That country is so well known to our nation, that I shall say nothing of it, nor shall I detain the reader with the story of my own affairs, and the troubles that befell me during the about 13 months of my stay'.

Dampier did reveal that he lodged with a 'gentlewoman', probably in Accomack County on the Eastern Shore.* About six months after his arrival he began suffering 'great

*We have been alerted to the possibility that Dampier may have contracted a bigamous marriage to a woman named Elinor at Accomack and that they had a son called Daniel. Virginia Land Office Patents Record No. 9 confirm that Elinor Dampour (or Dampier) was living in Virginia at the time. Dampier is certainly an uncommon name but we cannot yet establish her connection to Dampier and the birth of Daniel.

torment' from a swelling on his leg, which looked 'very red and angry'. He put a plaster over it to 'bring it to a head'. When he removed the plaster, out came three inches of brown, threadlike worm. Until that moment he had been unsure what was wrong with him. The 'gentlewoman' thought it was 'a nerve', but Dampier recognized the parasite as a guinea worm. He coolly spooled the protruding length of worm around a small stick. Then every morning and evening he patiently 'strained it out gently, about two inches at a time, not without some pain, till at length [he] had got out about two foot'. Yet his leg continued to hurt.

Learning that an acquaintance was on his way 'to a negro to have his horse cured of a galled back', Dampier went with him. He watched the black man, in a ceremony that seems to have owed something to the art of the witch doctor or voodoo, stroke the sore place, sprinkle it with a little coarse powder, like dry, crumbled tobacco leaves, mutter a few words, blow on the wound three times and wave his hands. The man then declared that the horse would soon recover and asked for a white cock in payment. The normally suspicious Dampier was evidently impressed, because he showed him his leg. The black man undertook to cure him in three days for the same fee. Dampier wrote admiringly, '[the man used] exactly the same method with me, as he did with the horse', and that he was completely cured. Years later, when Dampier reported on his voyages to a meeting of the Royal Society, the members showed particular interest in this cure.

The quiet rhythm of Dampier's life ended in the spring of 1683. In April, John Cook, the captain who had led Dampier

back across the isthmus, sailed up the Chesapeake, bringing Lionel Wafer with him. His large ship, mounting
eighteen guns, was named *Revenge* in jubilant reference to
Cook's seizure of her in retribution from French privateers
who had 'plundered the English of their ship, goods and
arms'. Cook planned 'a new expedition into the South
Seas, to cruise on the coast of Chile and Peru'. First he had
made for the Eastern Shore to trade wine from his prize for
provisions, relax in the taverns, refit his vessel and – most
important of all – recruit.

Dampier joined 'these new adventurers'. Still hankering
to seize a Spanish treasure ship, he also wanted to see more
of the Pacific. Thoughts of returning home to Judith do
not seem to have loomed large, even after four years. Or
perhaps he thought his reception would be warmer if he
brought Spanish gold to compensate for his protracted
absence.

Before sailing, the crew of seventy elected officers and
agreed on the usual articles, including some 'particular
rules' about 'temperance and sobriety' by reason of 'the
length of [their] intended voyage'. The elected quartermaster was Edward Davis, who had been with Dampier
and Cook on the isthmus. Effectively the second-in-
command, the quartermaster had considerable authority
on a buccaneer ship, often acting as a counterweight to the
captain's opinions. Serious offences aboard ship were tried
by jury, but the quartermaster judged minor offences and
'with an equality to them all' distributed food and plunder.
He could order sailors to be whipped as punishment but
would do so only in extreme circumstances given the
buccaneers' strong antipathy to such punishment, born of
aversion to the strict discipline of naval and merchant
ships. The quartermaster also usually led the boarding

parties when attacking enemy ships and often took command of captured prizes.

The ship's navigator was Ambrose Cowley. He claimed to have a master of arts from Cambridge University and, like Dampier and Wafer, would one day publish an account of his travels. Also like them, he did not then portray himself as a buccaneer, let alone a pirate. He was 'an ingenious Englishman' fallen into the buccaneers' company like 'a jackdaw amongst the rooks'. He claimed disingenuously that Cook had simply hired him to pilot the ship to Tortuga in the West Indies, and that only once they were at sea did he learn their true destination.

On 23 August 1683, the buccaneers sailed from Virginia southeastwards into the Atlantic, bound for the Cape Verde Islands. A few days out they encountered one of the worst storms of Dampier's life. It lasted more than a week, and they emerged 'like so many drowned rats'. Dampier blamed Cowley for incompetence in letting the ship go beam-on to the wind in a sea that was 'so high that every wave threatened to overwhelm [them]'. Cowley apparently 'raved like a mad man', calling for an axe to chop down the mizzenmast. Captain Cook, and Quartermaster Davis, told him to stay his hand. Instead, Dampier and another seaman, John Smallbone, whom Dampier praised in his book as their saviour, scrambled up into the forerigging. They spread their coats to catch enough wind to bring the ship around rather than risk trying to spread any headsails, which likely would have 'blown away' in the process.

They were thankful to reach Sal, one of the most easterly islands in the Cape Verde group and named for its salt pans. Dampier was not impressed by the barren little island with its scrubby vegetation and skinny goats. It did, however, provide his first sight of flamingos. The island's half-dozen impoverished Portuguese inhabitants had not seen a ship in three years. The governor nervously sent the buccaneers a few goats. Captain Cook, 'minding more the poverty of the giver than the value of the present', gave the man a coat in return. Dampier noted that he needed it, for 'he had nothing but a few rags on his back, and an old hat not worth 3 farthings'. The buccaneers traded a few more old clothes for some salt. Young surgeon Herman Coppinger excitedly bought what he believed to be ambergris from one of the islanders. A sceptical Dampier examined it. Noting its dark colour and 'very soft' consistency, he decided it was nothing but 'goat's dung'. Like many credulous tourists to this day, Coppinger, overeager for a bargain, had been conned.*

The buccaneers sailed on through the islands toward St Jago. Although Dampier did not say so, Cowley admitted they had 'no other intention than' to seize an even larger, stronger ship for the arduous voyage into the South Seas. Dampier apparently saw no irony in describing the inhabitants of St Jago, whom he recalled from his voyage of 1670, as 'very thievish'. If they saw a chance, they would 'snatch anything from you, and run away with it'.

Days later off the West African coast in an act of pure piracy, which, once again, Dampier did not describe, they seized a forty-gun Danish ship, ignoring the fact that she belonged to an ally of England and should have been left alone. Cowley called her a 'lovely ship'. She was 'very fit for a long voyage', sturdy, and crammed with 'good brandy, water,

*In his books Dampier would describe, for the benefit of future travellers, the look and smell of real ambergris, citing as his source 'a very diligent and observing person, and likewise very sober and credible', who had seen a large piece 'of a dusky color, towards black, and about the hardness of mellow cheese, and of a very fragrant smell'.

provisions, and other necessaries'. She was also carrying sixty female African slaves. The buccaneers renamed her the *Bachelor's Delight*. The fate of the slaves was never mentioned but was presumably a sad one. At best, the buccaneers may have sold the women to a slave trader on the coast.

The buccaneers filled their casks to the brim with precious fresh water essential to their survival and, in mid-November 1683, set out across the South Atlantic for the Strait of Magellan. The weather became stifling hot, relieved only temporarily and alarmingly by short, violent tornadoes bringing 'thunder, lightning and rain' in their wake. Many men fell ill with fever. There was little fresh food, so Dampier and others, who still had the strength, caught sharks. They boiled them, then squeezed them dry, before stewing the fishy flesh with vinegar and pepper and feeding it to the sick.

In late January 1684, they sighted the 'rocky, barren' shores of the Falkland Islands. The heaving seas were 'as red as blood' for about a mile across with small red shellfish 'no bigger than the top of a man's little finger', with lobsterlike claws. Dampier had been trying for a month to 'hinder' Cook's plan of 'going through the Strait of Magellan', which he feared would 'prove very dangerous' to them. He simply did not think his fellow seamen were up to negotiating the narrow, twisting strait between the South American mainland and Tierra del Fuego, where frequent strong winds and squalls blew down from the mountains on both sides. Dampier argued that they should instead go around Cape Horn, the island at the very tip of the continent.*

---

*Cape Horn was not named for its shape or geographic position, but rather after their 'beloved village of Hoorn', in Holland, by Jacob Le Maire and Willem van Schouten, who were the first to round it in 1616.

Not for the last time, Dampier's persuasive powers failed. Cook did not change course, but nature intervened. Strong westerlies buffeted the *Bachelor's Delight*, preventing her from entering the Strait of Magellan. Instead they headed south through the Le Maire Strait, which had its own hazards. The wind dropped, and they ran into 'a short cockling sea'. The waves ran first this way and then the other as if two tides were converging. Water crashed over the bows, and 'the ship tossed like an eggshell'. Dampier had 'never felt such uncertain jerks in a ship' and feared they would founder. At last, a breeze blew up that kicked them east of Staten Island and finally southwest around Cape Horn.

The fourteenth of February brought a 'violent storm'. Cowley described how, it being Valentine's Day, they were 'discoursing the intrigues of women' when the tempest began. It lasted for over two weeks and drove them down to a chilly latitude of sixty degrees thirty minutes south, 'farther than any ship hath sailed before south', as Cowley noted with pride.* The men warmed themselves with brandy, finding they could 'drink three quarts of burnt brandy a man in twenty-four hours, without getting intoxicated'. At least the storm gave them the chance to fill twenty-three barrels with rainwater. On 3 March, the wind, which had been blowing from the west, shifted around to the east, finally nudging them into the Pacific. The men concluded that 'the discoursing of women at sea was very unlucky' and 'occasioned the storm'.

On 19 March, off the coast of Chile near Valdivia, Dampier and his companions were startled to see another

---

*The previous farthest south was some fifty-seven degrees, achieved by Drake.

ship to the south. Furthermore, 'she was coming [after them] with all the sail she could make'. The buccaneers deceitfully lay 'muzzled', with gunports closed and guns run in. They hoped the vessel was a Spanish cargo ship. Instead, they were hailed in English. The ship was the *Nicholas*, commanded by Captain John Eaton. She had been fitted out ostensibly as a trading vessel, but she was a raider. Eaton told Cook and his men that he had recently parted from yet another English ship, the merchant vessel *Cygnet* under Captain Charles Swan. Swan had been equipped with £5,000 of goods by some 'very eminent merchants' in London who had sent him 'only to trade with the Spaniards or Indians'.

Cook and Eaton agreed to team up, swapping salt beef, bread and water, and sailing to Juan Fernandez to recuperate after the hardships of the voyage. On 22 March, they reached the islands, where a strange reunion took place. Dampier had never forgotten William, the Moskito Indian abandoned there three years earlier when the arrival of Spaniards had forced the buccaneers under Captain Watling to flee. Dampier was one of those who got into a canoe to go in search of the castaway. William was very much alive. He had watched the ships anchor the day before, peering cautiously from a vantage point high up in the forests. Concluding they were English, he awaited them on the beach, a wiry, weathered figure with a goatskin tied around his lean waist. As the buccaneers jumped from their canoes to wade through the surf, another Moskito Indian with them named Robin rushed forward and, 'running to his brother Moskito man, threw himself flat on his face at his feet'. William helped him up and embraced him before prostrating himself in turn at Robin's feet. Dampier described the 'surprise, and tenderness

Juan Fernandez Islands.

and solemnity of this interview, which was exceedingly affectionate on both sides'.

William had spent the intervening years dodging Spanish landing parties, who chased him with dogs. He had been left on the island with just a gun, knife, small powder horn and a few shot. When his ammunition ran out, he had made new weapons. He made notches in his knife to turn it into a saw and then hacked the barrel of his gun into chunks. Using his gunflint to make fire, he heated the pieces of metal until they glowed and then hammered them with stones to make 'harpoons, lances, hooks and a long knife'. He survived on goats and on fish – snapper and grouper – which he caught with ease using lines cut from the skins of seals. Dampier was full of admiration even years later, writing in his book: 'All this may seem strange to those that are not acquainted with the sagacity of the Indians; but it is no more than these Moskito Men are accustomed to in their own country, where they make their own fishing and striking instruments without either forge or anvil'.

The buccaneers inspected William's small hut, half a mile inland and lined with goatskin. His 'couch or barbecu of sticks' was raised two feet above the ground and spread with skins. They feasted on the three goats he had slaughtered and 'dressed' with cabbage in their honour. The sick men were carried ashore and fed by one of Eaton's four doctors on a diet of goat meat, fragrant, leafy herbs and cabbage. Dampier spent time watching the seals, which, he noted, 'swarm as thick about this island as if they had no other place in the world to live in'. They were 'big as calves, the head of them like a dog, therefore called by the Dutch the Sea-hounds'.* Parties of whiskery seal-like creatures with shaggy manes also lolloped ashore, with their 'great goggle eye[s]' and sharp teeth from which seamen made dice. Dampier's account is credited as the first to give them the English name of sea lion.

On 8 April, the buccaneers left Juan Fernandez to begin the serious business of raiding the South American coast. They sailed steadily north, keeping about forty miles from land to avoid detection. The 'vastly high' mountains of the Andes were clearly visible. Dampier noticed how they always looked 'blue when seen at sea'. He rightly believed that these were the highest mountains he ever saw.† On 3 May, Captain Eaton chased and seized a small barque carrying timber from Guayaquil to Lima and learned the unwelcome news that the Spanish knew all about the buccaneers' arrival in the Pacific. This was the result of Captain Swan's blunderingly futile attempts to trade at Valdivia, during which he had helpfully volunteered warnings that other, more aggressive, Englishmen were abroad. As a result, the viceroy of Lima had sent 'expresses to all the sea ports, that they might provide themselves against our assaults'.

---

*Seals and dogs have a common ancestor.

†Only the Himalayas, then unsighted by Britons, are higher.

The whole coast was on high alert. The Spaniards were highly indignant at the arrival of pirates in their midst. But they had been pirates too. In 1526 two small ships commanded by the pilot Bartolome Ruiz, on behalf of Francisco Pizarro, sailed south over the equator to encounter and capture an oceangoing raft fitted with fine cotton sails. This was Europe's first contact with the Inca Empire. A mouthwatering report about the booty was sent back to Spain:

> They were carrying many pieces of silver and gold as personal ornaments . . . including crowns and diadems, belts and bracelets, armour for the legs and breastplates; tweezers and rattles and strings and clusters of beads and rubies; mirrors decorated with silver, and cups and other drinking vessels. They were carrying many wool and cotton mantles and Moorish tunics . . . and other pieces of clothing coloured with cochineal, crimson, blue, yellow and all other colours, and worked with different types of ornate embroidery, in figures of birds, animals, fish and trees . . . There were small stones in bead bags: emeralds and chalcedonies and other jewels.

The incident was the prelude to a campaign far more bloody, sustained and merciless than anything perpetrated by these newer raiders.

The dismayed buccaneers realized there would be no such booty for them. As Dampier ruefully wrote, '[the Spanish] would send no riches by sea so long as we were here'. They headed further north for the rocky Lobos de la Mar, 'Seal' Island, to take stock. While they debated, Dampier watched penguins flip through the water. They were, he decided, 'a sea-fowl, about as big as a duck, and such feet; but a sharp bill, feeding on fish. They do not fly but flutter, having rather stumps like young goslings, than wings; and these are instead of fins to them in the water'. He dismissed their flesh as 'ordinary food', but their eggs were 'good meat'.

The buccaneers' hopes received a further knock when they captured three Spanish vessels that had unwittingly sailed too close to the island. Ransacking their prizes, they discovered a letter to the president of Panama from the viceroy of Lima. It warned that 'there were enemies come into' the Pacific. In consequence, the letter continued, the viceroy was sending him flour so that the citizens of Panama 'might not want' if besieged. In addition to an enormous cargo of flour, the buccaneers found '7 or 8 tons of marmalade of quinces and a stately mule', together with a huge carved and painted wooden image of the Virgin Mary. They were galled to learn that the ships had originally been carrying 800,000 pieces of eight, but that the money had prudently been ordered ashore.

There was no point attacking the heavily defended mainland, so the buccaneers sought refuge in the remote Galapagos Islands. They knew of these islands, some 600 miles west of Ecuador and straddling the equator, only by vague report. Their Spanish prisoners tried to dissuade them, claiming they were 'enchanted islands ... but shadows and not real'. Yet to the buccaneers they were real enough, although good navigation would be required to reach them successfully.

The ship's navigator had a number of aids to his art. Near land, he had the benefit of lookouts and of frequent soundings with the lead line to determine the depth of the

---

*The phrase 'plumbing the depths' comes from this operation. *Plumbum* is Latin for lead.

water.* He always had the use of magnetic compasses, which had been introduced to European ships from China via Arabia at the time of the Crusades. The ship's main magnetic compass, the steering compass, was mounted on gimbals to keep it upright, however much the ship tossed, and well protected from the elements in a wooden stand known as a binnacle. Both the helmsman and the navigator made sure they removed their knives and other metal items before they went to work to avoid compass deviation. The navigator also had a smaller azimuth compass: one with a means of taking sun sights to allow him to identify the variation between magnetic and true north.

The navigator could find his latitude with reasonable accuracy – in good weather at least – by taking sights of the height over the horizon of either the sun at midday or the polestar at midnight. Until recently he had only been able to use either the astrolabe or the cross-staff to do this. The astronomer's astrolabe had been simplified for use at sea. It was a large brass ring with a pivoting arm, at each end of which were pinhole sights to align on the relevant celestial object. The theory was that the latitude could be read off, but the astrolabe had to be held up to the eye by a very steady hand and was subject to much buffeting by wind. It was therefore mostly supplanted by the cross-staff, which allowed sights to be taken on the sun and the horizon. However, the cross-staff had a serious disadvantage: sun sights involved looking directly at the sun, which meant that 'there was not one old master of a ship amongst twenty' who was not 'blind in one eye by daily staring in the sun'. Fortunately, at the end of the sixteenth century, Jon Davis had invented the backstaff, which combined the good points of the astrolabe and cross-staff in a simple instrument that allowed the sun's position to be taken from behind the navigator's back while the elevation above the horizon was calculated.

The absence of an instrument for accurate timekeeping meant that longitude was extremely difficult to calculate at sea. The navigator had to work using 'dead reckoning'. He regularly made the best estimate he could of his course and speed, and how they were affected by wind and sea. Each day at noon he recorded his estimates in the logbook. The book took its name from the logline, the device used to measure speed. This was a line thrown over the side, with a piece of wood, or 'log', at the end, and with knots at every 'fathom'.* By counting the number of knots that were played out during the time it took a half-minute glass to empty, the navigator could calculate the ship's speed.† Because errors in assessing longitude were cumulative, the ship's position could be off by 100 or more miles at the end of an ocean voyage.

The difficulty in assessing longitude and the relative accuracy with which latitude could be measured favoured a strategy of what Dampier called 'running down the latitude' for long cross-ocean voyages. First, the ship would sail up or down a coast to a point on the same latitude as its destination and then attempt to sail along that latitude. It was in this way that the *Bachelor's Delight* made for the Galapagos. Dampier noted: 'We steered away NW by N intending to run into the latitude of the Isles Galapagos and steer off west, because we did not know the certain distance, and therefore could not shape a direct course to

*The fathom was the sailor's preferred measure of depth. Originally a rough measurement equating to the span of a man's outstretched arms, it was later standardized to mean six feet.

†In later days the term *knot* was applied to the ship's speed in nautical miles per hour.

them. When we came within 40 minutes of the Equator we steered west'. The method worked well, and on 31 May 1684 they sighted the islands: 'Some of them appeared on our weather bow, some on our lee bow, others right ahead'. They anchored in clear, blue water above 'clean, white, hard sand'.

VIII

THE ENCHANTED ISLANDS

The uninhabited Galapagos Islands were a haven to hungry, exhausted men suffering from scurvy and craving fresh water, fresh meat and 'salading vegetables'. Dampier did not identify where they landed, but it was probably Santiago Island, whose red-black cinder cliffs, washed by a swell of jade-green water, look inhospitable at first. However, after rounding a high, guano-covered rock shaped like a praying man, which pirates nicknamed 'the monk', the buccaneers would have found a wide, gently sloping bay – today named Buccaneer Cove. They quickly erected a tent for Cook, their captain, who had fallen ill on Juan Fernandez.

In the woods beyond the beach, the buccaneers found colonies of tortoises to plunder for food. The Spanish discoverers of these islands had named them Galapagos from the Spanish word for saddle, in tribute to the shape of the shell of the saddleback tortoises. An amazed Dampier wrote, 'I do believe there is no place in the world that is so plentifully stored with those animals'. The tortoises' succulent flesh was 'so sweet, that no pullet eats more pleasantly'. The buccaneers knew the creatures could survive without food or water for up to six months,* so they loaded their vessels with them, storing them upside

*Unknown to the buccaneers, this was because of their slow metabolism.

Ambrose Cowley's map of the
Galapagos Islands drawn in 1684.

down. Dampier calculated that none weighed less than 30 pounds, while the largest were 150 or 200 pounds. The fat could be rendered into oil and used instead of butter to eat with doughboys – a sort of dumpling.

Dampier was in a world where red-legged crabs with yellow and blue heads sashayed over the sand. Male man-of-war birds, inflating their red, balloonlike throat pouches to attract females, flashed through the trees. Spiky-skinned marine iguanas tramped slowly down to the sea to dive for algae, exhausted by demanding mating routines for which nature had thoughtfully given them two penises. Orange and brown land iguanas sunned themselves on rocks. The finches later made famous by Darwin darted hungrily from bush to bush.

Dampier watched and wrote. His descriptions became the first detailed account in English of the Galapagos Islands' famed flora and fauna. Nearly a century and a half later, Charles Darwin took Dampier's books with him on the *Beagle* and studied them carefully. Dampier closely examined stately green turtles paddling through the channels between the islands. He was fond of turtle meat and remarked that a good time to catch turtles was while they were mating in the water. It was possible simply to grab the males, which, 'while engendering, do not easily forsake their female'.

Later, Dampier concluded that, compared with those he had seen elsewhere, these were 'a sort of bastard green turtle; for their shell is thicker than other green turtle in the West or East Indies'. He described how in different parts of the world there were 'degrees of them both in respect to their flesh and bigness', but those of the Galapagos were the largest he had ever seen, some with bellies 'five feet wide'; by contrast, elsewhere in the South Seas there were other green turtles not 'so big as the smallest hawkbill' turtle.

A tortoise.

His consciousness of geographic variation and of degrees of difference and his use of the word *bastard* – which he used in similar contexts elsewhere – all suggest a willingness to conceive of the characteristics of related creatures being changed by local circumstances and by the selection of those with whom they mated. This revolutionary view was at direct variance with accepted religious doctrine. Scholars calculated in years, months and days the date of Creation, when every living thing had been created; since then, no change had taken place, nor would it until the millennium and beyond. The consensus, established in 1658 when Dampier was a boy, was that the six days of Creation had begun at 9 a.m. on Monday, 23 October, 4004 BC.

Dampier would later insert in his first book, alongside his comments about geographic variation, a detailed account of the migratory patterns of the green turtle in the Caribbean, Atlantic and Pacific. His understanding of the principles of migration and how it worked in practice is a further measure of his advanced thinking.

A green turtle.

In Dampier's time, Daniel Defoe's old schoolmaster seriously claimed in a pamphlet that swallows migrated to the moon in winter. More than eighty years later, in 1768, the great lexicographer Samuel Johnson maintained the still common thesis that swallows wintered under ice in ponds.

Dampier also noticed a phenomenon he had seen elsewhere: the rising and falling of the tides. But unlike in islands closer to the mainland, those in the Galapagos rose and fell only between one and a half to two feet. He would have liked the chance to explore the islands properly: 'I must confess my curiosity would have carried me further in search to find anything profitable on them', but, as he admitted with regret, 'our business was not to search places to settle in, only to find convenience to careen'.

Ambrose Cowley was also intrigued by this strange, volcanic archipelago. Most islands, he believed, had previously had 'sulphurous matter that had set them on fire, they having been burned formerly and some part of them burned up leaving piles of cinders'. Excited to see a hill on one of the islands that looked 'covered with gold', he rushed to investigate, only to find it was 'a fine brimstone as fine as flour'. He embarked on the first geographic survey of the islands, later producing the first detailed maps seen in England. His beautifully coloured sketches of the main islands show their dark-green slopes covered then, as now, in incense trees. With an eye to the main chance, he named the islands for the noblemen and politicians of England but could not resist reserving one for himself, calling it Cowley's Enchanted Island.

On 12 June, although Cook was still unwell, the buccaneers sailed northwest for the coast of New Spain (present-day Mexico), hoping that news of their arrival might not have spread that far. One of their Indian prisoners had been born in the port of Realeja and promised his captors easy pickings there. By early July, they were passing Cape Blanco, which reminded Dampier of Beachy Head. Here, near this comfortingly England-like coastline, Captain Cook suddenly died. Dampier believed 'it is usual with sick men coming from the sea, where they have nothing but the sea-air, to die off as soon as ever they come within the view of the land'.

The buccaneers anchored and carried Cook ashore 'to give him Christian burial'. The burial party, of whom Dampier was one, was surprised to see three Indians watching them. The buccaneers captured two, who confessed to spying for the Spanish. They tried to appease the buccaneers with tales of a 'beef estancion' some three miles away; these tales, Dampier later recalled, 'set us agog'. He and twenty-four eager, hungry buccaneers set off around the shore by canoe. Beaching their boats, they found a cattle ranch in the savannah. Many of the cattle were out grazing. Some of the men wanted to overnight there and next day slaughter twenty or thirty beasts. Dampier thought this highly imprudent. He argued that it was better to kill three or four and return on board immediately. This time he persuaded half the men to return with him. The others insisted on staying.

The next morning, there was no sign of them. A search party set out by canoe and found their comrades huddling on a small rock half a mile offshore, up to their waists in water. They had been attacked by forty or fifty armed Spaniards and had rushed back to their canoe, only to find 'their boat all in flames'. Spotting the rock and deciding it would make a good redoubt, they had managed to wade out to it on the ebb tide, dodging shots whistling from the shore. Their rescuers had arrived just in time to save them from the now swiftly rising tide, from which, Dampier recalled smugly, they were 'in as great danger' as from the Spanish.

On 20 July, the buccaneers resumed their voyage. Their new captain was Edward Davis, the moderate, sober quartermaster, who was appointed 'by consent of all the company'. As they neared Realeja, Dampier saw 'a high peaked burning mountain', known to the Spanish as 'the old volcano'. That evening, violent storms delayed their attack. They finally set out at 11 p.m., paddling by canoe up creeks thickly fringed with dripping mangroves to try to reach the town, but it was hard going. They soon discovered, from prisoners captured along the way, that the town governor had been warned of 'enemies come into the sea'. It was hopeless, and, as Dampier noted, they prudently 'thought it best to defer this design till another time'.

With the element of surprise denied them at every turn, the buccaneers headed for the Gulf of Amapalla to careen

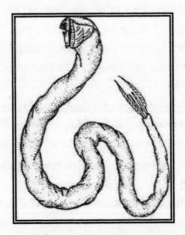

A teredo worm.

their vessels and take stock once more.* Careening was a lengthy and complicated process of cleaning and repairing the ship's bottom. In tropical waters barnacles and weeds built up rapidly, soon slowing the vessels' prized speed. Additionally, teredo worms (a type of mollusc) could quickly honeycomb a hull by boring into its timbers. A single worm could lay a million eggs a year and grow up to six inches in length.

To careen a ship, she had to be beached, preferably in the case of a buccaneer ship in a remote location, with nearby trees to use in positioning and holding her. The carpenter then took charge. First, the ship's guns and stores were removed, and her topmast was taken down. Sometimes the guns were mounted on hastily thrown up earthworks as a means of defence. The next step was to heave the ship first on one side, then on the other, using the trees and blocks and tackle so that weeds and barnacles could be burned or scraped off, rotting or worm-holed planking repaired or replaced, and the bottom coated with a protective goo of tallow, tar and wax, sometimes also mixed with sulphur and arsenic.

Captain Davis went in by canoe to check that it was safe and seek help from the Indians. On the island of Mangera, he captured a stout Spanish friar, whom he forced to guide him to an Indian hilltop town on the neighbouring island of Amapalla. Here Davis lied to the assembled Indians that he and his men 'were Biscayers sent thither by the King of Spain to clear those seas from enemies; that their ships were coming into the Gulf to careen'. The Indians agreed to help him and led him and his men to their

*The term *careen* comes from the Latin word for keel.

church, 'the place of all public meetings and all plays and pastimes'.

Dampier found it a poignant and compelling place. He later described how the churches in Indian towns had 'all sorts of vizards [masks] and strange antick dresses both for men and women'. The abundant musical instruments included 'strumstrums', an instrument he likened to a sitar 'made of a large gourd cut in the midst, and a thin board layed over the hollow fastened to the sides; this serves for the belly; over which the strings are placed'.

Dampier watched Indians dance and sing in their churches in the warm tropical night. Sometimes the moonlight was enough for them. At other times they lit torches, which filled the church with a smoky light and gave a spectral quality to their dance. The images of the Virgin Mary and other saints in churches in the Spanish Indian settlements were 'painted in an Indian complexion' and were partly dressed in Indian clothes to preserve something of the Indian identity in the religion their conquerors had pressed upon them.

Dampier again concluded that Indians living under the Spanish seemed 'more melancholy than other Indians that are free', their jollity and mirth 'rather forced than real'. He wondered whether it was the result of their subjection to the Spanish and decided that the cause was indeed the loss of 'their country and liberties and their ancient freedom'. He philosophized that the native peoples he met on his journey would attack only if they felt threatened and that it was not in their character to be naturally aggressive: 'There are no people in the world so barbarous as to kill a single person who falls accidentally into their hands, or comes to live among them, except they have before been injured by some outrage or violence committed against them'.*

Once they had careened their ships, the buccaneers were anxious to sail on, hoping their luck would change. However, at this critical point, Captain Davis and Captain Eaton decided to part. Dampier explained the reason: 'Eaton's men were but young beginners to the trade', but Davis's men valued their experience 'and would not agree on equal terms'. In other words, they wanted a larger share of the booty. In September 1684, Eaton sailed westwards, taking Cowley with him.

Dampier and Wafer remained with Davis, and on 3 September they sailed for Peru. The weather was vile, with daily storms. A few days later Eaton reappeared. 'He was', Dampier wrote, 'very willing to have made up those differences which first parted us'. Dampier tried to mediate, again unsuccessfully, later writing, 'I did what I could to persuade our men to it but could not'. The result: 'Captain Eaton seeing the unreasonableness of our men, he went away the next day and we never saw him afterwards'. Dampier knew that their chances would have been much better had they stayed together.

A few days later Davis sent men ashore under cover of darkness to seize some prisoners. They also seized a small barque, which those on board had immediately tried to set alight. From their captives they learned that the viceroy of Peru had ordered all seamen, if attacked, to burn their vessels and 'betake themselves to their boats'. He had also

---

*There are glimpses in this portrayal of the ideal of 'the noble savage' first set out by John Dryden in 1670 in 'The Conquest of Granada': 'I am as free as nature first made man, / Ere the base laws of servitude began, / When wild in the woods the noble savage ran'. Like Dampier, Dryden was an acute, independent observer, in his case of society. His words echo Dampier's own philosophy and aspirations.

ordered seaports to keep only the minimum of provisions and had sent Indians to the Isla de Plata, a common watering hole of the pirates, to destroy the goats there. Dampier derided these attempts to starve them, noting that it was 'impossible for them to do unless they could kill all the fish, turtle and seals and sealions in the sea and clear all the islands of boobies'.

It soon became apparent that Davis, Dampier and company might not be alone for much longer. Prisoners spoke of reports reaching the Spanish of a 'great many enemies . . . come over land thro' the country of Darien into the South Seas'. Near Plata, the buccaneers encountered Captain Charles Swan and his ship, the *Cygnet*, which had rounded South America. With him was a large body of men commanded by Captain Peter Harris, nephew of the captain killed in the 1680 expedition, who had crossed the Isthmus of Panama and sacked Santa Maria.

The stout, genial Swan was anxious to preserve some distance from his new companions. He claimed that, after his attempts to trade legitimately failed, his men had forced him to join Harris. He insisted that the *Cygnet*'s owners should receive ten shares of any prize money and wrote plaintive letters to his wife about the company he was forced to keep, overlooking the fact that buccaneering was not the new and horrible pastime he pretended – twelve years earlier he had been at Panama with Morgan. The fortuitous meeting near Plata caused 'much joy on all sides'. Dampier must have been pleased to discover that Basil Ringrose, his companion from the isthmus days, was aboard the *Cygnet* as Swan's supercargo, or commercial agent. In fact, Ringrose had originally proposed the voyage to Swan.

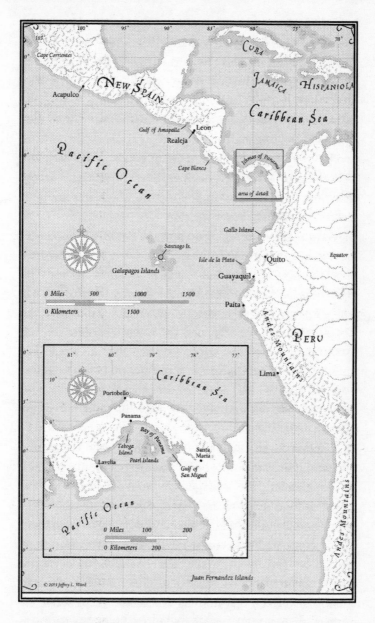

The South Sea (Pacific Ocean) and the North Sea (Caribbean) of the
buccaneers.

Davis tried to locate Eaton so that he could join the group as well. Dampier was scornful. They had had their chance and lost it. 'This', he wrote later, 'is the condition of those men never satisfied in their condition'. He grumbled that even if they had succeeded in finding Eaton, his comrades' pigheadedness would have ensured that they 'should not long have continued in consortship'. Meanwhile, Swan brought his remaining goods up on deck and sold them to Davis's eager men. Everything else – except fine silks, muslins, stockings, and iron, which was saved for ballast – was tossed over the side.

As time passed bringing no news of Eaton, the buccaneer fleet indulged in some fruitless raids. On 2 November they took the port of Paita but found little worth having. The Spaniards had been ordered by the viceroy to refuse to pay any ransom, not even jars of water and wine. The disappointed buccaneers burned the town. Dampier did not particularly regret the wine, realizing that it 'would but make us mad', but he did mind the fact that their food was running low. He and some companions went hunting for penguins, boobies and seals, for they 'had not tasted any flesh in a great while'.

Captain Swan urged all to eat, cheerfully 'comparing the young seals to roasted pigs and the boobies to turkeys' and applauding the strange selection of meats 'for the sweetest food that ever he tasted'. Swan's leadership skills impressed Dampier, who realized 'this he did to train them to live contentedly on coarse meat, not knowing but [they] might be forced to make use of such food before [they] departed out of these seas; for it is generally seen among privateers, that nothing emboldens them sooner to mutiny than want'. He also admired Swan's patience in coaxing the men. His own, more unyielding, philosophy was that 'men as cannot comply with any custom or cannot endure hardships or hard fare . . . should endeavour to live at home for they are apt to make mountains of molehills'.

Dampier described how the local Indians near Paita still made large seagoing rafts similar to the one seized by Ruiz over 150 years earlier. These rafts could carry sixty or seventy tons of cargo on long coastal voyages but were only good for sailing with the prevailing winds, 'which [were] always the same, not varying above a point or two all the way from Lima to Panama'. The rafts were used for just a single voyage. When they reached their northern-most destination, the crew abandoned them and returned home by ship.

Still failing to find Eaton, the captains prepared to attack the port of Guayaquil. Dampier knew the town as 'a place of no mean trade' but also as 'very sickly' and notorious for 'fevers, violent headache, pains in the bowels and fluxes'. Entering the Bay of Guayaquil, they passed the small island of Santa Clara. Ominously, its shape struck Dampier as 'like a dead man stretched in a shroud'. Many ships had indeed foundered on the shoals off its northern shores. Dampier was intrigued by tales of one 'very rich wreck' lying beneath the waters and occasionally plundered by Indians who dived down, risking vicious attacks from swarms of catfish looking 'much like a whiting' but, unlike them, 'very venomous'.

The buccaneers set out in canoes, but their progress was slow. As the dawn came up, they were still two leagues from the town, trapped among claustrophobic mangroves. All they could do was hide in a creek till darkness fell. As they lay concealed, tormented by mosquitoes, midges and flies, two barques laden with African slaves sailed out from Guayaquil. The Spanish sailors failed to spot the buccaneer canoes. But as the barques came out into the bay, they were seen by a group of buccaneers keeping watch in a small boat. Assuming their comrades had been captured or killed and that the two approaching vessels were manned by Spanish soldiers intent on seizing the buccaneer fleet, they opened fire. The sound, ripping through the hot, heavy air, caused 'a great disorder' among the buccaneers concealed in the creek. Not knowing the cause of the firing, some were for returning to the ships, other for marching at once on the town. Eventually, they agreed to wait for the next tide and row on.

It was hazardous negotiating the swift-flowing river at night. One canoe became caught on a concealed tree stump, but they freed it before it overturned. Then suddenly, or so it seemed, Dampier saw Guayaquil lying 'open before [them]' with 'but one light'. A single musket shot rang out, and the town lit up, suddenly brilliant with torch and candlelight. The buccaneers hesitated, uncertain whether they had been discovered or whether a fiesta which they knew was imminent was beginning with fireworks. Davis, with Dampier and the rest of his men, drove their canoes into the bank and crept ashore to investigate. At first, according to Dampier, Swan and most of his men 'did not think it convenient to attempt anything' but, nettled by charges of cowardice, followed reluctantly.

The buccaneers were still two miles from Guayaquil and found the going difficult through the thick vegetation. They decided to lie low until daylight and then to surprise the town. During the night, however, one of the buccaneers allowed an Indian they had taken captive to be their guide to escape. The men searched frantically and futilely, blundering around in the dark, knowing the escaped man would soon raise the alarm. As Dampier confessed, 'Not a man after that had the heart to speak of going farther'. They climbed back into their canoes, rowed out into the middle of the river, took a final look at the 'very pleasant prospect' of Guayaquil, then rowed reluctantly away. As Dampier wrote grumpily, 'They did not fire one gun at us, nor we at them'. Yet there were consolations. Sailing downriver into the bay, they captured the two barques loaded with slaves that had earlier caused so much confusion, together with a third, carrying 1,000 Africans in total, 'all lusty young men and women'. The buccaneers selected a number and took them aboard, then turned the rest ashore.

Dampier, however, was deeply disappointed. He knew that in crossing the isthmus, Harris and his men had 'routed the Spaniards away from the town and gold mines' of Santa Maria. Harris had taken 120 pounds of gold and had shown Dampier 'a lump as big as a hen's egg', assuring him 'there were lumps a great deal bigger'. The gold was there for the taking, and providence had just provided a labour force. Santa Maria itself could provide an 'abundance of iron crows and pickaxes' for the slaves to labour with. 'There was never a greater opportunity put into the hands of men to enrich themselves than we had, to have gone with these negroes and settled ourselves at Santa Maria', Dampier later recalled with real regret. Everything would have been in their favour to found a colony. They had good supplies of flour, and the concealed creeks along the broad Santa Maria River were an excellent place to careen and refit their ships. The buccaneers could have counted on the help of their old friends the Kuna Indians of the isthmus, who were 'flushed by their successes against [the Spanish], through the assistance of the privateers . . . and many thousands of privateers from

Jamaica and the French islands especially would have flocked over to [a buccaneer colony]'. They could have been masters not only of the richest gold mines in America but of all the coast 'as high as Quito'.

These were, as Dampier candidly admitted, his 'golden dreams', but they were not to be, though they would later, with his encouragement, lure the Scottish founder of the Bank of England to Darien.

IX

'WE RAN FOR IT'

On 23 December 1684, the buccaneers sailed north for Panama Bay, intending to plunder the town of Lavelia. A brisk wind filled their sails, and they scudded past a high, mountainous coastline clothed in trees of every size and hue. The effect, like sailing by 'a vast grove or wood', pleased Dampier's eye. The buccaneers scanned the shore, hoping to spot the mouth of some river unfrequented by Spaniards where they could seize more Indian canoes. This stretch of coast, beaten by frequent heavy rains and far from the Spaniards' usual sea routes, was relatively unknown. Dampier and his colleagues pored over the Spanish pilot-books they always took care to remove from captured ships. Though usually 'very good guides', they were no help because the coastline was such an intricate web of estuaries and creeks, so well camouflaged by lush vegetation, that only detailed personal knowledge could assist.

The perplexed buccaneers made for the mouth of the wide, swift-flowing St Jago River near the island of Gallo, about 400 miles south of Panama, which they knew had safe anchorage. Dampier was among those who climbed into four canoes to row upriver, reconnoitre, and forage. He was captivated by the 'great tall trees' along the river-banks, including the white cotton trees with their great silvery trunks, 'big-bellied like nine-pins'. Their gossamer-soft cotton, 'like the down of thistles', made the trees appear as laden with blossom as the 'apple-trees in England'.

The jungle's flamboyant beauty was not the only reason Dampier scrutinized the riverbanks closely. He had heard of 'the wildness and enmity of all the natives on this coast'. Screened by 'vast forests', unseen eyes could watch the progress of intruders and ambush them at will. The buccaneers rowed eighteen miles before spotting two small huts thatched with palm leaves. The local men hastily put 'their wives and little ones with their household stuff' into their canoes and paddled frantically away, far faster than the buccaneers could row against the fierce rippling current. Sweating, parched and hungry, they contented themselves with landing at the huts and killing and eating a hog and some chickens.

The buccaneers returned downriver, propelled by the current, and reached the mouth just before dawn. Here they seized an Indian and forced him to guide them to the small village of Tumaco. They reached it at around midnight and, stealing ashore in the darkness, captured all the Indian inhabitants and a frightened Spaniard, Don Diego de Pinas, who had sailed from Lima to load timber. After 'much persuasion', Dampier induced seven of his weary companions to row off with him to ransack Don Diego's ship. It was worth the effort: there were jars of 'good wine' with which the buccaneers 'made merry'. On 1 January, they departed, taking Don Diego with them. As they rowed their canoes towards Gallo to rejoin their ships, they intercepted a small packet sailing from Panama to Lima. Her Spanish crew hurriedly threw a bundle of letters over the side as the buccaneers leaped aboard. They managed to retrieve the sodden parchments and carried them, and their new prisoners, back to Gallo.

The letters contained the momentous news that 'the armada from Old Spain was come to Portobello and that the President of Panama had sent this packet on purpose to hasten the plate fleet thither from Lima'. This meant that the galleons loaded with Peruvian silver would soon arrive in Panama Bay so that the treasure could be unloaded and carried over the isthmus to Portobello. The buccaneers were 'very joyful of this news'. They at once abandoned their plans to attack Lavelia and made instead for the Pearl Islands in Panama Bay, a perfect place of ambush since 'all ships bound to Panama from the coast of Lima pass by them; so that being there we could not possibly miss the fleet'.

In late January 1685 they reached the islands, where they found a 'fine, small, sandy bay' in which to careen their ships. There were far more men than could usefully be employed in this process, so half of each ship's company 'were at liberty to go and do what they pleased'. At low tide the men gathered clams, limpets and mussels from the exposed rocks. Hungry for meat, some crossed to other islands to hunt for pigeons, turtledoves and iguanas, but two men were dragged away by Spaniards lying in ambush.

Not only did their capture make the buccaneers 'more cautious how [they] straggled abroad', but as soon as the ships were ready the fleet headed for the city of Panama to negotiate the men's release. Anchored off Panama, they despatched Don Diego de Pinas with a letter addressed to the city's president, suggesting an exchange of prisoners. Unknown to the buccaneers, the unfortunate Don Diego was 'killed before he got ashore', probably shot by Spaniards who mistook him for a spy. When Don Diego failed to reappear, the buccaneers sent the president another letter. It was, Dampier later wrote, 'full of threats', warning that if the Englishmen were harmed, 'by the help of God we will colour your land, rivers and sea with Spanish blood of men, women and children ... we will bring our ships near your walls, that you may have the pleasure of seeing them [the Spanish prisoners] hanged at our yardarms ... we will make you know that we are the Commanders of the whole South Seas ...' The prisoner-messenger carrying the letter ran 'raving' through the streets of Panama to the president's house, crying out that 'the prisoners on board were dead men' unless the president acted quickly.

With an astute eye to public morale, the buccaneers provided three or four extra copies of their alarming letter 'to be dispersed abroad among the common people' by the messenger. Unsurprisingly, this 'wrought so powerfully' upon Panama's inhabitants 'that the city was in an uproar'. Dampier appreciated the psychological impact, observing that 'people lying under any fearful apprehensions will term dwarfs giants, and men who are really great cowards would not be so accounted and therefore seek remedies to disguise the truth by excusing their own weakness'. The president at once despatched an emissary, and urgent bartering began. The buccaneers at first insisted on a 'man for man' exchange, but this was for form's sake only. As Dampier wryly noted, 'We had more [prisoners] than we knew what to do with'. As it turned out, they were happy to swap forty Spanish prisoners for their two companions.

The buccaneers withdrew a short distance to the island of Taboga in the bay, a nearer ambush point than the Pearl Islands. While they awaited the billowing sails of the treasure fleet, a 'pretended merchant from Panama' played them 'a scurvy trick'. He arrived 'by stealth', claiming that he wanted to trade privately with the buccaneers and thus to avoid the heavy Spanish import duties – the *averia*. Captain Swan, who was 'most desirous to sell his goods', leaped at the chance. The buccaneers arranged to meet the 'merchant' at a rendezvous point and established a secret password with him. Dampier thought they were gullible, writing of 'those who never had any experiences of the Spaniards'. As the pretended merchant's ship approached, he and his crew suddenly jumped down into canoes and set fire to their ship. '[The ship] blew up, and burnt close by us', Dampier reported, 'so that we were forced to cut our cables in all haste, and scamper away as well as we could'. He was struck that, before leaving the Pearl Islands, Captain Swan had been warned by the astrologer he carried on board to beware of fire. That very evening the astrologer had again warned Swan 'to be careful'.

Early the next morning, returning shaken to their anchorage, the buccaneers found 'many canoes full of men', clearly not Spanish, passing between Taboga and the other islands. Dampier and his companions manoeuvred cautiously within hailing distance to learn the cause of this 'new consternation'. They discovered that the new arrivals were a party of 200 French and 80 English 'privateers' who had recently crossed the isthmus from the Caribbean under the command of Captains Grogniet and Lescuyer. A further 180 Englishmen, under one Captain Townley, were building canoes at Santa Maria and would shortly follow.

The new arrivals, bobbing about on the swells of the bay in twenty-eight canoes, were clearly in need of more stable vessels. Swan and Davis at once offered to take all the Englishmen on board their ships and gave the Frenchmen a Spanish barque they had seized. In return, Grogniet offered the two captains a privateering 'commission' from the governor of the French colony of Petit-Goave on Hispaniola to legitimize their activities. Dampier noted disparagingly that the governor was in the habit of giving 'blank commissions' to his captains to hand out to anyone they pleased as a carte blanche 'for a general ravage in any part of America, by sea or land'. According to Dampier, he hoped thereby to enrich Petit-Goave by making it 'the sanctuary and asylum of all people of desperate fortunes'.

Davis gratefully accepted his commission, a useful replacement for a dubious document he had inherited from Captain Cook on the latter's death. Swan, however, refused. He insisted that he had an order from the Duke of York commanding him neither to give offence to, nor to suffer affront from, the Spanish. As the Spanish had 'affronted' him and his men at Valdivia by injuring or killing several of them, he claimed 'he had a lawful commission of his own to right himself'.

On 2 March, the buccaneer fleet went in search of Captain Townley, sailing towards the Gulf of San Miguel, some thirty leagues southeast of Panama, where the river from Santa Maria flowed into the sea. The buccaneers spotted two barques among the pattern of islands and found Townley and his men on board. They had captured these vessels, well laden with flour, wine, brandy, sugar, and oil, as they rowed down the swift-running Santa Maria River at night. Their prisoners had confirmed 'that the Lima fleet was ready to sail'. The buccaneers sailed together back to the Pearl Islands, where Townley distributed wine and brandy to all the other ships 'that [they] might be drunk out' because he wanted the great seven- and eight-gallon jars they were stored in for fresh water.

With their new recruits, the buccaneers numbered more than 600 men. Several days later, the occupants of an Indian canoe paddling out of the Santa Maria River reported that another group of some 300 Frenchmen and Englishmen were tramping across the isthmus. Peter Harris was sent to look for them. Dampier decided 'the isthmus of Darien was now become a common road for privateers to pass between the North and South Seas at their pleasure'. The result was the largest concentration of buccaneers ever to gather in the Pacific. The possibilities were exciting. In March, Swan wrote to a friend, with a blend of patriotism and personal interest so characteristic of buccaneering: 'The king might make this whole Kingdom of Peru tributary to him in two years' time. We now await the Spanish fleet that brings money to Panama ... If we have success against them we shall make a desperate alarm all Europe over'.*

The sheer numbers brought practical problems. The buccaneers raided the mainland 'to get coppers for each ship, having now so many men, our pots would not boil victuals fast enough, though they kept them boiling all day'. They also plundered a sugar works to get extra sugar to cook up with their cocoa.

However, this large, disparate band was not a cohesive force. They were riven with disagreements and could not agree on a single overall leader. Aboard the *Bachelor's Delight*, there was an attempt to oust Davis in favour of 'another commander of a rougher temper', but Dampier opposed the troublemakers and was this time persuasive in

---

*The king Swan was referring to was Charles II, but he had in fact died on 6 February. His Catholic brother, who as Duke of York had issued the order to Swan to accept no affront, had acceded to the throne as James II. The buccaneers would not hear this news for several months.

his arguments. With the help of another crewman, he 'made them quiet'. Also, the dry season was ending, and the sky was beginning to crack with thunder. Lowering skies and heavy humidity, combined with boredom, cannot have helped the mood. The buccaneers roamed the verdant islands of the bay, seizing and interrogating prisoners to discover more precisely when the treasure ships were due. Suspecting that a mulatto prisoner was on 'the fireship that came to burn [them] in the night', they promptly hanged him. In his unpublished manuscript notes Dampier reflected that ''tis hard falling into the hands of cruel men'.

Aboard the *Bachelor's Delight*, tension eased a few days later when she intercepted a Spanish ship carrying letters to Panama, from which the anxious men learned that the Lima treasure fleet was indeed coming. They continued to wait, making the occasional raid.

Dampier had plenty of time to observe the lush fruits on the islands of Panama Bay. He admired the Spanish as gardeners, regretting that his own countrymen were so 'little curious' about cultivating exotic fruits. He sampled everything from star fruit to avocado pears, of which he provided the first description in English. '[The fruit is] as big as a large lemon. It is of a green colour, till it is ripe, and then it is a little yellowish. They are seldom fit to eat till they have been gathered 2 or 3 days; then they become soft, and the skin or rind will peel off. The substance inside is green, or a little yellowish, and as soft as butter'. He recommended eating it mashed with sugar and lime juice to give it flavour and make it a 'gourmet' dish, or else with just a little salt and a roasted plantain to satisfy hunger.

Dampier noted the belief that 'this fruit provokes to lust, and therefore is said to be much esteemed by the Spaniards'. Any Spanish settlement he had ever seen had its avocado bushes, so he decided this was probably true.* Dampier also examined the sapodilla tree, which was 'as big as a large pear tree' and with 'an excellent fruit', the juice of which was 'white and clammy and it will stick like glue'.†

Yet by late April the buccaneers were again dispirited and on edge. Dampier caught the mood of men 'ever-weary waiting at one place and suspecting that [the Spanish vessels] might come another way and miss us which made us very uneasy'. They began to wonder whether they should attack Panama itself. After all, they numbered nearly 1,000 men and had a fleet of ten ships. Harris had located the additional group of buccaneers reported to be crossing the isthmus – numbering 264 and mostly French – and had brought them back to the main party. The buccaneers grilled their prisoners, demanding detailed information about Panama's defences, but their captives dissuaded them, warning that 'all the strength of the country was there' and that extra forces had arrived from Portobello.

On 28 May 1685, the impasse ended. The season had broken and torrential rain hammered the decks as 'all our fleet lay waiting for the Lima fleet'. At about 11 a.m. it cleared, and Captain Grogniet suddenly sighted an approaching huddle of ships. He signalled to the other buccaneer vessels lying about a mile off. Swan and Townley hurriedly boarded Davis's ship to decide how to engage the

*The word *avocado* originates from a Nahuatl Indian (Aztec) word meaning 'testicle', a reference either to its shape or to its aphrodisiac qualities.

†The latex of the sapodilla today provides chicle, the basis for chewing gum.

enemy, 'who we saw came purposely to fight' the buccaneer. The Spanish treasure fleet comprised fourteen vessels, including six 'ships of good force'. Several hundred men in periagos rode up and down in their wake.

The largest buccaneer vessel was Davis's *Bachelor's Delight* – with thirty-six guns and a crew of 156. Swan's *Cygnet* had sixteen guns and 140 men, but the other craft had only small arms. They faced a Spanish force of more than 3,000. But the British buccaneers, 'not discouraged . . . resolved to fight'. Davis and Swan expected Grogniet, with some 300 aboard, to weigh anchor and join them, but, as Dampier wrote, 'he took care to keep himself out of harm's way'. They gave up waiting for the Frenchman. The wind was in their favour, and at 3 p.m. they bore down on the Spanish. Night fell with little more than 'the exchanging of a few shot on each side'. During the hours of darkness the Spanish managed to confuse the buccaneers about the position of their ships by snuffing then relighting their stern lanterns to convince them the fleet had changed station. In the pink light of dawn, the buccaneers discovered that the Spanish 'had got the weather-gauge of us and were coming upon us with full sail'. As Dampier admitted, 'We ran for it.' After 'a running fight all day' and being chased 'almost round the Bay of Panama', they found themselves back at the very point where they had been anchored that morning.

Nevertheless, they had lost only one man and in Dampier's private view 'were all more scared than hurt'. He was philosophical: 'Thus ended this day's work and with it all we had been projecting for 5 or 6 months; when instead of making ourselves master of the Spanish fleet and treasure, we were glad to escape them: and owed that too, in a great measure, to their want of courage to pursue their advantage'. The buccaneers later discovered that, even had they vanquished the Spanish fleet, they would have found no glistening mounds of pieces of eight. The Spaniards had prudently unloaded their treasure at Lavelia and taken more men on board before sailing to do battle.

And that was that. The indignant English summoned Grogniet to account for his behaviour. He insisted that 'his men would not suffer him to join [them] in the fight'. French accounts hint at distrust, misunderstandings, and dissension between the English and the French as the cause, but Dampier wrote disgustedly that Grogniet and his men were 'like a company of small birds that have been chased by the hawk . . . the danger being over they again appeared'. The English buccaneers 'cashiered' their 'cowardly companion'. Grogniet was allowed to keep his ship and sailed ignominiously away, no doubt to English jeers.

In mid-June, the remaining captains consulted 'about new methods to advance their fortunes'. They had no hopes 'to get anything at sea' and decided instead to see 'what the land would afford'. The buccaneers took Pueblo Nuevo, where Sawkins had been killed in 1680, but found little there. The attack exacerbated tensions between the English and the remaining French, who accused the former of desecrating crucifixes and lopping limbs off holy images in the Catholic churches. Many of the French departed, and a largely English group led by Davis, Swan and Townley decided to assault the prosperous city of Leon, in present-day Nicaragua, twenty miles inland through 'long, grassy savannahs'.

Dampier did not see this for himself. He remained with a small party guarding the canoes among the mangrove swamps while a large force, led by the 'briskest men' under

Townley, set out for the city. It was a gruelling march under a beating sun, and a number lagged behind with heat exhaustion. Unsurprisingly, the stragglers included 'a stout, old grey-headed man, aged about 84, who had served under Oliver [Cromwell]'. He refused offers to stay with the canoes, claiming 'he would venture as far as the best of them'. When surrounded by the Spaniards, the determined old man refused to surrender. Summoning up his last reserves of strength, he kept firing his pistol until 'they shot him dead at a distance'.

In the end these efforts were for nothing. The Spanish, who had fled Leon, refused to pay any ransom, and the buccaneers burned down the town once described as 'the paradise of the Indies'. Regaining their canoes, they turned their attention to Realeja, the port for Leon. Again, they found the place deserted, but rummaged happily for provisions, undeterred by a pervasive noxious stench from the nearby swamps.

Dampier was delighted by Realeja's lovely gardens with their abundance of fruits, especially guavas, 'yellow, soft, and very pleasant'. The fruit 'bakes as well as a pear . . . and makes good pies'. He noted the guavas were 'binding' when green and 'loosening' when ripe. Prickly pears, full of 'small black seeds, mixed with a certain red pulp, like thick syrup', were also delicious and very 'cooling and refreshing', although if a man ate a large quantity they turned his urine red, 'making it look like blood'. He added reassuringly, 'This I have often experienced, yet found no harm by it'.

On 25 August 1685, the buccaneer force split up. Swan was keen to explore the northwestern coast of Mexico, perhaps to seek gold and silver mines, whereas Davis wanted to head south for Peru. Dampier decided to leave Davis and transfer to the *Cygnet*, 'not from any dislike to [his] old captain', but because he was eager 'to get some knowledge of the northern parts of this Continent of Mexico'. As Daniel Defoe would later write of Robinson Crusoe, he had become committed to a life of 'inimitable wanderings'; in Dampier's own words, '[I believed] no proposal for seeing any part of the world which I had never seen before could possibly come amiss'. He admitted in his first book that he had returned to the South Seas 'more to indulge my curiosity than to get wealth'. While this may be an exaggerated self-justification of his initial decision, Dampier was intent on recording assiduously, even obsessively, what he saw of nature in his wanderings and, as a good 'natural philosopher', trying to fit these observations within a logical framework. So Dampier packed his precious papers into his sea chest and moved across to the *Cygnet*.

Townley announced that he would accompany Swan. The two groups parted with a mutual salute of guns. Of Dampier's two long-term acquaintances, surgeon Lionel Wafer sailed off with Davis, but Basil Ringrose remained on board the *Cygnet*, which soon ran into 'violent tornadoes' with 'very frightful flashes of lightning and claps of thunder'. Also, increasing numbers were showing symptoms of a fever, probably typhus, which had started to dog them after Realeja. Before long, nearly half the buccaneers had fallen sick and a number died. Swan became so ill 'that the doctor could entertain no hopes of his recovery'.

Dampier does not appear to have suffered and quickly found sights to feed his consuming 'curiosity'. He gazed at the Volcano of Guatemala, belching flames and smoke, and ashore examined the bushy little shrub used to make indigo. Dampier found 'a great quantity of vinellos [vanilla pods] drying in the sun' in an Indian village. Vanilla was used to perfume chocolate, even tobacco, but the process of curing the pods was apparently a mystery. Dampier tried to cure some 'but could not'. He concluded that there must be 'some secret' known only to the Indians.

Dampier also examined cochineal, at that time thought to be made from seeds. However, Dampier identified the real source as a small insect infesting a plant that resembled a prickly pear. He watched the Indians beat the plant with sticks to drive the red insects into the air so that the heat of the sun killed them and they fell down onto large linen cloths they had spread on the ground. They left them to dry for several days, then scooped them up to make 'the much esteemed scarlet'.*

By October, according to Dampier, '[the fever] which had raged amongst us' was abating. Against all the odds, Swan

*In Dampier's day cochineal was particularly coveted by the Restoration lady for her toilette. She had a formidable battery of cosmetics, including cat dung mixed with vinegar as a depilatory and mouse skins cut into false eyebrows. Cochineal was a relatively innocuous part of her armoury. She applied it to her cheeks to give a becoming flush on top of the white lead compound, ceruse, used to create a delicate overall pallor and hide craters caused by smallpox. In 1703 Dutch microscopist and Royal Society fellow Antonie van Leeuwenhoek confirmed Dampier's observations that cochineal came from insects, not seeds. During Dampier's lifetime the use of microscopes was revealing whole new miniature worlds, just as astronomers were using telescopes to reveal the larger world of the cosmos, and Dampier's voyages were revealing the natural world outside the confines of Europe. The known scope of Creation was multiplying rapidly, leaving natural philosophers much to consider about the Creator's intentions.

had survived, and the buccaneers' appetite for action
returned. They decided to lie in wait for the 'rich ship' that
came annually to the 'very commodious' harbour of
Acapulco from Manila with a fabulous cargo of spices,
silks, calicoes and muslins. They hoped she would be a soft
target. The journey from Manila to Acapulco was the
longest unbroken trading voyage in the world and took
some five or six months. Before the galleon left Manila,
priests sang blessings and wafted clouds of incense across
her decks. The crew and passengers needed this
benediction as many would die in the days ahead.
Survivors would be tottering with scurvy and, the
buccaneers hoped, too weak to put up much of a fight. In
1656 an entire crew had perished en route from Manila.
Their floating graveyard had washed up on the shores of
Mexico.

While the buccaneers waited, squabbles broke out
between Townley and Swan, and for some reason a
prisoner was killed. The incident caused an indignant
Dampier to reflect privately 'how bloody-minded some
men are [yet] bloody, mad, swearing, flashy fellows are
commonly but ordinary fellows in the face of their enemy'.
He was also irritated that Townley and others had refused
to trust a female mulatto prisoner to be their guide,
because they dismissed her as a mere 'foolish woman',
whereas he wanted 'to make a trial of our female pilot'.

Some of Dampier's irritation was due to the fact that,
though normally robust, he had contracted 'a fever which
afterwards turned to the dropsy and brought me very near
my end'.* Many of his comrades were dying of the same

---

*His ailment was presumably not epidemic dropsy, first identified in 1877, but
it may have been beriberi, caused by a deficiency of thiamine and producing
dangerous quantities of serous fluid.

ailment, though their surgeons 'used their greatest skill to preserve their lives'. Dampier knew of an Indian remedy involving taking 'the stone or cod of an alligator', pulverizing it, and drinking it in water. Ever ready to experiment, he wrote with regret, 'I would have tried it, but we found no alligators here'. Despite his illness, Dampier was determined to keep on observing. While the buccaneers patrolled the waters off Cape Corrientes, Dampier tried to calculate their longitude.

He also retained an interest in food, writing plaintively, '[On 25 December] we were forced to send our canoes ashore to get a Christmas dinner for we had nothing but flour and water aboard'. They managed to catch 'three great Jew-fish' – enough for a feast. Dampier rated these huge codlike fish highly. He believed they were so named because, having scales and fins, they were considered 'clean' under Levitical law. He had often seen the Jewish community, which had established itself in Jamaica after the English takeover, eating them 'very freely'.

By early January 1686, there was still no sign of the Manila ship. Desperate for fresh provisions, the buccaneers landed and went hunting. They chose the wrong moment. The ship, the *Santa Rosa*, guided by a pearling vessel, slipped past them, so that 'our hopes of meeting the Philippine ship were now over'. It was a bitter disappointment. The buccaneers ranged disconsolately along the Mexican coast, looking without much conviction 'for rich towns and mines'. Townley, whose main ambition had been the Manila ship, departed south. Swan undertook a series of raids in which Dampier was too sick to participate.

In February 1686, while he lay feverish, swollen and aching on board, the buccaneers seized the town of Santa

Pecaque. This was despite warnings from Swan's astrologer of great peril. The buccaneers bivouacked in a church for the night but could not sleep for sinister 'grievous groanings'. Several days later, learning that a Spanish force was on its way to attack them, Swan tried to evacuate his men quickly, but some, intent on carrying off as much as possible, stubbornly resisted his orders. They continued determinedly back and forth, transporting provisions the considerable distance down to their canoes, and, as Dampier noted, 'their own folly ruined them'. The Spanish ambushed them as they struggled along the road and killed fifty-four men. Swan was shocked to come upon the bodies, which were 'stript, and so cut and mangl'd, that he scarce knew one man'. One of the dead was Dampier's 'ingenious friend Mr Ringrose', who, he reflected sadly, 'had no mind to this voyage; but was necessitated to engage in it or starve'.

The disheartened buccaneers withdrew to near Cape St Lucas in California to careen. Dampier noted that the Spanish had little knowledge of the Gulf, or 'Lake', of California, as he called it. Some believed that California was an island. Dampier was convinced that 'here might be very advantageous discoveries made by any that would attempt it: for the Spaniards have more [land] than they can well manage . . . yet they would lie like the dog in the manger; although not able to eat themselves they would endeavour to hinder others'.

The fact that it took so long for vessels to reach California around the Horn was a hindrance to colonization, but Dampier maintained, '[There might be] a nearer way hither than we came; I mean by the North West'. Although others had sought a Northwest passage, they had always explored westwards from the Atlantic. Dampier believed it would be better to start 'in the less known coast or the South Seas side and bend my course from thence along by California northeastwards around the coast'. He argued sensibly that in so doing one would be travelling from lesser-known regions of the Pacific to the more familiar ones of the Atlantic and would be without that 'dread and fear' which had beset others 'in passing from the known to the unknown' and 'having to provide for a long course back again for fear of being left in the winter'.

At this point Captain Swan stunned his men with his own innovative plan. He argued that their voyaging along the Mexican coast had brought nothing but disappointment and it was pointless continuing. Instead, they would cross the Pacific and 'go into the East-Indies'. He conjured the glory days of Drake and Cavendish, who had successfully passed that way, but even so he had a struggle. Two thirds of his men did not believe it possible. 'Such was their ignorance', wrote Dampier, that they were convinced 'he would carry them out of the world'.

Swan had sought the views of Dampier, who was probably one of his most senior navigators, 'a long time before', and Dampier had supported the scheme. In unpublished notes, he confided, 'Although I was sick I still had a mind to make further discoveries and my advice and counsel was ever accepted by the company as much as any one man's, and indeed it was ever a design between Captain Swan and myself to promote it and use our utmost endeavours to persuade the unthinking rabble to it'. Eventually, the 'unthinking rabble' was won over, largely by the hope of seizing the elusive Manila ship, this time in the Indies. Captain Swan's own motivation was apparently entirely different. According to Dampier, he 'often assured' him 'with his own mouth' that he had 'no intention to be a privateer in the East Indies' but thought that it would be easier there to find an opportunity of returning to England to slip back under the mantle of responsibility.

Before they set out, Dampier knew he had to rid himself of his debilitating illness. He tried the desperate remedy of being buried up to his neck in hot sand. He endured it for nearly half an hour before being dug out and 'laid to sweat in a tent'. This technique, also used to counter scurvy, sometimes proved fatal. Vitus Bering, discoverer of the strait and sea that bear his name, died after similar treatment in 1741. Luckily, it worked for Dampier, who later wrote, 'I did sweat exceedingly while I was in the sand, and I do believe it did me much good, for I grew well soon after'.

PART III

The Traveller

X

'YOU WOULD HAVE POISONED THEM'

On 31 March 1686, seven years after Dampier had left England and Judith, the *Cygnet* sailed out from Cape Corrientes in Mexico with 100 men on board. Alongside her was a captured barque commanded by Josiah Teat, previously mate of the *Cygnet*, with a crew of fifty. As the land slipped below the horizon, Dampier had few regrets. This 'little frequented coast' had brought the buccaneers only 'fatigues, hardships and losses', and he eagerly anticipated new discoveries and opportunities.

The plan was to make a landfall on the island of Guam, 'discovered' by Magellan in 1521, which had become a staging post for Spanish ships. No one was sure of the distance. Dampier noted that the Spanish, who should 'know best', believed it lay between 6,900 and 7,200 miles. The English pilot-books reckoned the distance at between 5,400 and 5,700 miles. Swan insisted to his apprehensive men that English calculations were correct. '[Yet even this] was a voyage enough to frighten us, considering our scanty provisions', Dampier later recalled. They had tried to make a 'computation' of 'the time that [they] should be running to Guam', knowing that Drake had taken some fifty days and Cavendish forty-eight. They had also carefully checked their stores of maize. Provided they could keep it from the voracious rats, it would last sixty days, at a rate of half a

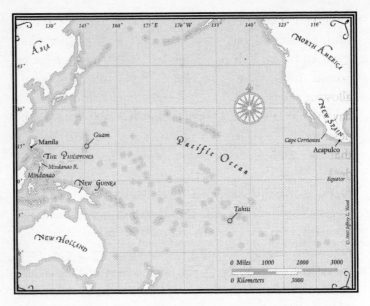

At the time of Dampier's voyages much of the coast of both New Holland (Australia) and New Guinea was unknown and many believed the two to be joined.

pint per man per day. Otherwise, all they had was a little salted fish, which they consumed within the first three days.

Soon everyone was focused on one thing: food. The prospect of drifting lost and starving in an endless, unknown ocean was every seaman's nightmare. There was no need 'to call men to victuals for the kettle was boiled but once a day, which being made ready at noon, all hands were aloft to see the quartermaster share' the food. He had to dole it out very precisely, 'having so many eyes to observe him'. The observing eyes included those of the *Cygnet*'s two cats and two dogs, which lived on 'what was given them and waited with as much eagerness to see it shared as [the men] did'.

After twenty days at sea with the brisk trade winds behind her, the *Cygnet* was making such good progress that the men felt confident enough to demand an increase in rations. Swan gave way against his better judgement, allowing them ten rather than eight spoonfuls of maize a day for their porridge. Dampier, still recovering from his illness, was perfectly happy with his austere diet. He thought that the semistarvation rations were doing him 'a great deal of good': 'I found that my strength increased and my dropsy wore off'. Others did not find it so easy. The hungry men were outraged to discover that one of their number had been stealing from the store. He was sentenced to three blows on his bare back with a thick rope from every crewman: 'Captain Swan began first, and struck with a good will whose example was followed by all of us'. It was a harsh punishment for a buccaneering ship and a sign of the rising tension as the sailors endured day after featureless day, with no way of knowing when the voyage would end.

Cramped conditions fed the malaise. The converted merchantmen used by buccaneers were not designed to carry large crews – often triple or quadruple those for which they were originally designed – on long voyages. The extra men were needed to man the guns and board prizes, and to provide ready replacements for losses through battle and disease, but the larger numbers made living conditions nearly impossible. The height between decks in the forecastles, where the crewmen lived and slept, could be as little as four feet, six inches.

The forecastles were gloomy caverns of damp, mildewing wood. The entrance hatch from the deck above had to be closed even in moderate weather or sea, as did the gun ports, which were often only six feet or so above the

waterline. This made for an even more 'foulsome, suffocating abode'. Men lay in swaying canvas hammocks, or
packed side by side on the floor, scratching at omnipresent
lice and breathing fetid air reeking of unwashed bodies and
rank breath. The deck itself was far from clean. One
traveller recorded how rainwater collecting on the decks
'smells and ferments because of the spittle, dung etc'. Even
nastier, he added, the sailors were often forced to drink this
water for want of an alternative.

Sometimes, the men attempted to clean their living
quarters by vigorous brushing with vinegar and sand and
burning pitch for fumigation. These efforts produced a
cleaner smell, but the improvement was only temporary
because the rubbish was often swept down into the bilges
onto the ballast. Here it fermented, adding to the putrid
stench and requiring the carpenter to take great care, when
entering the bilges to look for leaks, to avoid death by
asphyxiation from vapours fit 'to poison the devil' – a fate
to which the rats, cockroaches and maggots multiplying
there seemed entirely immune.

Whenever the weather was remotely good enough,
men lay 'kennelling like hounds' on the open decks or slept
in one of the ship's boats or even in the rigging or loosely
furled sails. Dampier himself often spread his bedding outside and lay observing the clouds above. It is truly
remarkable that Dampier managed to write and preserve a
journal and sketch maps in the cramped conditions of the
ships in which he served. Even before starting to write, he
would have had to stumble through the gloom to his sea
chest to find his quill pen, sharpen it with his penknife,
make up his ink, extract a piece of paper from his limited
store, and find a place not too damp or dark but relatively
stable. When he had finished, he would have used sand to

dry his work before restowing all his equipment in his chest.

Late one night, a month into the voyage, and perhaps feeling a little homesick, Dampier made some calculations in his journal. 'I reckoned myself 1800 from England which being half the circumference of the globe makes the difference of time twelve hours so that at that time it was between 12 and one o'clock in the afternoon here in England'. Perhaps his ever-active mind craved diversion. The boredom of a long voyage was killing.

During good weather, time hung especially heavy. The sailors mended their clothes, stiff and salty from being washed in sea water and perpetually damp because the residual salt attracted moisture. They used joints of sharks' backbones, even bits of hardened cheese rind, to fashion buttons and fastenings. They carved wood and bone for pleasure. They also played dice and cards. Music, singing and dancing were a great relief, and the *Cygnet* carried both trumpeters and violin players. The ship's pets also provided diversion. Some had pet parrots, while penguins were not unknown. The *Cygnet*'s crew were clearly devoted to their cats and dogs, sharing their frugal rations with them rather than adding them to the menu.

Those who could, read. The literacy rate among sailors was high – more than 70 per cent.* Some read worthy books, like the Greek Bible of Richard Gopson, who

---

*This means that almost three out of four sailors could sign their name rather than simply make their mark – the only consistent distinction on which academics can agree between literacy and illiteracy for this period. By comparison, the level of literacy was 97 per cent for goldsmiths, 60 per cent for carpenters ashore, and only 33 per cent for Thames watermen. The relatively high level among sailors reflected partly the intelligence of those sufficiently curious to want to see the world and partly the requirement to read charts.

crossed the Panamanian isthmus with Lionel Wafer. Others, the majority probably, preferred something lighter such as 'the obscene verses' recorded as causing a major argument aboard one ship.

Sailors were great practical jokers too, not only at boisterous ceremonies such as crossing the equator. When one man fell sick who was 'too apt to joke at other people in their illness', his shipmates 'resolved to affright him and finding him asleep . . . tied his legs fast together and fixed a great stone' to them. When he woke up, they said, 'We thought a little while ago you had been dead so we tied that great stone to your feet to sink you and were just going to throw you overboard and had done it now if you had not cried out'.

Pirate and buccaneer ships also held another ceremony unique to themselves: the gallows humour of the mock trial. With the aid of a few props, such as a mop for the judge's wig and a tarpaulin for his robe, the sailors would expiate their forebodings by taking turns playing the judge, lawyer or prisoner. Sometimes the charges were ludicrous, and the humour was broad. At other times, the sailors' pleas reflected what they might have said in reality before a stern-faced judge. Some swore they 'came from the sea' and so recognized no country and no authority. Some claimed to be egalitarian 'Robin Hood's men', righting social wrong, others that they were expansionist imperialists like Alexander the Great and that the only differences between them was the extent of their conquests, not their legitimacy.

As the *Cygnet* gusted her pinched and hungry men over the great expanse of the Pacific, Dampier was surprised to spot not 'so much as a flying-fish, nor any sort of fowl'. It was not until some 4,975 miles out from Cape Corrientes, by his calculation, that he at last saw a gaggle of big-footed boobies fly past. The sight may have cheered Dampier, but it did not make the other men less restive. After they had sailed what they reckoned to be 5,700 miles, the distance Swan had promised would bring them to Guam, his increasingly weak and miserable crew 'began to murmur' angrily, demanding to know why no land was in sight. Swan needed all his diplomatic skills to soothe them. He wisely admitted that the longer Spanish estimate of the distance had probably been correct but promised that the favourable winds would soon 'end [their] troubles'.

He was right. Not long afterwards, it began to rain. Dampier noticed clouds settling on the western horizon – 'an apparent token that we were not far from land'. Further evidence that they might be nearing land came on 20 May when Teat's barque, which was well ahead of the *Cygnet*, suddenly sailed over a rocky shoal teeming with bright fish in just four fathoms of clear water.

Teat waited for Swan to catch up; then the two ships sailed on together. Swan and Dampier were a little troubled that they were off course. According to Spanish charts, there were no such shoals around Guam. However, at 4 p.m., 'by God's assistance', they sighted a smudge on the horizon: Guam. Dampier reported, '[It was] as well for Captain Swan that we got sight of it before our provision was spent, of which we had but enough for three days more; for, as I was afterwards informed, the men had con-trived, first to kill Captain Swan and eat him when the victuals was gone, and after him all of us who were accessory in promoting the undertaking [of] this voyage'. When the story reached Swan, it amused him, and he remarked, 'Ah Dampier, you would have poisoned them, you are too lean . . . they would have [left] you alive for you have so little flesh that it will not give them a mouth-ful'. Swan was himself, by contrast, still 'lusty and fleshy'.

The voyage to Guam had lasted fifty-one days. Dampier had meticulously recorded the details of each day's run – the course, distance, latitude, wind and weather – which he later published in a neat table in his first book 'for the satisfaction of those who may think it serviceable to the fix-ing the longitudes of these parts or to any other use in geography or navigation'. His own calculations of longitudes during the voyage were, in fact, inaccurate, not only due to the imprecisions of dead reckoning but also because he had not measured magnetic variation. Swan, 'who had the instruments in his cabin', was not, apparently, much interested in the variation. However, Dampier's calculation of Guam's latitude was dead-on.

Toward dusk on 21 May, the two ships cautiously approached the land, uncertain what reception they would receive from the small Spanish garrison. Suddenly, a single canoe shot out from the shore and made for them through the gathering darkness. It contained a Spanish priest rowed by some native Chamorro islanders. Peering up at the dim outlines of the ships, the priest demanded to know 'from whence we came and what we were'. They replied in Spanish that they were Spaniards from Acapulco. The priest was deceived and came aboard. In the flickering torchlight, he realized his mistake and tried vainly to flee, but he was a prisoner.

Captain Swan courteously conducted the priest to his own quarters, 'the great cabin', where he explained that they had not come with hostile intent. All they wanted were pro-visions, and they were prepared to pay for them. He asked the priest to write to Guam's Spanish governor setting out their needs. The man agreed, but he warned the buccaneers that food on the island was scant. As they likely discovered, fourteen months earlier Captain Eaton had passed that way. His men had been full of scurvy, and many had already died, their mouths too sore to even try to eat 'their victuals of boiled bread and rotten peas'. He had been desperate to purchase fresh provisions, which he had done by means of 'many rich gifts to the Governor'.

Swan and his men would have been pleased to learn that Eaton's crew were still alive, but Eaton's sojourn on the island had ended in a bout of squalid cruelty. His men had soon recovered strength enough to pick a fight with the Chamorros, which had ended with them murdering some of the islanders with the apparent blessing of the Spanish. Not long after Eaton's departure, the Chamorros had risen, killing many Spaniards and rampaging though the plantations. They failed, however, to dislodge the Spaniards from their small fort on the west of the island, and the rebellion fizzled out. Many Chamorros had fled to other islands, leaving only about 100 islanders and a tense, uneasy atmosphere on Guam. The small Spanish garrison of no more than thirty were living a nervous existence in the fort.

The next morning Swan sent the priest's letter, together with 'a very obliging one' of his own, ashore to the governor. Taking the hint about 'rich gifts', he also sent four yards of brilliant scarlet cloth and 'a piece of broad silver and gold lace'. While they waited for an answer, the buccaneers despatched a canoe full of men to gather coconuts in great groves swaying along the shore. After their long, deprived voyage, the taste of the 'sweet, delicate, wholesome and refreshing water' inside the nuts was overwhelming. Dampier rated the Guam coconuts the best he ever tasted. He described the many other uses of the coconut palm – 'possibly of all others the most

Breadfruit.

generally serviceable to conveniences as well as the necessities of human life' – producing oil, fashioning utensils, spinning coir ropes and, perhaps a particular interest to thirsty sailors, making arrack. Dampier wrote that he gave such a detailed account 'for the sake of our countrymen in our American plantations' and the West Indies who, because ignorant of its uses, 'scarce regarded' the coconut palm. The laziness and narrow-mindedness of the English about cultivating and exploiting novel crops was one of his recurring complaints.

The governor's reply came more quickly than antici-pated. Promising to do what he could to help them, he sent a welcome present of six small hogs – 'the best I think, that ever I eat', Dampier later recalled. The governor offered to supply the buccaneers with as much baked breadfruit as they wanted. The breadfruit, which he had 'never heard of anywhere else', fascinated Dampier, and he wrote the first description in English of these handsome trees 'as big and high as [the] largest apple trees' in England, with their glossy dark-green leaves and fruits 'as big as a penny loaf'. He also explored the process that metamorphosed the fruits into bread: 'When the fruit is ripe, it is yellow and soft: and the taste is sweet and pleasant. The natives of this island use it for bread: they gather it when full grown, while it is green and hard; then they bake it in an oven, which scorcheth the rind and makes it black: but they scrape off the outside black crust, and there remains a tender thin crust, and the inside is soft, tender and white, like the crumb of a penny loaf. There is neither seed nor stone in the inside, but all is of a pure substance like bread'.*

The governor had no option but to humour the buccaneers. His small garrison was no match for the well-armed visitors. The Chamorros had reached the same conclusion. Despite their suffering at the hands of Eaton's men, they proposed to the buccaneers that they should join them in driving the Spanish off the island. Dampier admired these 'strong-bodied, large-limb'd, and well-shap'd people' who were 'stern of countenance' yet 'affable and courteous'. They were also fine boat builders. He watched them construct long outrigger canoes, or 'proas', noting how the small, wedge-shaped 'boat or canoe', which they fixed 'firm and contiguous' to the main craft with bamboo, helped 'keep the great boat upright from oversetting' in the brisk winds. Dampier believed 'they sail the best of any boats in the world' and decided to test their

---

*Dampier's glowing words, confirmed by his own observations, would cause Captain James Cook, seventy-five years later, to recommend transplanting breadfruit to the British West Indies as a source of food. Captain William Bligh was despatched on the *Bounty* in 1787 to transport breadfruit saplings from Tahiti to the Caribbean. Despite the mutiny, the determined Bligh successfully shipped breadfruit plants in a later voyage of 1792–93. In his account of his voyages Bligh quoted Dampier's pioneering observations in full as the prime inspiration for the voyage.

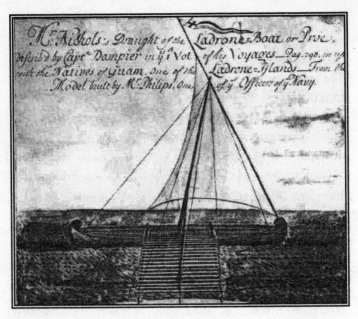

A proa.

speed 'for my own satisfaction' and to 'make an experiment of it'. He climbed aboard a proa and, using a logline as he zipped through the water, calculated that they were probably capable of twenty-four knots.

Swan 'was not for molesting the Spaniards here' and turned down the Chamorro offer. He was secretly hoping to obtain a letter of recommendation from the governor to merchants in Manila in the hope of trading there. The civilities and exchanges of gifts continued. The governor sent more hogs and more fruit, and Swan gave him powder, shot and weapons in return. He also agreed to the governor's request for one of the *Cygnet*'s two dogs – 'a delicate large English dog' – to which he had taken a fancy, although this much upset some of Swan's crew 'who had a great value for that dog'.

Swan might not have been so generous had he known that, while they were lying at anchor, the Spanish galleon bound for Manila from Acapulco had arrived off the island. The governor had despatched a swift boat to alert the ship to the buccaneers' presence. She had at once stood out to sea but had caught her rudder on the same outlying shoal that had surprised the buccaneers. She lay struggling for three days before managing to free herself. When the buccaneers finally learned that she was so near, it put them 'in a great heat to go out after her', but Swan refused. 'He was now wholly averse to any hostile action', reported Dampier. He later recalled with some regret that although the ship had fifty guns, only four were mounted and she was carrying '800,000 of merchants' money'.

Anxious to be rid of the buccaneers before things turned sour, the governor reminded Swan that 'the west monsoon was at hand'. On 30 May, a final exchange of gifts took place, during which Swan released the hostage priest after presenting him with an astrolabe and a large telescope. The priest advised the buccaneers to make for Mindanao in the Philippines. Not only was it very well stocked with provisions, but the Muslim inhabitants were at war with the Spanish. As Dampier wrote, this appealed to their men, 'who were very squeamish of plundering without licence'. They hoped to get a commission from the ruler of Mindanao to attack Spanish ships around Manila and to use Mindanao as their refuge. Swan, according to Dampier, was 'willing enough to go there as best suiting his own designs'. He had amassed some £5,000 in gold for himself and his sponsors by selling his goods to the buccaneers and thought Mindanao would be a safe haven for himself and his wealth, at least in the short term.

XI

'AS WHITE AS MILK AND
AS SOFT AS CREAM'

On 21 June 1686, three weeks after leaving Guam, the buccaneers sighted the first islands of the Philippines and wove through them to Mindanao, second largest in the group. They cruised along it, alert for any signs of life in the harbours and creeks, but there was nothing, no canoes, no people. Finally, they encountered a few islanders on the northeastern shore, but they were too timid to come on board. The buccaneers did not know the location of the island's main town, nor what reception to expect. The weather was becoming 'boisterous with rains and tornadoes'. They sailed around the island to find a safe anchorage and then sent a party ashore by canoe, which found wide savannahs teeming with deer and fertile, well-tended plantations. Once again the weathered, sea-hardened buccaneers with their muskets and pistols tried to question the few inhabitants, but – unsurprisingly in view of their appearance – as Dampier noted, 'they fled from us'.

Hoping for better luck, they coasted round the southern shore, which they found better populated. They saw canoes, full of lithe, wiry fishermen, and small villages built on stilts along the shoreline. These people were not so apprehensive of the visitors, but language difficulties posed problems: 'We could not understand them nor they us'. On 18 July, the buccaneers nevertheless managed to reach the

Mindanao River and anchored two miles offshore. To announce their presence to this sleepy island, they fired their guns. The booms were answered by three shots. A canoe put out from the shore carrying, as they discovered, important dignitaries: Raja Laut, brother to the local sultan and commander of his army, together with one of the sultan's sons.

The two men refused to come aboard but shouted questions in Spanish across the water. Who were the new arrivals? Where were they from? A buccaneer called Smith, who had learned Spanish while a prisoner in Mexico, explained that they were from England. The Mindanaons excitedly asked whether they had been sent by English East India merchants to set up a factory. Smith's truthful reply that they were simply hoping to buy provisions seemed to disappoint the islanders. The buccaneers later learned that a British captain named Goodlad had visited the island not long before and promised the Mindanaons 'an Ambassador from England'. To the north of Mindanao, most of the Philippines were under Spanish rule. To their south and west was the expanding trading empire of the Dutch. So the Mindanaons had hoped England would become their protector against the other encroaching European powers. The sight of Swan, pacing the deck in 'a scarlet coat with broad silver lace', looking the very picture of an ambassador, had raised their hopes.

Nevertheless, the exchange was friendly. Raja Laut and his nephew invited Swan ashore. They also advised him to shift anchorage and bring his ships into the river 'for fear of the westerly winds', which, in his present position, would become 'very violent'. Not to be outdone in courtesy, Swan sent three yards of scarlet cloth, three yards of gold lace, a Turkish scimitar and a pair of pistols to the sultan and a length of scarlet cloth with three yards of silver lace to Raja Laut. Swan chose Quartermaster Henry More as the gift bearer, and he became the first of Swan's men to enter what many would find a seductive world. More was taken to Raja Laut's house and later escorted by torchlight to the sultan's palace. This great structure was built on a platform supported by some 180 posts. In front of it was a smaller, lower house, where strangers were received. Here the sultan, seated on carpets and surrounded by his advisers, awaited his visitors. He quizzed More carefully in Spanish through an interpreter for about an hour before dismissing him.

The next day the sultan summoned Swan, who went ashore revelling in the pomp and ceremony with 'a flag flying in the boat's head, and two trumpets sounding all the way'. As Dampier later wrote, the sultan received his guest in his audience chamber, offering him tobacco and betel nut, wrapped in a leaf spread with lime paste, which the locals chewed with relish. He showed Swan two elegantly written letters, each line underscored in gold. The first was from the East India Company about proposals to set up an English trading base on Mindanao. The second, from Captain Goodlad, was 'directed to any English-men who should happen to come thither' and informed them of the rates he had established for the sale and purchase of goods. It concluded rather ominously, 'Trust none of them for they are all thieves.' Audience over, Swan and his men returned to Raja Laut's house. Over a dinner of boiled chicken and rice, they learned that their affable host was highly influential. Not only was he a renowned warrior, but he controlled all aspects of maritime trade.

Swan was convinced that if the East India Company were proposing to trade at Mindanao, the people were surely trustworthy. Goodlad's warning was a worry, but, as he soon learned, the reason for it seemed to be that he had been robbed by a thief who had subsequently fled into the mountains. Not long after the buccaneers' arrival, Raja Laut's men produced the miscreant, who they claimed had returned to the town coincidentally. Raja Laut invited the captain to punish the man 'as he pleased'. Swan declined to become involved. Dampier recorded the punishment his own people then meted out – 'which I did never see but at this time'. At sunrise the man was stripped naked and tied to a post 'so that he could not stir hand nor foot', facing the rising sun. In the afternoon the post was turned westward, 'and thus he stood all day, parched in the sun . . . tormented with the moskitoes or gnats'.

Raja Laut assiduously courted Swan. He provided scores of Mindanaon fishermen to help the buccaneers manoeuvre their ships up the shallow river to a safe mooring, while he himself directed operations from the deck of the *Cygnet*. Swan was soon dining nearly every day with Raja Laut, where he was joined by some of his men, Dampier among them. They fed on boiled rice, which was 'well dressed', and scraps of fowl and buffalo, which he thought were cooked 'very nastily'. They ate as the locals did, wetting their hand in water before taking a handful of rice from the common dish, squeezing it, then cramming it into their mouths. An apparent contest among the raja's followers to take the largest possible lump, 'so that sometimes they almost choke themselves', amused Dampier.

Swan dined apart on better fare, serenaded throughout by his two trumpeters. After dinner, he and Raja Laut would sit talking through an interpreter. The attention was going to Swan's head. He began punishing his own men, including his chief mate, Josiah Teat, who had captained

his accompanying barque, 'for the least offence' in full sight
of the Mindanaons. Teat and others were 'tied and
whipped at a coconut tree to show his power to the heathen
prince'. This was a stark departure from the buccaneers'
code, and Dampier later recalled that Swan 'had his
men as much under command as if he had been in a king's
ship'.

However, the buccaneers had compensations for their
captain's erratic behaviour. The islanders besieged them
with invitations to their houses. It was, as Dampier
acknowledged, a long time since 'any of us had received
such friendship'. The Mindanaons were particularly
anxious to know who had a 'comrade' or a 'pagally'. A
comrade was 'a familiar male friend', while a pagally was
'an innocent platonic friend of the other sex'. The visitors
soon realized that they were 'in a manner obliged to accept
of this acquaintance and familiarity', which must first be
purchased with a small present and later confirmed by a
more substantial gift. However, it was attractive to men
who had been long at sea. When they went ashore, they
were welcome to eat, drink and sleep in the comrade's or
pagally's house. Tobacco and betel nut, which made
Dampier giddy if the nuts were old, and cups of sweet,
spiced water were given gratis. Other things had to be paid
for.

The Mindanaon men had 'many wives', and, perhaps as
a consequence, the women were particularly 'desirous of
the company of strangers': 'Even the sultans' and the
generals' wives, who are always cooped up, will yet look out
of their cages when a stranger passeth by, and demand of
him if he wants a pagally'. In a short time those buccaneers
who 'had good clothes and store of gold' – mostly
those who had enriched themselves by sacking Santa Maria

as they crossed the isthmus before joining the *Cygnet* – had a comrade or two and as many pagallies. Many also had 'women-servants whom they hired off their masters for concubines'. Some rented houses to live full-time ashore. Dampier did not anywhere relate what liaisons he formed, but he could hardly have avoided them since, according to his own account, in time 'the very poorest and meanest' of the men could not walk down the street without being hailed by would-be friends and virtually forced into their houses. In any case, curiosity would have led him to seek the islanders' acquaintance. Their 'seeming sincerity' and 'simplicity' beguiled him. They signified that the English and the Mindanaons 'were all one' by putting their two fore-fingers together and saying, ' "Samo, samo," that is, "All one" '.

Dampier's writings about Mindanao, in his best-selling first book, went far beyond the laconic logging of times, dates, weather and distances that were the stuff of most seamen's journals. They were the fascinated and acute observations of a true traveller about exotic lands entirely unfamiliar to those in England who would later read his published works. He recounted how, although there were other peoples and rulers on the island, the sultan's subjects were the largest and most important group. He was keenly interested in language and noted that a number spoke not only Spanish but also Malay, Arabic and several local dialects. He observed their physical characteristics. The tawny-skinned males were 'of mean stature; small limbs, straight bodies and little heads'. Their faces were oval with flat foreheads, small, black eyes, short noses, large mouths, thin red lips, and teeth that were 'black, yet very sound'. The red and black discoloration came from chewing betel nut. They wore their thumbnails very long, 'especially that on their left thumb'. The women were fairer than the men, more round-faced, and 'generally well featured' and slender-limbed. However, he was disconcerted by their tiny noses and flat foreheads, writing that 'at a distance they appear very well; but being nigh these impediments are very obvious'. In perhaps the first English description of a sarong, he described their chief garment as 'only a piece of cloth' which they wound around their bodies.

The Mindanaons were 'ingenious, nimble and active' when they wanted to be, but prone to be 'very lazy and thievish' and reluctant to work 'except [when] forced by hunger'. Dampier blamed the sultan. By treating his people arbitrarily and overtaxing them, he dampened their industry 'so they never strive to have anything'. Dampier also wrote that they were implacable to their enemies and remorseless if injured. Their favourite means of revenge was 'poisoning secretly those that affronted them'.

Dampier examined the Mindanaon houses built high on stilts. The detritus was pushed down between the split bamboos forming the floors, where it bred maggots and made 'a prodigious stink', rather like the rubbish festering in the bilges of a ship. However, the people themselves were very clean. Only sick people urinated and defecated in their chambers, where a small, discreet hole allowed the ordure to fall through. Healthy people washed and relieved themselves in the river. Dampier was impressed that both men and women loved swimming and washing, reflecting, 'I do believe it is very wholesome to wash mornings and evenings in these hot countries, at least three or four days in the week'. After conducting an experiment of regular washing while 'very low' with a distemper and finding it worked, he later adopted the practice himself – an astonishing act, since seventeenth-century Englishmen washed much less often.

The Mindanaons were Muslims, and their religious rituals fascinated Dampier – from the sounding of a great gong in the sultan's mosque to summon the faithful to prayer to the elaborate purification rites and the celebration of Ramadan, which occurred while he was on the island: 'In this time they fast all day and about seven a clock in the evening they spend near an hour in prayer. Towards the latter end of their prayer, they loudly invoke their Prophet, for about a quarter of an hour, both old and young, bawling out very strangely, as if they intended to fright him out of his sleepiness or neglect of them'. He also watched a mass circumcision of boys between the ages of eleven and twelve, describing how the Muslim cleric 'takes hold of the fore-skin with two sticks and with a pair of scissors snips it off'. Immediately, a watching group of older men formed a great ring. One after another they ran yelling and grimacing into the centre to enact a wild martial dance, sword in one hand and lance in the other. It culminated in a decapitation of an imaginary enemy, after which the dancer was 'all of a sweat and [withdrew] triumphantly out of the ring', to be replaced by the next frenzied performer. But there was no dancing for the circumcised boys, who, Dampier later remembered, 'being sore with their amputation, went straddling for a fortnight after'.

When his son was circumcised, Raja Laut invited Swan and his men to join him in a grand procession to meet his brother, the sultan, who was coming to call on the young man. Dampier was among the forty who accompanied Swan. They joined some 1,000 Mindanaon men whose brightly burning torches 'made it as light as day'. The procession was led 'by two dancing women gorgeously apparelled with coronets on their heads, full of glittering

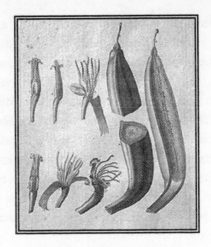

A plantain.

spangles, and pendants of the same, hanging down over their breast and shoulders'. The dancers, 'hands, arms, head and body were in continual motion', their movements so fluid 'you would think them to be made without bones'.

Swan and Raja Laut followed side by side, while behind them, in pride of place, marched Dampier and the buccaneers six abreast, 'with each man his gun on his shoulder, and torches on each side'. They met the sultan and his party and escorted them with due ceremony back to Raja Laut's house. The buccaneers were invited to remain while the sultan's family, male and female, danced. They sang as they sinuously twisted and turned. The only instruments to accompany them were a graduated set 'of a kind of bells without clappers sixteen in number' lined up in a row and struck with little sticks. The weary guests dispersed as festivities concluded with fireworks shooting into the starry night sky.

Sometimes the raja went off hunting with his men, claiming to leave his women in the buccaneers' care as a mark of his 'good trust and confidence'. In fact, 'he always left one of his principal men, for fear some of [the buccaneers] should be too familiar with his women'. Even so, Dampier had a chance to observe the women at close quarters. As soon as Raja Laut departed, they flocked to the buccaneers to ask them 'a thousand questions' about Englishwomen and English customs. They were amazed to learn that Englishmen were allowed only one wife, and debated the merits and disadvantages of such an arrangement. Dampier, in turn, learned that Raja Laut slept with his women 'by turns', but that the mother of his eldest son was entitled to 'a double portion of his company'. The woman with whom he was due to lie that night wore a striped silk handkerchief around her neck, by which they 'knew who was queen that day'.

Dampier was not immune to Mindanao's siren seductiveness, the valleys 'well-moistened with pleasant brooks and small rivers of delicate water'. He described the succulent-tasting durians with flesh 'as white as milk and as soft as cream', while adding in a not very exact description of their putrid smell that it was like 'roasted onions'.* His greatest praise was for 'the king of all fruit': the plantain, which was 'the colour of the purest yellow butter . . . of a delicate taste and melts in one's mouth like marmalet'. Years later, his book read like a cooking lesson, describing how plantains could be baked in everything from tarts to a boiled pudding of mashed plantains, which the buccaneers called 'a buff jacket' – no doubt a simulation of the boiled

*On this occasion he seems unaware of the claimed aphrodisiac qualities of the fruit, giving rise to the East Indian saying 'when the durians fall, the sarongs rise'.

puddings they relished in England. Dampier also warned that, if eaten raw, plantains caused wind. Accurately and precisely, he described how the plantain was cultivated and propagated, how when dried its leaves produced thread. The ordinary people of Mindanao wore 'no other cloth', but Dampier noted it 'wears out soon and when wet feels a little slimy'.

He roamed through forests of trees quite unknown to Europeans, like the 'libby', or sago, tree. He watched the islanders pound and then strain the soft white pith, from which they made sago to eat in place of bread. Centipedes 'as big as a goose quill' wriggled over the forest floor, and he saw a large, almost mythical creature 'like a guano [an iguana] both in colour and shape, but four times as big, whose tongue is like a small harpoon, having two beards like the beards of a fish-hook': perhaps a Komodo dragon.

Dampier believed that Mindanao was a place of commercial possibilities. The nutmegs there were 'fair and large'. The islanders were afraid to admit to cultivating them for fear of the Dutch, who jealously guarded their monopoly and would destroy spice trees outside their own sphere of influence. Dampier, a firm believer in 'a free trade', was sure that if the islanders thought the English would protect them, they would both cultivate and trade in nutmegs and cloves. Also, there was gold to be mined in the mountains, as well as the pleasing prospect of trading clandestinely with the Spanish in the other islands, who would be delighted to get their hands on cheap smuggled goods. Dampier would later write that 'upon mature thoughts' the buccaneers could not have done better than to settle here. It would have been more profitable than 'the loose roving way of life' and 'of public benefit to our nation'. Coolly reviewing the skills of his fellow crew members, he concluded that they had had the right mix to make a go of it: 'We had sawyers, carpenters, joiners, brickmakers, bricklayers, shoemakers, tailors'. The only craft lacking was 'a good smith for great work', whom they could have found among the islanders. The buccaneers had plentiful iron and lead, and every tool from saws and axes to hammers, as well as powder, shot and small arms. Dampier calculated that they could have built and defended a small fort. Moreover, their chances of survival and success would have been far greater than those of 'raw men' newly sent out from England. The latter would have proceeded 'too cautiously, coldly and formally', as well as endangering their lives by 'so great and sudden a change of air'. The buccaneers, by contrast, were 'daring men . . . inured to hot climates, hardened by many fatigues', who 'would not be easily baffled'.

The buccaneers were appalled to discover, after some weeks on Mindanao, that their river anchorage was 'a horrid place for worms'. The bottoms of their canoes were 'eaten like honey-combs', and their single-hulled barque was quite unseaworthy. The *Cygnet*, with her extra wooden sheathing, was still sound, but only just. The worms had not penetrated the main hull. Raja Laut, observing their efforts with interest, seemed surprised, even dismayed, that the *Cygnet* was double-sheathed, remarking that 'he did never see a ship with two bottoms before'. Dampier and his colleagues suspected that the reason he had been so insistent they moor in the river was that he knew the worms were bad. He did not want his visitors to be able to leave.

The buccaneers ripped off the worm-eaten planking and by December 1686, six months after arriving off

Mindanao, had resheathed the *Cygnet*'s bottom and coated it with tallow. They sailed her out of the river mouth and anchored in the open sea again. Swan seemed curiously vague about when he intended to sail. He had no intention of attacking Spanish shipping off Manila 'as his crew designed', but was plainly undecided what to do as an alternative. His crew found him 'commonly very cross' and equally uncommunicative.

Dampier, meanwhile, set out on a hunting trip with Raja Laut, who promised plenty of cattle to slaughter and salt as provisions for the buccaneers. After a week, all Dampier had seen were four cows, which were too wild to approach. He was further irritated by the behaviour of half a dozen young buccaneers. Unwilling to leave their 'Delilahs which made them fond of the place', they were plotting with Raja Laut to deceive Swan about the prospects of finding cattle and thus to detain him. Dampier discovered this and warned Swan. The captain stormed and raged against Raja Laut behind his back but dared say little in his presence, being, as Dampier wrote of the man whose skills he had once admired, 'a man of small courage'. In fact Dampier was growing thoroughly dis-illusioned with his captain, who had become 'so puffed up by the favour of a poor indigent prince that now he was clear another man than he had formerly been'. Swan's vain-glorious behaviour 'occasioned all those jarring discontents which happened and at last brought ruin and destruction on himself and most of his company'.

On Christmas Day, Swan summoned all his men aboard the *Cygnet* to celebrate the festival. Dampier waited expectantly for Swan to announce his plans. He wondered whether the captain intended to load the *Cygnet* with a cargo of spices from one of the Spice Islands. Swan said nothing. He simply dined and then immediately returned ashore. He was 'deaf to all their complaints and minded nothing but his pleasure'.

His men, though, were very restive 'for want of action' and argued among themselves about what they should do. As Dampier noted, 'the main division was between those that had money and those that had none'. A third were living the lotus-eating life ashore with their companions, concubines and pagallies. Like Fletcher Christian and others of Captain Bligh's crew in Tahiti 100 years later, they were mostly content to keep on doing so. A small group even absconded into the hinterland, to avoid being forced to sail. However, the majority of the crew, too poor to purchase comforts, were pressing Swan daily to be gone because it was the height of the easterly monsoon, the only wind that could carry them further into the Indies. Dampier gave little information about his own views, and it is not clear whether he took a leading role in the debates. Nevertheless, in the only surviving draft of his first book, but not in the book itself, he related how he was one of a group of fifteen men who, in desperation, 'bought a periago intending to go to Borneo'. Captain Swan discovered the plan and confiscated their boat. When they purchased another, he seized that too.

The crisis finally broke when a group of buccaneers based on the *Cygnet* became rip-roaring drunk. According to Dampier, this deterred him from going aboard: 'for I did ever abhor drunkenness which our men that were on board abandoned themselves wholly to'. He expected Swan to take control of what had become anarchy, but the captain ignored it until a merchant named Harthop, who had sailed with him from England, insisted he tell his men what he planned to do. Swan duly ordered all his men to be aboard the *Cygnet* on 13 January 1687.

Two days before this, however, he had sent his gunner to fetch something from his cabin. Rummaging about, the man had come across Swan's journal of the voyage from America to Guam. Somehow it got into the hands of a senior mariner, John Read, who had been keeping his own diary. According to Dampier, Read wanted to see how it matched his own account and read it eagerly.

The curious Read soon discovered that Swan's account was less of a journal than a catalogue of grievances 'against most of his men'. He showed it at once to his comrades, who, Dampier believed, were mostly 'ripe for mischief' and only awaiting an excuse. The diary provided it. Josiah Teat, erstwhile commander of the bark whom the captain unwisely had flogged, persuaded the buccaneers to depose Swan. It was not difficult; most 'were quite tired with this long and tedious voyage, and despaired of ever getting home, and therefore did not care what they did, or whither they went'. All those on board swore an oath to turn Swan out and to conceal their plan from those ashore. They would have sailed at once, but the surgeon and his mate were on land and it was not considered prudent 'to go to sea without a surgeon'. The next morning, they cunningly despatched a messenger ashore with a story that one of the men had broken his leg by falling into the hold. The surgeon sent his mate, Herman Coppinger. Dampier, Coppinger's friend, went aboard with him. According to Dampier's account, they discovered what was going on only once they were on the *Cygnet*.

On the morning of 13 January 1687, the mutineers fired a single gun. A startled Swan sent his chief mate, Nelly, aboard to ask what was happening. The buccaneers poured out their grievances and showed Nelly the offensive journal. He persuaded them to wait until the following day. The next morning, Harthop came aboard and pleaded with them to wait until early afternoon to give Swan and those still ashore the chance to decide whether they wanted to sail. They seem to have agreed, but the hours passed and Swan neither came himself – as Dampier thought 'a captain of any prudence and courage would have done' – nor sent a message.

Dampier claimed he hoped until the final moment that Swan would join them. In the unpublished draft of his book he wrote, 'Several of us were heartily sorry for Captain Swan and those that tarried behind'. Perhaps a little guiltily, he added that he would have stayed with Swan but lacked the money to keep himself or 'the liberty to leave the ship'. Again in the unpublished draft, he wrote, 'From me they would not part for fear they should want a man to navigate the ship'. As with Herman Coppinger, his presence seems to have been considered essential. Dampier added that he had hoped at some stage to persuade them to return for Swan. The flavour of these unpublished comments suggests that Dampier protested too much about his lack of involvement in the deposition of Swan. After all, he had no cause to love his captain after he had twice seized periagos in which he was hoping to desert.

The buccaneers sailed, with John Read as the new captain, Josiah Teat as master and Henry More remaining as quartermaster. They were abandoning not only Captain Swan but thirty-six men living in the town and the six or eight who had run off. They were also leaving the graves of sixteen men who had died, they suspected, from poisoning. According to Dampier, some of the buccaneers had provoked the Mindanaon men 'through their general rogueries, and sometimes by dallying too familiarly with

their women, even before their faces'. Some poisons were
thought to be so slow and lingering that they were to be
blamed for the deaths of others on board in the months
ahead.

XII

'THIS MAD CREW'

The buccaneers cruised along the coast of Mindanao before threading their way northwards through the Philippines. On one island they found a quiet, secluded bay, where they dragged the *Cygnet* onto the beach, scrubbed her hull vigorously, and coated it with tallow. Dampier explored the bay, penetrating dense clumps of hairy rattan canes. Each night towards sunset he watched 'incredible' battalions of dun-coloured bats 'with bodies as big as ducks' and massive wingspans come sweeping over the sea from a tiny offshore islet. They returned 'like a cloud' just before sunrise.

He made careful notes of how time appeared to have changed since they had begun voyaging westwards. He calculated that, given the respective longitudes of England and Mindanao, and the fact that Mindanao lay west of the Lizard in England, the time on the island must have been some fourteen hours behind British time. By 'keeping the same course with the sun', he realized, they had gained time. A day that in England would have been a Friday was on Mindanao still Thursday. Although he did not express it in such words, he had worked out that they had crossed the dateline.

In mid-February, as the buccaneers moved on, they hit rocks just below the water, which carved 'off a great piece' of their rudder. They were aground for two hours; in Dampier's opinion, '[We] more narrowly missed losing our ship this time, than on any other in the whole voyage'. Once the *Cygnet* was refloated, the relieved crew continued to hug the coastline, slinking past places where fires glowed in the night. Dampier guessed that the Spanish had spotted their ship and had lit beacons as a warning of 'danger or the like from sea'. They anchored off the mountainous island of Mindoro, where they intercepted a canoe carrying four Indians from Manila. The buccaneers addressed them in Spanish; '[we hoped] to get out of them what intelligence we could as to their shipping, strength, and the like, under colour of seeking a trade, for', as Dampier acknowledged, 'our business was to pillage'. In succeeding days, they captured several Spanish ships close to Manila and interrogated their crews also. They were dismayed to discover that it would be months before the next ship from Acapulco was due in Manila and decided to withdraw westwards to 'a little parcel of islands' – the Pulo Condore group (today the Con Son group) off the mouths of the Mekong River in the South China Sea – 'to lie snug for a while' and await the return of their 'prey' towards the end of May.

They reached their island hideaway in late March, dropped anchor, and went ashore to see what nature would provide. Roaming the humid forests in pursuit of hogs and wild fowl, Dampier sniffed a delicate, sweet fragrance borne on the breeze. He tracked it to some groves of wild mango trees, their branches drooping with ripe, yellowish fruits. He watched local people make mango pickle from them: 'When the mango is young they cut them in two pieces, and pickle them with salt and vinegar, in which they put some cloves of garlic. This is an excellent sauce, and much esteemed: it is called Mango-Achar'.*

Perhaps the piquant *achar* tasted good with the green turtle that Dampier so relished and which were plentiful here. The behaviour of the islands' turtles confirmed Dampier's thesis, first formed in the Galapagos Islands, that they migrated long distances to lay their eggs and then returned to their original feeding grounds. He dismissed the commonly held belief that they simply withdrew a little way out to sea from the breeding ground. How, he argued, could turtles possibly find enough food? Also, why were turtles seldom seen in such offshore waters after laying?

Dampier appraised the commercial potential of these islands, noting they were geographically well placed for trade. Running a practised, practical eye over the harbour where the *Cygnet* was moored, he concluded that it could easily be defended by building a few forts and would be an excellent place to establish a factory, as a trading station was known. As usual, the local people interested him. They were 'very civil people, but extraordinary poor'. They were also 'idolaters' – five-feet-high images of elephants and horses stood watch outside their thatched and wooden temples. Dampier conversed with an old man, using the 'smattering' of Malay he had acquired on Mindanao. He learned that the islanders survived by boiling the resin of the tall dammer tree – 'a sort of clammy juice' – which made 'perfect' tar and which they sold to the mainland of Cochinchina (now Indochina). They also hunted turtles, which they rendered down to make oil. They were 'so free of their women that they would bring them aboard and offer them to the buccaneers'. Many of the latter hired the

*This is the first reference in English to mango pickle, or chutney.

women 'for a small matter'. Again, Dampier did not mention in his book whether he was among them but coolly commended to merchants the taking of local mistresses to provide information and early warning 'to their white friends' of incipient trouble.

Once again, he and his colleagues set to work refitting the ship. They resheathed her bottom with fresh planks and coated it with tar, made from the pitchy spirit that they bought from the locals and mixed with lime. In the midst of all the hammering and sawing and slapping on of pitch, two men died. They had been ailing for a while and were themselves convinced that they had been poisoned on Mindanao. '[They were] open'd up by our doctor, according to their own request before they died, and their livers were black, light and dry, like pieces of cork'.*

On 21 April 1687, a warm day with a brisk wind to speed them, the buccaneers sailed for the Gulf of Thailand. Their destination was a group of islands that they had been told were inhabited by fishermen who could sell them salt-fish. They found the islands, but the fishermen had no fish to sell. Disconsolately, the buccaneers retraced their journey, encountering a Cambodian vessel on her way to trade with the Dutch at Malacca. Her crew of forty men, armed with swords, lances and guns, fascinated Dampier. They were 'idolaters' but 'some of the briskest, most sociable, without fearfulness or shyness, and the most neat and dexterous about their shipping of any such I have met in all my travels'. Sailing on, the *Cygnet* overtook a great junk laden with pepper from Sumatra. Dampier learned from the crew that the English had established a factory on Sumatra.

---

*Their deaths might have been the result of a fatal dose administered by an affronted pagally but were more probably caused by cirrhosis of the liver induced by heavy drinking.

It was the first he knew of it, and he tucked the information away in his mind.

Regaining Pulo Condore, the buccaneers dropped anchor, then noticed a small barque close to the shore. Captain Read feared it was Malay. Their crews had a reputation as 'desperate fellows, and their vessels [were] commonly full of men who all [wore] cressets or little daggers by their sides'. He sent a canoe-load of men to enquire where the barque was from, with strict instructions that none were to go aboard. Unfortunately, the sailors disobeyed. Leaving just one man in the canoe, the rest clambered onto the barque. The crew, who were indeed Malays, saw at once that their visitors were armed, drew their daggers and hacked and stabbed at the men, killing half a dozen, including quartermaster Henry More. The remaining buccaneers tumbled back into the canoe or leaped frantically into the sea. Dampier noted with grim humour that one man, Daniel Wallis, 'who could never swim before nor since', managed to swim 'very well' until help came.

The Malays, fearing revenge, holed their own barque, got into a canoe and raced for the shore, where they ran into the woods. An incensed Captain Read sent a party to flush them out, but with no success. However, a harsh wind made it impossible to sail on. Surgeon Herman Coppinger took the opportunity to sneak ashore, hoping to escape from the *Cygnet*, but the angry captain sent men to bring him back. Similar thoughts of escape had also been running through Dampier's mind. Like his friend the young doctor, he was 'weary of this mad crew'; '[I] was willing to give them the slip at any place from whence we might hope to get a passage to an English factory', but Dampier decided to wait 'for a more convenient place'.

On 4 June 1687, Captain Read took advantage of a brisk southwest wind to set course for Manila, but the wind swung perversely round, instead forcing them up the coast of China. Three weeks brought them to St John's Island near Hong Kong. Dampier went eagerly ashore, where he saw Chinamen walking in the bright sun. They were 'of an ashen complexion' and wore no hats or turbans but carried a small umbrella or a large fan made of paper or silk to protect them. Their beards were 'thin and long for they pluck the hair out by the roots, suffering only some few very long straggling hairs to grow about their chin in which they take pride, often combing them'. Their heads were shaved, 'only reserving one lock' of hair, the pigtail. Dampier learned that this was imposed on pain of death by a much resented order of the ruling 'Tartars' – by which he meant the Manchu, who had invaded from the north beyond the Great Wall to tumble the Ming dynasty some forty years earlier.

Dampier was also struck, even shocked, by the bound feet, or 'golden lillies' as the Chinese called them, of the women. He recorded how their feet were swathed in tight bandages from infancy 'to hinder them from growing' since the Chinese esteemed little feet as 'a great beauty'. This was, he wrote, an 'unreasonable custom', which made them 'in a manner lose the use of their feet'. Instead of being able to move freely, the women could 'only stumble about their houses, and presently squat down . . . being, as it were, confined to sitting all days of their lives'. He wondered whether it was 'a stratagem' of the men to keep the women from 'gadding about and gossiping'. He also thought the Chinese 'very great gamesters' who never tired of gambling, 'playing night and day until they have lost all their estates', whereupon, he added, 'it is usual with them to hang themselves'.

Nevertheless, during the ten days he spent there, Dampier came to admire the Chinese as 'very ingenious people' – his highest praise. An 'account of them and their country would fill a volume', he later wrote. He noted the Chinese use of ginseng and praised Chinese tea, or *char,* beyond 'any other for the colour and pleasant bitter taste'. He extolled their exquisite porcelain, the fine lacquer-ware, the supple, shimmering silks, the deft, delicate paintings and intricate carvings. He also admired the sturdy Chinese cargo junks with huge masts hewn from a single tree, unlike in Britain where such tall masts were pieced together from more than one tree. He was struck by the honeycomb of watertight partitions with which the Chinese divided the hull so that damage and water flooding in could more easily be contained.

Dampier watched men plough with buffaloes in preparation for the sowing of rice. A hunting expedition gave him a little insight into their religion. He and some companions were cooking a succulent 'young porker' that they had just slain, when a Chinese man approached them. Once the meat was cooked, they gave him a large piece. The man implored them to go with him into the woods, which, having eaten their fill, they reluctantly did. He led them to an ancient, brick-paved temple. A rusted iron bell, surmounted by iron bars shaped like 'the paw of some monstrous beast', stood in the middle of the floor. 'This it seems was their God', wrote Dampier. Earthernware vessels on an altar were filled with joss sticks. The man wished them to present some meat to the god as a sacrifice, but they refused.

Bad weather brought an end to such encounters. The wind began 'whiffling about from one part of the compass to another' – a sign that a bad storm was coming. The buccaneers decided to weigh anchor and ride out the tempest at sea, rather than risk the *Cygnet* being driven ashore. Soon the sky blackened, and a vicious wind rose from the northeast. Men scrambled barefoot into the rigging, swaying precariously on the tarred footropes beneath the bucking yardarms to reef and furl the sails. Rain poured down 'as through a sieve'. It 'thundered and lightened prodigiously, and the sea seemed all of a fire about us'. Waves broke foaming over the deck, washing away part of the ship's heads and dislodging an anchor, which nearly punched a hole in the hull. The crew had to put the ship's head to the wind to recover the anchor and dared not turn to put the wind behind them again 'for fear of foundering', as the storm was by then too violent to risk taking the wind abeam again.

When the tempest finally abated and the exhausted seamen had time to look about them, Dampier noticed 'a certain small glittering light . . . like a star' dancing round the top of the mast. He had seen this light before, creeping over the decks like 'a great glow-worm'. It was St Elmo's Fire – an electrical discharge which sometimes appears after storms at sea. Many of his contemporaries believed it was a manifestation of Christ or the Holy Spirit; it was often known as the *corpus sant*. Other sailors thought the radiant light was the cavortings of hobgoblins, fairies or 'the enchanted bodies of witches', or even the spirit of a dead comrade come to warn of mortal danger. Dampier, though, was convinced that it was a natural phenomenon with a rational explanation and disparaged 'ignorant seamen' with their 'dismal stories' about what it portended.

The weather had not done with them yet. For a while it was so perversely calm that 'the sea tossed us about like an egg-shell for want of wind'. Then a gale sprang up, this time from the southwest. Heavy rains battered them again as a fresh tempest broke. Waves seemed to be breaking in all directions. 'I was never in such a violent storm in all my life', Dampier later wrote. The men manoeuvred the ship so that she flew before the wind. Somehow they survived, but the experience had 'deadened the[ir] hearts' so much that when the wind finally dropped all they could think of was finding shelter 'for fear of another such storm'.

They consulted their charts and decided to make for the Pescadores Islands, between Taiwan and mainland China. It was risky. None had been there before, and their maps contained no information about safe harbours. However, they managed to navigate successfully and to their relief 'blundered' into a good harbour. The hilly, grassy landscape reminded Dampier of 'Dorsetshire and Wiltshire downs in England'. He was less delighted to see that the harbour seethed with Chinese junks, busily 'going and coming'. The buccaneers had hoped the islands were uninhabited. They 'did not expect, nor desire, to have seen any people, being in care to lie concealed in these seas', yet they had little option but boldly to send a party ashore by canoe.

A Chinese official was waiting for the men as they landed, and conducted them to the governor. At this time the Chinese saw their own country as the 'middle kingdom' and the fount of civilization. They had little curiosity about the world beyond their borders. They believed Europe to be a series of small islands on the periphery of the known world, from which they had nothing to learn and which owed allegiance as a vassal to the Chinese Empire. They believed England to be subordinate to Holland and inhabited by red-haired barbarians. Following the Confucian maxim enjoining 'tender cherishing of men from afar', they allowed Europeans to trade at a few strictly regulated ports for porcelain, silk, tea and rhubarb, considering the latter essential to the English to relieve their chronic constipation.

When the governor asked the *Cygnet*'s crew where they were from and what was their business, they replied that they were English and en route to Amoy to trade, but had put in to repair storm damage to their ship. The governor reiterated politely but firmly that there was no question of trading there and that they would do better to sail straight to Amoy or alternatively Macao, both of which were 'allowed to entertain merchant-strangers'. Nevertheless, he 'cherished' the strangers by sending aboard gifts of flour, bread, watermelons and pineapples.

The next day, an eminent Chinese official came on board. Dampier noted his rich, exotic garb of a black silk cap with a high plume of black and white feathers, a loose black coat over two garments of coloured silk, and a pair of handsome boots. His attendants were also clad in black silk. Their caps had no feathers, but a fringe of coarse hair, dyed pale red, dangled over their faces. They brought more gifts, including jars of arrack and of *hoc shu*, a type of beer. The buccaneers were delighted, particularly by the beer. 'Our seamen', wrote Dampier, 'love it mightily, and will lick their lips with it; for scarce a ship goes to China but the men come home fat with soaking this liquor'.

On 29 July, the buccaneers departed, deciding to make for a group of five small islands which, though unnamed on their charts, lay close to Taiwan.* Hoping these islands would be uninhabited and that they could 'lie there secure' for a while, they reached them a week later to find,

*These were the Batanes Islands of the northern Philippines.

contrary to expectations, an 'abundance of inhabitants'. They were still furling their sails when 100 small boats approached, each bearing three or four curious occupants who swarmed aboard the ship so that the *Cygnet*'s deck was soon 'full of men'. The nervous buccaneers stood ready to fire on their uninvited guests 'if they had offered to molest [them]'. However, they were quiet and friendly and seemed most interested in helping themselves to pieces of iron, which they clearly prized highly. One man even began to remove the linchpins out of the gun carriages. The buccaneers grabbed hold of him, making him yell out in panic. The others at once leaped overboard. Regretting that they had frightened them away, the buccaneers sensibly 'made much' of their trembling captive. They released him and gave him a small piece of iron. He dived over the side and swam off to rejoin his companions. The buccaneers beckoned them to return aboard, and soon the deck was swarming once more.

Anxious to trade, the buccaneers sent a canoe ashore. The landing party were welcomed with *bashee* – a type of beer made from sugarcane and berries – and a vigorous barter began. The sailors bought hogs, goats, yams and potatoes, and of course *bashee*, in return for pieces of iron. They also found a small, sandy bay, where they erected a tent, mended their sails and yet again scrubbed the ship. They decided to exercise the traditional 'seamen's privilege' of naming these 'unnamed' islands. Dampier called the island where they had first anchored the Duke of Grafton's Isle – 'having married my wife out of his Duchess's family and leaving her at Arlington House at my going abroad'. Another island was named 'Bashee', which the buccaneers 'drank plentifully every day'.

Dampier explored the islands, recording their cliffs and

harbours. He examined the rich soil and plentiful crops of plantains, pineapples, pumpkins, and potatoes. '[The local people were] the quietest and civilest people that I did ever meet with'. Seldom angry, they strove 'to help each other', and their children were not rude to strangers 'as is usual'. Their egalitarianism matched Dampier's own ideals for a just society: 'I could never perceive that one man was of greater power than another; but they seemed to be all equal; only every man ruling in his own house, and the children respecting and honouring their parents'. Even their methods of execution seemed quiet and orderly. He watched a young man convicted of theft being buried alive. First a great, deep hole was dug; then an 'abundance of people' came to take their last farewell of the condemned man. He was then placed in the hole. He did not struggle 'but yielded very quietly to his punishment; and they crammed the earth close upon him, and stifled him'.

An intrigued Dampier recorded nearly every aspect of the islanders' lives – from their harmonious, monogamous marriages to their minimal clothing. He watched them cook their favourite dishes – though the stewed contents of a goat's stomach, which they devoured with raw, minced fish, was too much even for Dampier, who wrote of its 'nastiness'. However, he 'liked well enough' the taste of the locusts they seared over the fire, turning them shrimp-pink. The plump bodies 'would eat very moist, their heads would crackle in one's teeth'.*

The heavy, pale yellow metal mined by the islanders

---

*Dampier was lucky that at almost forty he still had enough of his own teeth to 'crackle' them. Contemporaries wore false sets of elephant ivory, ox bone or hippo tusks. The latter were most prized because they stayed whiter longer. Human teeth were also sometimes implanted – there had been a glut of them after the Great Plague of 1665.

keenly interested Dampier. Both men and women wore large earrings made of it, and he wondered whether it could be gold. They called the metal *bullawan* – the word used on Mindanao for gold. However, he noticed that the metal's lustre soon faded and that it needed to be polished with a paste of red earth. He would dearly have loved to purchase some, if only to satisfy his curiosity, but he 'had nothing wherewith to buy any'.

These weeks passed pleasantly, and the crew's depression lifted. However, towards the end of September a storm brewed up, forcing them once more out to sea. In the rush, six men were left ashore, and it was several days before the buccaneers could return for them. They found that their comrades had been well looked after; the islanders had even offered them young wives and a piece of land to farm. However, the renewed bad weather had put the *Cygnet*'s crew 'quite out of heart again' and 'frighted them from their design of cruising before Manila'. Yet they knew if they did not go there, their chances of seizing any treasure would be negligible. Dampier caught the glum mood: 'Every man wished himself at home, as they had done an hundred times before'. At last, they agreed to sail west to Cape Cormorin, on the southern tip of India, and there to take stock. Dampier was pleased: 'The farther we went, the more knowledge and experience I should get, which was the main thing I regarded'. He also had another motive. It would provide him with 'the more variety of places to attempt an escape'. He was 'fully resolved to take the first opportunity of giving them the slip'.

On 3 October 1687, they sailed southwards, heading back through the Philippines and leaving all thought of their 'golden projects' behind. By the middle of the month, they were off the southeast coast of Mindanao, where a

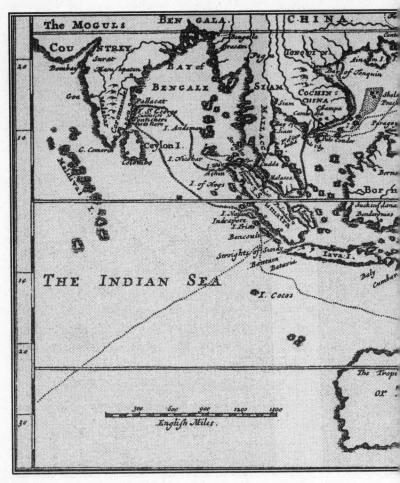

From the original 1697 edition of Dampier's A New Voyage.

young nobleman came aboard with news of Captain Swan. He related how Swan and several of the men who had remained with him had been fighting with Raja Laut against his enemies, but that Swan wished to leave. He had offered forty ounces of gold for a ship but feared that Raja Laut would not let him go until the wars were over. Dampier

A Map of the EAST INDIES

tried behind Read's back to persuade his comrades to rescue Swan, but one man betrayed him to Read, who squashed the plan. Instead, the captain 'made all possible haste to be gone'. Dampier later learned that Swan was murdered, probably on the orders of Raja Laut, at the mouth of the Mindanao River as he tried to reach a Dutch ship.

The *Cygnet* sailed on through the Celebes Sea into the arms of 'a hard tornado'. Dampier watched how the '[water]spouts', or whirlwinds, formed. His celebrated account provided the first detailed explanation. He described a 'spout' as 'a small ragged piece or part of a cloud hanging down about a yard, seemingly from the blackest part thereof'. Then, 'when the surface of the sea begins to work, you shall see the water, for about 100 paces in circumference, foam and move gently round till the whirling motion increases: and then it flies upward in a pillar, about 100 paces in compass at the bottom, but lessening gradually upwards to the smallness of the spout itself, there where it reaches the lower end of the spout, through which the rising seawater seems to be conveyed into the clouds'. Next, the swollen, blackening cloud begins to gust across the sky, accompanied by the spout still sucking up water until 'breaking off, all the water . . . falls down again into the sea, making a great noise with its fall and clashing motion'. It was highly dangerous for a ship to be under a spout when it broke, but it was hard to avoid them. Sometimes sailors would 'fire shot out of their great guns into [a spout]', hoping to break it up. Dampier was sceptical, stating, 'I did never hear that it proved to be of any benefit'.

Once again the robust *Cygnet* survived. In early December, the buccaneers anchored off the Celebes Islands.* A local sultan arrived in a large, stately proa with a white silken flag, depicting a griffin trampling a serpent, fluttering from the mast. He explained courteously and diplomatically that he was curious 'to have a sight of

---

*Named Sulawesi today, the main island has perhaps the most unusual shape of any island in the world – a bit like a starfish.

Englishmen, having heard extraordinary characters of their just and honourable dealing'. He complained bitterly about the Dutch, although, Dampier noted with some contempt, he did not hesitate to sell as slaves to the Dutch people from the interior whom he regarded 'as savages, just as the Spaniards do the poor Americans'. The sultan presented Read with a 'very pretty' and 'tractable' boy who was remarkable for his two rows of teeth in each jaw.

Leaving the Celebes behind them, the buccaneers battled strong tides and heavy winds with the constant risk of submerged reefs. On 29 December, sodden and exhausted, they reached Timor and – free at last of the web of islands – headed south, temporarily diverting from their voyage to India, 'intending to touch at New Holland to see what that country would afford [them]'. On 4 January 1688, they reached a finger of land projecting into a sparkling blue sea. Here they found a deep bay and the next day dropped anchor on 'good hard sand and clean ground'. They thus became the first Britons to reach the mainland of Australia.

XIII

'NEW-GOTTEN LIBERTY'

They had reached a land on the edge of the known world. Dampier wrote in his first book, 'It is not yet determined whether it is an island or a main continent, but I am certain that it joins neither Asia, Africa nor America'. Avoiding whirlpools and tideraces, they anchored in the northwest corner of the wide bay now called King Sound.*

There had been earlier voyagers to New Holland, as Australia was then known. In 1616, Dirk Hartog in the off-course Dutch East Indiaman *Eendracht* had landed for two nights on the large offshore island that now bears his name, just off the Western Australian coast near the modern town of Carnarvon. In 1623, Jan Cartensz landed briefly in the Gulf of Carpentaria in northern Australia, believing himself to be in New Guinea. Six years later, the Dutch East Indiaman *Batavia* had been wrecked on another island just off the Western Australian coast. Most significantly, in 1642 the Dutchman Abel Tasman had landed on the island now called Tasmania before going on to New Zealand, and in 1644 had sailed the northwestern coasts of Australia.

Both the Dutch East India Company and its trading rivals, the Spanish – who had sailed close to northern

*Northeast of the modern town of Broome in the northern part of Western Australia.

Australia – had kept knowledge of their voyages and of areas adjacent to the East Indies to themselves to protect their trading monopolies.*

That day in January 1688, Dampier gazed on 'low even land with sandy banks against the sea'. It looked an arid, unforgiving landscape. Spying men walking along the shore, the buccaneers eagerly despatched a canoe. They hoped to barter for provisions, but as the canoe approached the beach, the men ran off and hid. The frustrated buccaneers searched for them for three days but found no inhabitants nor houses, just the cooling ashes of abandoned fires. They finally gave up, though they left 'a great many toys ashore in such places where we thought that they would come' as a sign that they meant the people no harm.

Their search for ready supplies of fresh water also proved fruitless. There were no flowing streams or tumbling brooks. Nor did there seem to be much to eat. There were trees, some as big as apple trees, but none 'bore fruit or berries'. A few birds hopped about the branches and among the thin, tough and spindly grasses, but there was little sign of any animals – no fat hogs or cattle. The only tracks were 'the tread of a beast as big as a great mastiff dog' (probably the track of a dingo).

The buccaneers decided to search some of the islands in the bay, where, at last, they encountered around forty Aborigines,† men, women and children. The men at once

*The first Britons to land on what is now Australian soil were men of the English ship *Trial*, who, in May 1622, were wrecked on rocky islets about seventy miles off the northwest Australian coast, near the Monte Bello Islands. These rocky islets became known to mariners thereafter as the Trial Rocks.

†Dampier did not use the word *Aborigine*. During his time the word simply meant 'indigenous', in accordance with its Latin roots, and was applied to both people and things. Later, it usually referred to native inhabitants of areas before European colonization and only later still took its usual modern and specific reference to the native people of Australia.

threatened the buccaneers with 'their lances and swords'. Their lances were long, straight, sharpened wooden poles, while their swords were pieces of wood shaped, Dampier thought, 'somewhat like a cutlass'. (The latter were probably boomerangs.) The buccaneers first fired a gun in warning, scattering the people, and then ran into their encampment, where they found more people crouching around a wood fire. The sight of the buccaneers – the first white men they had ever seen – must have been terrifying. Dampier recorded how the Aborigines made a sound like 'gurry, gurry' when alarmed. The 'lustiest of the women' snatched up their babies and ran off, their toddlers running after them 'squeaking and bawling'. Others – male and female, too old, weak or frightened to run – lay still by the fire, making 'a doleful noise as if we had been coming to devour them'.

The buccaneers waited patiently. After a while, when the people saw that the visitors 'did not intend to harm them', their moaning grew 'pretty quiet'. Some who had run off began edging warily back into the camp. Gradually, the tension eased, and some of the Aboriginal men 'began to be familiar'. The buccaneers presented them with items of clothing – an old pair of breeches, ragged shirts – hoping for their assistance in return. They found some wells and began filling a quantity of six-gallon barrels, but they wanted help carrying them down to the canoes. They confidently led their 'new servants' to the wells and placed a barrel on each man's shoulders. Yet the men 'stood like statues, without motion', grinning 'like so many monkeys'. Dampier concluded that 'these poor creatures' were not 'accustomed to carry burdens'. Crossly, the buccaneers shouldered their burdens themselves while the Aborigines cheerfully and 'very fairly' took off the garments they had

An Aborigine.

been given and laid them on the ground 'as if clothes were
only to work in'. Their covering consisted of no more than
a string around their waists supporting 'a handful of long
grass or some small boughs before to cover their privities'.

Dampier was the first person to publish a description of
the Australian Aborigines. Those he encountered in King
Sound were probably members of the Bardi people. His
first book would depict them as 'the miserablest people in
the world'. The Hottentots of South Africa were 'for
wealth gentlemen' in comparison. Apart from their human
shape, he wrote, the Aborigines differed 'little from
brutes'. They were 'tall, strait-bodied, and thin, with small
long limbs'. They had 'great heads, round foreheads, and
great brows'. Their eyelids were 'always half-closed, to
keep the flies out of their eyes; they being so troublesome

here, that no fanning will keep them from coming to one's face . . . so that from their infancy being thus annoyed with these insects, they do never open their eyes as other people'. He described them as 'long visaged and of a very unpleasing aspect, having no one graceful feature in their faces', with 'great bottle noses, pretty full lips and wide mouths'. Their hair was 'black, short and curled like that of a negroe'. Their speech was guttural, rising from 'deep in the throat'.

These comments would be read almost a century later by James Cook and Joseph Banks. The latter wrote that, as they aproached the shores of southeastern Australia, they saw 'five people who appeared through our glasses to be enormously black; so far did the prejudices which we had built on Dampier's account influence us that we fancied we could see their colour when we could scarce distinguish whether or not they were men'. Dampier's vivid and uncompromising portrayal may also have contributed to Jonathan Swift's portrayal of the Yahoos.

Yet the unpublished draft of Dampier's book painted a different picture, more consistent with Dampier's usual objective style of observation. In it there were no comments about 'brutes' or 'unpleasing aspects' and he described the people as 'of good stature but very thin and lean', which he attributed to 'want of food'. He depicted their hair more accurately as 'matted-up like a negroe's', but this was 'for want of combs'. It would be long if combed out. Perhaps when Dampier's journals were being readied for publication, he was encouraged to sensationalize the physical descriptions of a people inhabitating a land so remote and unknown, or perhaps an editor did so for him. In such circumstances, nuance could easily have been lost and subjectivity equally easily introduced.

Both Dampier's book and draft showed a compassion, even admiration, for a people whose existence seemed hard. He looked on their landscape through European eyes. He did not realize that it was rich in 'bush tucker' if, like the Aborigines, you knew where to seek it. He knew nothing, for example, of the vinegar plum, whose fruit was richer in vitamin C than the orange, writing that 'the earth affords them no food at all'. There was 'neither herb, root, pulse nor any sort of grain for them to eat . . . nor any sort of bird or beast that they can catch, having no instruments wherewithal to do so'. He believed that the Aborigines depended for their food on the sea, but that apart from dugong and turtle the sea did not appear to be 'very plentifully stored with fish'.

He watched the thin, lithe, almost naked figures painstakingly constructing little stone dams across small coves and inlets to trap the 'small fry', which, with cockles, mussels and periwinkles, formed their staple diet. The fishermen then returned to the encampment, where the old people and 'tender infants' waited hungrily. The food was cooked over the fire, then carefully shared out. Dampier was impressed that – whether there was 'a plentiful banquet' or scarcely enough to give everyone 'a taste' – it was doled out equally so that the 'young and tender, the old and feeble' fared as well as 'the strong and lusty'. This was in tune with the buccaneers' code and Dampier's own strong belief in equality.

He wondered how the people made fire, and concluded that they used the Indian trick of taking a piece of flat, softish wood, putting a small dent in it, inserting one end of a small, hard, sharpened stick into the dent, and then furiously 'twirling the hard piece between the palms of their hands' until the soft wood began to smoke. He had personally 'tried the experiment'.

As far as he could tell, they did not 'worship any thing', and he was puzzled that people of both sexes and all ages had their two front teeth missing – unknown to him, the result of ritual tooth extraction. He noted that they had no houses but moved from place to place, sleeping in the open air with 'the earth being their bed and the heaven their canopy'. They lived in groups of twenty to thirty, but he could not discover whether they were monogamous or lived 'promiscuously'.

A curious man himself, he was, perhaps, most struck by the people's lack of curiosity. He described how a party of buccaneers out fishing encountered a group of men 'swimming from one island to another, for they have no boats'. They brought four of them on board the *Cygnet* and fed them boiled rice, dugong and turtle. The Aborigines greedily consumed the food but 'took no notice of the ship, or any thing in it'.

Dampier satisfied his own curiosity by wandering through the savannah among the spiky wattle bushes. He examined bloodwood trees with their knotted bark, dark leaves and rich, red gum which seemed to him like dragon's blood.*

But there was also work to be done: the ship had to be careened before they could sail on. The buccaneers searched out a small sloping cove with green mangroves and golden rocks on the north side of what is now Karrakatta Bay. They sailed in on a spring tide – the high tide that occurs when the sun, moon and Earth are directly aligned at a new or full moon. Dampier recorded that the difference between high and low water was about thirty

---

*The bloodwood tree – which he mistook for the dragon tree – would one day bear his name as *Eucalyptus dampieri*.

feet. As a result, the outgoing sea receded nearly half a mile, and the *Cygnet* was left dry. The perennial task of scrubbing the hull could begin, and tents were erected in the dunes for repairing the sails.

As the days passed, Dampier became restless and bored. This place held no magic for him. The beauty of King Sound with its clear, sparkling waters and glimmering white sands left him unmoved. He saw no prospect of trade or settlement here. The flies, the heat, the barren vegetation and the simple, incurious inhabitants grated on him. So did his fellow buccaneers, renewing his determination to escape them. He tried to convince the other buccaneers that they should make for an English factory, perhaps the one on Sumatra he had learned of from the crew of the Chinese pepper junk, rather than sailing aimlessly on. However, someone tipped off Captain Read about Dampier's seditious behaviour and he threatened him with being 'turned ashore and left'. Dampier could only desist and await 'some more convenient place and opportunity to leave them'.

The lengthy repair work completed, the buccaneers attempted to refloat the *Cygnet* on the next available spring tide, but the sea was slow to rise to the level they expected. This caused 'amazement and a great consternation'. Some feared they would only be able to free the *Cygnet* by digging a channel through the sand. Others despaired that they 'should never get her off at all'. Dampier was unperturbed. Unlike his less curious colleagues who 'had not taken notice' of such things, he had been carefully observing the pattern of the tides, particularly the 'great' spring tides. He realized that they did not 'keep the same time as they do in England'. It was no surprise to him when the tide finally 'rose so high' as to 'float her quite up'. They sailed thankfully out into the deep water of King Sound and, setting a northerly course, left Australia behind them.

Dampier and his companions had made the longest stay – some two months – on the mainland of New Holland of any Europeans to that date. Those weeks spent watching the play of the water with the complex flows of currents and tides had brought Dampier to a significant conclusion. Fully aware of where they were, he had become convinced that New Guinea was not, as the few available charts suggested, joined to Australia.* He was sure that a channel ran between them and would one day return to attempt to prove it.

The weather seemed set fair as they made for the Cocos Islands in the Indian Ocean, en route for Cape Cormorin. Yet soon they ran into 'thunder and lightning, rain and high blustring winds'. It took two weeks to reach the vicinity of the Cocos, but the winds were gusting against them. They decided to bear away towards some islands west of Sumatra, to the delight of Dampier, who was 'in hopes to make [his] escape from them to Sumatra'. Brisk winds blew them to a small wooded island that James Cook would, on 25 December 1777, name Christmas Island, and which he is often and incorrectly given credit for discovering. A party went in search of fresh water. Dampier was not among them, perhaps for fear he would abscond. The men returned with enough boobies and man-of-war birds to feed the entire company.

Reinvigorated, the buccaneers weighed anchor. On 7 April, they excitedly made out the distant outline of

---

*Including copies of Tasman's chart, which Dampier would get to see much later, after his return to England, and which showed New Guinea as an adjunct of Australia.

Sumatra to the north. Three days later, they found a mass of coconuts 'swimming in the sea'. Hauling them in, they eagerly devoured the sweet white meat and fragrant milk. Reaching a small, low island west of Sumatra, the buccaneers sent out canoes for more coconuts while their Moskito Indian strikers, or hunters, still with them, brought back a fine haul of fish and two crocodiles which were salted for the next day. Dampier was constantly on the alert for the chance of making a run for it but found 'there was no compassing this'. He could not get his hands on a boat.

They cruised up Sumatra's western coast, living on 'a pleasant mess' of rice and stewed coconut flesh, and crossed the equator. On 29 April, they spied a sail to the north. Overtaking the vessel, they discovered that it was a proa carrying coconuts and coconut oil to Achin (today, Banda Aceh), a town on the northwest tip of Sumatra. Captain Read seized the cargo and the frightened four-man crew, and then ordered the hacking of a hole in the bottom of the proa to sink it. Read's motive, according to Dampier, was not greed but 'to hinder me and some others from going ashore; for he knew that we were ready to make our escapes if an opportunity presented itself; and he thought that by his abusing and robbing the natives, we should be afraid to trust ourselves among them'.

The tension must have been palpable as they voyaged on. A tantalized Dampier learned from the prisoners that there was an English factory at Achin. However, Read altered course for the Nicobar Islands, north of Sumatra. On 5 May, they anchored off the west side of the main island. Big trees and coconut groves fringed every bay. Its 'tall, well-limbed' people led a pleasant life. Dampier was interested that they seemed to live under no government but 'to be equal without any distinction'.

There was, however, little time for observing the quiet tempo of island life. An impatient Read ordered the hull to be cleaned yet again and the water barrels filled. He was anxious to set course for Cape Cormorin before the westerly monsoon made it impossible. Dampier realized this might be his last chance of escape for a long time. It also seemed a good place to be left. He had heard that the Nicobar islanders traded in fragrant ambergris, a commodity highly prized in Europe. He later remembered dreaming of a life among them, learning their language and customs, including 'how they got their ambregrease . . . what quantities they get, and the time of year when most is found' and of making 'a considerable fortune'.

But Dampier knew that his chances of stealing a canoe and slipping ashore were slim. He decided instead to confront Read and demand his freedom. This was, after all, his right under the buccaneers' own rules. To his probable surprise, Captain Read agreed. Dampier decided that this was because he could hardly 'go ashore in a place less frequented by ships than this'. It would therefore be a long time before Dampier would be in a position to give 'an account' of Read 'to the English or the Dutch'. A delighted Dampier hurriedly gathered up his sea chest containing his papers and his bedding and was rowed ashore 'by some that wished me well' before Read could change his mind.

He landed on a small sandy bay, 'kneeled down and gave thanks to God almighty for his deliverance'. Looking around, he saw just two houses, both empty. Dampier guessed their occupants had fled for fear of the buccaneers. At last, the owner of one arrived by canoe. The man signalled Dampier to leave the beach and pointed insistently towards his house. Dampier could not understand what the man was saying but recognized the Malay word *matty*, signifying 'dead'. He realized he was warning him: 'Some beast or venomous creature . . . would come out of the woods in the night, when I was asleep, and kill me'. He wisely decided to accept his benefactor's counsel, retrieved his belongings from beneath the coconut palm where he had stowed them, and followed the man indoors.

Dampier had not been in the house an hour before the ship's master, Josiah Teat, and a group of armed men burst in. They demanded he return on board the *Cygnet* at once. Dampier later wrote that they need not have gone to so much trouble; sending the cabin boy to fetch him would have sufficed. It would have been suicide to remain on the island against their will: '[They] would have abused, or have killed some of the natives, purposely to incense them against me'. Disappointed but resigned, Dampier shouldered his possessions and trudged down to the canoe.

He found the *Cygnet* in 'an uproar'. Three more crewmen, inspired by Dampier's boldness, were insisting they be allowed to accompany him. These included surgeon Herman Coppinger – who, like Dampier, had long planned to jump ship – and two others, Robert Hall and a man named Ambrose. Read was not worried about losing the latter pair, but he was adamant that he would not part with the doctor. This goaded Coppinger into leaping into a canoe, seizing Dampier's gun and yelling that he would shoot any man who tried to prevent him going ashore. The luckless surgeon was overpowered by another crewman and dragged back on board.

Dampier, Hall and Ambrose were, however, taken ashore. A friendly crewman slipped them an axe he had stolen from the ship, knowing they would be able to trade it. It was dark by then, so Dampier lit a candle. By its flickering light, he led his fellow castaways up the beach to one of the houses, where they wearily slung their hammocks. Before long, though, the *Cygnet*'s canoe again returned. This time it brought the four sailors from Achin whom Read had taken prisoner just a few days earlier, and a Portuguese sailor who had joined the *Cygnet* at Pulo Condore. Instead of being able to pursue his own dreams of living among the islanders and learning the mysteries of ambergris, Dampier had become the leader of this motley group, all looking to him for help in surviving.

He calculated that at least there were enough of them 'to defend ourselves against the natives of this island, if they should prove our enemies', although he doubted it would be necessary. More important, they had 'men enough to row [themselves] over to the Island of Sumatra'. All they had to do was buy a canoe from the islanders. First, though, Dampier and his companions wanted to be sure that Read would not change his mind and snatch their 'new-gotten liberty' away from them. The men crunched anxiously down to the shore by moonlight to watch and wait. Not long before midnight, the *Cygnet* weighed anchor. The light of her lanterns faded as she merged into the deeper darkness beyond.

XIV

'OUR LITTLE ARK'

The next morning, the owner of the house returned with some friends. He expected to find only Dampier, swinging alone in his hammock, and was astonished to discover three Englishmen, four Achinese sailors and a 'mungrel Portuguese' making themselves at home. Yet 'he seemed to be very well pleased' and liberally shared the large calabash of toddy he had brought with him among his unexpected guests. They purchased a seagoing canoe from him in exchange for their axe and began loading their battered sea chests and clothes into it. According to Dampier, the canoe was about the length of the London wherries that whisked people and goods along the Thames, though deeper and narrower. The plan was to paddle to the south of the island, 'lie there till the monsoon shifted', and then launch out across the sea, over 120 miles to Achin on Sumatra's northern coast.

They climbed into the canoe 'with joy', pushed off from the shore, and within moments capsized. 'We preserved our lives well enough by swimming and dragged also our chests and clothes ashore', wrote Dampier, 'but all our things were wet'. Opening his dripping chest, he rummaged frantically for his 'journal and some drafts of land of my own taking which I much prized' and pulled the sopping parchments out.

He spent the next three days 'making great fires' to dry his books. He clearly recognized the value of his writings, some of which he had been carrying with him for nearly nine years – on foot back and forth over the Isthmus of Panama, by sea to Virginia, around the Horn and across the Pacific, sometimes in bamboo tubes, sometimes in sea chests – and never left behind whatever the haste to avoid the Spanish or to change ships. Despite his efforts, some loose papers were 'spoiled' beyond redemption, but he was able to save his journal. The four Achinese sailors meanwhile sensibly attended to the canoe, adding outriggers for greater stability, cutting a good strong mast and constructing 'a substantial sail' out of palm mats, so that they could take advantage of the winds rather than using muscle power alone.

They put to sea once more, intending, this time, to edge around Nicobar's eastern shore. To their annoyance, they had an escort. A little flotilla of canoes filled with islanders came bobbing in their wake. Dampier feared this would make it more difficult for them to bargain at their new destination. The islanders would relate the high prices the *Cygnet*'s crew had paid for provisions before she sailed. 'Ships crews', as Dampier lamented, 'were not so thrifty in bargaining . . . as single persons or a few men'. To scare the islanders off, Robert Hall fired a warning shot over their heads. The islanders leaped from their canoes into the sea but, seeing the buccaneers making off, climbed quickly back in and resumed pursuit.

Firing the gun had been a poor idea – it 'made all the inhabitants of the island our enemies'. When the buccaneers landed in a small bay, the inhabitants fled from them. And so it went wherever they came ashore hoping to buy provisions: '[The islanders] came not to us; nay they opposed us wherever we came, and often shaking their lances at us, made all the show of hatred that they could invent'. The buccaneers rowed glumly on, surviving on coconuts that their Achinese companions shinned up palms to gather. At last, goaded by sharp, gnawing hunger, they decided to head for the north of the island and to 'use force to get some of their food, if we could not get it in other ways'. They were followed by seven or eight canoes, which soon overtook them and landed before them, ready to repel the unwanted visitors. The buccaneers rowed to within 100 yards. Then Dampier picked up his gun and pointed it at the islanders, at which they 'all fell down flat on the ground'. He swivelled round and – 'to show that we did not intend to harm them' – fired out to sea so that they could see the shot graze the surface of the water. He then reloaded, and the buccaneers rowed cautiously towards the beach.

Some of the islanders ran off, but others held their ground, cutting and hewing the air with their lances as 'signs of their hatred'. Dampier fired harmlessly once more, and all but half a dozen ran away. The buccaneers rode through the surf to the shore, and Hall jumped out brandishing his sword. Dampier had again reloaded and stood ready to fire if Hall was attacked. It was a tense moment as Hall advanced up the beach. Then slowly, carefully, he shook each of the islanders by the hand, and 'peace was concluded' at last.

The relieved buccaneers traded 'old rags and small strips of cloth' for food. They would have liked to buy some of the small hogs they could see rooting about, but did not wish to offend their 'Achinese friends, who were Mahometans [Muslims]'. The buccaneers soon rowed south again to provision themselves for the voyage across to Achin. They loaded food and filled coconut shells and bamboos with water, reckoning this would give them a supply of seven or eight gallons. These modest supplies were, Dampier wrote, their 'sea-store'.

His experienced eye scanned the sky for signs of the expected western monsoon that would speed them on their way. It seemed to be at hand, 'for the clouds began to hang their heads to the eastward, and at last moved gently that way'. On 15 May 1688, at around four o'clock in the afternoon, the small party set out. Looking back years later, Dampier recalled that their canoe was very 'thin and light', but the outriggers lashed tightly to its sides with poles convinced him it 'could not overset' so long as they remained in place.

All the same, Dampier knew it would be risky and that only he and Hall really understood the danger. The others were trusting in them completely to bring them through. Dampier, who had plotted his escape for so long, had while still on board consulted the *Cygnet*'s only chart of the East Indies. He had made furtive notes in his pocketbook 'of the bearing and distance' of all those places, including Sumatra, which he thought he might need in his bid for freedom. He had also carried off with him 'a pocket compass for my direction in any enterprise that I should undertake'.

The weather was 'fair, clear and hot', and the clouds gusted gently eastwards as the men struck out from the shore. Dampier planned to reach Achin before the western monsoon really set in, bringing 'very blustering weather' that would buffet their fragile craft. They rowed with four oars, taking turns. Dampier and Hall also took turns steering, 'for none of the rest were capable of it'. On the second day, there was wind enough for the men to lay down their oars as the canoe skimmed over the water with Dampier at the helm. The sea rippled alarmingly as they encountered a strong current, making 'a great noise that might be heard near half a mile', but they managed to sail on.

By the morning of the third day, Dampier expected to see the shores of Sumatra. Instead, to his grief, he saw the Nicobar Islands once more. A powerful current had nudged them off course during the night. All they could do was alter course and try again. The next day at noon, heavy clouds prevented Dampier and Hall from taking observations of the sun to calculate their latitude. Not long after, Dampier saw 'a great circle about the sun' – an ominous sign of coming 'storms of wind or much rain'. He wished heartily that they were nearer land, but concealed his anxiety, putting 'a good countenance on the matter'.

The wind rose, just as he had feared. They reduced their sail, 'but it was still too big, considering the wind', which was now catching them broadside on, pushing the canoe down into the rising sea. The poles of the outriggers were bending under the pressure and appeared close to snapping. Desperately, they manoeuvred around so that the wind was behind them. For the next few hours the tempest drove them through swelling, tumultuous waves. Dampier and Hall, taking turns as helmsman in the narrow stern, braced themselves to take the full force of the breaking waves on their backs and 'so kept it from coming in so much as to endanger the vessel'. The others bailed frantically to get rid of the water that did get in.

That evening, dark clouds scudded over a 'very dismal' sky. The wind blew hard, and the seas ran frighteningly high, 'roaring in a white foam' around the little craft. A 'dark night' was coming on, there was 'no land in sight to shelter us', and 'our little ark in danger to be swallowed by every wave'. There was a good chance they would not

survive. But 'what was worst of all', Dampier later recalled,
'none of us thought ourselves prepared for another world'.
He was in 'great conflicts of mind'. Although he had been
'in many eminent dangers before now', the most awful of
them was 'but a play-game' compared with this 'leisurely
and dreadful solemnity'. Unlike 'a sudden skirmish or
engagement' when 'one's blood was up', it left a man time
to think. Dampier had 'a lingering view of approaching
death, and little or no hopes of escaping it', and confessed
that for once his courage failed. '[I made] very sad
reflections on my former life and looked back with horror
and detestation on actions which before I disliked, but now
I trembled at the remembrance of'.

'I had long before this repented me of that roving
course of life, but never with such concern as now', he
later wrote in an unusually frank passage. His plight also
turned his mind to God, who, like his wife, was not often
in his thoughts. He generally believed that men – not God
– were responsible for their actions and what befell them,
but not now. '[I recalled] the many miraculous acts of
God's providence towards me in the whole course of my
life, of which kind I believe few men have met with' – and
for which he gave thanks. He 'once more desired God's
assistance' and composed his mind as well as he could 'in
the hopes of it'.

At 10 p.m. thunder and lightning boomed and cracked,
bringing welcome rain to the parched seamen, whose
water had run out. Illuminated by the ghostly lightning
flashes, they drank greedily. The wind was blowing harder
than ever but then began to abate. Gradually, the sea lost its
fury. By the flickering light of a match, Dampier consulted
his compass. To his relief, he saw that they were still heading eastwards. Angling their small sail round in the velvet

dark, they managed to adjust their course to south-south-east for Sumatra.

At 2 a.m. the wind once more began to howl, and the thunder, lightning and rain returned. Again they were forced to run before the wind. They were exhausted, with 'not one dry thread about them', and chilled to the bone by the rainwater, which was 'much colder than that of the sea'. 'In this wet, starveling plight', wrote Dampier, in one of the rare passages where he ever complained of discomfort, 'we spent the tedious night', longing for the dawning light. But dawn brought no comfort. Dark, black clouds piled ominously on the horizon. Shivering and numb, they were carried eastwards.

Suddenly at around 8 a.m. on the fifth day of their journey, one of the 'Achinese' shouted, 'Pulo Way'. The three exhausted Englishmen looked at one another in puzzlement, wondering what he meant. They thought he had said, 'Pull away' – 'an expression usual among English seamen when they are rowing'. Then they saw that the man was talking excitedly to his fellow Achinese and pointing. Following his outstretched hand, Dampier made out a smudge of land on the hazy horizon. It was, the Achinese insisted, an island called Way. *Pulo* meant 'island', making the place 'Pulo Way'. (It is now called Weh Island.)

'We, who were dropping with wet, cold and hungry, were all overjoyed at the sight of the land', Dampier later recalled. They trimmed their already small sail to 'no bigger than an apron' and steered for it. However, towards noon Dampier was surprised to spy land even nearer. Altering course again, they headed slowly for it and towards dusk realized that it was the coast of Sumatra. The Achinese had mistaken Golden Mountain on Sumatra for Pulo Way. The wind was dying away now, and the weary men once more took to the oars, doggedly determined to reach dry land. Thirty exhausting hours later, the aching muscles of the men so long suspended between fear and hope and life and death propelled their waterlogged craft into the mouth of the Passanjan River. The Achinese recognized it and told their wasted companions that a fishing village lay a mile upriver. They were too weak to make it unaided. 'The hardships of this voyage, with the scorching heat of the sun, at our first setting out, and the cold rain, and our continuing wet for the last two days . . . [had cast all of us] into fevers, so that now we were not able to help each other, nor so much as to get our canoe up to the village'.

Villagers found them lying half dead. They carried the scarcely conscious men first to a hut and then to a large house, where they were allowed to lie 'till we should be recovered of our sickness'. The Achinese sailors gave such a glowing account of the courage and skill of Dampier and his companions that the local people ensured that they lacked for nothing, lavishing so many gifts on them that they were embarrassed. The buccaneers resorted to surreptitiously turning buffaloes and goats they had been given loose at night after the donors had left.

The Europeans lay at one end of the house, but the Achinese sailors withdrew to the other. While tossing about in the canoe, the men had shared everything, drinking out of the same coconut shells. On land the Achinese wished to resume 'their accustomed nicety and reservedness'. As Muslims this meant not eating or drinking with unbelievers or even touching 'anything that we used'. They were, however, quite as sick as the buccaneers, and one who was probably delirious threatened that, if any of the Achinese should die, 'the rest would kill' the Europeans for having brought them on this voyage. Dampier did not take the threat seriously. He was more preoccupied with curing himself. His head was pounding; he was running a high temperature and so dizzy he could hardly stand. He tried to bleed himself, whetting and sharpening his penknife with trembling hands, but the blade remained 'too blunt' to open a vein.

Twelve days later, the Europeans were still no better. The local people – 'though very kind in giving us any thing we wanted' – would not come near them. There was no one even to prepare their food. The sick men took turns, depending on who 'had strength to do it, or stomachs to eat it'. Their only chance was to reach the English factory at Achin, 100 miles away to the northwest. At first the villagers tried to detain Dampier and Hall, hoping the two skilled navigators would help them sail to places where they wished to trade. However, realizing that they were determined to be gone and also that they were too weak to travel alone by canoe, the locals relented and generously provided a large proa to take them. Three of the Achinese sailors chose to remain, but Dampier, Hall, Ambrose, the Portuguese sailor and the fourth Achinese climbed thankfully in.

Three days' sailing in fair weather and soft, gentle breezes brought them to Achin. Dampier was at once taken before the *shabander*, or chief magistrate. Irishman Dennis Driscal, an employee of the English East India Company's factory there, acted as interpreter. Dampier would normally have been required to sit on the floor in the *shabander*'s presence, 'as they do cross-legged like tailors', but he was allowed to stand since he had not 'the strength then to pluck up my heels in that manner'. The magistrate asked how he had dared attempt the crossing from the Nicobars to Sumatra, to which Dampier replied that he was inured 'to hardships and hazards'. The magistrate then asked a potentially far more awkward question. Where, he enquired, was the *Cygnet*? Dampier replied that she had come from the South Seas, had ranged round the Philippines, 'and was now gone towards Arabia and the Red Sea'.

The question had particular significance for Driscal. Elihu Yale, founder of the university that bears his name, was then head of the East India Company's factory at Fort St George (today Madras/Chenai), on the southeast coast of India. Only a few weeks earlier, he had written to the captains of the company's ships trading east from India to China and Southeast Asia, alerting them to the dangers from English pirates and the 'ignominy' that their 'notorious villainies' had brought on the company to the detriment of its trade.

Driscal provided a room in the East India Company's factory and food for the new arrivals, who he could see were very sick. The Portuguese sailor died soon after. Hall was so weak that Dampier did not believe he would recover. Dampier himself, who clearly had a remarkable constitution, was 'the best', but still feverish. Driscal and some Englishmen persuaded him to 'take some purging physic of a Malayan doctor'. He took their advice and drank three large calabashes 'of nasty stuff' with no effect. He was urged to take a fourth dose. This time, the effect was dramatic. In fact, it was so violent that Dampier thought the doctor 'would have killed me outright'. 'I struggled till I had been about 20 or 30 times at stool: But it working so quick with me, with little intermission, and my strength being almost spent, I even threw myself down once for all, and had above 60 stools in all before it left off working'. The colonic frenzy left Dampier weak as a kitten, but his fever abated, if only for a week. Fever and an accompanying 'flux' – diarrhoea – would afflict Dampier for the next twelve months.

Reviving a little, Dampier began to totter about. He was befriended by a captain named Thomas Bowrey whose ship was anchored in the harbour but who lived ashore. He was a long-term English resident in the East Indies with good contacts among the secretive Dutch trading community. Bowrey was 'extraordinary kind' to Dampier. He 'cossetted' him 'with wine and good cheer' and tried to persuade him to go as his boatswain on a voyage to Persia (present-day Iran). However, Dampier still felt too weak. He hoped to secure 'a better voyage' on another English ship. Luck was with him. Not long after, a Captain Welden arrived on board the *Curtana* bound for Tonquin (today known as Tonkin, northern Vietnam). Not only would this be a more agreeable voyage, but Welden had a surgeon on board. He also promised Dampier command of a sloop he intended to buy in Tonquin. In July 1688, after six weeks of recuperation, Dampier left Achin for yet another new land.

XV

GUT ROT AND GUNPOWDER

By late summer 1688, skilful Tonquinese pilots were guiding the *Curtana* across the treacherous sandbar at the mouth of the Tonquin River and through swirling currents to a safe anchorage twenty miles upriver. Captain Welden had business to attend to, leaving Dampier a free man. He decided to sail eighty miles further upriver to Cachao (Hanoi) and went enthusiastically aboard a riverboat. For the first time since leaving Jamaica in 1680, he was simply a traveller. His motivation had nothing to do with prospects of financial gain. His account of Tonquin – the first in English to describe the country – was objective, open-minded and spiced with telling detail.

The 'large level fruitful country' with its pastures and paddy fields pleased his eye. It was a picturesque journey, except for the beggars who besieged the boat in pathetic little craft made of twigs plastered with clay. Dampier discovered that they were lepers, forced to live in isolation but allowed to beg. They pursued the riverboat with eerie 'doleful cries', and Dampier threw rice to them.

When they reached Cachao, Dampier set about exploring the city for the next week with the thoroughness – and economy – of a modern backpacker. He squelched through streets thick with 'black, stinking mud' because of the continuous rain and past low, thatched buildings

From the original 1697 edition of Dampier's A New Voyage.

of mud or wattle, which looked 'mean' compared with
European dwellings. The city's teeming byways quickly
became familiar. He learned to jump aside when he heard
the beating of a gong or drum heralding the approach of

'an unruly elephant'. He watched dextrous blacksmiths and goldsmiths, whose rhythmic hammering echoed in his ears. He studied how the exquisite lacquerware was made, though he recognized the human cost, for the artisans worked with noxious substances 'which fume[d] into the brains . . . making them break out in blotches and biles'.

The money changers surprised Dampier most. They were mainly women and sat in the markets and on street corners behind piles of 'leaden money called cash, which is a name that is generally given to small money in all these countries'. They were, he decided, 'as crafty as the cunningest stock-jobber in London'. They were not the only women involved in commerce. Many European merchants had Tonquinese concubines, whom they prized for their business acumen as well as their other skills, and in whose hands they happily left their businesses while voyaging overseas. Often they returned to find the women had improved their profits 'mightily' by 'buying raw silk in the dead time of the year' when no foreign ships were in port. Silk was the country's chief trade, and Dampier carefully noted how the young mulberry trees were cultivated to nourish silkworms.

Walking the oozing riverbanks, sixteen years after he had first served on an English warship, Dampier appraised the Tonquinese navy. The heavily carved and gilded flat-bottomed galleys were 'very graceful and pleasant' to look at but not, he judged, well suited to war. They carried only a single brass cannon and were too shallow, drawing just two and a half feet of water, making them useful only on rivers and the most placid of coastal seas. The captain sat in the stern on 'a little throne' facing his rowers, who were naked except for a narrow fillet of black cloth, which they wound around their waists, then passed between their thighs and tucked in. Each man stood upright behind his oar, thrusting and pushing with 'great strength' and keeping exact time thanks to the striking of a small gong. The rowers answered each stroke with an impressive 'sort of hollow noise, through the throat, and a stamp on the deck with one foot'.

Dampier peeked into the dark interiors of ancient pagodas spicy with incense and saw offerings of rice and betel leaves piled high in the shadows. He watched people jostling to have their fortunes told by the priests, who, though supposed to abstain from women and alcohol, did not seem 'to confine themselves much to these rules'. He learned that the Tonquinese acknowledged one supreme power, but to him their concept of an omnipotent being was 'very obscure'. He ran a critical eye over their 'idolatrous' statues: 'Some are very corpulent and fat, others are very lean; some also have many eyes, others as many hands, and all grasping somewhat'. Yet, he acknowledged, a friend had been 'much affected' by an image of a lean, sorrowful deity, eyes mournfully lifted heavenwards. In schools, he watched earnest young students painstakingly and deftly writing lines of characters from top to bottom and right to left.

Dampier liked the Tonquinese, finding them 'good-natured in general, and kind enough to strangers'. They were also handsome – 'straight and well-shaped' – although, whatever their class or sex, their teeth were black, the result of assiduous dyeing in adolescence with the juice of a herb. The 'great fault' of all, Dampier reported, was gaming. The whole population was obsessed, particularly Cachao's Chinese community, who would 'stake down their wives and children', even 'mortgage their hair'.

Many could ill afford to gamble. Unemployment levels were high in this populous country, and many faced starvation. The precariousness of people's daily lives struck Dampier. Like 'most silk countries', Tonquin was 'stocked with great multitudes of poor people who work cheap and live meanly on a little rice'.* If the price of rice went up, a man might be forced to sell wife and children to survive. Unsurprisingly, the poor were 'addicted to theft'. Like many a traveller before and since, Dampier needed 'to keep good watch in the night' over his few possessions. Cachao itself was policed at night by 'a strong watch' armed with staffs who had the right to challenge passersby. Any 'night ramblers' trying to slip past were liable to be 'soundly banged' by the watch, who knew exactly where to aim their staffs to 'dextrously break a leg or thigh-bone'. Stealing was punished by lopping off a body part, sometimes only one finger joint, but if the offence was serious, an entire finger or even a whole hand.

Lesser crimes were punished by bambooing. As Dampier observed, 'The criminal is laid flat on his belly on the ground, with his breeches plucked down over his hams: in which posture a lusty fellow bangs his bare breech with a split bamboo, about 4 fingers broad, and 5 foot long'. A man so punished could 'never obtain any public favour or employment'. Dampier witnessed malefactors weighed down with heavy iron chains. Others had their heads forced between 'two great heavy planks made like a pillory but moveable', which they were forced to carry wherever they went and to sleep in as best they could. There was also the bamboo *gongo*, which made a man look 'as if he were

*By the time Dampier published this observation, he had visited India, as well as China and Southeast Asia.

carrying a ladder on his shoulders, with his head through the rounds [rungs]'. Corruption was rife, and the magistrates often pocketed the fines they imposed.

Dampier did admire the Tonquinese method for resolving legal disputes between poor men. Instead of imposing a heavy fine on the offender, the magistrate would order him to 'treat the injured person with a jar of arrack and a fowl or a small porker, that so feasting together, they may both drown all animosity in good liquor and renew their friendship'.

Coming from a country that had seen revolution and rebellion to uphold the people's rights against the divine right of kings, Dampier was more than a little curious about Tonquin's system of government. It was, he discovered, 'an absolute monarchy', but there were two rulers. The *'boua'*, or hereditary king, lived the twilight 'life of a kind of prisoner of state' confined within his ancient palace and deeply venerated by his people. He passed his days elegantly and aimlessly boating on his fishponds. The real power over 'all the magistracy and soldiery, treasure, and the ordering of all matters of peace or war' was exercised by the *'choua'* – descended from an 'upstart' general who had deprived the royal line of everything except the nominal title of king. The *choua* had some dozen wives and was 'an angry, ill-natured, leprous person' who ruled his subjects with 'great tyranny'. He kept his money buried in great water cisterns guarded by soldiers. Dampier watched these 'lusty strong well-made men' drill on the hot dusty parade ground before the *choua's* palace. A key factor in their selection was their ability to consume vast amounts of food, which was taken as a sign of manhood. To be successful, applicants had to swallow at least eight or nine cups of boiled rice, 'each containing a pint'.

The 'greatest eaters' were appointed to the *choua*'s personal bodyguard.

Some men went to greater lengths to gain advancement in the Tonquinese bureaucracy. As in China, magistrates and other high officials were mostly eunuchs. 'Not only [were they] gelded', but 'their members [were] cut off quite flat to their bellies'. This group was extremely powerful and exercised a 'closed shop'. Dampier heard tales of an ambitious man with a wife and clutch of children who was so distraught at being excluded from high office that he 'took up a sharp knife' and hacked off his own genitals. His self-mutilation brought him the office of master of the king's ordnance.

The eunuch mandarins lived pampered lives and were 'generally covetous beyond measure, and very malicious'. Despite being gelded, some were 'as great admirers of the female sex as any men, and not satisfied without them, but they all keep several handsome young wenches to dally withal'. They took a vicarious satisfaction in being 'courted by strangers' to find women for them. While disparaging the common bawdy houses as 'hateful and scandalous', they delighted in procuring a woman for a foreigner for a night or two or for several months and thought it 'very decent and honourable' to do so. Dampier thought such pandering base.

The mandarins loved to be visited, treating their guests with 'the best cheer they [were] able to procure'. This included hot 'rack' – a spirit in which, like some contemporary Eastern medicines, snakes and scorpions had been infused. Tonquinese nobles relished it both as 'a great cordial' and as a prophylactic against leprosy and poison. At one of their feasts, Dampier saw some strange implements laid out 'as knives, forks and spoons are in

England'. They consisted of 'two small round sticks about the length and bigness of a tobacco pipe', some tipped with silver. He watched carefully as his hosts held them 'in the right hand, one between the fore-finger and thumb; the other between the middle-finger and the fore-finger'. They could pick up 'the smallest grain of rice with them'. Dampier had just had his first sight of chopsticks, which he would be the first to name and describe in English, and he resolved to master the technique of using them.

Unchauvinistically, and unlike many later English-speaking travellers, he did not expect the Tonquinese to conform to Western habits. He believed that 'persons that reside here ought to learn this, as well as other customs of the country, that are innocent, so that their company may be more acceptable'. In line with his philosophy, he also hoped to learn something of the Tonquinese language and thus to discover even more about the country. He listened closely to their speech, detecting 'a great affinity' between the language, religion and customs of Tonquin and China.

One custom Dampier could not get used to was the Tonquinese predilection for eating 'a huge mess' of great yellow frogs newly pulled from the pond as a culinary treat. He wrote of other 'dishes that would turn the stomach of a stranger', like one consisting of raw minced pork. He reported with amazement that cats and dogs were commonly eaten 'and their flesh [was] much esteemed by people of best fashion', noting also the taste for horse and elephant flesh. Indeed an elephant's trunk was a gift fit for a nobleman, even if 'the beast die[d] of age or sickness'. Yet, he acknowledged, the Tonquinese dressed their food 'very cleanly', and he enjoyed the piquancy of soy sauce, recording with accuracy and fascination the process whereby fermenting soya beans and wheat kernels were mixed with water and salt. He also described how prawns and small fish were fermented with salt and water to make fish paste and fish sauce, both staples, then as now, of Southeast Asian cookery. He found the paste 'rank-scented yet the taste was not altogether unpleasant'. The sauce was 'very savoury and used as a good sauce for fowls, not only by the natives but also by many Europeans who esteem[ed] it equal with soy'. He tasted 'delicate lychees'. Dampier eschewed kumquats, believed to cause flux, but introduced their name into the English language, describing them in detail and recognizing their kinship to the orange.

Cachao captured Dampier's mind and his senses, and he returned to his ship seven days later with real reluctance. Captain Welden was planning a six-week voyage to fetch rice from the neighbouring provinces, but Dampier was too weak for the enterprise. Welden sailed, leaving Dampier behind to recuperate. He consoled himself by planning a second trip to Cachao as soon as he felt well enough. This time he would go on foot. He was 'desirous to see as much' of the country 'as he could' and hired a Tonquinese guide for a Tonquinese dollar. It was a small enough sum, he acknowledged, yet it was half of all he possessed in the world. He had made the money by teaching young sailors on Welden's ship the art of 'plain sailing' – a simple method of calculating a ship's position. Any profits made from buccaneering had clearly long been spent.

Dampier and his guide – who spoke no English – set out towards the end of November 1688. Dampier's frailty forced him to make only 'short journeys every day'. Although free of the 'fever and ague' he had brought from

Achin, his stomach remained delicate. He unwisely ate some small oranges, which gave him diarrhoea, but he soldiered on, 'weary of lying still, and impatient of seeing some[thing] that might further gratify my curiosity'. There were no inns on the road, and every night they stayed in a village house. To describe a Southeast Asian bed, he used a South American term and wrote how people lay on 'a barbecue of split bamboos' with a log for a pillow.

The days fell into a pattern. Dampier walked for as long as he felt able, then looked for lodgings. After supper, if there was still enough light, he would go for a ramble round the village, dodging dogs, children and curious onlookers, 'to see what was worth taking notice of'.

One day, Dampier spotted a small tower ahead. Drawing nearer, he found crowds of people, mostly men and boys, milling round the base and nearby stalls spread temptingly with meat. Deciding this must be a market and that the flesh was for sale, he plunged into the crowd to inspect it. He reckoned some fifty or sixty hogs had been cut up. The pork looked as if it were 'very good meat', although the pieces were far too large for him. He grabbed a quarter and signed that he wanted a hunk of two or three pounds. The result was unexpected.

Dampier was immediately assaulted on all sides by furious, screaming people. His clothes were ripped, and someone snatched his hat from his head. His guide did what he could to appease the angry, muttering crowd and managed to drag Dampier away. Men followed them, shouting abuse and threatening further violence, but the guide managed to quiet them, even to retrieve the crest-fallen traveller's hat. He then hurried Dampier off as fast as possible. However, due to his lack of English, he was unable to explain what the problem had been. Dampier later discovered that he had interrupted a funeral feast and that the tower was the pyre, which was about to be burned. For the moment, though, a chastened, puzzled Dampier was left hungry and weary. The sight of the meat had whetted his appetite, but all he could look forward to was yet another meal of boiled rice or perhaps a roasted yam with some eggs. There were chickens at every house they slept in, but his pocket 'would not reach them'.

Two days later – '[as] my flux increased and my strength decreased' – Dampier reached the town of Hean, which he remembered from the boat trip to Cachao. He struggled to the low, neat, pretty house on the riverbank that was the palace of the French bishop who headed a Catholic mission there. No one answered his calls, and Dampier went tentatively inside, where he found a bell and rang it. The lonely clanging, echoing through the quiet house, brought a French priest, who received him kindly in a finely appointed room hung with European paintings. The two men tried to communicate in Spanish, and, when that failed, in Latin. Dampier still had 'some smatterings of what I learnt of it at school'. The priest explained that the bishop was ill, then poured them both some wine.

It must have seemed a strange interlude. The priest asked his help in making gunpowder, bringing him sulphur and saltpetre. Dampier had once read a recipe in *The Mariner's Magazine*, an instructive book written by Captain Samuel Sturmey, and got confidently to work. He carefully weighed out portions of both substances and then mixed the result with coal dust and put it through a sieve. They tested the powder, which worked spectacularly well. The delighted priest ordered a chicken to be roasted for Dampier's dinner, even though it was a 'fish-day' in the bishop's house. Then he found his guest lodgings in the house of some Tonquinese Christians.

The experience made Dampier reflect on the effectiveness of the vigorous attempts by the French to convert the Tonquinese to Roman Catholicism. He admitted that the Catholics were the only religious people 'to cross sea and land' to gain 'proselytes', and that the Protestant 'English and Dutch were in this part of the world too loose-living to gain reputation for their religion'. Showing his Protestant roots, however, he decided that 'the gross idolatory of the Papists is rather a prejudice, than an advantage' to their mission. Why should the Tonquinese want to swap their own idols for images of saints? In a suggestion more redolent of cool logic than religious fire, Dampier decided that the Catholic priests would have done better to 'bring the people to be virtuous and considerate' and then to 'give them a plain history and scheme of the fundamental truths of Christianity'. In the first English use of the concept, Dampier believed that many of their converts were rice Christians – 'alms of rice have converted more than their preaching'.

The following day, Dampier felt restored but decided, nevertheless, to part from his guide and complete the remaining twenty miles to Cachao by riverboat. At first, he sat in the thick of his fellow passengers, but the flux 'would not suffer [him] to rest long in one place'. He was forced to find himself a more discreet place. At midnight, the boat moored by a huddle of candlelit inns, which dispensed rack, tea and small meat kebabs to the travellers before they voyaged on. Under a star-splashed sky, the people chatted and sang songs that sounded to Dampier's ears more 'like crying'. Or perhaps illness was making him melancholy. Racked by stomach cramps, he felt truly lonely and isolated, forced to 'be mute for want of a person I could converse with'.

The next morning, a pale, shaking Dampier was put ashore about five miles short of the city. He reached it by noon and went in search of a house belonging to a merchant named Bowyers, who was an acquaintance of Captain Welden. To his relief, Bowyers welcomed him kindly. The flux had become so bad that it confined him to bed. The long strolls around the city, which he had anticipated with such eagerness, were impossible. All he could do was wait until he was strong enough to return downriver to rejoin his ship.

In February 1689, Dampier sailed out of the Bay of Tonquin on the *Curtana*. Captain Welden had not, after all, purchased a sloop and, even if he had, Dampier would not have been strong enough to take command. Several ships were accompanying them, including the *Rainbow*, bound for London. The *Rainbow*'s mate was Edward Barlow, with whom Dampier seems to have become friends. Dampier entrusted him with a packet of papers to deliver to the *Cygnet*'s owners. These papers contained a painstaking account by Dampier of 'all the course and transactions of their ship' from the time Dampier first boarded her in the Pacific to his escape in the Nicobar Islands. No doubt it covered the abandonment of the vainglorious Swan on Mindanao. However, the papers would never see England. Although Barlow reached home safely, he lost his sea chest in which the papers were stored.

The *Curtana* arrived back at Achin in early March. Welden offered to take Dampier with him to Fort St George, but he was still too ill. He sensibly decided to stay where he had friends rather than voyage in a weakened state to a place where he was unknown. Also, he had never really explored Achin. Once he felt strong enough, he found much to satisfy his curiosity. He bit into juicy mangosteens – 'the most delicate' and 'delicious' of Achin's kaleidoscope of fruits. He noted with keen personal interest that the rind was known 'to be binding'. As well as many purely medicinal herbs, which he thought were 'wholly' out of his sphere, he examined a hemplike herb he had never seen before 'called ganga or bang'. He provided one of the first two descriptions in English of its effects. Infused in liquid, it would 'stupify the brains of any person that drinks thereof'. Its effects varied 'according to the constitution of the person'. It made some people sleepy, some cheerful, 'putting them into a laughing fit', but 'others it [made] mad'. It was 'much esteemed here, and in other places to whither it is transported'. It was marijuana.

Ranging through the savannahs, he recorded everything from buffalo to wood lice to the flavourful porcupines and squirrels that were 'accounted good food by the English'. Despite his fragile digestion, Dampier relished the local dishes of rice supplemented by chicken, fish or buffalo, which were 'dressed very savourly with pepper and garlic, and tinctured yellow with turmeric, to make [them] pleasant to the eye'. There was no shortage of 'good achars and sauces' to give them extra bite.

He also listened attentively to accounts of rich gold mines inland over high, hazardous mountain passes, which only Muslims were allowed to visit. Soldiers were stationed below the passes to ensure that 'no uncircumcised person' passed that way. The profits from trading clothing and spirits with the miners for gold were apparently enormous, and he wrote wistfully that merchants could make 2,000 per cent profit. Gold was certainly the lure for the foreign merchants, whose ships crowded the harbour with cargoes of silks, chintzes, muslins, calicoes and rice.

Dampier again studied the system of punishment. As in

Tonquin, loss of a hand was the punishment for theft.
Afterwards, pieces of leather were clapped over bleeding
stumps to staunch the blood and make it clot. But
amputation did not deter the hardened, who, in Dampier's
view, would 'steal with their toes' if they could.*
Dampier noted that the usual Achinese penalty for capital
crimes was beheading. In England this form of punishment
was reserved for the nobility. Humbler people were usually
hanged. Dampier was, however, horrified to discover that
in Achin certain crimes were punishable by impaling on a
sharpened stake stuck in the ground, which penetrated up
'the fundament through the bowels', coming out 'at the
neck'. He saw one man thus 'spitted' and left for three days.
Tonquinese noblemen, however, were allowed 'more
honourable' deaths. They were permitted to fight for their
lives, albeit against overwhelming numbers of well-armed
men.

Dampier tried to visit the handsome, stone-built palace
of Achin's queen, but to his regret he 'could not get into
the inside of it'. The queen, he discovered, was always 'an
old maid, chosen out of the royal family'. She lived a
closeted life behind the walls of her palace except when,
once a year, she dressed all in white and rode down to the

---

*Dampier was less shocked by the amputations than people would be to-
day. It was not practised in England, but punishments were still un-
compromisingly brutal. You could be hanged for stealing more than a
shilling's worth of goods. Lesser thieves were branded (although if they
had thirteen pence to spare, they could pay for the red-hot iron to be first
dipped in cold water to lessen the damage and pain). In England and its
colonies, prisoners who refused to recognize the court by entering a plea
were stretched out on the ground with cords and progressively crushed
with heavy stones. Those who suffered such a death usually did so for their
families, since, if they did not plead, the court could not confiscate
their possessions.

river on the back of a swaying elephant for a ritual washing ceremony. Like the Boua of Tonquin, she was a figurehead only. Real power lay in the hands of twelve powerful lords, or *oronkeys*. A constitutional crisis involving the queen ended Dampier's quiet tourist ramblings. While he had been away in Tonquin, the former queen had died and a new one elected in her place. Not all the *oronkeys* supported her. Four wanted a king instead and marched an army to the city, camping with banners flying on the east bank of the river directly opposite the palace. The queen's army hurriedly formed up to resist any attack across the water. Trumpeting elephants hauled great tree trunks down to the riverbank to make barricades. Soldiers trained brass guns on the enemy.

The foreign community was nervous, fearful for their goods if not their lives. Their situation was complicated further by the rash behaviour of an English captain named Thwaite. He had recently arrived from Bengal aboard his ship, the *Nellegree*, with a cargo of butter made from buffalo's milk, 'much esteemed' by the Achinese. As was the custom, he had taken a present to the queen, returning to his lodgings on a royal elephant with a gift of two dancing girls. However, instead of settling down to enjoy their supple 'antic gestures', he decided to attack a ship belonging to the Great Moghul of India, moored at Achin and reputedly loaded with treasure. The East India Company was currently in conflict with the Great Moghul, and it seemed too good an opportunity to miss.

Thwaite duly seized the ship, sending her indignant crew flocking to the royal court to demand satisfaction. Given her own precarious position, the queen could do nothing for them, but the brouhaha was enough to alarm Dampier. He feared he might be thrown in prison, which, in his weakened state, 'would have gone near to have killed me'. He sought sanctuary on the *Nellegree* but found the ship so crammed with goods that he could not find a space to sling his hammock. He decided instead to sleep in one of the ship's boats. His flux turned so 'violent' that he slept little. Gazing up into the warm night sky while awaiting the next spasm, he was amazed to see 'the moon totally eclipsed'. However, for once he was too ill to record the details.

Although he must have felt depressed, dehydrated and uncertain whether he would see home again, Dampier did not view the eclipse as any kind of portent or omen. Nor did he do so on other occasions. His lack of superstition was at variance with the mood of many of his country-men, who believed that the upheavals of the previous fifty years portended the imminent arrival of the millennium, when Christ would return to rule on Earth for 1,000 years before the end of the world. In addition to the rebellions and revolutions, the millenarians saw the plague and the great Fire of London as portents. So too was the rare appearance of the northern lights over London and the rash of comets like the one identified in 1682 by Edmund Halley, which he correctly predicted would return every seventy-six years.

Dampier spent three or four days lying weak and help-less in the boat, provided with 'necessaries' by the ship's crew. During this time the affair of the Great Moghul's ship was settled; Captain Thwaite returned the stolen vessel. In the following days, the dispute over the new queen was also resolved without bloodshed, and she was accepted by all her people. A relieved Dampier thought it was safe to go ashore and began a determined bid to regain his health. He munched dishes of 'binding' salt-fish and boiled rice mixed with 'cooling' sour milk, regarded by the Achinese as the 'proper food for the common people when they have fluxes'. Like the local people, but most unlike the English at home, he started washing morning and night in the river. He waded out up to his waist, then stooped down to allow the water 'so cool and refreshing' to flow over his feverish body.

The treatment worked. The bland, clotting diet soothed his stomach, and the river water relieved the 'great heat' within his aching bowels so much that he was 'always loath to go out again'. Feeling 'pretty well recovered' at last and his wanderlust returning, Dampier looked around for a suitable ship. In September 1689, he left Achin as mate on board an English trading vessel bound southeast for Malacca.

XVI

THE PAINTED PRINCE

Threading through islands several days after leaving Achin, Dampier and his new shipmates spied a river mouth and sailed in closer, hoping to find fresh water. As Dampier later recalled, ''Tis an ordinary thing in several places to take up fresh water at sea, against the mouth of some river where it floats above the salt-water'.* He warned against dipping too deep, since 'if the bucket goes but a foot deep it takes up salt-water with the fresh'. The men lowered their buckets, found sweet water, and filled their casks, keeping an anxious eye out for 'pirates living on rapine'.

There were no pirates, but, as they sailed on, a strange coincidence awaited Dampier. They noticed a ship lying at anchor, which they identified as a Danish vessel they had passed a few days earlier. One of Dampier's shipmates, a man named Coventry, said that he knew the captain and that Herman Coppinger – the young surgeon whom Dampier had last seen aboard the *Cygnet*, screaming to be set ashore on the Nicobar Islands – was aboard. Dampier set out with Coventry to investigate. The Danes, however, suspected their intentions. As Dampier's boat drew near, every Danish crewman had 'his gun in his hand'. Dampier yelled in English that he and his colleagues were

*This phenomenon occurs because freshwater has a lower specific gravity.

friends, outward bound from Achin, but to no avail. Only when Coventry also began to shout did the captain suddenly recognize him, and the Danes lowered their weapons. Dampier was helped aboard and found Coppinger safe and well. Coppinger told him how, after at last fleeing the *Cygnet*, he had found sanctuary in a Danish trading station and was employed on this ship as the doctor.

Dampier reached the neat, pretty town of Malacca in mid-October. Wandering the streets past 'fair Dutch houses', he learned that 'King William and Queen Mary were crowned King and Queen of England'. It was his first intimation of yet another upheaval at home: the 'Glorious Revolution'. This had toppled from the throne Catholic James II, a strong believer (like his father) in the Divine Right of Kings, in favour of James's own Protestant daughter, the more tractable Mary, and her husband, the Dutch ruler William of Orange. Dampier noted how the change in monarchs had altered the atmosphere: the Dutch had become more polite, even friendly, towards the English.

Dampier pondered the politics and morals of the European rulers of this part of the world and the reasons behind their rise and fall. The Portuguese had been the first explorers of the East Indies. They had established flourishing settlements and built sturdy forts to defend them. Then, drunk with their own power, they had 'insulted over the natives: and being grown rich with trade, they fell into all manner of looseness and debauchery'. This was, Dampier decided, 'the usual concomitant of wealth and as commonly the forerunner of ruin'. He learned that in Malacca itself the Portuguese colonizers had 'made use of the native women at their pleasure whether virgins or married women; such as they liked they took without control'. The justifiable result of such lustful practices had been to goad the Malayans to join forces with the Dutch to oust the Portuguese here as elsewhere.

Returning to Achin in late 1689, Dampier encountered another member of the *Cygnet*'s crew, Edward Morgan, who told him more about the traumatic fate of the ship and her 'mad fickle crew'. Pushed off course by strong monsoon winds, they had found shelter on the south-eastern shores of India – the Coromandel coast – where Morgan had fled the ship with Coppinger. A sizeable number of others also deserted. Lured by 'fine stories' of the fortunes to be made, they enlisted in the service of the Great Moghul. Captain Read – without 'the best half of his men' – sailed to Madagascar. When a vessel arrived there from New York to purchase slaves, Read and half a dozen others slunk aboard. This left Josiah Teat in command of the *Cygnet*, but he too decided to abandon her in favour of serving the Great Moghul.*

Perhaps Morgan's tales of India whetted Dampier's appetite, for he soon took passage to Fort St George on the southeast Indian coast. Approaching the East India Company settlement towards the middle of January, he saw the gentle swell washing against the high stone walls of the fort and was 'much pleased with the beautiful prospect this place makes off at sea'. He spent the next few weeks wandering and observing until, in April 1690, the merchant ship *Mindanao* arrived. She was carrying three crewmen from the *Cygnet* who had remained with Swan on Mindanao. She was also carrying someone else whom

---

*Dampier later learned from another mariner that the ship, which had carried him all the way across the Pacific, finally foundered off Madagascar.

Contemporary engraving of Jeoly.

Dampier had not seen since Mindanao – a slave named Jeoly – 'the painted prince'. Intricate tattoos – the word *tattoo* was not then known in England – covered nearly every muscular inch of the young man's body, except his face, hands and feet. Dampier admiringly described how he 'was painted all down the breast, between his shoulders behind; on his thighs (mostly) before; and in the form of several broad rings or bracelets, round his arms and legs'. The tattoos were not representations of animals but a 'very curious' graphic design, 'full of great variety of lines, flourishes, chequered work'.

Dampier had met Jeoly while visiting his master's house on Mindanao and also aboard the *Cygnet*, where the hungry young slave had gratefully accepted victuals. He learned that the *Mindanao*'s supercargo, a man called

Moody, had purchased both Jeoly and his mother, who was also tattooed, and brought them to Fort St George. Dampier became 'very intimately acquainted' with Moody, admiring his ready intelligence. Moody could speak Malay fluently, and Dampier was not surprised when the governor of Fort St George appointed him head of an English factory at Indrapore on the west coast of Sumatra. Moody urged Dampier to go with him to be the gunner of the fort, but Dampier was not keen. Curious as ever, he instead felt 'a great desire' to explore an area new to him: the Bay of Bengal. Moody coaxed him, promising that if Dampier would go to Indrapore he would buy a small vessel there, appoint Dampier its captain, and send him with Jeoly and his mother to Meangis, the small island of their birth between the Celebes and Mindanao. On Meangis, Dampier could explore how he might 'gain a commerce with [Jeoly's] people for cloves'. Such an offer proved irresistible.

In July 1690, Dampier and Moody sailed for Sumatra with Jeoly and his mother. As they approached the coast, a ferocious wind forced them south to another English factory at Bencouli. Its governor, an irascible, incompetent alcoholic named James Sowdon, greeted Dampier with joy. His own master-gunner had just died, probably of dysentery or typhoid, which ravaged the garrison, and he urged the post on Dampier, arguing that Bencouli was more important than Indrapore. The salary – twenty-four dollars a month – was very acceptable to Dampier but did not compare with Moody's promise of a ship of his own. However, Moody told him that he was free to choose, confessing frankly that he did not know whether he could honour his promise to purchase a ship. Furthermore, since Dampier had left Fort St George only on his account, he offered Dampier a 'half share of the two painted people'.

He would leave them in Dampier's possession and at his disposal. Dampier accepted, and the two men scratched their signatures on papers confirming the deal. 'Thus it was', Dampier later wrote, 'that I came to have this painted prince.'

Curious to know the young man's history, Dampier managed to communicate with him in Malay, which Jeoly had learned on Mindanao and spoke 'indifferent well'. When words failed, Dampier held things up, pointing and gesticulating. He showed Jeoly cloves, spices and something that had interested him keenly ever since his buccaneering days: gold. The young man falteringly replied, *'Meangis hadda madochala se bullawan'*, which Dampier joyfully translated as 'There is abundance of gold at Meangis'. Jeoly also indicated that Meangis was rich in spices. To emphasize this, he pointed to his hair, a sign Dampier had seen used by other peoples to 'express more than they can number'.

Dampier discovered how Jeoly's body had been painted. One of his five wives had painstakingly pricked his skin, then rubbed in pigment made by beating the gum of the dammer tree to a powder. Jeoly told him that most of the islanders, male and female, were decorated in this way and wore heavy gold earrings, bracelets, and anklets. He also described how he had become a slave. He and his family had been crossing to a neighboring island when stormy winds blew them instead onto the shores of Mindanao, where fishermen seized them, stripped them roughly of their gold, and sold them. Dampier could see the empty holes and gashes in Jeoly's lobes where his earrings had been torn off. He and his mother had been purchased by a Mindanaon who spoke Spanish and served Raja Laut as an interpreter. The Mindanaon had beaten and abused 'his painted servant' for five years until Moody had purchased both him and his mother for sixty dollars.

Dampier installed Jeoly and his mother in a house beyond the fort walls. The woman busied herself mending and making clothes, while Jeoly begged some boards and a few nails from Dampier and set about making a chest. It was 'an ill shaped odd thing', but, Dampier wrote with some affection, 'he was as proud of it as if it had been the rarest piece in the world'. Dampier was distraught when, soon after, both fell ill. He nursed them 'as if they had been my brother and sister', but the mother died. He had her 'shrouded decently' in a piece of new calico, though the grief-stricken Jeoly insisted on rewrapping the corpse in all the clothes she had possessed. Dampier dared not argue for fear of 'endangering' Jeoly's life.

Dampier came to dislike Bencouli. Not only was it a fetid, unhealthy spot that had killed Jeoly's mother, but his task as gunner proved frustrating. He inspected the fort's gunpowder supplies and found thirty barrels, yet the contents had absorbed so much moisture that they had turned to the consistency of mud, with all the saltpetre sunk to the bottom. On ships, powder kegs were carefully turned at least once a month to stop this from happening, but no one had had the good sense to take such a precaution here. Governor Sowdon was planning to send the powder to Fort St. George 'to be renewed there', which Dampier thought was both foolish and unnecessary. What would happen if the fort came under attack and they needed powder before it was returned? He persuaded the governor to 'let me first try my skill on it'. He set to work beating the saltpetre back into the other ingredients, and drying then sifting the result through sieves made of his 'old parchment drafts'. To his delight, he managed to retrieve '8 barrels full of very good powder'.

Looking for other activities deserving of his energies, Dampier decided that the fort – 'the most irregular' he had ever seen – needed remodelling. He drew up plans for a fifth bastion. He was also keen to face the mud fort in stone or brick, but Sowdon thought this far too costly and proposed simply to patch things up. An irritated Dampier decided that the governor might just as well save himself the trouble – the fort would continue to 'moulder away every wet season', leaving the guns to tumble down 'into the ditches'.

His relationship with the governor soon spiralled downwards. He considered the 'brutish and barbarous' Sowdon 'much fitter to be a book-keeper than governor of a fort', reflecting sourly that the East India Company should, for the good of its own trade, take more care over those it appointed to positions of authority. Men like Sowdon had neither the education nor the experience. Dampier was particularly disgusted by his arrogant treatment of the local people, who were 'best-managed as all mankind are, by justice, and fair-dealings', and who, if roused, might well assault the fort. Equally deplorably, Dampier realized that Sowdon was trying to cheat him of his wages.

Dampier plotted his escape. As well as a determined desire to get away from Sowdon, he was beginning to 'long after my native country'. It had been twelve years since he had left England as an eager young man bound for Jamaica on a trading trip that should have lasted only a matter of months. He hoped that he had a means of supporting himself – and Judith, if she was still alive. Despite his affection for Jeoly, he planned to exhibit his 'painted prince' in England. People would flock, coin in hand, to see such an exotic spectacle. Then, when he had made his money,

Dampier intended to buy a ship 'to carry [Jeoly] back to Meangis and re-instate him there in his own country'. It was a romantic notion, but it also contained a pragmatic element: Dampier hoped by Jeoly's 'favour and negotiation to establish a traffic for the spices and other products of those islands'.

He confronted Sowdon, demanding to be discharged and allowed to depart on the next ship bound for England. Sowdon – somewhat to his surprise – agreed. In January 1691, the *Defence*, under Captain Heath, arrived from Indrapore, and Dampier discovered that the chief mate, a man named Goddard, had purchased Moody's share of Jeoly from him. Dampier asked Goddard to take Jeoly onto the ship and made him swear as well that, if Sowdon tried to block his own leaving, he would help Dampier get aboard and hide him. It was a wise precaution. Just as Dampier feared, at the last moment Sowdon changed his mind and refused to let his gunner go. After several abortive attempts, and within hours of the ship's sailing, a determined Dampier squeezed through 'one of the port holes of the fort' and ran down to the shore, where a boat awaited him. He was carrying with him his most precious possessions: his journal of the last eleven years and most of his papers. It is scarcely credible that he would have left without them. He was forced to abandon books, bedding, clothes, intruments and all his furniture, but he did not care. He was at liberty, with high 'hopes of seeing England again'.

The *Defence* nosed out into the warm Indian Ocean bound for the Cape of Good Hope. Yet it soon seemed that he had 'leapt out of the frying pan into the fire'. A 'sort of distemper stole insensibly' through the ship, leaving men listless and drained. Men almost too weak to hold a quill began making their wills. Every morning, two or three bodies were thrown overboard, and before the Cape of Good Hope was sighted, thirty had died. Dampier suspected the cause to be 'unwholesome' water taken aboard at Bencouli. Instead of filling their casks from the clean spring supplying the fort, the crew had lazily scooped up fetid river water, which 'looked more like ink than water'.

Lack of fresh food was also making men ill. A worried Captain Heath broke open some of his own jars of tamarinds, which the men consumed gratefully with their rice. '[The tamarinds] contributed much to keep us on our legs'. Nevertheless, two months into the voyage, the captain, sick himself, was struggling to keep his ship afloat. Strong winds pounded the vessel, and there were not enough men to handle the ropes. In desperation, the captain promised a month's extra salary to any men 'that would engage to assist on all occasions, and be ready on call'. Dampier, who would have worked for their 'common safety' rather than any reward, was by then too weak to do anything. It seemed like a miracle when, shortly afterwards, 'it pleased God to favour [them] with a fine wind', and they at last approached the cape, firing a gun every hour to signal that they were in distress. A Dutch captain came aboard and was horrified by the men's desperate condition. He sent ashore for 'a hundred lusty men' to bring the *Defence* safely into the harbour. The sick were taken ashore, while those strong enough to stay on board were revived by daily supplies of 'good fat mutton' and 'fresh beef'.

Dampier recovered quickly and before long was roaming the cape. The 'very temperate climate' was sweet. He dismissed the 'common prejudice' of European seamen who believed the south wind blowing over the cape was cool simply because it was a sea wind. His own view, reflecting his understanding of meteorology, was that the temperature at the wind's source and along its path were what mattered, not whether the wind blew over land or sea.

Dampier wrote approvingly of the neat Dutch East India Company settlement with its fine stone houses and wonderful gardens with 'the largest pomegranates that I did ever see'. The grapes, too, were luscious, the wine they produced 'pale yellow, sweet, very pleasant and strong'. Dampier ate ostrich eggs so large that one egg would 'suffice two men very well'. The sheep were pleasingly fat, but one animal in particular caught his eye: 'a very beautiful sort of wild ass'. Its body '[is] curiously striped with equal lists of white and black; the stripes coming from the ridge of his back, and ending under the belly, which is white. These stripes are two or three fingers broad, running parallel with each other, and curiously intermixt'. His description of a zebra in his book would be the first in English.

He also scrutinized 'the natural inhabitants of the Cape', the Hottentots. 'Of a middle stature' with 'small limbs and thin bodies, full of activity', they had faces 'of a flat oval figure, of the negro make', with 'great eyebrows' and 'black eyes'. Their skin was paler than that of the New Hollanders, and their hair less frizzled. They smeared their bodies with pungent-smelling grease to keep themselves supple and to protect their semi-naked bodies from the elements. They also rubbed soot over the greased parts, especially their faces. Their heads were bare, and their hair was decked with small shells. Their clothes consisted of sheepskins, which they wrapped round them 'like a mantle', woolly side next to their skin. The men also wore a small sheepskin apron, while the women had skins wrapped round their waists and descending to their knees 'like a petticoat'.

Dampier was puzzled that the Hottentots wound sheep's guts two or three inches thick round their calves. When they first put them on, they were fresh, but they became 'hard and stiff on their legs' like boots. Dampier was told by the Dutch that the Hottentots removed them only when they had 'occasion to eat them', perhaps while journeying far from home when they had no other food. Their houses were 'the meanest' that Dampier had ever seen – flimsy structures supported by small poles and with sides and roof made of boughs covered with long grasses, rushes and pieces of hide. From a distance a house looked 'just like a hay-cock'.

Just as he had in Southeast Asia, Dampier inquired into the people's religion. He could see no sign of any 'temple nor idol nor any place of worship'. Yet 'their mirth and nocturnal pastimes at the New and Full of the Moon' seemed to have 'some superstition about [them]'. At the time of the full moon especially, they sang and danced all night, 'making a great noise'. Several times Dampier walked out in the moonlight to their huts to watch men, women and children 'dancing very oddly . . . faces some-times to the east, sometimes to the west'. Drawn back in the grey of the morning by a consuming curiosity, he found them still swaying and chanting. He was fascinated by the Hottentots but also exasperated, as he had been by the Australian Aborigines. He concluded that they were 'a very lazy sort of people'. They lived in a fine, fertile country with enough land for all, 'yet they chose rather to live as their fore-fathers, poor and miserable, than be at pains for plenty'.

On 23 May 1691, the *Defence* finally sailed for home.

Soon 'a great tumbling sea' caught her broadside on. Water casks and barrels of 'good Cape wine' broke free, rolling about below-decks and splitting open. Dampier feared that some of the guns would break loose, even that the masts would crash down. He was relieved on 20 June to see the rough-hewn outline of St Helena take substance on the horizon.

The tiny Atlantic island – more than 1,000 miles off the west coast of Africa – was administered as a staging post by the English East India Company. Sailors weakened by 'scorbutic distempers' could bathe in infusions of 'delicate herbs' to ease their joints and feast on 'fruits and herbs and fresh food' to bring them back to health. The cure was reputedly so effective that in just a week skeletal men carried ashore in their hammocks too feeble to move could 'leap and dance'. The islanders, who profited from providing this tender care, were somewhat put out to discover that Captain Heath and his men were actually quite healthy after their stay at the cape. They were even more annoyed to discover, as Dampier chronicled, that many sailors had spent most of their money there.

Nevertheless, some were 'extremely kind, in hopes to get what was remaining'. The punch houses were soon full to bursting, and the next five or six days passed in general roistering. One consequence was that many of the men fell 'over head and ears in love'. Some got married there and then. Others signed contracts confirming they would wed their sweethearts as soon as they reached England and carried their new loves joyfully aboard. Dampier, who spent only two days ashore gathering provisions for himself and Jeoly, cast an ironic eye over the proceedings. He concluded that the 'Saint Helena maids', born on this remote island, 'very earnestly desired to be released from that prison' by finding husbands among the seamen and passengers who called here. The girls were, he acknowledged, 'well shaped, proper and comely', but needed better clothes 'to set them off'.

On 2 July 1691, the *Defence* departed, and ten weeks later Dampier and his painted prince at last reached England. Dampier had been away for more than twelve years – an extraordinary length of time, even in an age when trading voyages could take a year or more to complete.* He did not record his feelings.

*Even Drake's circumnavigation had taken just three years.

PART IV

The Celebrity

XVII

THE ROVER'S RETURN

The *Defence* anchored in the Thames, and Dampier made his way to London. Not only the occupants of the royal palaces and parliament buildings had changed during his twelve-year absence, but much else besides. The city had grown in population, expanse and commerce. It provided nearly half of the new government's revenues and had almost 500,000 citizens – about one-tenth of England's total population. Only two other cities – Norwich with 30,000 and Bristol with 20,000 – had populations of any size. Even so, there was still only one bridge spanning the Thames: old London Bridge, completed in 1209, over 905 feet long and with nineteen large stone pillars. When the tide ebbed or flowed, the water boiled between them alarmingly. Most river travellers preferred to disembark, rather

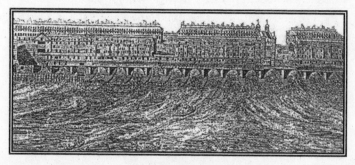

Old London Bridge.

than trust themselves to these rapids. By 1691, the houses on the bridge, burned down in the Great Fire of 1666, had been replaced by tall, handsome structures with shops on their lower storeys selling everything from clothes to 'counterfeit damask', a fashionable 'flocked' wallpaper with which Mrs Pepys papered her chamber. Carts, carriages, and hawkers clutching bundles pushed their way over the bridge in a ceaseless stream.

Activity on the river itself had burgeoned since Dampier left. Upriver from the bridge at least 10,000 boats plied between London and Windsor and beyond. In the twenty miles downriver to Gravesend were another 14,000 vessels. In the pool of London itself, between the bridge and the Tower of London, swayed the great masts of seagoing ships, waiting to unload cargoes from silks and spices to pepper and porcelain. A mass of small craft plied busily from bank to bank. Wherries, a sort of river bus, ran on regular timetables between major landing places. Those who could afford one hired small craft rowed by a single waterman, the taxi drivers of their day. Their insults were considered particularly 'coarse and dirty', even at a time when, according to a visitor, it was 'the custom for anyone on the water to call out whatever he pleased to occupants of other boats, even were it to the king himself, and no one had a right to be shocked'.

The increase in trade and prosperity was evident in other ways. The Thames was even fuller of rubbish and waste from industries like the tanneries along the banks which discharged into it their acrid vats of dog turds and urine used to soften the leather. The river smelled horribly, particularly when the ooze and its decaying contents were exposed at low tide. John Evelyn wrote, 'Dirty and nasty it is at every ebb . . . so as next to the hellish smoke of the town there is nothing doubtless which does more impair the health of its inhabitants'. These smoggy and insanitary conditions meant that the capital's energetic population was not self-sustaining: more people died than were born there. London's dynamic growth relied on immigration from all parts of Britain and Ireland to a city that offered wages 50 per cent higher than elsewhere. The population had been further swelled by numbers of Protestant Huguenots, fleeing religious persecution in France, and whose arrival had accelerated dramatically following the revocation in 1685 of the Edict of Nantes, which had protected their civil freedoms.*

During Dampier's absence, new land to the west of the old city had been developed to house the increasing population, including areas like Soho, the former hunting ground named after a hunting cry, and Carnaby Street, laid out in 1683 by the bricklayer Richard Tyler. Henry Jermyn, Earl of St Albans, had developed St James's Square and the adjacent street bearing his name to provide lodgings for the changing bands of ambitious courtiers attending successive monarchs. Piccadilly (named after 'Pickadillies', the borders to ruffs and collars sold by its original inhabitants) was also newly built up.

Another large-scale developer whose ambitious projects included the area around Soho Square was the son of the famous Puritan Parliamentarian Praise God Barebones. His father christened him If-Jesus-Christ-Had-Not-Died-For-Thee-Thou-Hadst-Been-Damned Barebones. Unsurprisingly, for business purposes he preferred to be known as Nicholas Barbon. He had trained as

---

*The word *refugee*, which has come to mean anyone seeking refuge from persecution, was first used in the minutes of a London Huguenot church meeting in 1681 to describe their own plight.

a physician but, spotting an obvious opportunity after the Great Fire, had become a successful speculative builder. To protect his own, and others', investments against the all-too-recently demonstrated fire risk, in May 1680 he had set up Britain's first fire insurance company.

Although he would later move to Soho, Dampier probably first returned to one of the older areas clustered on both sides of the Thames below London Bridge. Limehouse, Wapping and Rotherhithe, in particular, with their warrens of narrow-fronted houses, were the sailors' neighbourhoods. Dampier would have found relaxation and convivial company in alehouses like the still-surviving Angel or the Prospect of Whitby.* The alehouses provided food, drink and a chance to gamble at cards, dice or ten-bones. Here sailors gossiped and exchanged information on what voyages were recruiting, wage rates, good and bad captains, and the activities of the press-gang. Here too were the lawyers or agents whom the sailors hired to try to get wages owed them by avaricious shipowners. Dampier would soon have occasion to resort to them.

On his return Dampier, perhaps with some trepidation, sought out the wife he had not seen for so long. During his wanderings he may have asked fellow sailors to carry letters for her home to England, but it seems unlikely that any letter from Judith could ever have reached him. He would not even have known whether Judith was still alive. There was a good chance she was not. The average life expectancy was around thirty-five years. Perhaps the papers

*The term *public house*, short for *public alehouse*, was first used around 1700. The shortened version – *pub* – was first recorded 150 years later.

recording Dampier's purchase of the small estate in Dorset had reached Judith, and this estate had provided her with some means of subsisting. Whatever the case, she was probably still in London in the Duchess of Grafton's household in Arlington House, where Dampier had left her before sailing to Jamaica. He did not describe their reunion, but it did take place and must have been a strange one. He was forty, and she probably not much younger. They may not even have recognized each other at first. More significantly, a gulf of experience separated them.

Dampier's main priority was to find a means of support for them. His plan of exhibiting Jeoly had failed. Almost immediately after reaching England, the painted prince had caught the eye of 'some eminent persons', who pressured Dampier to part with him. According to his first book, 'want of money' forced him to agree. His manuscript draft was more forthright, suggesting that he was cheated. He had, he wrote bitterly, fallen 'amongst rooks'.

The loss of Jeoly not only dashed Dampier's business schemes but was also an emotional blow. He had looked after him for months, tending him through bereavement and illness. Even though he had himself planned to exhibit Jeoly, it must have been a wrench to abandon him to strangers in a bewildering new land to the uncertain fate of being 'carried about to be shown as a sight'. He would describe Jeoly in his book with greater feeling than anyone else, including Judith, to whom he referred only once and in passing.

Jeoly's new owners lost no time in exploiting their acquisition. Their printed flyer promised: 'The famous painted prince is the just wonder of the age, his whole body is curiously and most exquisitely painted or stained, full of variety and invention with prodigious skill performed. Insomuch, that the ancient and noble mystery of painting or staining upon human bodies seems to be comprised in this one stately piece'. In contrast to Dampier's honest admission that he could not 'liken the drawings' to anything in particular, the flier boasted that 'the more admirable back parts afford us a lively representation of one quarter part of the world, upon and betwixt his shoulders where the Arctic and Tropic circles centre on the North Pole on his neck'. According to the flyer, the process of painting had rendered Jeoly invulnerable to the bites of venomous snakes and insects – a claim Dampier dismissed as rubbish, having seen Jeoly as terrified of snakes and scorpions as himself. The flyer concluded: 'This admirable person is about the age of thirty ... extremely modest and civil, neat and cleanly, but his language is not understood, neither can he speak English. He will appear publicly every day at his lodgings at the Blue Boar's Head in Fleet Street'.

Jeoly's owners faced stiff competition. There was an appetite for the 'freak show', a chance to goggle at exotic or grotesque 'curiosities' like 'a prodigious monster ... from the Great Moghul's country, being a man with one head and two distinct bodies, both masculine', or 'a living skeleton ... a fairy child aged nine years not exceeding a foot and a half high. ... You may see the whole anatomy of its body by setting it against the sun'. Even the Royal Society had a museum of 'rarities', including an Egyptian mummy, tiger claws and human skulls. Other competing attractions included executions. Londoners could escort the condemned to the gallows and trade banter and insults with them. They could also mock the insane in Bedlam or pelt criminals in the pillory with rotting filth. They could elbow in among roaring, jostling crowds to watch cockfights or the blood-soaked baitings of bears and bulls by mastiffs. Or they could go to a play. Theatres were flourishing, with the added realism that women, not boys, now played the female roles. The plays might be witty, amoral comedies celebrating extramarital relationships like those crafted by Sir John Vanbrugh, William Wycherly and William Congreve. The latter wrote of Jeoly in his play *Love for Love*. Some plays, though, were less accomplished. One theatregoer complained, 'Character is supplied with a smutty song, humour with a dance, and argument with lightening and thunder, and this has often reprieved many a scurvy play from damning'.

Faced with such rival attractions, Jeoly's owners published 'a book of the exhibit', to drum up extra interest and as a money-spinner in its own right. They claimed that a Dutch merchant who knew Jeoly's language had, before conveniently departing again, taken down his story 'from his own mouth'. It was a romantic production told in the first person. Jeoly represents himself as a king's son, captured at sea by Celebean pirates and sold as a slave to the sister of the king of another island. Predictably, they fall in love, but the king gets wind of it and banishes the princess to a remote castle. He hands Jeoly to a favourite of his, who uses him 'with all the severity imaginable'. Jeoly escapes and by chance encounters his princess, who is 'struggling with the mighty onsets of a bold ravisher'. Jeoly despatches the would-be rapist and revives the swooning princess 'by stealing one gentle kiss from her dear lips'. They spend their single night of passion together, falling asleep in each other's arms, but are once more betrayed. The princess is dragged away 'with scarce leisure' to wish him well or 'give a parting look'. Jeoly is carried off back into slavery. Dampier dismissed these titillating confections as 'stories indeed'. He later learned that there had been no fairy-tale ending for his 'painted prince'. In 1692, Jeoly 'died of the small-pox at Oxford'.

Dampier meanwhile was looking for employment and was, perhaps, once more hankering for the sea. If he had hopes of recouping his fortunes by returning to Jamaica to trade, they had been dashed when, some nine months after his return, he heard that Port Royal had been destroyed. On 7 June 1692, massive earthquakes and a tidal wave obliterated the brash, bawdy, bustling town. The sand in the unpaved streets rose up in great rippling waves. Stone buildings collapsed, and two whole streets simply vanished beneath the sea. Too few were left living to bury the dead. To the millenarians, it seemed yet another portent. To others, it was a fitting judgement on the wickedest city in Christendom.

In the summer of 1693, Dampier learned of a proposed 'Spanish Expedition' sponsored by the influential Huguenot financier Sir John Houblon. Its purpose was to trade with Spanish colonists in the West Indies and to salvage treasure from Spanish wrecks off Central America. Dampier signed up for this further opportunity to satisfy his 'sacred hunger' for gold, giving Judith power of attorney to act for him in his absence. He was among 200 men carried by a squadron of four ships – the flagship *Charles II*, the *James*, the *Dove Galley*, and the *Seventh Son* – to La Coruna, in Spain, in early 1694 under the overall command of Admiral O'Byrne. In his first book, Dampier later made a single, studiedly casual comment that in July 1694 he 'lay at anchor at the Groin [La Coruna]'. He was in fact participating in a bizarre venture whose failure would result in the most blatantly successful example of out-and-out piracy of his day and would dog Dampier for years.

The expedition's sponsors believed that they had secured a charter for their activities from King Carlos II of Spain. Yet weeks turned into months, and still the expedition received no formal sanction. Aboard the four ships tempers frayed in the cramped, sweaty conditions. There was no sign of the six-monthly wages the crews had been promised or of 'necessaries' like 'wine and fresh provisions' – essential for the recovery of 'several poor sick men'. In May 1694, eighty-five men, drawn from all four ships, lost

Henry Every, better known as Captain John Avery.

patience and mutinied. Dampier, second mate on the *Dove Galley*, was not among them. The mutineers' leader was chief mate aboard the *Charles II*, Devonshire sailor Henry Every, shortly to become known to contemporaries as Captain John Avery. He and his followers seized the *Charles II*, rechristened her the *Fancy*, and sailed off.

Avery took the *Fancy* south and east. An increasing naval presence in the West Indies was forcing pirates to seek new hunting grounds. Stories of easy pickings in the Indian Ocean like the fleets of the Great Moghul, and in particular the pilgrim fleets crossing from India to Arabia via the coffee port of Mocha, prompted many to make Madagascar their base. It was from here that Avery set out to raid the pilgrim fleet. His greatest prize was the *Ganj-i-Sawai*, the largest ship in the Great Moghul's fleet, which the pirates quickly captured, committing, as one later confessed, 'the most horrid barbarities'. They raped the women, who, rumour had it, included a close relative of the Great Moghul, and tortured men and women alike to make them reveal the whereabouts of their treasures. The plunder in gold, jewels and precious cloths was immense, with each man receiving about £1,000. Avery wisely quit while the going was good, disposed of his loot cheaply and discreetly in the West Indies, and sailed to Donegal in Ireland. No more is known for certain of his fate.

The repercussions of Avery's marauding for the East India Company were severe. When the news of the taking of the *Ganj-i-Sawai* and the brutalizing of those on board reached India, rioters besieged the houses of English residents and invaded the company's factories. It took much diplomacy and much money to persuade the Great Moghul to allow the company to remain in his domains.

Dampier may have met Avery when hewing logwood

in the creeks of Campeachy in the 1670s, if some accounts of Avery's early life are to be believed. They would certainly have got to know each other during the months at La Coruna, where the crews of all the ships were 'very conversant together'. Dampier may well have known about the planned mutiny but decided not to join it, remaining on the sidelines as he had so often before during shipboard disputes. Dampier knew that going with Avery would put him irrevocably outside the law, never able to return home to England and to Judith and never able to indulge in legitimate trade. Avery's was no privateering expedition with a commission from the king to capture enemy shipping. It was not even the increasingly anachronistic buccaneering, the tacitly tolerated plundering of enemy settlements and shipping in the distant New World. Even though Avery's exploits were to excite some popular admiration, they were overt piracy, stealing before witnesses in a European port an English ship belonging to an influential member of London's merchant community. Such piracy could not attract even tacit toleration.

Another reason Dampier chose to remain may have been that he was beginning to work up his journals into a book. It is not clear when he first began to think of writing for publication, but perhaps it had been in his mind from the start of his travels. For twelve years he had obsessively made observations and kept notes in the most impossible of situations. He had rolled his parchments in tubes of bamboo sealed with wax to protect them from the tumbling rivers and sticky mud of the Darien. He had plucked his manuscripts from the waves when his canoe capsized in the Nicobar Islands, and carefully dried them. He had guarded his journals through turbulent days on mutinous ships, fighting for physical and mental space to mix his inks and record his thoughts, making sure that whatever else he lost, they always came with him.

It seems likely he took advantage of the company of so many experienced seamen at La Coruña to validate facts, compare experiences and seek information about regions unknown to him to make his knowledge as complete as possible. One of those he consulted was John Canby, chief mate of Dampier's own ship, the *Dove Galley*, whom Dampier 'much esteemed as a sensible man' and whom he would cite four times in his books as an authority.

Dampier meanwhile hoped that the Spanish Expedition might still proceed and at least that he would receive his wages. However, Avery's flight had made the expedition's sponsors suspect the remaining crewmen of planning mutiny. On 29 June 1694, they ordered the sailors of the *James* and the *Dove Galley* 'to be kept on shore'. Dampier was one of fifty to sign a letter angrily protesting their innocence. They insisted that they had no intention 'notoriously and feloniously to take carry and run away with' their ships, complained indignantly about 'that evil opinion' which the sponsors had 'hitherto too unjustly harboured' against them, and demanded their wages. Problems with Spanish officialdom and growing discontent among the crew made matters even worse. In February 1695, they were still in La Coruña, and the men's employment contracts had expired. A frustrated, angry Dampier returned to London and within six weeks was embroiled with fellow crewmen in a lawsuit before the High Court of Admiralty to recover back wages.

Merchant seamen were the first working men to be able to sell their services in a truly free market. A sailor could usually count on pay equivalent to that of a tailor or weaver on land. In addition, he was entitled to food and drink when on a voyage. Complaints about poor-quality beer 'as bad as water bewitched' and biscuits consisting mainly of dust and weevils were commonplace. Pursers and captains were invariably suspected of enriching themselves by 'pinching the bellies' of their men. Before a voyage, sailors had to outfit themselves and to make provision for their families ashore. To do so, they sought advances from the ship's owners, who, in turn, might require bonds from the crewmen against desertion and for their good behaviour, as they did in the case of the Spanish Expedition.

Such arangements provided a fertile source of litigation in a litigious age.* Between 100 and 200 claims for unpaid wages were brought annually before the High Court of Admiralty. Usually, the sailors joined forces to pay a single lawyer and to bring a single case – a kind of class action. This allowed most plaintiffs to return to sea and earn a living while the case proceeded. Those with wives also trusted to them to protect their interests.

The gist of Dampier's claim was that he had been hired at a monthly rate of £4 10s. and that of the £82 2s. 6d. owed him in total, £77 3s. 6d. was still outstanding. Testifying on behalf of other plaintiffs as well as himself, Dampier vigorously refuted all accusations that the officers and men had either assisted Avery or disobeyed orders themselves. He claimed that the expedition's sponsors had 'promised to pay off all the company their full pay every six months'. The sponsors argued that the plaintiffs had resisted their commander's authority and thus violated their contracts. The well-documented accusations and counteraccusations

*About 1½ per cent of the country's total population were trained lawyers.

are evidence of the relentless bureaucracy of the High Court of Admiralty. A faded paper in its archives, covered with neat lines of sloping writing, accuses Dampier specifically. His name appears at the head of a list of supposedly unruly crewmen charged with resisting orders. Dampier and his companions fought back, arguing firmly and convincingly and producing witnesses to back their claims, but to no avail. On 16 January 1696, the court ruled their evidence insufficient and dismissed their case.

At some point Dampier re-established contact with his old friend Lionel Wafer. Dampier had last seen the surgeon on 25 August 1685 when the *Bachelor's Delight*, with Wafer aboard, had separated from the *Cygnet* bearing Dampier away. Wafer would have told him of the difficult times that had followed. Like Dampier, he had had 'troubles' in Virginia. In June 1688, together with the captain of the *Bachelor's Delight*, Edward Davis, and others, he had been quietly rowing a small boat along the backwaters of Chesapeake Bay when Captain Rowe of HMS *Dumbarton* stopped and thoroughly searched their boat. He found that, in addition to 'some foul linen', the sailors' sea chests were full of silver of all sorts, including what looked like chalices and other dented altar vessels. The total haul was later valued at £2,316 19s. Rowe arrested the men on suspicion of piracy, a charge they vigorously denied. Nevertheless, they remained in Jamestown Jail.

That August a royal proclamation was published offering a pardon to pirates who surrendered. Wafer and his companions tried to take advantage of it, but their application was at first rejected since they had not surrendered but had been arrested. Wafer and Davis were finally released, but their goods were not returned. In July 1690, Wafer was allowed to sail to England to pursue his case. In March 1693, he finally received restitution, but more than £300 of the original haul seized with Wafer and his colleagues was held back 'to be employed towards the erecting of a free school or college in Virginia'. Thus the renowned College of William and Mary at Williamsburg was partly founded with pirate loot.

Dampier clearly discussed his literary ambitions with Wafer, who gave him an account of the time he had spent living with the Kuna Indians of Darien after being wounded. Dampier had it transcribed with suitable acknowledgement into the surviving draft of his first book. It would not appear in the published version, so the two men must have agreed not to compete. In his book Dampier would state that he left descriptions of Darien to Wafer and explained why: '[Wafer] made a longer abode in it than I; and is better able to do it than any man that I know, and is now preparing a particular description of this country for the press'. In the meantime, though, Dampier found a more immediate practical use for Wafer's account. He showed a copy to William Paterson, a Scot of humble origins but by then prosperous and one of the leading entrepreneurs of the day.

Paterson had traded in Jamaica in the late 1670s and early 1680s, around the time of the buccaneer raids across the isthmus, and certainly knew some of the buccaneer captains. Dampier probably first met him at this time. Paterson later took part in the development of property to the west of London and himself lived in Denmark Street in the parish of St Giles on the edge of the newly developed Soho. He was a humourless, serious, but strictly honest man who promoted new commercial ideas persistently and garrulously. He had propounded to the Committee of the House of Commons his ideas for the creation of a Bank of England, which would give credit and take loans on government security. The bank had been established on this basis in 1694, with the financial backing of, among others, the Houblon family, business associates of Paterson. England for the first time assumed a national debt, to the considerable relief of the impoverished exchequer. It also issued promissory 'bank notes' to acknowledge its debts: England's first paper currency. Paterson was one of the first directors of the bank but soon resigned.

Paterson had ambitions for his native Scotland. Scottish commerce was by then at a low ebb, and Paterson was hoping to found a Scottish overseas trading company to rival such English ventures as the East India Company. He and his fellow directors were as yet undecided about their sphere of operations, but Paterson's personal preference was for the Caribbean and Central America. Dampier's expert and unique knowledge of the region therefore interested Paterson. In particular, Dampier's ideas for commercial ventures, especially his 'golden dreams' of a settlement at Santa Maria on the Isthmus of Panama, chimed with his own vision.

Paterson used information from Dampier and Wafer to develop a proposal for a Scottish colony on the isthmus to provide a trading route and trading post between the Pacific and the Atlantic. He believed that 'the time and expense of navigation to China, Japan and the Spice Islands and the East Indies will be lessened by more than half and the consumption of European commodities will soon be more than doubled. Trade will increase trade and money will beget money and the trading world shall need no more to want work for their hands but will rather want hands for their work. Thus the door of the seas, and the key of the universe ... will enable its proprietors to give laws to both oceans without being liable to the fatigues, expenses and dangers, or contracting the guilt and blood of Alexander and Caesar'. On 16 July 1696, Paterson expounded his proposal to the committee of investors and left with them a bundle of papers, certainly including a copy of Wafer's draft that Dampier had given him and probably some of the latter's writing as well. The members of the committee were convinced, and the Scots Company was henceforth committed to a colony in Darien.

At this time the kingdoms of Scotland and England were still separate. (The fact that they had the same ruler was constitutionally simply coincidence.) The English government and its merchant companies feared Scottish competition. Learning of the proposal for a Scots settlement in Darien, they began to block and discredit it, using any means they could. In particular, they attempted to smear the Scots with accusations that they were recruiting pirates, including some of Avery's men, and, as a consequence, had plans for piracy themselves.

As a traveller in the region known to have been advising Paterson, Dampier became drawn into the political struggle. In June 1697, he was called before the Honourable Council of Lords of Trade and Plantations in London to give his views on the Scots' proposal. He said that Lionel Wafer knew more than he, and the two friends appeared together a month later. The council quizzed them about the 'conveniency of settlement' on the isthmus and how much land was 'possessed by the wild indians independent of the Spaniards'. Dampier and Wafer suggested that a colony of around 500 people would be viable. The council, of which philosopher John Locke was a leading member, accepted their view and proposed the pre-emptive annexation by England of Golden Island and some of the neighbouring mainland, although nothing ultimately came of this proposal.

In the spring of 1698, Lionel Wafer became more closely involved with the Scots Company as an adviser, travelling clandestinely to Edinburgh as 'Mr Brown'. He offered to delay publication of his manuscript and allow the Scots exclusive use of the information it contained for a fee of £1,000. He received only £70 for his trouble. Furthermore, despite his use of a cover name, news of Wafer's actions quickly reached the English government through its spy network. On 13 July 1698, only a week before the Scots Expedition finally sailed, the Honourable Council of Lords of Trade and Plantations called Dampier before it again and quizzed him vigorously about Wafer's doings and his likely utility to the Scots. Dampier denied any knowledge of Wafer's dealings and loyally did his friend a great favour by saying that he doubted whether Wafer could do the Scots 'any great service', which was clearly untrue given the extent of Wafer's knowledge of Darien. Dampier's views were accepted, and Wafer was not harassed further.

Paterson, his wife and 1,200 other prospective colonists landed in Darien in November 1698. They established their colony only three miles from Golden Island and reinforced it with additional colonists, but their 'New Caledonia' failed disastrously through starvation and disease. The desperate Scots, surviving on lizards and roots, appealed to the English colony of Jamaica for provisions but were refused on the express orders of a smug English government. By the time the colony was abandoned, 2,000 Scots lives and 300,000 Scots pounds had been lost, the latter a high proportion of the nation's financial resources. The resultant financial and commercial weakness was a major factor in the Scots' acceptance of the Treaty of Union with England in 1707. William Paterson's wife died in Darien, but he returned to Britain, dying there in 1719.

Lionel Wafer remained in touch with Paterson about further settlements in Panama until his own death, believed to be around 1705. His book, *A New Description of the Isthmus of Darien*, recounting his time with the Kuna, was finally published in 1699, by the man who had become Dampier's publisher, James Knapton. It bathed in Dampier's reflected glory. Dampier was by then an established bestselling author, lionized in London's salons and sought out by the leading intellectuals. His *A New Voyage Round the World*, published two years earlier – the first account in the first person of a circumnavigation of the world – had been an immediate and dramatic hit.

Of all William Dampier's travels, this swift journey from obscurity to celebrity was perhaps the strangest and least expected.

XVIII

'GOOD COPY'

*D*ampier had been working on *A New Voyage* for some time before its publication in early 1697. He had clearly been discussing his work with shipmates like Lionel Wafer and John Canby, but the content of his book showed other, wider influences. In particular, it reflected the philosophy of the Royal Society, whose fellows were begining to take a close interest in the sailor who had rambled around the world. He was exactly the type of seaman they had had in mind in drawing up their *Directions for Seamen Bound for Far Voyages*. These directions asked seamen to 'study nature rather than books and from the observations made to compose such a history of her, as may, hereinafter, serve to build a solid and useful philosophy upon'. The comprehensive data the society was seeking exactly matched Dampier's interests. They wanted data on magnetic variations, the topography of coastlines, weather patterns, the direction of tidal streams, and fluctuations in sea level between high and low water. Dampier, in turn, must have been flattered by the society's interest. As William Whaley had observed many years earlier in Jamaica, he was a 'self-conceited' rather than a modest man. He had a passion for information and believed that he had 'many things wholly new' to impart.

Dampier's obscure background was less of a hindrance

to his progress than might be imagined. Seventeenth-century society was relatively fluid, and the era was one of intellectual and political ferment where ideas could transcend status. London's lively coffeehouses, where Dampier probably pursued his contacts, exemplified this. England's first coffeehouse had been opened by a Jewish immigrant in Oxford in 1650. The first in London had followed two years later and proved so popular that by 1700 there were more than 2,000 in the city. They were convivial, democratic establishments where men of all pursuits and backgrounds rubbed shoulders. Entrance cost a mere penny, and a man could spend much of the day drinking a dish of coffee costing about one and a half pence and debating the state of the world with other drinkers.*

Some men were spending so much time in coffeehouses that their wives got up a petition against this 'nasty, bitter, stinking, nauseous puddlewater' which kept their men from home. Even worse, they claimed, 'never did men wear greater breeches, or carry less in them of any metal whatsoever . . . [the] heathenish liquor has so eunuched our husbands . . . that they are become as impotent as age', returning home with 'nothing moist but their snotty noses, nothing stiff but their joints, nothing standing but their ears'.†

We do not know how much time Dampier spent in

---

*If a man was in a hurry, he made sure that the server saw him drop some coins into a box marked 'T.I.P.', short for 'To Insure Promptness' and reputedly the origin of the word *tip*.

†A male response half conceded the case by suggesting that coffee helped men avoid being only a 'flash in the pan, without doing the thundering execution which your expectations exact', but went on, 'you may as well permit us to talk abroad, for at home we have scarce time to utter a word for the unsufferable din of your over-active tongues'.

coffeehouses nor what Judith thought of the amount of attention he paid her. One of his likely haunts was Jonathan's, in Change Alley in Cornhill and soon to become home to the embryonic stock exchange. Jonathan's was a well-known meeting place for shippers, merchants and others engaged in sea trade. Paterson and his friends met there while discussing the establishment of the Bank of England. Another regular was Herman Moll, a German-born mapmaker of about Dampier's age who was rapidly becoming Britain's best-known cartographer. He had already done much work for the Royal Society and was to draw the maps for Dampier's books on the basis of sketches provided by Dampier himself.

A friend of Moll's, who also frequented Jonathan's, was the Royal Society's gregarious curator of experiments, Robert Hooke. He loved chocolate and gossip, which the coffeehouses served in equal measure with coffee. Hooke was probably one of the first Royal Society members whom Dampier met in London, along with the two old Jamaica hands Hans Sloane and Lord Vaughan. Sloane shared Dampier's enthusiasm for plants and natural history. Vaughan, Jamaica's governor from 1674 to 1678, had been president of the Royal Society from 1686 to 1689. According to the normally broad-minded Pepys, he was 'one of the lewdest fellows of the age', but he was also an influential patron of the arts, in particular of Dryden. Lord Vaughan took a keen interest in Dampier's travels. He and Dampier discussed 'a sort of white cocoa' used by the Spanish to 'make their chocolate froth' – Vaughan was the only other person Dampier could find who had actually seen this early version of a cappuccino. Sloane and Vaughan would certainly have told Dampier about the Royal Society's *Directions for Seamen Bound for Far Voyages*.

Dampier also discussed his work with Sir Robert Southwell, president of the Royal Society from 1690 to 1695. Under his presidency the society had encouraged one of its members, geologist and physician John Woodward, to produce *Brief Instructions for Making Observations and Collections in All Parts of the World in Order to Promote Natural History*. Published in 1696, while Dampier was working on his draft, it went much further than the society's earlier *Directions for Seamen*. The new guide covered all aspects of natural history and topography, as well as the native inhabitants of 'remote' countries. Examples of the detailed instructions covered in its twenty pages were:

> As to the vegetable and animal productions observe whether the country be fruitful or barren; what kinds of trees, flowers and herbs it produceth that we have, and what kinds that we have not, in England . . . Also, what fowls, what beasts, serpents, lizards; what flies, moths, locusts . . . what other insects; what tortoises, snails or other creatures covered with shells are found living upon the earth . . . As to the bodies [of the native peoples] observe the features, shapes and proportions of them . . . their eyes whether large or small . . . their hair, long or short and curled or woolly . . . observe likewise whether they paint their bodies. Enquire into their notions touching the supreme God . . . whether they pay any worship or reverence to the sun, the moon . . . Get an account of their lives and civil government, their language, their learning . . .

In the months before his book's publication, Dampier significantly expanded his text to include more of precisely this sort of data. The evolution of *A New Voyage* can be traced by comparing the published version with the much shorter only surviving draft. Now in the British Library, it was written by a copyist but contains neat corrections and additions in Dampier's own hand. Many vivid passages detailing the natural history and inhabitants of the places Dampier visited are simply not there. Dampier added them later, probably at the suggestion of his new acquaintances, who may have provided extra snippets of information from their resources. As he later acknowledged, like 'the best and most eminent authors', he was not ashamed to have had his work 'revised and corrected by friends'. However, the finished product was very much Dampier's own, centred on his unique personal observations and experiences of far-flung places.

Dampier's amendments changed the character of his book. While the draft resembled the 'true account' type of adventure narrative like that published anonymously a few years earlier about Captain Barthlomew Sharp's voyage and by Alexander Exquemelin about the buccaneers in the Caribbean, *A New Voyage* offered the reading public a detailed and accomplished travelogue of a type not seen before, combining action with natural wonders and experiences of everyday life in exotic places.

Dampier added a preface and dedicated his book to the new president of the Royal Society and chancellor of the exchequer, Charles Montague, Earl of Halifax. Both the dedication and the preface showed how thoroughly Dampier had understood the society's objectives, which, in any case, mirrored his own approach. He expressed 'a hearty zeal for the promoting of useful knowledge and of anything that may never so remotely tend to my country's advantage'. He was also 'desirous to bring in my gleanings here and there in remote regions to that general magazine of knowledge of foreign parts' of which the Royal Society had 'custody'.

★ ★ ★

Dampier had chosen a good time to publish. The period from the Restoration of Charles II in 1660 to the end of the seventeenth century saw a publishing explosion, stimulated by the culture of curiosity and a greater freedom of thought and expression. This was the dawn of the Age of Enlightenment. People were becoming outward- and forward-looking, rather than turning inward and backward to supposed 'golden ages'. Reflecting the fluidity of society, authors were valued for what they wrote and what they knew, not for their position in society. For example, Britain's first female professional playwright, Aphra Behn, began to write plays such as *The Rover* to support herself. Following their success, she turned to writing prose romances, developing them into the forerunners of the novel. Her book *Oroonoko*, or *The Royal Slave*, drew on her own colourful experiences as an impoverished young woman supporting herself as best she could in the West Indies, to portray life there authentically.*

Such romances were, however, only one among many new publications, some of which were aimed at special-interest groups. The published account of the Royal Society's work, the *Philosophical Transactions*, became the world's first scientific journal. Royal Society fellow John Houghton in 1692 produced the first agricultural journal. The first report of crop circles merited a pamphlet of its own, *The Mowing Devil*, or *Strange News Out of Hertfordshire*. The phenomenon was attributed to 'some infernal spirit

Oroonoko was the first work in English literature to express sympathy for the lot of the slave.

[since] no mortal man was able to do the like'. Britain's first general magazine – the monthly *Gentleman's Journal* of 1692 – contained articles, poems and an original composition each month by composer Henry Purcell. The first guide-book to London appeared in 1693, complete with a five-day programme of suggested sight-seeing. At about the same time, book lovers welcomed their first periodical, the *Works of the Learned*, dedicated to reviewing books 'newly-printed, both foreign and domestic'.

Newspapers, too, were proliferating. In March 1691, at the sign of the Black Raven in a street in London known as Poultry, John Dunton produced the *Athenian Gazette* (later the *Athenian Mercury*) to answer 'all the most nice and curious questions proposed by the ingenious of either sex'. Questions included what became of the water after the Flood and whether mermen existed.* As a spin-off, Dunton produced the first women's magazine – the *Ladies' Mercury* – which consisted solely of 'problem pages', explicitly answering women's questions about relationships ranging from adultery to man-management. Dunton was quick to appreciate Dampier's contribution to the flood of literary innovation, writing a little enviously that in purchasing Dampier's work his publisher, James Knapton, showed he knew how 'to value good copy'.

Dunton was right. Dampier's literary success was extraordinary. *A New Voyage Round the World* ran to three printings within nine months and was rapidly translated into several foreign languages. It spawned a market for travel books, which for many years thereafter remained the public's favourite reading. As is usual for this period, there

---

*Answer 'yes', but they were part of original Creation, not monsters got 'in unnatural copulation'.

A

New Voyage

ROUND THE

WORLD.

Deſcribing particularly,

The *Iſthmus* of *America*, ſeveral Coaſts
and Iſlands in the *Weſt Indies* , the
Iſles of *Cape Verd*, the Paſſage by *Terra
del Fuego*, the *South Sea* Coaſts of *Chili,
Peru*, and *Mexico*; the Iſle of *Guam* one
of the *Ladrones*, *Mindanao*, and other
Philippine and *Eaſt-India* Iſlands near
*Cambodia, China, Formoſa, Luconia, Ce
lebes*, &c. *New Holland, Sumatra, Nicobar*
Iſles ; the *Cape* of *Good Hope*, and *Santa
Hellena.*

THEIR
Soil, Rivers, Harbours, Plants, Fruits, Animals, and Inhabitants.

THEIR
Cuſtoms, Religion, Government, Trade, &c.

By *William Dampier.*

Illuſtrated with Particular Maps and Draughts.

LONDON,
Printed for *James Knapton*, at the *Crown* in St *Paul's*
Church-yard. M DC XCVII.

The title page of Dampier's A New Voyage, *1697.*

are no records of print runs, but some measure of
Dampier's success can be gauged by comparison with
Daniel Defoe's *Robinson Crusoe*. Published twenty years
later and the most popular secular book of its time, it built
on the appetite for travel first created by Dampier and
borrowed heavily from him. Even so, it sold only slightly

better than *A New Voyage* (four printings in eight months).

The Royal Society also thought *A New Voyage* was 'good copy'. Robert Hooke immediately produced a summary for the society's *Transactions*. He commended the 'diligence' of Dampier's observations in places 'for the most part unknown to English navigators' and praised his 'very intelligible and expressive' style. The society invited Dampier to address its meeting on 10 March 1697. The recorded discussion centred mainly on the worms that had infested his leg, both during his time at Campeachy and in Virginia. His findings were subsequently mentioned a number of times in the society's deliberations, and they received through him a paper from his brother George suggesting a possible, if unlikely, cure for rabies, to which they gave considerable attention and credence.

Robert Hooke also noted in his summary that Dampier had promised a more extended work on winds and the sea. Many of the Royal Society's major figures had contributed to its marine work, including Hooke himself. He believed that much of England had once been under the sea, and that earthquakes had been responsible for raising above sea level those areas where marine remains were found. Contrary to religious teaching, he was convinced that certain species of plants and animals had become extinct, and that their demise might have been caused by climate change and other natural catastrophes. Hooke also believed that the motion of the sea was caused by the shock passed to it by movements of the Earth, in much the same way as Galileo had supposed that tidal forces were generated.

Hooke's implacable adversary Isaac Newton had published his definitive work *Principia Mathematica* in 1687. This established, among many other things, that the tides were caused not by the Earth's movements but by the gravitational attraction of the sun and moon. Seminal as Newton's work was, it was in Latin and did not gain ready acceptance, not least because the intensely reclusive, paranoid Newton detested 'smatterers' bothering him with their questions. He much preferred to immerse himself in his experiments on alchemy.

However, the desire to express findings in clear, simple English, not the increasingly outdated and academic Latin, was central to the Royal Society's aims. Writing in 1667, the society's first historian, Thomas Sprat, described its wish for prose to return to 'primitive purity'. The fellows believed their role was to promote 'a close, naked, natural way of speaking . . . preferring the language of artisans, countrymen and merchants before that of wits or scholars'. Therefore, because the original was 'very little understood by the common reader', the more gregarious and flamboyant Edmund Halley felt compelled to produce an English summary of Newton's work on the tides in the Royal Society's *Transactions* for March 1697. This was the same month that he attended the Royal Society meeting at which Dampier spoke.

Halley himself benefited seamen by giving them better star charts and researching how winds arose and where they occurred. He also produced and tested a series of novel diving bells.

Before his death in 1691, Robert Boyle had established the framework of modern chemistry and formulated his law on gas pressure, but he had worked on marine topics too. Using information from travellers who had habitually cooled wine in the tropics by lowering bottles deep into the sea, he concluded that the sea was generally colder the deeper one descended. He disproved the old theory that

Edmund Halley.

water was weightless in its proper position through experiments that showed how water pressure increased with depth. He argued that the sea floor had to resemble the land, with peaks, plains and precipices.

Encouraged by the Royal Society's interest, Dampier was soon hard at work fitting a 'second part for the press'. His publisher James Knapton was, according to his rival John Dunton, a conscientious businessman, 'not the sort of animal that flutters from tavern to playhouse and back again'. He had lost no time in signing up other writers of travel books such as Lionel Wafer and a certain Captain William Hacke, who produced a compendium including

Voyages and Descriptions.

Vol. I I.

In THREE Parts, *viz.*

1. A *Supplement* of the *Voyage round the World*, Describing the Countreys of *Tonquin*, *Achin*, *Malacca*, &c. their Product, Inhabitants, Manners, Trade, Policy, &c.

2. Two Voyages to *Campeachy*; with a Description of the Coasts, Product, Inhabitants, Logwood-Cutting, Trade, &c. of *Jucatan*, *Campeachy*, *New-Spain*, &c.

3. A Discourse of Trade-Winds, Breezes, Storms, Seasons of the Year, Tides and Currents of the *Torrid Zone* throughout the *World* : With an Account of *Natal* in *Africk*, its Product, Negro's, &c.

By Captain *William Dampier*.

Illustrated with Particular Maps and Draughts.

To which is Added,

A General I N D E X to both Volumes.

LONDON,
Printed for *James Knapton*, at the *Crown* in *St Pauls* Church-yard. M DC XCIX.

The title page of Dampier's Voyages and Descriptions, 1699.

Captain Sharp's account of his voyage and Ambrose Cowley's account of the *Bachelor's Delight*. Knapton judiciously whetted readers' appetites by advertising Dampier's sequel eight months before publication.

This second book, *Voyages and Descriptions*, appeared in early 1699, the same year as Wafer's and Hacke's books, which Knapton was careful to associate with Dampier's voyages. *Voyages and Descriptions* contained three separate sections, all prefigured in Dampier's first book: 'A Supplement to the Voyage Around the World', providing further exotic details about his time in Tonquin and the East Indies; 'A Voyage to Campeachy', about his time among the logwooders; and his main technical work, 'A Discourse of Trade Winds, Breezes, Storms, Tides and Currents'.

Dampier designed the 'Discourse' primarily for the practical benefit of voyagers, relating, for example, 'I took notice of the risings of the tides; because by knowing it, I always knew where we might best haul ashore and clean our ships'. However, he went much further than providing highly useful accounts of previously unknown coasts and landing places. On the basis of his worldwide soundings and observations, Dampier provided evidence that validated Robert Boyle's theory about the variations of the sea floor. Dampier stated that where there were sea cliffs, anchorages were always deep, and that where the coast was uneven, so was the ground offshore. While this relationship may appear obvious today, at the end of the seventeenth century people knew very little of the undersea world and could see no reason for such detailed work by their Creator in an environment impenetrable by man. Evidence that the sea floor resembled the land also gave credence to Hooke's theories about changes in sea level.

The breadth of his experience meant that Dampier could authoritatively compare and contrast phenomena and thus demystify them. He was, for example, the first to recognize that 'only the name' differentiated the hurricanes of the West Indies from the typhoons of the East Indies. 'I am apt to believe', he wrote with almost academic acerbity, 'that both words have one signification, which is, a violent storm'.

Most important, Dampier in the 'Discourse' produced major advances in the knowledge of how tides, winds and currents are distributed and the mechanics of their global interaction. The reasons for the movement of the sea and its tides and currents had long been debated, as had the reason that water flowing from rivers into seas did not cause them to overflow. As recently as 1665, an influential and respected academic, the Jesuit Athanasius Kircher, had suggested that the entire world's oceans were regulated and saved from stagnation only by the circulation of their water through the Earth's centre, entering at the North Pole and out through the South, as well as by gurgling sub-terranean passages between seas. Dampier dismissed the possibility of such a passage beneath the Panamanian isthmus in his 'Discourse'.

Dampier provided detailed information on tides, which he described as running forwards and back again twice daily and being most strongly felt near coasts. He also generalized on differences in tide patterns, observing that 'islands lying far off at sea, have seldom such high tides as those that are near the Main'. He distinguished between tides and currents. He found currents flowed farther out from shore and were much more constant in their direction of flow. He identified that 'in all places where the trade [wind] blows, we find a current setting with the wind'. He then deduced that the winds were the causes of the currents, the first time this key connection had ever been made. He was also the first to describe what hydrographers now call the monsoon currents in the Indian Ocean, the Benguela Current, the North Brazil Current, the Gulf Stream, the Peru Current, the southern end of the California current, and the

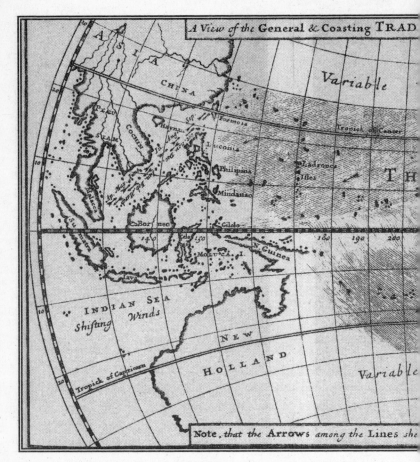

*From the original edition of Dampier's 'A Discourse of Trade Winds,
Breezes, Storms, Tides and Currents', part of his Voyages and
Descriptions of 1699.*

equatorial currents around the world. Dampier's descriptions of all these currents were essentially correct and a major advance in hydrography.

Dampier's 'Discourse' included for the first time careful maps of the winds across the world's oceans, produced on the basis of his data and drafts by Herman Moll. Unlike the

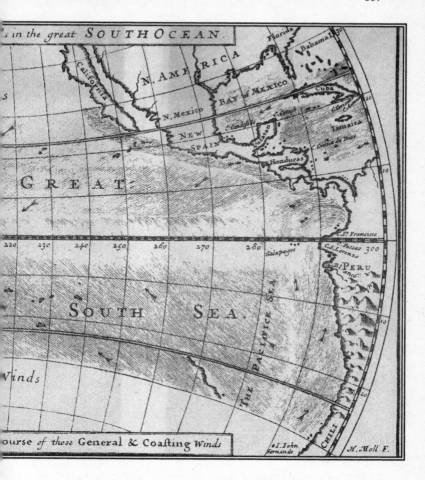

maps produced at this time by Edmund Halley, they
included the winds of the Pacific Ocean and thus provided
the first integrated picture of wind flows round the world,
becoming the model for the many globes showing the
winds produced throughout the eighteenth century.
Another innovation was to use shade and arrows to 'show

the course of the shifting trade winds'. Dampier gave much greater detail of coastal winds. His maps uniquely indicated the reversal of the monsoons 'wherein rains follow the sun and begin on either side of the Equator within a little while after the sun has crossed the Equinox and so continues till after his return back again'. Since Dampier correctly associated winds and currents, his wind maps are often regarded as giving the first clear and integrated picture of ocean current flows, in particular round the tropics.*

A few years later, Edmund Halley suggested that rain derived from water vapour evaporated from the sea. Condensed by cold, it fell again as rain, often in mountainous regions, feeding the streams and rivers and eventually returning to the sea in a self-sustaining cycle. Therefore, within a period of less than twenty years, the great issues relating to the movement of the sea were solved by Newton's and Halley's work on tides and the origin of rain and by Dampier's work on winds, tides and currents.

*Modern hydrographers have been especially impressed that, in the chart of the Pacific, the zone of intertropical convergence is correctly shown north of the equator.

XIX

'DAMPIER'S *VOYAGE* TAKES
SO WONDERFULLY'

The reviewers in the new literary magazine the *Works of the Learned* praised the vicarious spice and excitement that Dampier brought the armchair traveller. They correctly recognized that what made Dampier's new kind of travel writing a best-seller was the accessibility of his writing and the exoticism of his experience, not information about subterranean channels, winds and tides, nor even details of the migration patterns of turtles.

Dampier acknowledged in his preface to *A New Voyage* that he was writing for the general reader by including more information than the learned reader might need, 'rather than to omit what I thought might tend to the information of persons no less sensible and inquisitive, though not so learned or experienced'. He offered his reader 'many things wholly new to him and many others more fully described than he may have seen elsewhere'. He explained how his relatively random wanderings as a real traveller gave him considerable advantages over others journeying with a particular purpose on a particular timetable. 'One who rambles about a country can usually give a better account of it than a carrier who jogs on to his inn without ever going out of his road'.

Dampier confessed, 'As to my style, it cannot be expected that a seaman should affect politeness . . . for were

I able to do it yet I think I should be little solicitous about it in a work of this nature . . . for I am persuaded that if what I say be intelligible, it matters not greatly in what words it is expressed'. These sentiments were in line with the Royal Society's thinking, but they underrated Dampier's abilities as a writer and obscured the considerable pains he took to polish his draft. He wrote with credibility and originality and did not sensationalize. Using familiar comparisons and known reference points, his works conjured vivid pictures of a variety of scenery, people, experiences and actions, both good and bad. The texture of the durian in the mouth was, for him, like cream, part of the South American coastline looked like Beachy Head, cotton was like thistledown, a centipede was as big as a goose quill, and the stormy petrel 'not much unlike a swallow'.

Dampier brought many words into the English language, such as *posse*, *parade* (as in a row of buildings), *serrated*, and *tortilla*, but he also developed and extended the meaning or use of numerous others. He introduced *stilts* to describe house supports, *rambling* as an adjective to describe a life given to wandering, *caress* as a verb, *gentle* to describe the angle of a slope, *fair* to describe handwriting, and *slope* as an intransitive verb meaning 'to assume a sloping position'. He also brought together the words *sea* and *lion* and *sea* and *breeze*.

One of the joys of his books was his somewhat naive authorial voice directing the reader back and forth between the voyage narrative and detailed digressions on his experiences of nature. For example, he contrasted the characteristics of the crocodile and the alligator in meticulous scientific detail, then plunged straight into a hair-raising tale of an Irish logwooder seized by the leg by an alligator. The man 'waited till the beast opened his jaw to take better hold because it is usual for the alligator to do so and then snatched away his knee and slipped the butt-end of his gun in the room of it' and then shinned up a tree until his friends chased the alligator away with firebrands. Dampier ended reassuringly, 'This was all the mischief that ever I heard was done in the Bay of Campeachy by the creatures called alligators'.

The draft of *A New Voyage* was in some ways more revealing of Dampier's personality than the published version, for it contained more personal comment and cynical asides. It was more sardonic and censorious of the actions of his colleagues, often reflecting Dampier's belief that, had they only paid him more heed, events would have turned out better.

Many of the deletions and changes to the draft reflected Dampier's struggles about how much to reveal of his companions' more dubious activities. He was clearly anxious to distance himself from them and to present his own role in the best possible light to respectable society – as an innocent voyager, tagging along with the buccaneers merely to satisfy his curiosity. He talked disparagingly of 'pirating fellows' and omitted descriptions of the arguments about divisions of spoils that had led to the separation of Davis's and Eaton's ships and his own part in them and in foiling a mutiny against Davis. Perhaps because he remained troubled and uneasy about it, his role in the desertion of Captain Swan on Mindanao was the subject of much crossing out and amendment in his own hand in the draft and further changed in the final text, including the introduction of new material emphasizing how, later in the voyage, he tried to persuade the *Cygnet*'s crew to return and rescue Swan.

At the end of the draft Dampier wrote in his own spiky hand a justification of his suitability to write about his voyages. Nervous pride and conceit, mock and real humility, petulance and paranoia all seem to have bubbled through his stream of consciousness as he scrawled his scarcely puncuated note. Despite, he wrote, being 'neither master [captain] nor mate of any of the ships . . . all that knew me well did ever judge my accounts were kept as exact as any man's'. In any case, he believed that most of the commanders 'besides Captain Swan were wholly incapable of keeping a sea-journal and took no account of any actions. Neither did they make any observations . . . Yet such is the opinion of most men that nothing pleases them but what comes from the highest hand though from men of the meanest capacities'.

Then Dampier seemed to realize that this self-promotion and denigration of others might not create the right impression. He continued: 'But I fear I am too prolix in this discourse. I am only to answer for myself and if I have not given a description of those places to the satisfaction of my friends I must beg pardon and desire them to blame the defects they find in these my writings on the meanness of my information and not in me who has been faithful as to what is written of my own knowledge or in getting the best information I could'. Wisely Dampier included none of his apologia in his final text.

In his preface to the published work Dampier did, however, rather disingenuously remark, 'As for the actions of the company among whom I made the greatest part of this voyage, a thread of which I have carried on through [the book], it is not to divert the reader, much less that I take any pleasure in relating them'. His implication was that the buccaneering backdrop was there only to explain why he was travelling.

Yet both he and his publisher well knew that action and adventure would attract more readers. There was a ready market for adventure books among the growing reading public, who thrived on accounts of derring-do on the edge of the law and the defiance and defeat of England's 'natural enemies', the French and the Spanish. Accordingly, in the revisions to his draft, Dampier took trouble to polish some passages about action so that the reader would experience and empathize with his adventures. For example, in his description of the open-boat voyage to Sumatra, he added his intimate reflections on life and fate to heighten the dramatic effect.

The published *A New Voyage* also displayed more of Dampier's thoughts about the cultural and intellectual movements of his day than did the draft. His thinking was liberal and sophisticated, impressively so for one whose opportunities for debate had been so constrained aboard ship. Perhaps his receptive mind had benefited from his recent coffeehouse discussions. Dampier may have met the philosopher John Locke in the coffeehouses through Herman Moll, who had acted as a courier for Locke during the latter's exile in James II's reign. He certainly met Locke – a fellow Somerset man – during the hearing over the Darien scheme and probably had the chance to trade ideas with him at first hand. Locke's view of a virtuous citizen as a man of 'large, sound, roundabout sense' who lived in a just society under laws made with his consent and who acquired 'all the materials of reason and knowledge' from experience matched Dampier's own. In 1690, Locke had written, in a passage with overtones of 'the noble savage',

that 'the state of nature' was 'a state of perfect freedom . . .
also of equality'. This gelled with Dampier's own belief in
man's 'natural liberty', though Dampier recognized that it
might sometimes conflict with another of his dearly held
convictions – the benefits of trade.

Trade was, to Dampier, a civilizing influence and a force
for good: 'For the more trade, the more civility; and on the
contrary, the less trade the more barbarity and inhumanity.
For trade has a strong influence upon all people, who have
found the sweet of it, bringing with it so many of the conveniences of life as it does. And I believe that even the poor
Americans, who have not yet tasted the sweetness of it,
might be allured to it by an honest and just commerce:
even such of them as do yet seem to covet no more than a
bare subsistence of meat and drink, and a clout to cover
their nakedness'. Dampier was convinced that it was man's
duty to better himself. Like others of his time, he believed
in a natural order with man at the pinnacle. The Earth and
its resources were there for him to exploit.

At the same time, Dampier perceptively worried that
trade could bring oppression, writing that some peoples
'who are still ignorant of trade' might be 'happier now,
than they may hereafter be, when more known to the
avaricious world. For with trade they will be in danger of
meeting with oppression: men not being content with a
free traffic and a just and reasonable gain, especially in
these remote countries: but they must have the current run
altogether in their own channel, though to the depriving
the poor natives they deal with, of their natural liberty: as
if all mankind were to be ruled by their laws'.

In displaying his store of knowledge, Dampier reported
only with 'the greatest caution' anything he had not been 'an
ear or an eye witness of' or tried out for himself, always

John Locke.

making clear what he knew from personal experience and what he had learned secondhand. For example, he wrote, 'I cannot omit to tell my reader what I learned from Mr Hill a surgeon upon his showing me once a piece of ambergris'. Dampier scrupulously acknowledged his sources, typically assuring his readers that his informant was 'a very intelligent person' or 'very sober and credible' and therefore to be trusted. In fact, Dampier's highest commendation of a colleague was to call him 'ingenious'. By contrast, his most severe condemnation was of a lack of rationality or curiosity. Chinese foot binding was 'unreasonable'; so too were the antics of his drunken comrades. The Aborigines' and the Hottentots' lack of curiosity and industry seemed to Dampier their greatest failings.

When analysing information, he was careful to compare and contrast experiences in different locations. He was able to tell his readers that the nuts of the coast near Caracas, though smaller than those of Costa Rica, were 'better and fatter in [his] opinion'. He described the different uses that different peoples from the Kuna of the Darien to the Mindanaons made of the plantain. He contrasted the behaviour of the Spanish, Dutch and Portuguese as colonists and analysed the reactions of the native peoples to their new rulers.

As in the case of St Elmo's Fire, which he dismissed as 'some jelly', Dampier always looked for a rational relationship for unusual phenomena. He would have had no sympathy with his contemporary, the sailor Edward Barlow, who attributed strange phenomena or unseasonal weather to 'witches' and 'evil spirits', capable of 'conjuring winds'. For Dampier such stories were merely the gossip of 'ignorant sea-men'.*

Whether he knew of the Royal Society's precepts at the time or not, Dampier intuitively followed them during his twelve-year circumnavigation by relying on experiment as well as observation to validate his facts. He tested the speed of native canoes by trailing a logline from one as it cut through the surf. He waited with interest to see whether it was true that eating prickly pears turned the urine red. Even his attempt to cure himself of dysentery by frequently washing in river water or drinking yogurt, or of dropsy by having himself buried up to the neck in sand, was a form of experiment.

---

*The Salem witch trials took place only five years before the publication of Dampier's first book.

Paradoxically, despite his success, Dampier's writing is unlikely to have made him much money. Both *A New Voyage* and its sequel, *Voyages and Discoveries*, cost six shillings each – a price which would have restricted purchases, even of a best-seller, to the better-off at a time when a live-in maid received only thirty shillings a year and an ordinary seaman only thirty shillings a month. However many copies were sold, Dampier's publisher, James Knapton, would have paid him a flat fee, and probably a low one, for *A New Voyage* since Dampier was, before its publication, an unknown mariner.* Although there are no surviving records, because of *A New Voyage*'s success, Dampier would have been paid a little more for his next books.† However, the shrewd Knapton would have been entitled to produce repeat printings without paying Dampier any more money. He almost certainly made more than Dampier from his works, even leaving aside the profits from books he published by Wafer, Hacke and others, profits which were considerably increased by their association with Dampier and the travel vogue he had created.‡ In the absence of copyright until 1710, Dampier would have been subject to 'pirate' editions and anthologizing as well, without further payment. For

*The current system of advances and royalties on books sold was not introduced until the nineteenth century.

†The highest sum paid in the seventeenth century to an author was £1,000 paid to Dryden for his *Virgil*, which astonished his contemporaries. Milton received only £20 for *Paradise Lost*, and Dampier may well have got less.

‡Others, too, borrowed Dampier's name and reputation. The third edition of Alexander Exquemelin's *Buccaneers of America* appeared nearly twenty years after its first publication and contained, as an additional feature, Basil Ringrose's account of his travels with Captain Sharp. The preface justified its worth, as publishers often do today, with a plug from a better-known writer, boasting that Ringrose was 'said by Mr. Dampier to be very exact'.

example, an anonymous writer produced a bowdlerized amalgam of Dampier's and Wafer's work when interest in Panama was at its height. Such imitation and the inclusion of Dampier's work in several anthologies were, however, symbols of success.

Despite the lack of pecuniary reward from the books themselves, Dampier did benefit from the reputation as a navigator and traveller that the books gave him. His work found its way into the libraries of many influential people, from that of the Helyar family of East Coker to those of Hooke and Locke. Dampier became something of a celebrity. Even official records refer to him as the 'celebrated author'. Thomas Murray was commissioned, probably by Hans Sloane, to paint Dampier's portrait, which still survives and which was for a long time in Sloane's own collection. Dampier must have been highly gratified by his new status. He met many well-known people, including the intellectual elite. If the main surviving accounts – those of John Evelyn, the celebrated diarist, author and Royal Society fellow, and man-about-town Charles Hatton – are typical, they were pleasantly surprised by both Dampier's intellect and his demeanour. Hatton, who had written with some surprise to his brother that 'Dampier's Voyage takes so wonderfully', conceded he was 'of better understanding than would be expected from one of his education'.

In August 1698, just three weeks after Dampier had appeared before the Honourable Council of Lords of Trade and Plantations and rescued Wafer, he was invited to dine at the house of Samuel Pepys. John Evelyn was also there and wrote that this once 'famous buccaneer' was 'a more modest man than one would imagine by the relation of the crew he had consorted with'.* Dampier brought with him a map of the winds in the South Seas and confidently assured his fellow dinner guests that 'the maps hitherto extant were all false as to the Pacific Sea'. He also told them that the Pacific lived up to its name only south of the equator, being 'extremely tempestuous' to the north. John Evelyn was impressed by his 'very extraordinary' adventures and 'very profitable' observations. In his *Numismata: A Discourse of Medals*, he recommended that a medal be struck to commemorate Dampier as one of the nation's 'illustrious persons' and 'great travellers', whose 'famous actions' should be acknowledged.

Official recognition was not far away. In January of the following year, 1699, just a month before the publication of his second book, Dampier was once again at sea. This time he was in command of a Royal Navy ship. His mission was to explore New Holland and the East Indies for his nation's benefit. His reputation and future prosperity seemed assured.

*Pepys had, by then, ceased keeping a diary himself because of poor eyesight.

XX

KISS MY ARSE

*I*t was not to be. The transition from buccaneer to naval captain was to prove uncomfortable. Three and a half years later, on 8 June 1702 in the great cabin of HMS *Royal Sovereign*, Dampier would stand to hear the verdict of the court martial convened to investigate accusations against him of brutality. Dampier would be found guilty of beating his lieutenant and confining him in irons. The court would rule that he was 'not a fit person to be employed as commander of any of Her Majesty's Ships'.

The expedition had begun auspiciously enough. Shortly after the publication of *A New Voyage* in 1697, the man to whom Dampier had dedicated it, Charles Montague, introduced him to the plump, choleric-complexioned Lord Orford, the somewhat corrupt, if highly efficient, first lord of the Admiralty – the head of the navy. Impressed by Dampier's achievements, Orford provided him with a sinecure as a 'land-carriage man' at the customs house paying thirty-five pounds a year. He also invited him to propose an expedition that would be 'serviceable' to the nation. Dampier pondered, then suggested a voyage of exploration to 'Terra Australis'. There was 'no larger tract of land hitherto undiscovered . . . if that vast space

Lord Orford.

surrounding the South Pole, and extending so far into the warmer climate be a continued land', he argued. Also, it was 'a country likely to contain gold'. Dampier held the common belief that gold was more often found in hot climates. Dampier assured Orford that he had spent much time 'among unknown shores and savage nations' and was fully competent to lead such an ambitious venture. Orford agreed.

Terra Australis was still shown on maps as a mythical land emerging far out into the South Atlantic and South Pacific from the polar region. The credulous believed it peopled with grotesque creatures whose heads sprouted from under their shoulders and who shaded themselves from the sun by lying on their backs and spreading their giant feet parasol-like above them. Dampier intended to begin his exploration of this mysterious southern region by returning to New Holland. Probably relying on accounts of Tasman's voyage round the west and south coasts of Australia, and New Zealand,

An English East Indiaman of the early eighteenth century, thought to have some similarities to the Roebuck, *of which no illustration exists.*

he apparently saw New Holland as separate from Terra Australis, but as blocking an approach from the west to that region and to further unexplored, unclaimed spice islands.

Dampier insisted on a free hand. A 'thousand accidents' could occur, and he wanted 'unlimited' discretion 'with respect either to time or place'. He was not sure how far the voyage would take him nor how long it would last, though he estimated three years. These uncertainties prompted him to ask, as Cook would seventy years later, for two ships, not one. He also sensibly suggested that his crew be offered some inducement to complete the voyage. No doubt thinking of Avery, he wrote that this was essential 'considering the temptations our seamen have had of late to break loose and turn pirate'. He also requested a good supply of iron bars, axes, hatchets, knives, beads, looking glasses 'and such like toys' to trade for supplies.

As it turned out, Dampier was offered only one ship, the *Jolly Prize*. He 'strictly surveyed' her and found her wholly wanting. Casting aside the courtesy and humility with which he had addressed Orford, he fired off terse notes to Admiralty officials, protesting that the ship was far too cramped and would never hold the necessary men and stores. The parsimonious, debt-ridden Admiralty listened and offered him a slight improvement: the 290-ton, twelve-gun *Roebuck* built in 1690 as a fire ship but in 1698 a fifth-rate warship.

Dampier insisted his salary as a junior customs official be paid during his absence. Mindful of the wife he was deserting yet again, he arranged for Judith to receive it quarterly. He then turned to the serious business of provisioning the ship with enough beer, water, beef and pork to last twenty months if necessary. He knew that nothing was more likely to undermine seamen's morale than 'pinching their bellies'.

By late October 1698, the *Roebuck* was in the Downs amid the pomp and glory of a royal naval squadron under Admiral Sir Cloudesley Shovell about to sail for Holland. Yet things were going amiss. The Admiralty refused to increase the *Roebuck*'s complement of men from fifty to the seventy Dampier believed he needed given the risk of sickness, which might 'disable' the expedition. A disappointed Dampier reviewed the officers chosen by the Admiralty. They included George Fisher, as lieutenant and second-in-command, and Jacob Hughes, as master. Feeling the need for some familiar faces round him, Dampier also included in the crew three former comrades from the Spanish

Expedition. John Knight, former gunner of the *Dove Galley*, was transferred at Dampier's request from HMS *Dunwich* and appointed chief master's mate. Andres Garsia Cassada, the Spanish former pilot of the *Charles II*, was made a quartermaster and James Gregson a midshipman.

Knight and Gregson quickly proved not to be the steady and reliable allies Dampier had hoped for. Drinking with the boatswain, Robert Warren, they were overheard swearing that 'when they came to sea they would heave the master overboard and run away with the King's ship'. While this may just have been drunken, vainglorious talk, it set up dangerous undercurrents before the expedition had even begun. Dampier gave Knight and Gregson the benefit of the doubt but decided that Warren – who seemed 'unwilling to go on the voyage' and 'very mutinously inclined' – had to go. The final crunch came over the discovery of a woman whom Warren had somehow smuggled on board. On 17 November Dampier had the boatswain confined to his cabin in irons until he could 'learn the truth of this matter'. Four days later he was removed from the ship to be court-martialled and dismissed from the navy.

Warren was not, however, Dampier's main problem. In early November, he had written anxiously to the Admiralty, hoping Sir Cloudesley Shovell would report favourably on the calibre of the men he had recruited and ignore comments from 'any ill affected person'. The 'ill affected person' he had in mind was Fisher. As a regular Royal Navy officer, he despised Dampier. To use his own words, 'he did not care a fart' for his captain. Dampier 'did not understand the affairs of the Navy'. Worse still, Dampier had been a pirate and probably intended to be one again. Fisher probably knew about Dampier's background because he had served in the Royal Navy under the captaincy of Kerrill Roffey, one of those abandoned on Mindanao with Captain Swan. After his return to England, Roffey had joined the Royal Navy and risen swiftly.

Fisher was also influenced by the scandal of Captain Kidd, Dampier's reputed shipmate of twenty years earlier. Kidd was an arch opportunist. From 1689 to 1690 he had been a privateer captain attacking the French in the West Indies. When his crew mutinied, he had swiftly recouped his fortune by marrying the wealthy, twice-widowed New Yorker Sarah Oort – just eleven days after the death of her second husband – who brought him New York property, valuable then as now.*

Dissatisfied with this wealth, Kidd hankered to command a British man-of-war and went to London to lobby. He failed to secure a naval post but, in 1695, became involved in a novel venture with Lord Bellomont, governor of both New York and the Massachusetts Bay Colony, and with the leaders of England's Whig government, including not only Dampier's sponsor, Lord Orford, but also the secretary of state, the Duke of Shrewsbury; the government's leading lawyer, Lord Somers; and the handsome, womanizing Earl of Romney, the master fixer of the age.†

---

*New York then occupied only the tip of Manhattan, below Wall Street, where a turf barrier, the width of the island, protected its landward approach. Kidd owned 56 Wall Street and other properties on Water, Pine and Pearl Streets, as well as a farm on the East River where Seventy-fourth Street now is.

†The Whigs were the first political party in English history, founded some fifteen years earlier. The name Whig, awarded them by their opponents, had apparently first applied to 'sour, bigoted, money-grubbing Scots Presbyterians'. The Whigs had been instrumental in the Glorious Revolution, which toppled James II and brought William and Mary to the throne, and, as a result, had formed the government thereafter.

These grandees secured King William's approval for commissions for Kidd to attack pirates and the French in the Indian Ocean.

Instead, Kidd, like Avery before him, turned pirate and harassed the pilgrim fleet, sailing from Mocha at the mouth of the Red Sea. Although repulsed by an English vessel detailed to protect the fleet following Avery's seizure of the *Ganj-i-Sawai*, in January 1698 he had seized the *Quedah Merchant*, stuffed with gold, jewels, silks, opium and sugar. Kidd confidently expected his powerful allies in England to protect him, but the political climate was changing. The Whigs' opponents, the Tories,* eager for any stick to lambast the Whigs, lampooned them as 'a corporation of pirates' for backing Kidd. They hastily disowned him, and he was arrested in New York by his business partner, Lord Bellomont.

Fisher feared that, like Kidd, Dampier was an 'old rogue' who would steal the king's ship.† Dampier's decision to appoint former comrades from the Spanish Expedition – men who had known Avery and one of whom was a foreigner and a Catholic – aroused the chauvinistic Fisher's suspicions. So did Dampier's retention of the buccaneer's distaste for corporal punishment and his consequent reluctance to have crewmen who had offended Fisher severely flogged, in line with naval practice. Dampier's reputation as a writer and celebrity mariner

---

*Like the Whigs, the Tories were named by their opponents, in this case after 'Irish Catholic brigands'.

†Ironically, in September 1698, just a few months before the *Roebuck* sailed, and prompted by Kidd's activities, Dampier had been summoned to advise the Honourable Council of Lords of Trade and Plantations on plans for an expedition to root out pirates operating in the Red Sea, but Fisher was probably unaware of this.

meant nothing to Fisher. Thus he failed to understand that Dampier had a status in society to protect and enhance through a successful voyage and no incentive to throw it away by turning pirate.

Dampier recognized that he was an outsider. He acknowledged frankly to Lord Orford that he was 'much a stranger to his Majesty's service'. The rough-and-ready world of the buccaneers had been little preparation for the formal bureaucracy of the Royal Navy. In particular, the final preparations were taking far too long. His plan had been to leave England by mid-September 1698 and go round the Horn so that he might have begun his discoveries 'upon the Eastern and least known side of the Terra Australis', as Cook would later do. He then intended to go northwards till he reached New Guinea. But, as he wrote with some bitterness to Lord Orford, the time of year was now 'too far spent', and he could not risk losing his ship by sailing round the Horn 'in the depth of the winter'.

In late November, Dampier at last received his final orders from the Admiralty, which reflected the letters previously exchanged. Because it was too late to brave the Horn, he was ordered to round the Cape of Good Hope, then to 'stretch away towards New Holland' and on to New Guinea and the unknown Terra Australis. He had, as he wished, complete freedom to alter his course as he saw fit, but the Admiralty underlined his duty to spare no effort to make discoveries for 'the good of the nation'.

This was to be the Royal Navy's first expedition dedicated to both science and exploration – the direct forerunner of royal naval voyages from James Cook to James Clark Ross, Sir John Franklin and Robert Falcon Scott. Dampier was to bring back specimens from the places he visited, including the inhabitants, 'provided they shall be willing to come along', and to keep 'an exact journal'. The Admiralty had provided 'a person skilled in drawing' who would be able to sketch birds, beasts, fishes and plants 'for the greater satisfaction of the curious reader'. Dampier replied that he was 'ready to sail with the first opportunity of wind'.

On the cold pale morning of 14 January 1699, the *Roebuck* set out. On 28 January, pushed on by fair winds, the crew sighted the Canaries. Dampier made for Tenerife to buy brandy and Verdona – a 'green, strong-bodied wine, harsher and sharper than Canary' – which he knew from his days in the West Indies kept well in hot climates. He anchored off the town of Santa Cruz, and the governor invited him to dine the next evening. However, Dampier spent so long exploring the nearby town of Laguna with its orange- and lime-scented gardens and pleasant green pastures, like the 'meadows in England in the Spring', that he arrived only in time for a late supper. The crew went carousing in the tippling houses.

The stay in Tenerife was marred by rows between Dampier and Fisher. According to one crewman, 'upon a very frivolous occasion' Fisher 'gave the captain very reproachful words and bade him kiss his arse and said he did not care a turd for him'. He finally apologized, but the truce was uneasy.

On 4 February, the *Roebuck* departed south for her next staging post: the Cape Verde Islands, due west of Senegal. A stormy northeast wind whipped up the sea. The cable broke as they struggled to weigh anchor under a darkening sky. Once under way, the *Roebuck* ran before the wind, ripping through the water and making good time. Only a week later, they dropped anchor off Mayo in the Cape Verde archipelago, frequented by English ships for its salt pans. The local inhabitants, 'round and plump as little porpoises', loaded some seven or eight tons of salt aboard.

Dampier had time to look round the islands, where, as a young man sixteen years earlier, he had watched 'brick-red' flamingos pick their dainty way across a lagoon. He recorded the birds he saw on this occasion with un-diminished interest, noticing that the heavy-bodied, short-tailed guinea fowl could not fly far and concluding that the only birds to fly long distances were those with long tails, which they used to change direction 'as a rudder to a ship or boat'. Some things, though, had changed. The number of bulls and cows was far smaller than when he had last visited the islands. Without a trace of irony, Dampier blamed 'the pirates who have since miserably infested all these islands'.

Dampier knew that the long voyage to New Holland would be both physically and mentally taxing to an already fractious crew. He therefore decided 'to touch once more at a cultivated place . . . where my men might be refreshed'. He also hoped that breaking the voyage would enable them to adjust 'gradually and by intervals to the fatigues that were to be expected in the remainder of the voyage, which was to be in a part of the world they were altogether strangers to; none of them, except two young men, having ever crossed the line [equator]'. The 'cultivated place' he chose was Brazil, and on 22 February the *Roebuck* set out across the Atlantic at its narrowest point, blown by the trade winds.

The atmosphere on board was worsening. Two days later, Dampier invited Fisher, together with the purser, doctor and clerk – all of whom the lieutenant disliked and distrusted – to share a bowl of punch. To the chauvinistic Fisher, the doctor and clerk had the particular disadvantage of being 'Scots dogs'. The purser was simply 'a great rogue'. According to Fisher, conversation turned to 'a pirate's life which my captain called privateer and he said their life was the best of lives'. Fisher indignantly replied that being in the king's ship was better 'for there every man could have justice'. He reminded Dampier of the fate of Avery's men: some hanged, others forced to skulk 'in strange countries' to escape justice. Dampier swore that if he were to meet any of them, 'he would not hurt a hair of their heads'. Fisher's pious response was that, as a commissioned officer, Dampier's duty to the Admiralty was to arrest 'all such rogues and pirates'. The exchange left the relationship between captain and lieutenant at rock bottom.

Dampier faced many problems without the support of his second-in-command. He had to keep his men healthy, despite humidity and increasingly heavy tropical rainstorms as they approached the equator. Yet some were 'ill-provided with clothes'. Others were simply too idle to change after a drenching or believed 'the heat of the weather' meant there was no point.* Dampier, who had seen scores of men sicken and die at sea, fussed over his already small crew with drams of brandy and ordered them to change their wet garments. Few listened. Instead they lounged in their hammocks 'with their wet clothes; so that when they turned out they caused an ill smell wherever they came'. The hammocks reeked horribly.

Dampier debated which Brazilian port to make for and decided on Bahia, 'the most considerable town in Brazil',

---

*The Royal Navy had no formal uniform until 1748, when they were introduced at first for officers only. Sailors wore the usual seafarers' dress of checked linen shirts and short baggy canvas breeches, sometimes tarred to protect against the wet.

which had a fine harbour guarded by a strong fort. He
hoped the governor would help preserve his ship from the
mutiny he feared was imminent.

On 10 March, the day the *Roebuck* crossed the equator,
Dampier and Fisher finally came to blows. The superficial
cause was Fisher's order to open a new cask of beer. Both
merchant and Royal Navy ships celebrated crossing the line
with rough humour, 'misrule' and heavy drinking. The
Roebuck was no exception. Late in the humid afternoon,
the men complained to Fisher that 'the beer was out' and
'they were a dry'. Without consulting, as he should have
done, either Dampier or the 'great rogue' of a purser in
charge of stores, Fisher gave the go-ahead to the ship's
cooper. As soon as he heard, an enraged Dampier sent for
his cane and for the cooper and 'broke' the cooper's head
for obeying Fisher rather than referring back to him. Next
he summoned Fisher, asked him why he had ordered the
cask to be broached and, according to Fisher, before he
could answer 'fell to caning' him. Fisher fled to the fore-
castle, pursued by Dampier, who ordered him to be taken
to his cabin, where, according to Fisher, he assaulted him
again.

Dampier's violent reaction seems to have been caused
by the rumours rife through the ship that there was a plot
to murder him. Dampier suspected Fisher was the ringleader and was both flouting his captain's authority and
currying favour with the men when he ordered another
beer barrel opened. Rather than releasing Fisher the next
day, as might have been expected if the effect of the day's
high spirits had been the cause, Dampier kept Fisher confined. Several days later, he ordered both the lieutenant's
legs put in irons. He would not even release him from his
cabin to visit the heads. Fisher shrieked abuse from the

stifling, stinking cabin, where he was forced to relieve himself. Dampier was an 'old pirating dog' who had 'only got a ship to cheat his king and nation'. When Dampier asked him to moderate 'his scurrilous language', he yelled that 'the captain might kiss his arse for while in confinement he would speak as he pleased'.

Dampier summoned the rest of his crew and demanded to know whether they were planning to mutiny, which the men denied. Dampier nevertheless took the precaution of sleeping 'with small arms upon the quarterdeck' with those of his officers he thought he could trust – 'it scarce being safe for me to lie in my cabin, by reason of the discontents among my men'. On 23 March, he was relieved to spy the Brazilian coastline. Patches of white sand glimmered 'like snow' in the distance. Dampier steered south for Bahia and was guided towards the harbour mouth by the lights of a Portuguese vessel ahead. The next day, Dampier sought permission from Portuguese officials to bring the *Roebuck* into the harbour. He anchored under the watchful eye of the fort in 'hot sultry weather with much rain', which probably did nothing to soothe tempers.

Dampier was soon walking through streets lined with tall, balconied houses to the governor's palace to lay his problems before him. The governor agreed to put Fisher in the common jail until a vessel could be found to carry him back to England. Dampier believed he was fully within his rights. His instructions from the Admiralty had given him licence to remove from the ship anyone who caused 'any disturbance' and to send them home to England to be 'brought to trial and punished for their offence'. On 28 March, master Jacob Hughes made a laconic entry in his log: 'This morning the lieutenant sent on shore and put here in prison'. He omitted to mention that Fisher was in irons and under an armed guard. Dampier later sent him his pistols, his servant and his journal, out of which, Fisher claimed, he had torn some pages.

Fisher languished in his cell for weeks, shouting abuse about Dampier into the street through his cell bars to anyone who would listen. He would finally be released and taken aboard a Portuguese man-of-war bound for Lisbon. He spent that voyage penning lengthy letters to the Admiralty, charging Dampier with everything from piracy to trying to have him murdered in Tenerife. He also accused Dampier of carousing with and failing to arrest a trio of Avery's men who were then in Bahia.

Careless of the problems that Fisher was storing up for him, Dampier did what he most enjoyed: roaming the countryside with his notebook. During the *Roebuck's* month-long stay, he catalogued Bahia's crops – from indigo to the cotton trees, whose pods burst open to reveal great lumps of cotton 'as big as a man's head'. The inhabitants used it to stuff pillows and bolsters. He craned his neck at soaring timber trees and examined 'bastard' coconut trees smaller than those of the East and West Indies. Perhaps reliving his brief days on the Bybrook plantation in Jamaica, he investigated the seasons for cutting the high fields of waving sugarcane. The sugar produced in Brazil was 'much whiter and finer' than 'that which [the English] bring home from [their] plantations'. In accordance with his instructions to preserve specimens, he plucked 'a good number of plants', which he 'dried between the leaves of books'.

The vivid, varied birdlife fascinated him. The four types of 'long-legg'd fowls' he saw wading in the swamps were, he decided, as 'near a-kin to each other, as so many sub-species of the same kind'. This reference to *sub-species*, in the first volume of the book he would publish on the voyage in 1703, was the first public use of the term and indicated Dampier's continuing interest in the order and degrees of relationship within Creation. His view that some types of animals and birds were more closely related than others was revolutionary and formally heretical. The accepted doctrine was that each had been created in precisely its present form and entirely independently during the seven days of Creation.

Dampier wrote careful descriptions of animals and reptiles from armadillos and musky-scented monkeys to alligators and venomous serpents. Some of the latter were 'vastly great', like the crafty anaconda which lurked in pools and tried to lasso passersby with its tail. Yet the green snake, no bigger than the stem of a tobacco pipe, was, he warned, among the most venomous and 'very common'.

Dampier observed the soft, idle life of the citizens of Bahia, pampered by slaves so numerous that they made up 'the bulk of the inhabitants'. He watched wealthy merchants borne over the cobbled streets in large, fringed blue hammocks suspended from long bamboo poles resting on the muscular shoulders of their slaves. Many kept black mistresses, who, Dampier was informed, made love potions from crows and were so passionate and possessive that they resorted to poisoning if given 'any occasion of jealousy'. A man 'who had been familiar with his cook-maid' confessed to Dampier that he 'lay under some such apprehensions from her'.

The mood on board the *Roebuck* eased. Not only was Fisher out of the way, but Cassada and Gregson, Dampier's former comrades from the Spanish Expedition whose presence had been unsettling, deserted. Perhaps they realized that Dampier had no intention of running off with the ship to turn pirate. Perhaps they thought celebrity and power had gone to his head. Whatever the reason, Dampier could reflect that 'in some measure the ferment that had been raised among my men' had been allayed. At least he had not felt compelled to take such strong measures as Sir Francis Drake, who, at a similar point in his round-the-world voyage in 1578, had executed his second-in-command, Thomas Doughty, for insubordination. Dampier set himself to 'provide for the carrying on of my voyage with more heart than before'. He had the empty beer casks cleaned and refilled with fresh water. Oranges, sugar and rum were loaded aboard.

In the midst of this activity, one of Bahia's leading merchants warned Dampier that he risked being murdered in the streets or poisoned. He had become too inquisitive for the Inquisition, which was watching him closely. His long rambles, insatiable questions and omnipresent note-book had roused suspicions. Once 'in their clutches', he was warned, not even the governor could help him. The merchant told Dampier 'to stay aboard' his ship, advice Dampier took. He spent his time composing a letter to be sent home to the Admiralty, reporting that 'the crew [was] healthy' but then in sombre language cataloguing the 'insolence' of Fisher. He explained that his only option had been to 'return home or get rid of him'. Probably antici-pating Fisher's accusations, Dampier also informed the Admiralty that three of Avery's men were then in Bahia. He would have arrested them, but he dreaded the effect of 'such infectious company' on his men. Instead, he had alerted the governor to their presence, with the hope that, like Fisher, they would be conveyed to Lisbon and thence to London for trial.

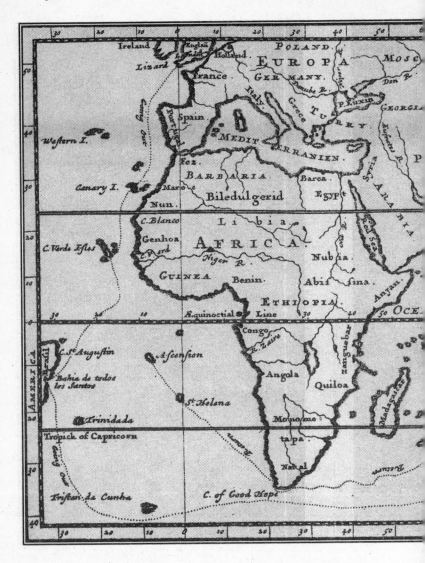

Map of the voyage of the Roebuck from the original edition of the first volume of Dampier's A Voyage to New Holland, *1703.*

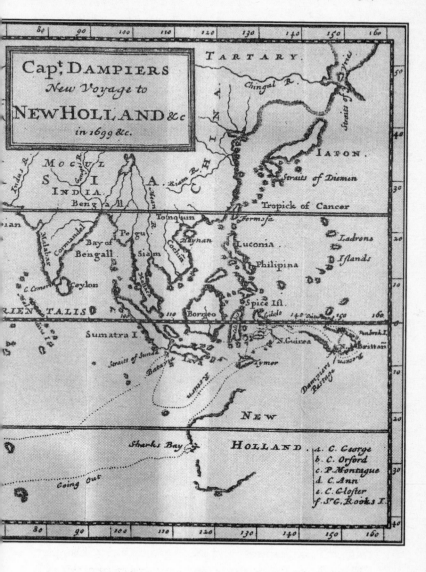

Cap.t DAMPIERS
New Voyage to
NEW HOLLAND &c
in 1699 &c.

On 23 April, the *Roebuck* rode to sea to begin her 'long run to New Holland'. The men amused themselves catching small sharks, which they boiled, pressed, then stewed with vinegar and pepper. Some of Dampier's men had been afraid to sail 'because their heads were generally filled with strange notions' of the 'southerly winds that were now setting in'. He had reassured them that these were only 'coasting trade winds' and would not hinder their voyage. Farther out to sea, when the 'true' trade winds began to gust them on their way, the men realized that Dampier had been telling the truth.

Dampier took great care with his navigation. In line with good practice and Royal Society guidance, he measured the variations of the compass at least once a day. However, the results puzzled him. He knew it was difficult to take exact readings at sea because of the motion of the ship and the inevitable deviations in steering made by the helmsman. '[But] what was most shocking to me, I found that the variation did not always increase or decrease in proportion to the degrees of longitude east or west', as he thought it should. He did not speculate in print as to the cause. Yet he continued to keep a careful table of all the variations he observed beyond the equator throughout his voyage for the benefit of future travellers and for analysis by the Royal Society.

The ship 'jogged on' eastwards towards the Cape of Good Hope, passing the putrid corpse of a whale on which thousands of seabirds were feeding voraciously. Dampier had 'never seen so many fowls at once' in his life. By 19 May, the daily water allowance was down to three pints per man, but Dampier had no intention of delaying further by putting in at the cape. Instead he steered east-southeast into the Indian Ocean, down towards the Roaring Forties, surrounded by the seabirds of the southern oceans, the albatrosses, shearwaters and giant petrels, soaring and swooping as they rode the air currents with their 'very long wings'. By early June, the weather had turned stormy. Dampier watched the sun set through a smoky black cloud radiating 'dusky beams'. Then it 'gilded' the cloud immediately above 'very prettily to the eye' like 'pure gold'. Higher up, other clouds were 'very bright' red. Dampier knew such gaudy light effects presaged trouble. Anticipating 'a violent blast of wind', he ordered the topsails reefed. Soon the wind was howling, and the seas surged high and white-capped. To Dampier's relief, the *Roebuck* was 'running so violently before wind and sea' that she shipped little water. By the time the winds dropped on 19 June, she had been blown some 1,800 miles in only twelve days.

Progress was slower thereafter, but in late July the water began to swim with seaweed, cuttlefish and minute jellyfish like 'white peas'.* By 30 July, grey birds 'big as lapwings' with black-rimmed eyes and sharp red bills – 'the like of which we had not seen in the whole voyage' – flapped round the ship. That afternoon, the sea began to ripple, as if they were passing over a shoal. Sailing on, they took soundings, but the water was still deep. Dampier ordered his crew to keep sailing eastwards and to keep a sharp lookout. At midnight he sounded again. This time he found the seabed at a depth of forty-five fathoms. Eagerly, he examined the sample adhering to the wax of the sounding line – 'coarse sand and small white shells'. Land could not be far.

---

*Darwin was particularly intrigued by these observations, reflecting on them in his famous red notebook when he visited the area in the *Beagle*.

XXI

SHARK'S BAY

Before departing on the *Roebuck* voyage, Dampier had obtained a copy of a chart made by Abel Tasman of his voyage round the Western Australian coast more than half a century earlier.* According to this chart, he should have been well south of the notoriously dangerous Abrolhos Islands, nearly fifty miles off the Western Australian coast, but increasingly shallow water and samples from the seabed showing coral mixed with the coarse sand convinced him Tasman's chart was wrong. He was still north of the Abrolhos and heading straight for treacherous shoals. Hastily, he gave the order to turn back to deep water and then set a northeasterly course.

As the light came up, a 'fine, brisk gale' pushed the *Roebuck* along. At 9 a.m. excited men high up the mast

---

*It is highly probable that Dampier had been given the chart in London by the prosperous merchant captain Thomas Bowrey, who had been 'extraordinary kind' to Dampier when he was ill in Achin in 1688. Bowrey certainly prized such a map from the commercially secretive Dutch during his long time in the East Indies and brought it home with him to London. It is now in the British Library, and, because of similarities in the misspellings of Dutch place-names between it and Dampier's book of the *Roebuck* voyage and other internal evidence, it seems clear that Dampier's map was based on Bowrey's. Bowrey had, since his return, been promoting business ventures in the South Seas and may well have advised Dampier on his plans.

sighted the coast of New Holland,* and by midday the shore was visible from the quarterdeck. Dampier's priority was to find a safe harbour. He could have turned south towards present-day Perth, but instead, continued northwards. As if to meet anticipated criticism, he would later explain in his third book that the areas closer to the equator and 'more directly under the sun' were those he most associated with abundance and wealth. There was also his old dislike of cold weather. Had he stood southwards, he feared he would have had to cope with 'a great deal of winter weather, increasing in severity ... in a place altogether unknown'. Furthermore, his men, 'who were heartless enough to the voyage at best', would not have borne it after the long run from Brazil.

Standing in towards land the next day, 1 August 1699, Dampier made out 'some red and some white cliffs'. As the *Roebuck* sailed cautiously up the coast, high winds and squalls of rain buffeted her. On 6 August, Dampier spotted an opening and made for it. The passage through labyrinthine shoals proved difficult and not dissimilar to the landfall he had made eleven and a half years earlier in the *Cygnet* in King Sound. He lowered the ship's boat to go ahead and take soundings – in one place the water was just nine feet deep. But on 7 August he entered a large bay and on its west side found a perfect anchorage – two miles from the shore in seven and a half fathoms over clean sand. He named the great, shining expanse of water, with its streaming ribbons of seagrass, Shark's Bay (today known as Shark Bay) because of the 'abundance' of these predators 'in this particular sound'.

*Probably what are now known as the Zuytdorp Cliffs north of the Murchison River in Western Australia.

Dampier at once despatched men ashore to look for water, but they returned empty-handed. The next morning, he went himself, taking pickaxes and shovels to dig wells and axes to hew wood. Although he did not know it, he had landed on the northeastern shore of a long finger of an island forming the bay's western boundary. He and his men trudged along a beach of brilliant white sand into the dunes beyond. Again finding no water, they wearily gave up the search to concentrate on cutting timber. Dampier also began to make observations of the bay and to collect specimens. The land rose gently from the sea. A white-flowered shrub resembling samphire grew close to the shoreline. Further inland, in the coarse reddish sandy soil, he found great tufts of grass. There were several trees and shrubs but none above ten feet high, their leaves whitish on one side and green on the other. Most had 'either blossoms or berries' – red, white, yellow, 'but mostly blue' – which smelled 'very sweet and fragrant'. There were also 'very small flowers growing on the ground that were sweet and beautiful, and for the most part unlike any I had seen elsewhere'. He was correct in recognizing their uniqueness: nearly all these plants were entirely unknown to botanists.

Dampier saw eagles and several kinds of small birds – the largest 'not bigger than larks', others 'no bigger than wrens', and all singing 'with great variety of fine shrill notes' – as well as 'waterfowl such as I have not seen anywhere besides', and asked his artist to sketch them. He searched for mammals but found only 'a sort of racoon' with 'very short fore-legs', which was 'very good meat'. (This was probably the banded hare-wallaby.)

He was less enthusiastic about the large, ugly, 'guanos'

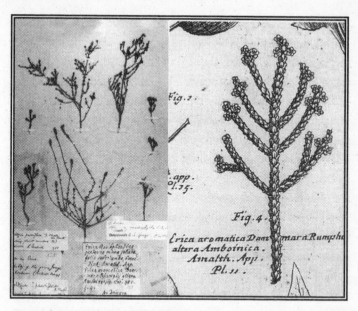

A specimen of **Thryptomene baeckeacea** *brought back by Dampier from New Holland and preserved in Oxford University, next to the illustration of the plant contained in Leonard Plukenet's book.*

– bobtail lizards – whose stump of a tail gave them the appearance of having two heads and which were speckled 'black and yellow like toads'. 'I have eaten of snakes, crocodiles and alligators, and many creatures that look frightfully enough and there are but few I should have been afraid to eat of, if pressed by hunger', Dampier later wrote, 'yet I think my stomach would scarce have served to venture upon these New Holland guanos, both the looks and the smell of them being so offensive'.

Green turtles, though, were consumed with relish. The crew caught two, weighing 200 pounds apiece, which had been left trapped on a rock ledge by the ebb tide and which fed the men for two days.

They also caught many sharks, which Dampier's men

ate 'very savourily'.* One was eleven feet long according to his reckoning and twenty feet long according to the more fanciful record of Jacob Hughes, the ship's master, in the logbook. Its stomach was like a leather sack, so thick they could hardly slice it with their knives. Inside they found 'the head and bones of a hippopotamus; the hairy lips of which were still sound and not putrefied'.† Dampier saved some of its teeth and the shark's great jaws.

Wandering the shores, he found mussel and oyster shells but also scooped up many 'very strange and beautiful shells . . . such as I have not seen anywhere but at this place'. They were 'most finely spotted with red, black, or yellow'.

On 11 August, with his men 'well refreshed' and 'much brisker than when he came in hither', Dampier decided to probe further into the bay, not only to continue his quest for water but also 'for the sake of discovering this part of the coast'. Slowly, cautiously, he explored the south and southwest of the bay, taking frequent soundings in shallow water that was never more than ten fathoms deep. The land looked unpromisingly barren, so Dampier decided to steer eastwards to see what lay there. The approach was hazardous through shoals and shallow water. The shore itself looked 'extraordinarily low', dotted with a few mangroves. It was 'very unlikely', he decided, that he would find fresh water there. Making for the entrance to the bay, he found two islands and a coral reef. He anchored and

---

*In Australia today the fish in fish-and-chips is often 'flake', as shark meat is euphemistically known.

†It was almost certainly the remains of a dugong, or sea cow, a mammal that is common in the area and, oddly enough, shares an ancestor with the hippo.

ordered the ship to be scrubbed, while sending men to reconnoiter the smaller island, which they found covered with 'green, short, hard, prickly grass' – spinifex – and without timber or fresh water. Dampier decided it was 'very improbable I should get any thing further here' and tried to regain the open sea by sailing east of the islands, but the water was not deep enough. Nor was there a deep enough channel between the islands. Anxiously, he returned to the westward channel where he had first entered Shark's Bay and finally sailed out on 14 August.

Ironically, Dampier had not noticed the evidence that he and his men were not the first European visitors to the bay. High on the cliffs of the island on which he had first landed was a pewter plate nailed to a wooden post. In 1616, Dirk Hartog had left a marker plate recording his brief visit to what he believed to be one of a series of barren, un-inhabited islands. In 1697, two years before Dampier's arrival, Willem de Vlamingh, who was seeking survivors from the wrecks of other Dutch ships, had entered the bay. He found and took Hartog's plate, leaving a pewter one of his own commemorating both visits.

Unlike the two Dutchmen, Dampier had made a thorough scientific record of the area and its 'unknown' flora and fauna – the first of any part of Australia. Besides his notes, he had with him both sketches and specimens. The plants were pressed between the pages of books, ready to be studied by the learned, 'ingenious', and 'curious' on his return.

The *Roebuck* continued northeasterly. Yellow, brown-spotted sea serpents thick as a man's wrist and four feet long swam through the clear water as the *Roebuck* shadowed the coastline. At times, rising winds pushed them out of sight of it, but Dampier was anxious not to be 'too far off from the land, being desirous to search into it where-ever I should find an opening'.

On 18 August, he recorded a previously unknown and dangerous 'shole-point stretching from the land into the sea' and took care to stay well clear. That night as they coasted the unknown shore in the soft darkness, an 'abundance' of humpback whales, all round the ship, made 'a very dismal noise'. It was unnerving to men whose nerves were already taut with uncertainty. Even Dampier was affected, writing, 'The noise that they made . . . was very dreadful to us, like the breach of the waves in very shoalwater, or among rocks'.

On 21 August, a day when the sea had seemed positively alive with sea serpents, they anchored at sunset on clean sand off the easternmost end of an island – later named Enderby – in a sea dotted with small islets, later to be called the Dampier Archipelago. Dampier suspected that they stretched all the way back to Shark's Bay. He even wondered whether there might be a passage through them 'to the south of New Holland and New Guinea into the Great South Sea eastward'. None of this fitted with Tasman's chart, which showed no islands. Dampier concluded that Tasman had not come in so close to the shore, which explained why he 'could not so well distinguish the islands'.

Weighing anchor next morning, Dampier sailed in among the islands, 'sounding and looking out well, for this was dangerous work'. He despatched a boat to an island to search for water, but his disconsolate men reported it 'very rocky and dry'. Gazing about in frustration, Dampier could see 'nothing but islands', some large, some small, but 'all appeared dry, and mostly barren', with 'rusty yellow' rocks. He landed, probably on what is now East Lewis Island, to dig for water, but found none.

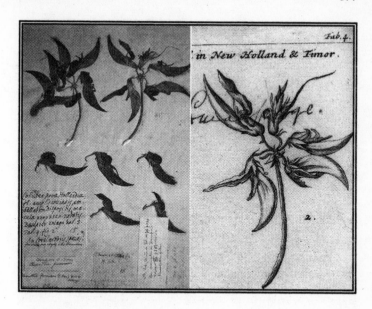

Dampier's specimen of Willdampia formosa, *the sturt pea, preserved in Oxford University, together with the illustration of it in Dampier's* Voyage to New Holland.

Several shrubs, however, interested him, and he plucked specimens from them. One was 'just like rosemary', though without that herb's pungent fragrance, and he named the island for it. He noted other shrubs with blue and yellow flowers and two types of grain 'like beans'. One grew on a bush, but the other was 'on a sort of creeping vine' with 'very beautiful', large, 'deep red' blossoms – the sturt pea.*

Flocks of 'a sort of white parrot' flew in clouds overhead. Along the shoreline the mariners found growing on the rocks an 'abundance of oysters', whose flesh was 'very sweet' and succulent.

While gathering specimens, Dampier noticed that some

*Preserved in Oxford University, Dampier's specimen retains its red colour.

A monkfish as sketched by Dampier's artist.

of the bushes had been burned, although there was no sign of inhabitants. However, a few miles away, a hazy trail of smoke rose from another island, suggesting it was inhabited and might have the fresh water they needed. At dawn the next morning, 23 August, they made for the island, but strong, persistent sea breezes frustrated them. Instead, they fished with hook and line, catching a monk-fish. Dampier thought it so unusual he asked his artist to sketch it, an image he included in his book.

On 30 August, after several days of gentle coasting, Dampier made for the mainland shore, anchoring in what is now Lagrange Bay. That night, there was a partial eclipse of the moon. The horizon was at first 'very hazy', but as the moon rose, Dampier and ship's master Jacob Hughes observed how 'there was two-thirds of his body darkened'. The next morning, Dampier and his men climbed into the ship's boat 'armed with muskets and cutlasses for our defence, expecting to see people'. Replenishing their limited supplies of fresh water was a constant pre-occupation, and they were also carrying shovels and pickaxes for the usual attempts to dig for wells.

As their boat was carried in on the swell, they saw '3 tall black naked men' standing on the sandy beach ahead of them, but they ran off. Dampier left two of his crew in the boat with orders to withdraw a little way out 'to prevent being seized' and set off with the others in pursuit of the three Aborigines, who reappeared with eight or nine others atop a small hill a quarter of a mile away. As Dampier and his men climbed through the sand towards them, they fled once more. Gazing down from the now-deserted hilltop, Dampier saw a savannah dotted with what looked to him 'like hay-cocks', which, on closer inspection, he decided were just 'so many rocks'. (They were probably termite mounds.) They searched for water but found 'none, nor any houses nor people', and plodded back to the beach to try digging for water there.

They were labouring hard in the heat when a group of Aborigines appeared on a nearby hillock and began 'menacing and threatening them' and 'making a great noise'. Finally, one bravely advanced towards the sailors. Dampier moved cautiously towards him, making 'all the signs of peace and friendship', but when they were still fifty yards apart, the man suddenly turned and sprinted off. Dampier tried several more approaches, to no avail. The people were 'so very shy' and would not let him near.

Dampier changed his tactics. Taking two crewmen – a 'nimble young man' named Alexander Beale and another – he set out along the shore. His plan was to capture an Aborigine, so they could learn where to find fresh water. At first it seemed their trap was working. A dozen or so followed at a distance. Reaching a sand dune, which momentarily concealed them, Dampier and his men hid. The Aborigines began searching, 'beating about the sand-hills'. Beale jumped up, cutlass in hand, and ran out at them. They fled and he quickly overtook them, but they turned and attacked him with their wooden lances. He was stabbed through the chin and struck out wildly with his cutlass, 'cleaving one part' of his assailant's head, but others closed in on him. Dampier, who had been chasing two others, saw that Beale was outnumbered and, 'fearing how it might be with my young man', came leaping over the dunes to his aid.

One Aborigine hurled a lance at Dampier, missing narrowly. Realizing that Beale was 'in great danger' and that he himself was 'in some', Dampier fired his gun in the air to frighten them off. The Aborigines wavered, but only for a moment. 'Tossing up their hands, and crying "pooh, pooh, pooh,"' they came on afresh 'with a great noise'. In desperation, Dampier reloaded and fired again, this time taking aim. One of the men fell to the ground, and in the confusion a blood-soaked Beale was able to stagger over to Dampier, who managed to get him safely back to the main group of sailors. The Aborigines picked up 'their wounded companion'. Dampier did not pursue them, 'being very sorry for what had happened already'.

During the skirmish, Dampier had noticed that 'among the New Hollanders' was a 'young brisk man' who seemed to be their chief. Although not very tall nor 'so personable as some of the rest', he was 'more active and courageous'. He was also the only one painted with a white paste or pigment. His eyes were rimmed, and a white streak ran from his forehead to the tip of his nose. His chest and parts of his arms were also adorned 'not for beauty or ornament' but, Dampier assumed, to make himself appear more fierce.

Dampier concluded that these people were 'probably the same sort' that he had encountered on his first visit to

New Holland. They were 'much the same blinking creatures (here being also abundance of the same kind of flesh-flies teasing them) and with the same black skins, and hair frizzled, tall and thin', he recalled, although he was unable to see whether they also lacked their two front teeth. Echoing his previous descriptions, he wrote, '[They had] the most unpleasant looks and the worst features of any people that ever I saw'. Dampier examined the traces of their fires, where piles of shells were always to be found. He concluded that 'these poor creatures' lived chiefly on fish.

Although his men had dug some nine feet down, they found no water. The next day, Dampier sent another party ashore to try burrowing yet deeper. While some dug, cursing the 'abundance of small flies . . . tickling their faces and buzzing about their ears', five armed sailors walked into the bush to stand sentry. They encountered about thirty Aborigines, 'many of them painted'. They were 'very shy' and kept their distance, 'leaping and dancing on the land'. Meanwhile, on board, Dampier observed the swift flow of the tide, wondering again whether there might be a strait or passage extending east to 'the great South Sea'. The landing party returned with some 'brackish water' from a well they had dug about half a mile inland. Although not fit to drink, the crew could at least use it to boil oatmeal for their porridge, or 'burgoo'.

As was his habit, even in extreme conditions, Dampier turned his attention back to gathering botanical specimens. The terrain was similar to the land he had seen on his first visit – low with long chains of sand dunes running like barricades down to the sea. Close to the shore the soil was sandy and dry and peppered with bushes and shrubs. Some were in flower with fragrant blossoms of yellow, blue and white; others had 'fruit like peascods'. He opened one to find in each 'just ten small peas'. Dampier was also struck by some 'strange shells'; not large, they were covered with spikes. Further inland the ground was 'very plain and even', part savannnah with thin coarse grass, and part woodland. On the banks of sea creeks he found small, black mangrove trees. They saw disappointingly few animals. His crew encountered just 'two or three beasts like hungry wolves, lean like so many skeletons, being nothing but skin and bones'. (They were probably dingoes.)

Dampier decided it was time to leave New Holland. He had failed to find 'any good fresh water', there was no 'convenient place' to careen the ship, and his men were 'already, and to my great grief, afflicted with the scurvy' and beginning 'to droop'. They needed 'fruits and other refreshments'. On 5 September the *Roebuck* put to sea, blown on her way by 'a gentle gale'. Dampier was leaving a place that instinct told him promised more, though he would not land there again. However, he had gathered unique scientific specimens and made observations, which fulfilled the goal of the first scientific exploration of Australia. As he later wrote with pride, he had 'found some things undiscovered by any before'.

XXII

'A FLAME OF FIRE'

$\mathcal{D}$ampier planned to revisit the spot further north in New Holland where he had landed on his first 'voyage round the world' aboard the *Cygnet*, if the need for 'sweet water' grew desperate. The 'brackish' stuff his men had dug out of the ground was making them ill. But reefs, dangerously shallow water, and 'great and uncertain tides' whirling about the ship forced them out to sea. Dampier consoled himself that 'better hopes of success' in finding fertile new lands suitable for settlement and trade lay in exploring New Guinea.

First, though, Dampier set a course northwards for the island of Timor to reprovision and give his crew some respite. Small white clouds hung in the sky, the first since Shark's Bay and a sign of the coming northwest monsoon. On 14 September, under a sky that had become threateningly black, Dampier and his men saw, to their 'great joy', Timor's high mountaintops 'peeping out of the clouds'. Dampier knew that both the Dutch and Portuguese had settlements there. He anchored about a mile off the low shore and took stock. Mangrove swamps stretched away towards mountains, where smoke rose lazily skywards and houses and plantations were visible. Ordering the ship's boat to be lowered, Dampier and some crewmen struggled through the mangrove swamps to reach solid land but

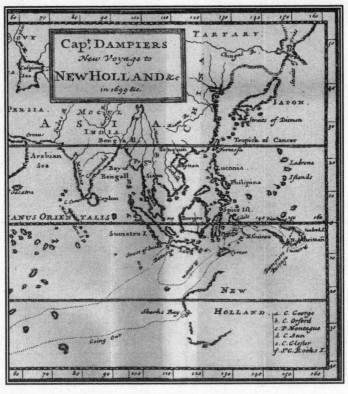

From the original edition of Dampier's
A Voyage to New Holland, *volume one, 1703.*

found them impenetrable. With darkness falling, they gave up, battling 'a rough short sea' to regain the *Roebuck*.

At dawn the next morning, they sailed eastwards, scouring the coast anxiously but finding only 'straight, bold, even shore' still 'barricaded with mangroves'. These trees – the only ones capable of surviving with their roots in salt water – continued to prove a formidable obstacle. Eventually, Dampier retraced his course, tantalized by rising wisps of smoke by day and the orange glow of fires by night. At last, a week after arriving, he spied 'an opening' and sailed cautiously in to find a good anchorage. Not long after, a sloop flying Dutch colours appeared. She was carrying the governor of a nearby Dutch fort, who, as Dampier wrote, informed the men of the *Roebuck* that he was most unwilling 'that we should come near their fort for water'. He added for good measure that the only place on that part of the island with fresh water was the fort, and that if the *Roebuck*'s men tried to land, 'the natives would kill us'.

Dampier assumed that the governor had taken his men for pirates, and that all would be well if he could convince him otherwise. He sailed towards the fort and anchored. On the beach were '2 or 300 Indians' armed with lances, swords and shields. They 'made a great noise all night'. Dampier took 'little notice of them', suspecting that the Dutch had sent them 'to scare us from landing'. The next morning, he despatched his clerk, James Brand, to assure the governor that the *Roebuck* was a Royal Naval vessel and to ask again for water.

The governor – whose little stone fort, in what was the Timor kingdom of Cupang, had been bloodily assaulted two years earlier by French pirates – remained suspicious. He harangued Brand, telling him his orders were to supply only the ships of the Dutch East India Company. He insisted that the *Roebuck* had come with the sole purpose of spying on Dutch 'trade and strength'. Brand replied that they were desperate for water. Even had they 'been enemies', they would have been forced to come ashore. At this, the governor relented. Provided Dampier did not sail closer, he would refill the *Roebuck*'s water casks. Dampier agreed, and the casks were replenished.

In gratitude, Dampier presented gifts to some Dutch officers who came aboard, while the governor sent him a

'very fat' little lamb. However, one of Dampier's officers –
he did not name him, but it was probably boatswain John
Norwood, whom Dampier subsequently confined to his
cabin – was fomenting trouble. Determined 'to make
everything in the voyage . . . seem as cross and discourag-
ing to my men as possible, that he might hasten our
return', this officer convinced his fellow crewmen that they
were about to be seized by the Dutch and flung in jail.
'Although I knew better', Dampier later recalled, he
decided to assuage his crew's fear by weighing anchor to
search for the Portuguese settlement instead.

Constantly seeking somewhere to land to search for
water, they made slow progress. On one occasion, the
Roebuck was pushed out to sea by the current, leaving a
scouting party marooned onshore. Dampier burned fires
on deck throughout the night and periodically fired a gun
to signal the ship's position. He was hugely relieved the
next morning to see the longboat making its way towards
them. Even better, the men brought two casks of 'very
good water' drawn from a small lake. They had also
identified a suitable anchorage for the *Roebuck*, where the
crew repaired their leaking ship and loaded more water,
which, though 'pale', was fresh and 'boiled peas well'.

Wandering around the lake, Dampier found signs of
human habitation – the rudder of a proa and a barbecue
over which fish and buffalo flesh had been dried. He led a
group into the forest to cut timber and was able from his
own experience to show his men which trees were worth
felling and how to strip the bark to make rope and twine.
They also went 'a fowling' through groves of sandalwood,
returning with the limp, gaudy bodies of parrots and
cockatoos slung from their belts.

Ship repaired, they sailed on, reaching on 12 October the

Portuguese trading enclave on a small offshore island with 'a great many houses' and large numbers of soldiers on the shore. Dampier sent a party to announce that they were English 'and came hither for refreshment'. The Portuguese replied that the visitors were 'welcome and should have anything that the island afforded'. Those of Dampier's men that were 'sick of the scurvy' quickly 'grew lusty'. Dampier's greatest concern, after the health of his men, was the increasingly parlous condition of his ship. He knew he must yet again clean and repair her before he 'could prosecute my voyage farther to the eastward'. He found a suitable careening place in late October. The *Roebuck*'s supplies of pitch were almost exhausted due to the carpenter's 'wilful waste and ignorance', but Dampier showed his men how to make lime out of shells, which they then mixed with water and smeared on the ship's hull. While they worked, they feasted on 'very fat and sweet' cockles 'as big as a man's head' and oysters so large and succulent that three or four were all a man could eat.

They had returned to near the Dutch settlement. A messenger arrived unexpectedly from the governor to invite Dampier to dine. Dampier afterwards wrote appreciatively of 'very good victuals and well-dressed', eaten off china plates. The evening ended amicably with the governor's earlier suspicions about Dampier's intentions apparently resolved.

Dampier had developed suspicions of his own. He believed the rival Dutch and Portuguese settlements around Timor were the 'greatest occasion' of continued wars between the natives, among whom each made allies to make war against each other by proxy. The Indians of Cupang, allies of the Dutch, were avid headhunters who displayed the heads of their enemies on the roofs of their houses or deposited these ghastly trophies in houses specially built for the purpose. One such house near the Dutch fort was 'almost full of heads'. Dampier suspected that the Dutch 'encouraged' them to such 'inhumanity' when it suited them. He politely declined the governor's offer of supplies, believing it would be safer 'to fish and hunt for provisions, than to be beholden to the Dutch and pay dearly for it too'.

On 12 December 1699, Dampier and his men left Timor, sailing eastwards into the rising sun. They ate sharks as they navigated cautiously through a maze of islands. On New Year's Day 1700, they sighted high, mountainous land 'very well clothed with tall flourishing trees'. Dampier had brought them safely to the unfrequented western coast of New Guinea.

Portuguese sailors had first sighted the northern coast of New Guinea in 1512. They named it Papua – land of the Fuzzy Hairs – but in 1545 the Spaniard Ynigo Ortes de Retes named it New Guinea because it reminded him of Guinea in Africa. No European nations had attempted to colonize this land of difficult terrain and warlike inhabitants, and it was still generally believed to be attached to New Holland. Dampier's is the first published work to describe the people and nature of New Guinea.

Soon, Dampier sent men ashore to look for water and hunt for fresh food. One man killed a bird of a kind Dampier had never seen before – a 'stately land-fowl', sky blue with white and red spots on its wings and a luxuriant crest of long feathers on its crown. They found signs of habitation – a 'shattered canoe' and a small barbecue – but no people. Two weeks later, continuing around the coast, they saw smoke rising from islands to the west and made towards them, hoping to trade.

As the *Roebuck* approached, two canoes paddled out to greet them. Dampier tried speaking to the occupants in Malay, but to no avail, and the natives retreated ashore. Dampier pursued them in the ship's boat. Nearing the shore, he saw men lying 'in ambush behind the bushes'. He threw 'some knives and other toys' onto the beach as a sign of goodwill and waited. Slowly, the men emerged, flinging down bows and arrows, swords and bone-tipped lances and 'making signs of friendship by pouring water on their heads'. They were almost naked except for a small cloth around their waist and bracelets of blue and yellow beads. Dampier signed that he wanted food.

The next day, the islanders ferried plantains, coconuts and other fruit to the *Roebuck*. They shared a communal cup of brandy with the sailors 'without scruple'. From this, Dampier deduced they could not be 'Mahometans', but he 'could not tell' their religion. Dampier wished to establish the potential for a spice trade, as well as to secure the information the Royal Society and others sought about religion. Therefore, he bought several nutmegs, 'which did not seem long gathered', but could not discover from his visitors whether they actually grew on the island. Searching for himself, he found no spices but encountered 'an abundance of bats', big as rabbits, with a four-foot wingspan and the acrid, gamey smell of foxes. He watched the islanders catch fish using a lure, a 'piece of wood curiously carved and painted much like a dolphin'. They attached a small weight to it, lowered it into the water, then suddenly and speedily yanked it up, tempting the fish to rise in pursuit so they could spear them.

By 4 February, the *Roebuck* was off the northwest cape of New Guinea among a scattering of islands. Dampier sent his men to forage, and they returned with a giant

Strange & large Batts on I. Pulo Sabuda in New Guinea described

A bat drawn by Dampier's artist.

cockle, the shell of which weighed 258 pounds. Sailing eastwards along the coast, the *Roebuck* crossed the equator, cutting through a sea that seemed littered with 'great logs' and full of dolphins and sharks. Another flotilla of canoes streamed out to greet the ship, their handsome occupants wearing ornaments of crab claws and white shells stuck through their noses and their hair 'cut in ridges upon their heads' and, like their faces and hands, spectacularly painted. Night was falling fast, and with 200 men bobbing in canoes in the seas around them and the shores 'lined and thronged' with many more, the *Roebuck* put back out to sea. Pursuing canoers used catapults to bombard the ship with stones as large as 'hens' eggs'. Dampier ordered his men to fire one of the ship's cannons, killing or wounding several canoers. The rest, 'amazed', remained where they were. Dampier, 'unwilling to cut off any [more]', continued out to sea.

On 3 March, they reached a large, hilly island with shores clothed in coconut groves. It was populated by 'very black, strong and well-limbed people' who shaved their hair into patterns, dyeing it red, white, and yellow. They had 'broad round faces with great bottle noses', which were 'agreeable enough' in Dampier's view, except for the ornaments they wore in their noses. 'As big as a man's thumb and about four inches long', the ornament ran 'clear through both nostrils, one end coming out by each cheek-bone; and their noses so stretched, that only a small slip of them appears about the ornament. They also have great holes in their ears, wherein they wear such stuff as in their noses'. Their canoes, handled expertly, were decorated with carvings and paintings of fish, birds and human hands. Though 'but rudely done', to the ever-observant Dampier, the artwork showed 'an ingenious fancy'. In line with Royal Society guidance, Dampier listened carefully to the words the canoers were shouting. He later reported in his book that their speech was 'clear and distinct'. Though he could not understand the words, it was obvious they were urging the crew to come ashore. Dampier was not prepared to risk it, but he did allow small groups aboard. He showed the native men nutmegs and gold dust, 'which they seemed to know', raising his hopes about possible riches to be discovered.

But wherever the *Roebuck*'s men tried to land, they found their way blocked by warriors on the beach or riding the waves in their canoes. On 18 March 1700, Dampier summoned his officers to determine whether they should stay longer and 'endeavour a better acquaintance with these people' or return to sea. Dampier's own preference was to remain. Perhaps aware of their captain's wishes, his officers agreed 'unanimously'. The next day, they managed to get on shore, where they encountered a group of forty male and female natives who simply made signs of

Natives of New Guinea.

friendship and walked on. The men were 'finely bedecked with feathers of divers colours about their heads'. The women 'had no ornament about them nor anything to cover their nakedness but a bunch of small green boughs, before and behind stuck under a string which came round their waists', and were balancing large baskets of yams on their heads. Dampier, eager as ever to make comparisons from across his travels and to understand the structures of the lives of those he met, recalled, 'This I have observed, among all the wild natives I have known, that they make their women carry their burdens while the men walk before [ahead] without any other load than their arms and ornaments'.

Dampier's men insisted on visiting another bay to hunt for hogs. Here they found 'great companies' of men menacingly brandishing lances. The nervous sailors discharged their muskets to frighten them away, then managed to shoot some hogs, to be cut up and salted for the voyage ahead. They also brought back wooden idols 'in the form of a man's face painted', which Dampier took possession of.*

On 24 March, as the *Roebuck* entered a strait, Dampier saw an erupting volcano – 'a great fire . . . blazing up in a pillar'. Sometimes the flames were dazzlingly high, at others they were scarcely visible. The curious Dampier brought his ship closer and recorded a formidable sight: 'The island all night vomited fire and smoke very amazingly; and at every belch we heard a dreadful noise like thunder, and saw a flame of fire after it, the most terrifying that ever I saw'. Meticulous observer and recorder for the Royal Society that he was, he timed the intervals between each 'belch' and noticed how some 'pulses or eruptions' were faint and others 'more vigorous', making a roaring noise, spewing flames thirty yards high, and sending streams of fiery lava burning their way down to the shoreline.

Dampier studied his charts in puzzlement. The passage ran between the 'easternmost part of New Guinea' and a tract of land yet further east that no other far-voyager had identified as separate. Dampier had discovered new land, which he named Nova Britannia, or New Britain. He hoped it would 'afford as many rich commodities as any in the world'. He began to bestow names on geographic landmarks, including those of King William and of Sir George Rooke, under whom Dampier had served twenty-seven years earlier on the *Royal Prince* and who was by then one of the lords of the Admiralty, as well as his patron, Charles Montague, for whom he named a cape.†

*Dampier also required a finely honed axe head of black stone, which is now in the Sedgwick Museum of Earth Sciences at Cambridge University.

†Dampier too was commemorated here. The strait between New Guinea and New Britain was named Dampier Passage. There is also Cape Dampier, Dampier Island and, on the south coast of New Britain, Roebuck Point.

Dampier could have sailed on southwards to fulfil what had been his original desire: 'to have begun my discoveries upon the eastern and least known side' of New Holland. Yet he reckoned that the *Roebuck*, in her ever-more-rotten, worm-eaten condition, might not last the course. This, he wrote, 'was one great reason why I could not prosecute my discoveries further'. Other compelling reasons to turn back included 'the fewness of my men and their desire to hasten home'. And so Dampier headed north again, showing an ability to calculate risk in abandoning his quest. A further seventy years would pass before another Royal Naval expedition under James Cook would seek, and find, the more hospitable eastern seaboard of New Holland. Dampier had been cruelly close.

XXIII

'NOT A FIT PERSON'

Dampier intended to touch once more on the west coast of New Holland, but currents pushed him westwards. He decided, instead, to seek the Trial Rocks, where the English ship of that name had been wrecked in 1622. He thought that pinpointing the location of these dangerous reefs would be 'of great use to merchants trading to these parts'. However, he had to abandon his plans because he fell ill. 'Having been sick 5 or 6 days, without any fresh provision or other good nourishment aboard, and seeing no likelihood of my recovery', he made for the Dutch entrepôt of Batavia, the modern Jakarta, on the west coast of Java. Batavia was notoriously unhealthy, but it was the nearest suitable place. The *Roebuck* arrived at the end of September 1700.

As Dampier's strength returned, he had the ominously leaking *Roebuck* careened. He learned that on 16 October a convoy of ships would be departing for Europe and joined them. By 30 December, they were at the Cape of Good Hope; by early February, at St Helena, the last leg of the journey lay before them.

In England, on 1 February 1701, the diarist Narcissus Luttrell was writing, 'Captain Dampier is daily expected home in the "Roebuck" from Batavia having (as tis said) been successful in discovering those lands he went in search of.' However, in the early evening of 22 February off

Ascension Island, the *Roebuck* sprang 'a great leak'. Dampier and his men pumped frantically, and he tried to sail in closer to the shore. The wind was in the right direction, and the next morning he anchored in a bay on the northwest of the island. Dampier ordered his gunner, Philip Paine, and his boatswain, John Norwood, the latter having been released from confinement sometime before, to clear the powder room, which seemed closest to the leak. As soon as it was empty, they began the search. The results were not encouraging. The leak was low down and inaccessible. Dampier's men suggested that the only way to reach it was to cut the inner lining of the ship, 'which I bade them do'. They sliced through and found a leak in the exterior planking round one of the curving wooden rib timbers bracing the ship. It was 'very large', and water gushed through with great force.

John Penton, originally the carpenter's mate but by then the sole surviving carpenter, insisted that this timber had to be cut away before a repair could be attempted. It seemed a desperate measure and was against Dampier's instincts. He 'never was in any ship where timbers were cut' to deal with leaks, but with water pouring in 'very violently' he felt he had no choice but to trust his only specialist. He sent his own bedclothes to be used to plug the hole if necessary and spent an agonizing afternoon overseeing the pumping of the ship. As he had feared, when Penton cut into the timber, sea water surged in, partly flooding the powder room. Dampier hurried down. He tried everything he could think of, even ordering his men to ram 'some pieces of beef' into the breach. Nevertheless, the water 'flew in', filling the powder room so that men could not work at the leak. Hurriedly, Dampier ordered a neighbouring bulkhead to be cut open to lower the water level by allowing the water to flow elsewhere in the ship so that they could reach the leak once more. Then he told his men to bale as well as pump. The water level began to drop, but at 11 p.m. boatswain John Norwood informed Dampier that 'it was impossible to save the ship'.

A terrible, unthinkable catastrophe stared Dampier in the face. At first he would not accept it. He urged his sodden, exhausted men on, comforting them with 'drams'. He heaved with them on the long handles of the great chain pumps. The handles were like the spokes on a horizontal wheel, just like those on the capstan. Turning them raised and lowered a chain with buckets, which discharged water onto the decks, whence it flowed away into the sea through the frayed leather flaps of the scupper holes. Yet by morning on 23 February, Dampier knew he could think of 'nothing now but saving our lives'. He coaxed the

The bell of the Roebuck, *recovered in 2001.*

waterlogged *Roebuck* closer to the beach, helped by a sea breeze that nudged her in. He then had a raft constructed to ferry ashore his men, their sea chests and their bedding.

By eight o'clock that night, he had the satisfaction of knowing that his men were safe. The *Roebuck* had settled in the water with only her masts and yardarms still visible. The next morning, as the tide ebbed, Dampier ordered her sails to be stripped off to make tents, and sent casks of fresh water and a large bag of rice ashore. He lost many of his books and papers but, as on previous voyages, managed to save his journals as well as some of his plants and other specimens. Many larger specimens, such as giant shells, remained on board.*

On this uninhabited, 'desolate island', about 500 miles below the equator and midway between Africa and South America, Dampier and his shaken men searched for water. With relief, they found a spring beyond the mountains. There were also plenty of turtles, goats, land crabs and boobies to eat and rocks to shelter their tents. Exploring their new home, Dampier discovered that they were not the first castaways. Carved on a tree were an anchor and cable and the date, 1642.

Ascension lies in the path of the southeast trade winds,

*In Fremantle, near Perth, we met Dr Mike McCarthy of the Western Australia Maritime Museum, leader of the team that in 2001 discovered the wreck of the *Roebuck* lying in twenty feet of water off Ascension Island. Timely storms had whipped up the seas, shifting the sandbanks to expose the remains of the ship, and then abating, providing a window to allow them to locate and retrieve the *Roebuck*'s bronze bell and a giant clamshell. Dr McCarthy is convinced that the shell, which is of a type not native to the Atlantic, is 'one of Dampier's specimens for the Royal Society, probably garnered off the coast of New Guinea'. The ship's bell and the clam shell are now back on Ascension Island after restoration in Portsmouth in England, by the conservationists responsible for the *Mary Rose*. Replicas are on display in Australia.

and a week after coming ashore Dampier and his men saw two ships making for the island. An excited Dampier ordered twenty turtles to be gathered to feast their rescuers, but by morning the ships had vanished and Dampier released the turtles. On 2 April, they had the frustration of watching the sails of eleven vessels blown past by the trade winds. However, the next day three Royal Naval vessels and an East Indiaman, the *Canterbury*, arrived in the bay where the *Roebuck* had sunk. Dampier and his men went gratefully aboard the naval ships. Later, learning that his vessel was bound for Barbados, Dampier transferred to the *Canterbury*. His only desire was 'to get to England as soon as possible'. By August 1701, he was home, thirty-one months after the *Roebuck* had departed.

Dampier's first task on landing was to report the sinking of the *Roebuck* to the Admiralty. They held an investigation on 29 September 1701 and accepted Dampier's explanation that the ship had sprung a terminal leak. He might reasonably have expected to concentrate on reporting his findings to his influential acquaintances in the Royal Society and rejoining Judith. But Dampier soon discovered he was in deep trouble. The abusive lieutenant he had ordered ashore in chains and deposited among the riffraff of the common jail in Bahia – George Fisher – had arrived back in England and spent the intervening two years preparing a case against him.

Fisher had begun writing letters and collecting statements while still in Brazil. Despite their previous arguments, Fisher had secured from John Gregson, who had deserted at Bahia, a vitriolic and spiteful denunciation of Dampier as 'a very ignorant man'. As soon as Fisher had arrived back in England in December 1699, he had presented his case to the lords of the Admiralty, who promised to investigate on the *Roebuck*'s return. When Dampier arrived home, Fisher was back at sea as a merchant captain. However, Fisher's wife 'renewed his petition for justice', asking that Dampier's wages be stopped until the case was heard. Back in England himself by April 1702, Fisher began firing off blunt letters to senior officials. These letters pointed out his unblemished career and the 'nastiness' of Dampier's treatment of him and petitioned for Dampier to be court-martialled 'as soon as possible'.

A formal system of courts-martial to judge offences against the naval disciplinary code had been established only thirteen years earlier, in 1689. The Admiralty alone had the right to institute proceedings and judged that, based on the evidence available, Dampier had a case to answer for his treatment of Fisher.

Dampier's only defence so far was the detailed letter he had sent to the Admiralty from Bahia on 22 April 1699. This catalogued a series of disputes over everything from Dampier's refusal to allow Fisher to bring 'two little boys' on board as servants to spats over the quality of the ship's bread. He detailed the events leading up to his caning and confining of Fisher, asserting that he struck the lieutenant only in self-defence, fearing he would 'collar' him. He also catalogued the abusive names Fisher had hurled at him. The only way to prevent Fisher from rousing the crew to mutiny, he insisted, had been to remove him from the ship. Even in prison in Bahia, Fisher had told anyone who would listen that Dampier was a pirate who had tied men 'back to back' before throwing them overboard. He had also incited the 'ghostly padres' – by which he meant the Inquisition – against him. Dampier forwarded six separate accounts of the quarrel with Fisher written by crewmen who supported him, together with a petition signed by several crewmen and stating their unanimous opinion that it would not have been 'safe or expedient' to allow Fisher to continue aboard. Dampier added that he could have sent evidence from his purser or his surgeon, but had not done so in case they were considered 'partial' because they had been at loggerheads with Fisher.

Surviving papers reveal Dampier's spirited and determined efforts to gather further evidence in his defence. They also show his anxiety. He tried to track down 'as many of the seamen as can be found', scouring London and beyond, but finding them was difficult. Some had gone back to sea, while others, like Alexander Beale, the young man Dampier had rescued from attack by Aborigines, had disappeared.

In his detailed refutation, Dampier also hinted at Fisher's relations with younger members of the crew. Adding to the tale of the 'two little boys', he told the Admiralty how Fisher had ordered his bed and bedclothes to be placed in the ship's pinnace in defiance of Dampier's orders that no one should get into it. Dampier, summoned by the boatswain, had found Fisher and 'a boy in the boat'. He had admonished Fisher for not showing a better example, but the lieutenant had threatened him with his fist, shouting that 'he did not care a fart for him'. But if Dampier did suspect Fisher of making homosexual advances to subordinates, and if this had contributed to the tension between them, he did not accuse him directly. 'The detestable and unnatural sin of sodomy', as Admiralty documents called it, was a serious charge and, since Fisher was a married man with a good service record, Dampier would have needed to produce irrefutable evidence.

★ ★ ★

The date set for the hearing was 8 June 1702. Dampier was shocked when, shortly before the trial, a new charge was added to the list against him. Dampier's former boatswain, John Norwood, had sailed from Ascension Island with the royal naval vessels to Barbados, where he had died. Ursula Norwood, his widow, presumably learning of his treatment from her late husband's returning shipmates, and perhaps incited by Fisher, accused Dampier of causing his death 'by barbarous and inhuman usage'. She claimed that by confining him for four months in an airless, suffocating cabin, Dampier had caused his death ten months later.

As far as can be judged from surviving records, such charges against captains were not uncommon. The journals of Edward Barlow, whom Dampier knew, record his involvement on both sides of the issue of shipboard violence. Barlow was reckoned by his contemporaries to be 'too mild' to become a captain yet was accused by the wife of a seaman whom he had caned of bringing about his death. She made 'a great bustle', and to prevent his name being paraded through the courts, Barlow paid her off with fifty pounds. As he wryly noted, she 'received more by his death than ever she had seen together since he had been her husband'. Barlow had also twice been a victim of authoritarian rule himself, confined and subsequently put ashore by 'proud and scornful' captains, to whom he was second-in-command, and one of whom had threatened him with a carpenter's adze.

It did not help Dampier that there had been a change of government. Whigs such as Orford, who had sponsored his expedition, were no longer in power in Parliament, and their rivals, the Tories, provided the government's ministers. They were highly doubtful about the conduct of their opponents and their protégés. Dampier had hanging over him a particular shadow – that of the Whigs' other maritime protégé, William Kidd, whose tarred body was still dangling from a gibbet at Tilbury Point, in the lower reaches of the Thames, 'as a greater terror to all persons from committing the like crimes'. Kidd had eventually been sent from New York to England for trial in 1700. He was imprisoned without proper lawyers and access to his papers and called briefly before Parliament to give evidence in an unsuccessful Tory attempt to impeach Lord Somers and Lord Orford.

At his own trial, the jury found Kidd guilty not only of piracy but also of the murder of the *Adventure Galley*'s gunner, William Moore. Kidd admitted killing Moore by

The body of Captain Kidd hanging in chains.

hitting him with a heavy bucket. However, he claimed that Moore was inciting mutiny and that he had no desire to kill – 'it was not designedly done but in my passion, for which I am heartily sorry'. On 23 May 1701, just after Dampier's rescue from Ascension Island, Kidd was hanged at Execution Dock at Wapping at the second attempt – the rope breaking on the first. Kidd died as a scapegoat for the greed of the Whig rulers, his notoriety coming much more from exaggerated Tory propaganda than from his relatively minor piracies.

Dampier may have feared that he, too, was to be scape-goated by the new government and by a naval establishment intolerant of outsiders and outside inter-ference. Even the astronomer Edmund Halley, when given command of a naval ship, HMS *Paramore*, in 1698, to make observations in the South Atlantic, had suffered severe insubordination and 'uneasy and refractory conduct' from naval officers. Because of the 'unreasonable behaviour' of his second-in-command, Lieutenant Edward Harrison, Halley relieved him of his duties and returned home prematurely in early 1699, just after Dampier's departure. A court martial reprimanded Harrison, but Halley thought that his complaints had not been taken seriously. He was very careful to take no second-in-command when he resumed his voyage.

Dampier could not have been confident as the court martial convened aboard HMS *Royal Sovereign* at Spithead, on 8 June. Admiral of the Fleet Sir George Rooke, after whom Dampier had named an island between New Guinea and New Britain, was presiding. Unfortunately for Dampier, he was a more recent shipmate of Fisher's than Dampier's. As captain of a ship on which Fisher had served, he had in 1693 written him an excellent testimonial, praising his sobriety, diligence and obedience. Rooke was assisted by Admiral Sir Cloudesley Shovell, who had been in the Downs with his squadron when the *Roebuck* was there, two other admirals and as many as thirty-three captains. It must have seemed to Dampier, the outsider, the ex-buccaneer, that the entire naval establishment was ranged against him. Of all the accusations Fisher flung at Dampier, the most consistent and vitriolic remained that he was at heart a pirate and, like many others, including Dampier's own former captains Sharp and Davis, only awaiting a profitable opportunity before reverting to type.*

Dampier, Fisher and seven crewmen gave sworn evidence. Some defended Dampier; others took Fisher's side. Their collective testimony presented a confused and confusing tale of suspicion, insults and intrigue. The court concluded that some of the accusations and counter-accusations were 'frivolous' or could not be proved. It was not interested in arguments about mouldy bread or abusive language. It gave no credence to Fisher's accusations that Dampier had been a 'very mean artist' – a bad navigator – for Dampier had taken the *Roebuck* everywhere he had intended to go, often through uncharted waters. Nor had Dampier been responsible, the court ruled, for the death of boatswain John Norwood, who had not died in confinement, nor even on the *Roebuck*, but many months later and was regarded by other crew members 'as sickly both before and after his confinement'.

The main issue, the court believed, was how Dampier had treated Fisher, an officer, and his grounds for doing so. By the standards of the day, Dampier's assault of Fisher

*Edward Davis, by then grown stout, had been imprisoned with Kidd, after joining his ship on his return from the pirate haven of Madagascar.

was relatively mild. Admiralty records are littered with cases of protracted sadism, of men being fatally flogged for offences as trivial as stealing a chicken. But the verdict was unequivocal: 'The matter of fact of his beating his lieutenant on board, his confining him . . . and then sending him home in irons to be imprisoned' was 'past dispute'. Dampier's counter-claim 'of mutinous practices' fomented by Fisher was judged only 'suppositions and surmise' and no justification for his behaviour. The court found him guilty of 'very hard and cruel usage' of Fisher, ruling him 'not a fit person' to command a naval vessel and fining him all his salary for the previous three years.*

Perhaps this was the best that Dampier could have expected under the circumstances. His only surviving direct comment on the debacle related to the loss of his ship, rather than his fight with Fisher. He wrote briefly and without melodrama that the *Roebuck* 'foundered through perfect age' and that 'I suffered extremely in my reputation by that misfortune'. He also observed that it was almost always the fate of 'those who have made new discoveries' to be 'disesteemed and slightly spoken of' by those who have 'no true relish and value' for new discoveries or some 'prejudice against the person by whom the discoveries were made'.

Although Dampier's reputation with Admiralty grandees had been tarnished, his standing remained high with the intellectual and scientific world, who would have learned from Halley how difficult the naval establishment could be.

---

*Ironically, the money was to be paid into a charitable fund for sailors established by Sir Francis Drake, who had executed his own second-in-command.

Shortly after his arrival back in England, Dampier had presented the plant specimens he had collected from around the world and carefully preserved from his shipwreck to 'the ingenious' Dr John Woodward.

Woodward was the author of the Royal Society document of 1696 about making 'observations in all parts of the world, as also for collecting, preserving and sending over natural things', which had so influenced Dampier's first books. A practising medical doctor, he had a special interest in collecting fossils and minerals. He was also a colourful eccentric, later expelled from the Royal Society for insulting Hans Sloane when the latter was president. Woodward and Dampier clearly knew each other quite well. It may be that he personally had asked Dampier to bring back specimens, or perhaps Dampier saw the author of the Royal Society's guide as the person best placed to be custodian of the precious specimens he had saved from the wreck. Woodward did not let him down.

Botany was then at an early stage of development. Its origins lay in the search by doctors and apothecaries for plants that would provide new remedies to rebalance the humours of their sick patients. In the mid–sixteenth century, Luca Ghini, a professor at Bologna University, had prescribed two simple new approaches to the study of plants that would have far-reaching effects. He encouraged his students to study real plants in the wild, and not just illustrations in books, and to preserve for later reference the specimens they had seen by picking them and pressing them between the pages of a book or in the simple flower presses he invented. The specimens were then mounted on paper and preserved in collections in what became known as herbaria.

By providing better reference materials, herbaria led

naturally to a greater consistency in the knowledge and naming of plants. In London, the Society of Apothecaries took the leading role in plant collecting, organizing field trips to teach medical students about plants and their properties. Members of the medical profession preserved their secrets carefully, writing about their researches always in Latin and for their own sole use. They continued to rely heavily on the Doctrine of Signatures in selecting specific plants to cure specific diseases. This doctrine stated that God had put plants on Earth to help cure human illness and that they carried secret signs or symbols to reveal their therapeutic purposes.* However, in the mid-1600s, one of their number, Nicholas Culpepper, broke ranks and earned the wrath of the medical community by publishing in English his hugely popular *Herbal* on the worthy grounds that the poor, who neither had money for physicians nor could read Latin, should not suffer on this account. He believed that 'things grown in England' were not only cheap but 'the most fit for English bodies'. He explained how to extract opium from 'our own country poppy' and described simple remedies such as the use of a fig turned inside out, oiled and salted as a cheap suppository. He also mixed his prescriptions with astrology in books that still sell well today.

Although the 'curious' culture of the age had later led others to collect and draw plants, doctors and apothecaries were still suspicious of interlopers. This may explain why in his earlier books, when describing the medical uses of plants, Dampier was quick to disclaim expertise and why he passed his specimens to a doctor, pausing only to

---

*For example, because of their resemblance to brains, walnuts were thought to cure brain diseases. Henbane, with its rows of teethlike fruit, was believed to cure toothache.

John Ray.

arrange for some of them to be drawn as illustrations for his book about his voyage.

Woodward immediately lent a number of Dampier's plant specimens to Dr John Ray, the greatest naturalist of the seventeenth century. Unlike the apothecaries and Culpepper, who looked at plants according to their medical uses, Ray examined them as scientific specimens and classified them accordingly into three main kinds: those without flowers, those with one seed leaf, and those with two – categorizations that are still used today. Ray is often said to be the inventor of 'the species'. A prolific writer, he named and described eleven of Dampier's plants in a new book published in 1704. Dampier's introduction of the word *sub-species* in his own book on the *Roebuck* voyage,

John Flamsteed.

A Voyage to New Holland, likely built on conversations with Ray and Woodward as well as on his own observations on this and previous voyages. Woodward also lent Dampier's specimens to the queen's botanist, Leonard Plukenet, who described and illustrated six of them in his book of 1705. Finally, Woodward passed nearly all of the specimens to William Sherard, founder of the Sherardian Herbarium at Oxford University, where they remain.

John Flamsteed, the meticulous and cantankerous astronomer royal, also had a high regard for Dampier. In July 1701, just before Dampier's return to England, he wrote to Woodward, who was to meet Dampier on his arrival, 'You will oblige me much if when you see Mr. Dampier you please to procure of him a copy of what variation of the compass he observed everywhere in his voyage with the latitudes of his ship and meridinal distances from the port from whence he last took his departure at each'. He asked for the material to be put into the newly created penny-post to reach him while he was out of town.

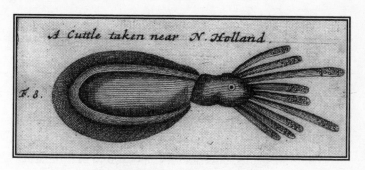

A drawing of a cuttlefish taken near New Holland, from Dampier's Voyage to New Holland.

Flamsteed had given Dampier guidance before he sailed about the information on magnetic variance and other matters he required. He had also included surprisingly practical advice, better befitting an astrologer than an astronomer. He warned 'that when he came to the coast of Brazil his men would mutiny'.

Flamsteed was interested in Dampier's findings to understand how the lines of magnetic variation changed across the globe and to disprove the still common theory that they followed those of the meridians. Dampier's results, together with contemporary work by Edmund Halley, showed that they did not.*

In February 1703, James Knapton published the first volume of Dampier's *A Voyage to New Holland,* again with maps by Herman Moll, to an enthusiastic response. There

*It was, however, a hundred years before Matthew Flinders and William Bain completed their analysis of the magnetic pattern. Both men cited Dampier in their works and used data from the *Roebuck* in reaching their conclusions. Flinders, who in 1814 was also the first man to apply the name Australia to the land Dampier knew as New Holland, used the data to help work out in 1810 the placing of the Flinder's Bar – a bar of iron on compasses that corrected the deviation in nearly all latitudes.

was no reference to the fighting and feuding that had dogged his expedition. The voyage had been 'vexatious', and Dampier had faced 'many difficulties', but he did not, he said, propose to trouble his readers with them. Instead, Dampier's clear, vivid prose immersed them once more in new sights, sounds and experiences described in familiar language and against well-known reference points. The delicate copper engravings of plants, birds and fish 'not found in this part of the world', including the first known portrayals of Australian fauna and flora, enhanced the mental journey. So did the detailed commentary on the plants, which, perhaps, owed something to John Ray. It was certainly written with a botanist's knowledge and insight. The review in the *Works of the Learned* particularly praised the woodcuts as an advantage over Dampier's previous volumes.

Yet the story recounted Dampier's voyage only until the day he and his scurvy-ridden men had left the shores of New Holland in their rotting ship for the island of Timor. Dampier apologized in his dedication of the book to the Earl of Pembroke for offering him 'so imperfect a present'. He had not had time 'to set down all the memoirs of [his] last voyage' because 'the particular service' he was about to perform had prevented him. What Dampier meant was that he was going back to sea.

PART V

The Ancient Mariner

XXIV

'BRANDY ENOUGH'

On 16 April 1703, less than a year after Dampier's court martial, the *London Gazette* reported that 'Captain William Dampier, being prepared to depart on another voyage to the West Indies, had the honour to kiss Her Majesty's Hand, being introduced by His Royal Highness, the Lord High Admiral'. 'Her Majesty' was Queen Anne, who had succeeded King William III on his death, a year previously. The 'Lord High Admiral' was her none too bright husband, Prince George. Dampier had not been deserted by his powerful friends.

England was again at war, allied with the Dutch against France and Spain, this time in the War of the Spanish Succession, which had broken out in 1702. So there was no imminent prospect of further voyages of scientific discovery, whether privately or publicly funded. However, privateering against enemy shipping was again a favoured and potentially profitable activity. Dampier's expedition was a privateering one, backed by a business consortium led by the Bristol merchant Thomas Estcourt. In the background were former Royal Society president Sir Robert Southwell, until his death in autumn 1702, and subsequently his son, Edward, secretary of state for Ireland and also a fellow of the society. The fifty-two-year-old Dampier was bound not for the West Indies – that was a subterfuge – but for the east coast of South America to seize the Spanish Atlantic treasure fleet. If that mission failed, he planned to round the Horn into the Pacific to secure 'the vast profits and advantages' he had promised his sponsors by seizing the Manila galleon.

The expedition was to consist of two ships. Dampier himself commanded 'an old ship but in very good condition and strong', the *St George*, of 200 tons and mounting twenty-six guns, none larger than five-pounders. A crew of 120 men were crammed into a ship designed to take scarcely more than a quarter of that number. At first, her companion was to be the *Fame*, commanded by Captain John Pulling, but following some disagreement she sailed off on other ventures.

The letters of marque, the government documents confirming the expedition's privateer status, were issued in April 1703. Dampier was preparing to leave the Thames Estuary at the end of the month when George Fisher had him arrested 'in a very boisterous, rude and unusual manner' in pursuit of a civil claim for damages of '300 shillings or some other greater sum' relating to Dampier's actions against Fisher on the *Roebuck*. Two other members of the *St George*'s consortium, William Price and a London vintner, Richard Collett, posted bail for Dampier, and he sailed on time. However, the arrest, its manner, and its cause – unjust treatment of an officer – must have severely embarrassed Dampier and, as it was certainly intended to, prejudiced his position with his men.

Dampier's crew were, in any case, a disparate and desperate bunch, by no means all British, nor all experienced sailors. He had seen 'better crews' and 'stouter men' in his buccaneering days. Unsurprisingly, in such circumstances he again wanted old friends around him. Again he did not choose wisely. He had insisted on delaying the expedition until Edward Morgan, his shipmate from the *Cygnet*, could be released from prison to serve as the owner's agent and expedition purser. Why Morgan was in prison and where he had again encountered Dampier are unknown. At one time he seems to have served as a government agent; at another he was accused of attempting to smuggle French prisoners of war out of the country.

He was by Dampier's side on the *St George* at the beginning of what was to be a difficult voyage.* The ship first sailed across to the small port of Kinsale on Ireland's southeast coast, where the Southwell family had considerable interests. Here, Dampier reprovisioned, while awaiting a new consort ship. He took advantage of the delay to write to Southwell about the financial provisions to be made for Judith during his absence. He had left £200 with Southwell for her use but asked him to use it to buy him a share in the venture. Judith would have to live on his sinecure salary as a customs official. 'I have not yet written to my wife about it . . . and I know it will not please her', he added nervously. Judith was obviously a strong personality whom he, once again, preferred to advise of difficult decisions from a distance. This is the last surviving mention of her, and she may well have died while Dampier was on the voyage.

Even at this early stage, all was not well among the

---

*The main account of the voyage was provided by William Funnell, whom Dampier first took aboard as a steward and then made a midshipman. In his book, denounced by Dampier as a 'chimerical relation', Funnell claimed, 'The success . . . was not such as might at first have been expected from the skill of our commander and the resolution of our men; disagreements and mismanagements having broken our measures and defeated our most promising hopes'. Dampier responded with a short, hastily written *Vindication*, which was, in turn, countered by another junior officer, John Welbe.

crew, nor in Dampier's relations with the owners and their agents. The latter were concerned about extravagant financial demands being made by Dampier, complaining that they had 'conceived so ill an opinion of Captain Dampier's conduct and management, that they begin to despair of the voyage and give over for lost what they have already laid out'. They also queried the competence of his senior lieutenant, Samuel Huxford, to handle financial affairs and suggested that Morgan take on more responsibility for this. Meanwhile, the *St George*'s new consort, the newly built *Cinque Ports* galley, had arrived in Kinsale. Commanded by Charles Pickering, she weighed ninety tons and had sixteen guns and a crew of sixty-three. Because she was a galley, she had the advantage that she could be rowed into action against becalmed targets.

The expedition finally set off on 11 September 1703. On the first night out, according to junior officer John Welbe, Dampier quarrelled with Huxford and ordered the ship to be turned around to put Huxford ashore, an instruction that was not obeyed. However, after further arguments in which both drink and Edward Morgan seem to have played some part, Dampier did indeed abandon Huxford in the Cape Verde Islands. He appointed James Burnaby, one of his companions from the *Roebuck*, as the new first lieutenant, but he hardly lasted longer. After reaching a Portuguese island off Brazil in early November, Burnaby and Morgan fell out. Dampier took Morgan's part, accusing the lieutenant of mutiny. Burnaby promptly decamped with eight others, who sneaked their chests and clothes ashore while – according to Welbe – Dampier was in his cabin 'quite drunk'.

At this difficult point, Captain Pickering of the *Cinque Ports* died. His inexperienced, twenty-one-year-old first lieutenant, Thomas Stradling, took command, and a cantankerous, twenty-three-year-old seaman from Fife, in eastern Scotland, Alexander Selkirk, was appointed quartermaster.

The reprovisioned ships set off again in December but spent little time searching for the Spanish Atlantic fleet. Instead they headed for the Pacific, losing touch with each other in foul weather off the Falkland Islands and rounding the Horn independently. They were reunited on 10 February on the Juan Fernandez Islands, which the *Cinque Ports* had reached three days before the *St George*. In that short time a serious dispute had broken out on the galley. Forty-two of the crew refused to serve further under Stradling and demanded to be put ashore. Funnell, although no friend to Dampier, acknowledged his skill on this occasion as a peacemaker: 'By the endeavours of Captain Dampier they were reconciled and returned aboard their own ship again'.

After four weeks, refreshed and again reprovisioned, the two ships set sail in pursuit of prizes. Soon the eager, excited men sighted and chased an armed French merchantship. Realizing her nationality, Dampier did not wish 'to pursue her any further', presumably preferring to wait for the real goal of Spanish treasure. However, his men would not listen, and the attack became a fiasco. The two privateers got into each other's line of fire. Welbe wrote accusingly that 'Captain Dampier himself the whole time of the engagement neither encouraged his men nor gave any regular command ... but stood upon the quarterdeck behind a good barricade which he had ordered to be made of beds, rugs, pillows, blankets etc. to defend him from the small shot of the enemy'. Dampier asserted that after nine of his crew were killed during an exchange of broadsides, the rest deserted their posts at the very moment the French ship might have been boarded.

Deprived of their prize, the privateers sailed up the South American coast. The crew were resentful that the regular councils of war, which Dampier had promised, were not being held. Instead, as Alexander Selkirk testified in later court documents, Dampier, Stradling and Morgan were making decisions secretly 'hugger mugger among themselves without the knowledge of the ship's company'. Welbe alleged that, on the rare occasions when councils did take place, although it was usual 'for the youngest officer to give his opinion first', Dampier would 'always give his own opinion first; and then if any of the officers gave their opinion contrary to his he would fly out in a passion and say "if you know better than I do take you charge of the ship." He was always a man so much self-conceited he would never hear any reason'.

The *St George* and the *Cinque Ports* succeeded in capturing two medium-sized Spanish vessels, but Dampier's crew were openly critical that he let them go without searching them thoroughly. Some suspected that he and Edward Morgan took 'a private consideration' from the Spanish captains to release them. They also believed Morgan secreted a valuable silver dinner service from one of the ships among his clothes in his sea chest. Dampier's defence of his actions was that 'he would not cumber up his ship for that he intended to make a voyage at one stroke upon some rich town on which he had a speedy design'.

This 'design' was once more to attack Santa Maria – the town of Dampier's 'golden dreams', upriver from Panama Bay. The two ships arrived off the river mouth on the night of 27 April 1704. Rain poured down as the privateers climbed into their boats, soaking their clothes and dampening their gunpowder. According to Welbe, Stradling suggested to Dampier that they should give each man a tot of brandy to warm them and provide Dutch courage. Dampier's ironic response was 'If we take the town they will get brandy enough but if we don't I shall want it myself'. The attack failed because, as they paddled towards the town, one of Dampier's crew fired at an Indian canoe, which escaped to raise the alarm. The privateers were not strong enough to attack alerted defenders.

Ten days later, the privateers' luck changed dramatically. A large 500-ton Spanish vessel, the *Assumsion*, anchored close to the *Cinque Ports* and *St George*, believing them to be friendly. Dampier's men quickly seized her and found her full of bales of linen and wool, brandy, wine and thirty tons of quince marmalade. Yet after searching the ship in what some of his men thought was only the most cursory fashion, Dampier let her go. Again, some suspected 'a private consideration had changed hands' and that Morgan had appropriated yet another ship's dinner service for his own use. Stradling and Dampier seem to have argued about the rigour of the search and their future plan of action. Contrary to the agreement with the owners governing the voyage, they divided up some of the spoils and went their separate ways.

Stradling headed back towards the Juan Fernandez Islands in the by-then-leaking *Cinque Ports*. There, while the men attempted repairs, Stradling quarrelled with his Scottish quartermaster, Selkirk, about the seaworthiness of their ship. The upshot was that Selkirk asked to be left behind. In October 1704 he was set ashore with bedding, food, some books, and gunpowder and shot. As the ship departed, he changed his mind, waving frantically from the shore, but Stradling would not re-embark him.*

The *St George* continued her patrol in Panama Bay. She too was leaking. According to Funnell, 'The bottom was in many places eaten like a honeycomb . . . in some places we could thrust our thumbs quite through with ease'. Soon Dampier's unruly mate, John Clipperton, and twenty other men took the opportunity afforded by the capture of a small prize to mutiny and go off in her on their own account.

After the split with Stradling, and Clipperton's mutiny, Dampier's authority over the remaining men must at best have been fragile. To encourage them, he held out the prospect of capturing the Manila galleon – the holy grail of a privateer cruise. For a short while, it seemed they might succeed. On 6 December 1704, the *St George* sighted the unsuspecting galleon, whose gunports were closed. Behind them lay twenty-four-pounder guns, compared with the *St George*'s five-pounders. Given the disparity, the *St George* needed to get in close before her intentions were discovered, but somehow the element of surprise was lost. The enemy ran out their large guns and inflicted severe damage below the waterline on the *St George*'s already leaky hull, forcing Dampier to break off the action. Welbe and Funnell blamed Dampier for hoisting the ensign and firing an opening shot too soon, as well as for drunkenness and cowardice in action. Dampier, in turn, blamed his 'drunk and bewitched' crew for failing to obey his orders to close in and board.

---

*Selkirk was fortunate. Not long afterwards the *Cinque Ports* was wrecked. The eight survivors, including Stradling, were imprisoned by the Spanish. It was several years before Stradling reached home.

He nevertheless managed to persuade his men to cruise a further six weeks on the Mexican coast in the hope of at least capturing a more seaworthy vessel in which to return home. They seized a brigantine, but at the end of January 1705 there was a final mutiny, this time led by Dampier's old comrade Edward Morgan and supported by Funnell and Welbe. According to Dampier, it was a violent affair. He was taken 'by the throat' and was threatened: 'If I spoke a word they would dash my brains out'. When he angrily refused to hand over the keys to the arms chest and the powder room, Morgan simply said, 'We have iron crows on board, they are as good keys as we desire and with that broke 'em open'. Funnell and Welbe, in their accounts, unconvincingly claimed that the separation was by mutual consent. (They were hardly likely to convict themselves of mutiny – a hanging offence.)

The mutineers set off in the prize brigantine. As they departed, Dampier recalled, 'that buffoon Toby Thomas, said "Poor Dampier, thy case is like King James's, every-body has left thee." Dampier remained in the leaking *St George* with twenty-seven men, 'most of them landsmen'. Surgeon John Ballatt was his only officer.

From this low point Dampier's fortunes unexpectedly improved. As he later wrote, 'They reported . . . I should never come home; it is a miracle in nature how I did'. He and his skeleton crew succeeded in sacking the island of Puna in the Gulf of Guayaquil. Then they seized a Spanish brigantine to replace the *St George*, which they abandoned. In this new vessel they crossed the Pacific. There are no details of their voyage since neither Dampier nor anyone else kept a record, but they reached Batavia safely. Here, the suspicious Dutch authorities threw them into prison because Dampier could not produce his privateering commission. According to some accounts, it had been stolen by Clipperton; according to others, he had lost it at Puna. Finally, Dampier was released, and he returned to London in late 1707.

His arrival, eighteen months after that of Funnell and Clipperton, finally blasted the hopes of the expedition's sponsors. They had previously been buoyed by mouth-watering reports in the papers, recorded by Narcissus Luttrell, of Captain Dampier seizing 'French prizes of great value' and of Spanish prisoners interrogated by the governor of Jamaica reporting that 'one Dampier' with 'a letter of mark ship was fallen in with the Spanish plate fleet' and was making for the East Indies 'with three millions of silver'. An exhilarated Helen Southwell had written to her brother Edward, 'I believe I shall very soon have the manteau and petticoat you promised, for I dreamt Captain Dampier was come home with a very good cargo'.

The disappointed owners debated what legal action they could take to recover some of their outlay. The most severe of Welbe's and Funnell's charges were, however, unproven and clearly fuelled in part by malice and self-preservation.* The owners eventually brought a case against Dampier and others in 1712, but it seems to have been inconclusive. One macabre consequence of the affair was that Thomas Estcourt's sister Elizabeth, who had inherited from him his share of any profits, was rumoured to have been murdered by an avaricious sister eager to secure some of the loot.

For Dampier, the *St George* expedition – his second

---

*In fact, some years later, Welbe would write to the English government, pinning the major blame on Morgan, not Dampier.

round-the-world voyage – was a bruising experience. By having him very publicly arrested at the beginning of the voyage, the vindictive Fisher had raised questions in the crew's minds about his competence and character, making it easier for them to challenge doubtful decisions and draw invidious comparisons. For his part, Dampier never succeeded in allaying his men's concerns or in learning the lessons of the *Roebuck*. His treatment of Huxford and Burnaby recklessly mirrored his handling of Fisher and gave Welbe the ammunition to write, 'I wonder not at the captain's monstrous barbarity, knowing the like scene of cruelty was acted by him, when commander of the *Roebuck*'.

Dampier displayed a combination of arrogance, conceit and bluster, which failed to control his unruly officers in the hothouse atmosphere of the privateers' confined quarters. Old friends like Morgan let him down, and, with the exception of surgeon John Ballatt, he failed to make new allies. Heavy drinking was rife and seems to have brought out the worst in all concerned and Dampier in particular, despite his pious claim in *A New Voyage* that he 'abhorred all drunkenness'. It was, perhaps, the result of inner insecurities and of boredom and frustration. The voyage had done nothing to satisfy his intellectual appetite. The only thing that would have made it worthwhile would have been a great prize. For the first time Dampier did not publish a book about his voyage.

Though Dampier's reputation for leadership had suffered once more, his repute as a navigator was undiminished. Even the vitriolic Funnell conceded, 'I cannot in justice but take notice that upon all this coast [of South America] and during our whole stay in the South

Seas we found Captain Dampier's descriptions of
places very exact, and his account of winds, currents etc
very extraordinary'.*

*The recent fate of Sir Cloudesley Shovell, who had sat on Dampier's court
martial, served as a sharp reminder of navigational problems before longitude could be calculated accurately. In October 1707, when the fleet under his
command was returning from Portugal, it ran at night and under full sail
into the Scilly Islands. Four ships and 2,000 men were lost. Sir Cloudesley
made it ashore, but as he lay exhausted on the beach he was murdered by a
local woman for the emerald ring on his finger.

XXV

THE MANILA GALLEON AT LAST

$\mathcal{D}$ampier's final voyage – and third circumnavigation of the world – was, once again, in pursuit of Spanish gold. The chimeric image of Spanish treasure galleons still tantalized him. Despite the failure of the *St George* enterprise, and despite his fifty-six years, Dampier retained in 1707 the authority and enthusiasm to convey his dreams to others and to convince them of their commercial viability. As one member of the new expedition, Edward Cooke, wrote, Dampier did not give up 'till he had prevailed with some able persons at Bristol to venture upon an undertaking, which might turn to a prodigious advantage'.

Bristol was England's second-largest port, thriving on the growing trade with the American colonies. Among the 'able persons' of Bristol whom Dampier persuaded to become involved was twenty-nine-year-old merchant and sea captain Woodes Rogers. His attention had already been caught by accounts of the spectacular profits recently made by French traders in the Pacific. The War of the Spanish Succession was still under way, and Rogers was therefore receptive to Dampier's depiction of the plunder to be gained from privateering in the Pacific against England's enemies, the French and the Spanish. Private profit and public patriotism coalesced nicely. Once convinced by Dampier, Rogers joined him in persuading a

Woodes Rogers with his family in later life.

group of prominent Bristol citizens to finance a privateering expedition.

The consortium purchased two ships: the 320-ton, 30-gun *Duke* and the 260-ton, 26-gun *Duchess*. Such was Dampier's continuing celebrity with the public that diarist Narcissus Luttrell, eagerly scanning the daily newspapers for material to fill his chronicle, automatically but incorrectly ascribed the command of the expedition to him.

Instead, Woodes Rogers commanded the *Duke* and Stephen Courtney the *Duchess*. Courtney was a courteous, sensible man, occasionally troubled by gout. Dampier was to be the 'pilot for the South Seas', appointed for his unrivalled expertise as a navigator and as the only living Englishman to have been thrice to the Pacific and twice round the world. The owners promised Dampier, as a prime mover behind the venture, one-sixteenth of their net profits, the only officer to whom they made such a commitment. Dampier was also able to reward his faithful surgeon from the *St George*, John Ballatt, with a berth as third mate and ancillary surgeon.*

Dampier was so busy promoting this new venture that he had little time to work on the second volume of his book about the *Roebuck*. James Knapton did not publish it until 1709, when Dampier was once more at sea. Its main feature was Dampier's pioneering and detailed description of New Guinea and its people.

The owners tried to forestall the vicious arguments and mutinies which had bedevilled the *St George* expedition by doubling the number of officers aboard each ship. Also, they stipulated that the expedition should be managed by an officers' committee aboard each ship, itself subordinate to a joint council. Dr Thomas Dover, Bristol's leading doctor and one of the largest investors, was appointed president of the council. Despite his lack of maritime experience, this conceited man sailed as second captain on the *Duke*, as well as senior physician and captain of marines. Both his temperament and inexperience would cause friction as the voyage progressed.†

The *Duke* and *Duchess* left Bristol on 2 August 1708, bound for Cork, with all 'necessaries' on board for a long voyage. The crew – 117 on the *Duke* and 108 on her consort – were less satisfactory. Rogers estimated that he had 'not

*Dampier wrote no book about the voyage. If he kept a journal, it has not survived. What we know of the progress of the voyage comes from the accounts produced by others, in particular Woodes Rogers and Edward Cooke.

†Dover later made a fortune from his Dover's Powder – an addictive concoction of opium and ipecac. Over 160 years later, Henry Stanley would claim that Dover's Powder saved his life during his search for Dr David Livingstone in Africa.

20 sailors in the ship', and because of the crew's ineptitude the ships made slow progress. Nevertheless, they reached Cork safely, limping into port in dark, foggy weather. Here Rogers discharged forty incompetents and recruited 150 more able men. They were still 'a mixed gang'; one-third were foreigners, and the British component included 'tinkers, tailors, hay-makers, pedlars and fiddlers'. The ships were so crowded that Rogers feared that they would not be able to fight 'without throwing provision and stores over-board'.

On 5 September, with a naval ship standing close by in case Rogers needed to get rid of any 'malcontents', he summoned the crew and broke the news that had been kept from the majority: they were bound for the South Sea. Some were shocked, but he quieted their fears and all hands 'drank to a good voyage'. Nevertheless, the first mutiny took place five days later, under circumstances Dampier must have found eerily familiar. It was sparked by Rogers's decision to allow a Swedish vessel to sail on rather than seizing her. He and his officers reacted swiftly, whipping the ringleader and putting ten men in irons. Rogers armed his chief officers in case of further trouble, and in succeeding days other malcontents were whipped and confined until all was 'quiet again'. However, at Tenerife, where the expedition called to collect supplies of Canary wine, Rogers fell out with one of the owner's agents, Carleton Vanbrugh, cousin of the famous architect and playwright. Vanbrugh had rashly gone ashore and been seized by the Spanish authorities, who demanded that the privateers give up a barque they had captured in return for his release. Rogers's tart response was that 'it was Mr. Vanbrugh's misfortune to go ashore; and if he is detained, we can't help it'. Vanbrugh – eventually and ignominiously sent back with a consignment of wine, grapes and hogs – was furious that Rogers had been prepared to abandon him.

The *Duke* and *Duchess* struck out on the long haul to Brazil, just as Dampier had done on the *Roebuck*. As they crossed the Tropic of Cancer, those whose first time it was were ducked on ropes from the yardarm. Rogers joked, '[This] proved of great use to our fresh-water sailors, to recover the colour of their skins which were grown very black and nasty'. The good mood did not last. Soon the men demanded, and obtained, a promise of a larger share of any spoils. Rogers wrote glumly that otherwise he would have needed a near miracle 'to keep the men in both ships under command, and willing to fight resolutely' and avoid the 'continual scenes of mischief and disorder' that 'not only tended to the great hindrance, but generally to the total disappointment of all voyages of this nature'. In an effort to maintain order, Rogers and Courtney 'began to read prayers in both ships mornings and evenings'.

On 14 November, in heavy, humid weather, they sighted the coast of Brazil. Dampier went turtle hunting along the shore to provide the weakened men with fresh meat. Showers turned to a 'heavy tornado', with lightning falling like 'liquid'. Five more days brought them to the island of Grande, where two men deserted, running into the jungle only to be so frightened 'with tigers as they thought, but really by monkeys and baboons that they ran into the water, hollering to the ship till they were fetched aboard again'. While the carpenters and sail makers worked to repair and refit the ships, Rogers and his officers visited the little town of Angre de Reys, with its mud-covered, palm-thatched houses. A festival was taking place, and Rogers summoned the ships' musicians. They played 'Hey Boys

Up We Go!' and 'all manner of noisy, paltry tunes' and then, 'half-drunk', led a long procession through the streets. Rogers, Courtney and Dampier joined the revellers with long, lighted candles in their hands to follow a swaying, flower-decked, candlelit bier carrying an image of the Virgin Mary.

Reprovisioned and refitted, the privateers sailed south. With advice, no doubt, from Dampier, who much preferred this route, they chose to round the Horn rather than face the surging tides and treacherous channels of the Strait of Magellan. Soon the air grew colder. The ships' tailors hacked rough garments out of woollen blankets to clothe the shivering men. The crews of the two ships celebrated New Year's Day with music and 'a large tub of hot punch' and cheered each other across the chill, pewter-grey waters. The following days brought violent gales and towering seas. The ships tossed wildly while aloft men struggled with raw, frozen fingers to adjust the sails, and lookouts scanned the pale horizon for ice. The *Duchess* fared worst. Waves smashed her stern windows, and she was shipping water, leaving her men 'intolerably cold' and everything wet. Nevertheless, on 15 January 1709, an exhausted Rogers wrote, 'We now account ourselves in the South-Sea'.

The owners had instructed Rogers and Courtney that once in the Pacific: 'Consult your pilot Captain Dampier in Council on whose knowledge in those parts we mainly depend upon for satisfactory success'. Heading north, Dampier held the ships close to the shore until he came to a landmark he recognized. Then he set course due west along the latitude for the Juan Fernandez Islands to find much-needed fresh food and water.

Early on 31 January, the familiar, spiky, mountainous

outline of the main island lay before him. The island was supposedly uninhabited, so the privateers were alarmed to see a large fire burning on the shore. An armed landing party cautiously approached the beach. No French or Spanish soldiers appeared, only a hairy, agitated figure clad in goatskins and looking 'wilder than the first owners of them', who waved a white rag in greeting. The privateers surrounded him, shouting questions, but the only word he could fashion was *marooned*. It was Alexander Selkirk.

Four years and four months before, the peppery-tempered Scot had been left behind by Captain Stradling from the leaking *Cinque Ports*. Now nearly twenty-nine years old, he had adapted, and in a sense thrived. He had become so fit and wiry that when his ammunition ran out, he had been able to outrun any goat, leaping from rock to rock on agile, leather-soled feet. The amazed privateers inspected his two neat, grass-decked huts of pimento wood lined with goatskins. He had used nails for needles and stitched goatskins together with thongs to replace his clothes. He had ground new blades for his knife using the iron hoops of barrels washed up on the shore. He had even discovered a black pepper growing on the island that was excellent for expelling wind from the bowels and curing diarrhoea. Selkirk's greatest problem had been the utter, desolate loneliness. He had, indeed, nearly lost the power of speech, stammering his words 'by halves'. His only companions had been wild goats and cats and voracious rats that had gnawed his feet as he slept.

Selkirk played host to the privateers, some so weakened by scurvy they could not walk. They were hoisted through the ships' hatches and lowered in canvas slings over the side into the boats. Stews of goat, seal meat, cabbage and turnips, cooked over fires of fragrant pimento wood,

A statue of Alexander Selkirk in Fife, Scotland, his birthplace.

revived them. Meanwhile, Selkirk took Dampier and others hunting for goats.

Two weeks later, they were ready to sail again. The tongue-tied, traumatized Selkirk had been made mate aboard the *Duke*, thanks to Dampier's endorsement that he had been the 'best man' on the *Cinque Ports*. Selkirk's worst problems were that when he tried to wear shoes again, his feet swelled painfully, the food on board made him ill, and he lost his 'strength and agility'. It caused Rogers to philosophize about the evils of 'excess and plenty'.

The *Duke* and *Duchess* bore northeast for another island group well known to Dampier: the Lobos Islands near Lima with their teeming, acrid-smelling seal colonies. The capture of several small trading vessels did nothing to ease the men's complaints that they had 'met with no prize in these seas'. Disturbing phenomena like a sea 'as red as blood', the result, in fact, of plankton, fed the men's edginess, which, as weeks passed, lack of food exacerbated. Rogers, not at all tender about corporal punishment, had two men 'whipped and pickled' for stealing meat. His decision to attack the town of Guayaquil brought discontent to a head. The crewmen argued that they had signed on to attack ships, not towns. It was a riskier undertaking than they had bargained for. They would take part only if their share of the booty was increased. Again, the officers had no option but to agree. 'All bedding and clothes, gold rings, buttons and buckles, liquors and provisions' would 'be allowed as plunder, to be equally divided to everyone'.

Under a moonlit sky on 17 April, the privateers landed on the marshy, mosquito-infested island of Puna in the Gulf of Guayaquil, which Dampier knew well. They seized its inhabitants and smashed their canoes to prevent them from raising the alarm. Ransacking the houses, they discovered a letter from the authorities in Lima to the governor of Guayaquil. It warned of an expedition 'under the conduct of an Englishman named Dampier' and exhorted the governor 'to keep constant watch'. The main force pressed on through dense, claustrophobic mangrove swamps croaking with toads and up the tidal estuary to Guayaquil. They were dismayed to find the town ablaze with light, with a great beacon flaring on the hill. Within moments church bells were peeling and cannons boomed into the night as the inhabitants frantically sounded the alarm.

For Dampier, it was like stepping back in time to the December night of 1684 when he had rowed upriver to find 'lighted torches, or candles, all the town over'. A hesitant

Rogers asked an equally hesitant Dampier, what should they do? Never a particularly reckless man, Dampier cautiously advised that the buccaneers never 'attacked any large place after it was alarmed'. Rogers disagreed, arguing for an immediate attack while the town was in confusion. He called a meeting in the stern of one of the boats, where, according to Edward Cooke, a 'hot dispute' broke out. Finally, they decided first to negotiate a ransom with the Spaniards, and if that failed, to attack. They sent a demand to the governor, who promised 50,000 pieces of eight if they would spare the town. The privateers waited as deadline after deadline passed.

On 24 April, they lost patience. Hoisting the Union Jack, they attacked, pouring off boats onto the stone quay. The town's militia and cavalry made a brief sortie, then turned tail. Within half an hour the privateers had seized the town without a man lost. Dampier took charge of the captured guns, which he turned on the fleeing enemy. But it proved an unsatisfactory victory, for the citizens had had time to remove the bulk of their wealth. Furthermore, a 'contagious distemper' had recently killed a large number of citizens, whose bodies had been piled under the church floor or thrown down a nearby hole 'almost filled with corpses half putrefied'. His men wanted to pull up the church floorboards 'to look amongst the dead' for concealed treasure, but Rogers refused. He feared his men, already weak from the 'sultry, hot, wet and unhealthful weather', would catch the disease.

Some pickings were had from robbing the town's 'handsome genteel young women'. A party under Selkirk discovered that 'some of their largest gold chains were concealed and wound about their middles, legs and thighs etc, but the gentlewomen in these hot countries being very thin clad with silk and fine linen ... our men by pressing felt the chains etc., with their hands on the outside of the lady's apparel, and ... modestly desired the gentlewomen to take 'em off and surrender 'em'. Rogers meanwhile took hostages and demanded money or he would burn the town. Negotiations once more proved sterile and protracted.

With Spanish forces regrouping in the woods, Rogers decided they should 'be gone from hence' with their booty and hostages and await the ransom money at Puna. They slithered down the muddy riverbank to the boats, clutching everything from clothing, silver plate and jewellery to bales of cloth, jars of liquor and bags of rice. Some fainted in the heat. Others discarded their pistols and cutlasses so that they could carry more loot. Rogers brought up the rear, retrieving the arms from the oozing mud and angry that his men 'were grown very careless, weak, and weary of being soldiers'. On 28 April the laden boats pulled away from the shore to the sound of trumpets and drums to follow the fast-flowing river down to the sea.

Ransom money arrived at Puna, and the privateers released their hostages. However, the total yield from the attack had been far less than expected. The expedition sailed on for the Galapagos Islands. Within days 'a malignant fever' was cutting a swath through the crew, no doubt contracted at Guayaquil, just as Rogers had feared. By 14 May, over 120 were ill; by 17 May, the figure was closer to 150. Rogers noted bleakly, 'There is hardly a man in the ship, who had been ashore at Guayaquil, but has felt something of this distemper'. Rogers found that 'punch did preserve' his own health and 'prescribed it freely' to those who were still well, but it was 'a melancholy time'.

They finally reached the Galapagos after some difficulty

locating them. Edward Cooke blamed their charts rather
than Dampier, who may well have been among the sick –
he had been on guard in the noisome church in Guayaquil.
They searched but could find no water on the parched
islets. Rogers had read accounts, including Dampier's, that
'good water, timber, land and sea turtle' were to be found
here, but dismissed them as mere 'stories' concocted by
those who 'imposed on the credulous'. They were in a
desperate situation, with barely enough men capable of
clambering from their sweat-soaked hammocks to handle
the boats. A dozen men died on the islands. Water was fast
running out, and it became 'absolutely necessary' to make
again for the mainland.

They left 'these unfortunate islands' for Gorgona.
Rumours reached Rogers that prisoners aboard one of
their prize ships planned to murder the crew and seize the
ship. Burning matches were rammed between the
prisoners' fingers to make them confess, and they were dispersed among the other ships. On 7 June, the fleet reached
Gorgona and found respite at last. There was plenty of
water and plenty to hunt in the forests – Dampier urged his
comrades to eat monkeys and baboons, telling them that
'he never ate anything in London that seemed more
delicious to him', but without success. The men caught a
sloth and brought it on board. They watched amazed as it
took two hours to climb the mast.

The sick recuperated in tents erected onshore, while
those with enough strength cleaned and overhauled the
ships. A large ship, the *Havre de Grace*, captured just before
the assault on Guayaquil, was converted 'with much
fatigue and trouble' into a fighting ship and renamed the
Marquess. Edward Cooke was appointed her captain. The
men toasted her new identity. They now had time to

inspect her hold and discovered glistening silver plate and pearls, but also '500 bales of Pope's bulls', dispensations to eat meat in Lent on receipt of a suitable payment. Another ship yielded thirty tons of saints' relics – 'bones in small boxes' – which were tossed into the sea with Protestant disdain. Rogers did, however, allow his Spanish prisoners freedom of worship. On Sundays, a Protestant service was held above decks, while a Catholic mass took place below, enabling Rogers to quip that 'the Papists here were the Low Churchmen'.

There were further bitter arguments about the distribution of plunder. Sixty men from the *Duke* refused to leave Gorgona until their demands were met. Rogers dealt severely with the ringleaders but had to mollify the rest since 'there were too many guilty to punish them at once'. Problems among the officers were more serious. Rogers and Dover were no longer on speaking terms, and the doctor had decamped to the *Duchess*. There was such 'a general misunderstanding' among the officers that Rogers feared 'a separation' as had taken place between Dampier's *St George* and the *Cinque Ports*. He longed for reconciliation and 'good harmony' and in desperation made some of his officers – Dampier was not among them – swear on the Bible to aid and protect each other in extremis.

Rogers tried to focus his men's minds on the challenges ahead, in particular the prospect of seizing the gilded, teak-framed Manila galleon, which should soon be approaching these waters. He organized mock engagements. Blank shot was fired, and men dripping with red lead mixed with water to simulate injury were carried to the surgeons for mock operations. He divested the ships of unnecessary encumbrances. Prisoners were released, sometimes on the promise of a ransom; others were simply let go.

On the basis of his considerable experience of previous ventures, Dampier advised that the best place to intercept the Manila galleon was Cape St Lucas in lower California. After many long weeks of being blown by the prevailing westerlies in a great arc across the Pacific, the exhausted crews of the galleons commonly made their landfall in California before sailing south past the cape to Acapulco.

Rogers took Dampier's advice, and the privateers sailed for Cape San Lucas, fanning out to prevent the Manila ship from slipping by. Aboard the *Duke* there was a diversion when a black slave girl gave birth to a baby girl 'of a tawny colour'. Rogers warned the women aboard to 'be modest' or face 'severe punishment'. A woman on the *Duchess* had recently been whipped at the capstan – '[to show] we don't countenance lewdness'. Arriving off the cape, they took up their stations, eyes straining to the horizon, but time passed and nothing came. November went by without sight of another vessel. Food stocks declined. The ship's steward took the precaution of sleeping with the storehouse key 'fastened to his privy parts'. Even so, a nimble-fingered thief stole it and helped himself to bread and sugar. He was caught because he lacked the finesse to reattach the key 'to the same place' where he had found it without rousing the steward.

By mid-December, the galleon was a month late. Rogers wondered whether she had evaded their net. There began to be despairing talk of giving up and making for Guam while they still had sufficient supplies and the increasingly worm-eaten ships were still strong enough for the voyage. Cooke had already had to take the *Marquess* to the mainland for repairs. He was still away when, on 21 December, to their 'great and joyful surprise', the *Duke* and *Duchess* sighted a sail. Shadowing the vessel until certain she was the Manila ship, the privateers ran out the guns, battened the hatches and issued muskets. On a dark night, guided by flares from the ships' boats, the *Duke* and *Duchess* bore down on their quarry. At dawn, just before the attack, the men were given 'a large kettle of chocolate' as there was no 'spiritous liquor' left. Then they knelt on the deck and prayed.

A brief but fierce fight ensued. The *Duchess* overshot the galleon and could not tack back, leaving the *Duke* to attack alone. Rogers manoeuvred his ship up close under a hail of musket fire and ordered his gunners to fire broadsides. The galleon fired back. Her guns were larger, but her sailors could not reload as quickly. Within half an hour, she struck her colours in surrender. Only two privateers had been wounded, one of them Woodes Rogers, whose left cheek had been hit by a musket shot; '[it] struck away a great part of my upper jaw and several of my teeth'. Though he was in great pain, spitting blood and teeth all over the deck, the injury was not life threatening. He could not speak but scratched orders with a quill pen on a piece of paper. The privateers soon learned that their prize, the *Nuestra Senora de la Encarnacion Disengano*, was not the main galleon. Another larger and richer vessel had sailed with her, but the two ships had become separated in bad weather.

Rogers ordered his ships to keep watch. On Christmas Day, the 900-ton *Nuestra Senora de Begona* sailed into view, but she proved quite a different proposition. She mounted forty twelve-pound guns, and her hull was too thick for shot from the privateers' six-pounders to penetrate. Unlike her sister ship, she carried a large and experienced crew, including English and Irish former pirates whose own property was on board. Nevertheless, the *Duke*, *Duchess*

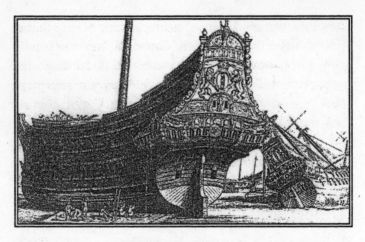

A Spanish East Indiaman.

and *Marquess* attacked doggedly. Dampier's part in the engagement is unknown, but some privateers managed to board, clambering up the shrouds. However, the odds were too great. Edward Cooke decided that they 'might as well have fought a castle of 50 guns'. A box of gunpowder on the *Duke's* deck exploded, killing or wounding thirty privateers. The unfortunate Rogers was hit again; this time a flying splinter sliced through the heel of his left foot and half severed his ankle. He lay on his back, blood flowing from the wound. With masts broken and rigging flapping and useless, he ordered the privateers to withdraw. The *Nuestra Senora de Begona* sailed on for Acapulco.

It took a week to repair their ships. Meanwhile, the privateers inspected their loot, finding some consolation for the loss of the greater prize. The *Encarnacion's* hold was stuffed with jewels, silver plate, musk, cinnamon, cloves, soft sinuous silks, damasks and taffetas, and Chinese porcelain. They renamed her the *Batchelor* in honour of one of the expedition's sponsors. Her captain told them that they had been warned before leaving Manila that an English expedition of which 'Captain Dampier was pilot' would be hunting them. She was placed under the formal command of Thomas Dover, despite angry protest notes sent by Rogers from his sickbed that Dover was utterly unsuitable because of his lack of experience and 'violent' temper. A compromise resolved this paper war: two officers were appointed to serve under Dover and oversee the day-to-day sailing of the ship, assisted by Alexander Selkirk as master.

On 10 January 1710, the little squadron plunged out across the Pacific to Guam. Dampier was the only officer to have made the crossing before. The voyage was tense, with illness, storms and the threat of starvation. A pound and a half of flour and a scrap of meat were the daily rations for five men. Pilferers were whipped, and men became so weak that they collapsed at their posts. However, Dampier's navigation did not fail. He had estimated the 6,000-mile crossing at between sixty and seventy days, and sixty-nine days after setting out they saw ahead of them the lush coastline of Guam. Red-painted proas, fast as 'a bird flying', escorted them in. They faced some awkward questions from the Spanish authorities. However, seeing that their visitors were well armed, the officials did not probe too deeply.

At dawn on 21 March 1710, the reprovisioned privateers departed for Batavia. Soon, adverse winds and treacherous currents drove them off course. Tropical storms battered them. The *Duke* was leaking so badly that the men were 'wearied almost to death with continual pumping'. Dampier warned that there were few places where they would be able to find provisions, and that they must try to find the island of Ternate or Tula. By May, food was

running out again. Men traded rats for sixpence each, eating them 'very savourly'. They sailed on amid violent
showers and flashes of lightning, lost among a myriad of
islands. Dampier was aboard the *Duchess*, leading the way,
trying to identify where they were, but his memory seemingly was failing. Rogers complained about navigating
these difficult waters without good maps or 'an
experienced pilot'.

On 20 June, as the sun set gaudily in the tropical sky,
they finally reached Batavia. Rogers obtained permission
to reprovision and careen his ships. The rotting *Marquess*,
eaten 'to a honeycomb' by worms, was too far gone and
was sold for $575. While his men joyously drank punch,
'hugging each other and blessing themselves', a weak, thin
Rogers had his wounds tended. A doctor 'cut a large
musket shot' out of his mouth and plucked slivers of bone
from his foot. It would not have helped his recovery to
know that owner's agent Carleton Vanbrugh was busily
writing angry letters to the owners, bemoaning the 'great
jarring among us' and how badly Rogers had treated him.
Vanbrugh would not survive to make his complaints in
person but would perish of dysentery contracted at
Batavia. Another man died more quickly, bitten in two by
a shark during an ill-advised swim.

The booty was carefully catalogued and packed.
Dampier was given responsibility for deciding what was
plunder aboard one of the prize ships. He was also
advanced 200 pieces of eight – half as much as Rogers and
Courtney – to buy 'necessaries' for the long voyage home.
Four months later, the three ships set out again. An 'ugly
swelling sea' buffeted them, but on 29 December they
reached Cape Town safely. They spent the next three
months awaiting the arrival of Dutch and English East

Indiamen to convoy them home. The delay provided further opportunity for acrimonious letter writing. Thomas Dover complained to the owners that Rogers was 'a dead weight' whose behaviour had been characterized by violent threats to cut men's throats and make 'bloody noses'. Rogers, still in miserable pain, wrote plaintively that despite this 'successful long voyage', his shares amounted to 'little more than what's given to nine common sailors'. He contrasted this with 'the agreement which I promoted for Captain Dampier very much to his advantage'.

The convoy departed from the cape on 5 April 1711, and on 23 July the privateers anchored off the Dutch coast. An excited British agent sent the headline news to London: 'Dampier is alive'. The privateers awaited orders from the owners in Bristol. Rogers was pessimistic about his reception after the complaints of his colleagues. He wrote pleadingly to the owners, 'For Christ sake don't let me be torn to pieces at home after I have been so racked abroad'. Dover reported in a letter signed also by Dampier, '[Rogers is] disposing of what he thinks fit out of this ship. . . . we called a Council and would have had a chest out of him of pearl, jewels and gold but he swore by God we should not upon which I proposed to the Council to confine him . . . and was threatened with death'.

Several owners hurried to Holland to take control of this highly charged situation. Despite his endorsement of Dover's letter, Dampier seems wisely to have kept to the sidelines. He was by then sixty. He must have derived a certain wry amusement that, despite good intentions and careful planning, Rogers had been tormented by the same problems of maintaining discipline, trust and morale and stamping out mutiny that had bedevilled his own expeditions. Rogers was soon facing a further difficulty. An 'incensed' English East India Company claimed that the privateers had illegally encroached on the company's monopoly in the East and threatened to seize the ships when they arrived in British waters.

However, with the crew growing ever more restive, the owners finally decided to bring their vessels home. In October, the battered little squadron sailed up the Thames towards the new St Paul's Cathedral, completed only a year earlier. They received an enthusiastic reception. The papers had been eagerly reporting the successes of 'Captain Dampier's' privateers in sacking Guayaquil and, more fancifully, the capture of a Spanish fleet crammed with '6 millions of eight'. In fact, the Manila galleon finally yielded nearly £150,000. Half of this was consumed by legal fees, customs dues and £6,000 to buy off the voracious East India Company, but there was still a fortune left.

Dampier had at last fulfilled his ambition of seizing a Spanish treasure ship. He must have believed his share of the spoils was assured and that a comfortable old age awaited. Instead, he once again became embroiled in litigation. The owners claimed that, contrary to the agreement so envied by Rogers, Dampier's share of one-sixteenth of net profits should come out of the general pot and not the owners' share. The papers of the Court of Chancery reveal a tangled web, complicated by cash advances to Dampier and by his claims for special additional payments, like 'storm money' for participating in attacks. He clearly received some form of advance settlement, which, with his modest customs house salary, saved him from poverty while the dispute rattled on. With

Judith having apparently died during the *St George* expedition, the money enabled him to live quietly with his 'dear cousin', Grace Mercer, in Coleman Street in the parish of St. Stephen in the City of London.

Woodes Rogers's account of the voyage, *A Cruising Voyage Round the World*, appeared in 1712 and urged his nation to set up trading posts in the Pacific. The expedition had certainly whetted commercial appetites. The South Sea Company, later to fail disastrously in the world's first stock market crash, was founded the summer that Dampier and Rogers returned. However, Dampier's own energy for new ventures was spent. He was too old. From the scant information available it seems that, although he had guided the expedition through some critical stages, especially across the Pacific to Guam, his astonishing clarity of mind and memory were failing. He no longer had even the inclination to write. His vitality, and possibly also his eyesight – ruined by years of staring into distant sparkling horizons – were ebbing.

Almost nothing more is known about Dampier's life except that by the end of 1714, 'diseased and weak in body', he thought it prudent to make his will. He left one-tenth of his estate to his brother George and the rest to Grace Mercer. By early 1715, at the age of sixty-three, he was dead. Neither the cause nor the precise date of his death is known, but his will was proven on 23 March 1715. Two years later, his outstanding share from his final voyage, £1,000, was finally paid. It went towards his debts.

Dampier's place of burial is unknown. For a man who spent two thirds of his life restlessly travelling the world and covering more than 200,000 miles in his lifetime, this is sad but perhaps not inappropriate.

EPILOGUE

By the time of his death, William Dampier's name conjured instant images of exotic lands and distant windswept seas. His face was familiar through the circulation of engravings of his portrait by Thomas Murray. Journalists quoted from his works to illustrate their themes. As is the way with journalists, some, like Richard Steele in the *Tatler*, embellished them to make a better story. Others, like Joseph Addison in the *Spectator*, cited Dampier as an unimpeachable, immediately recognizable authority on such subjects as the inbred 'sagacity' of birds and animals in their response to their environment (what Darwin would have called 'cognate behaviour').

Dampier's literary legacy was considerable. Most important, his books provided a new kind of travel writing. They gave fresh substance to the armchair reader's journey by appealing to all five senses. As the reader went 'round the globe with Dampier', as Defoe put it, he not only saw what an anteater looked like but smelled its musky scent; he heard the sound of Aboriginal words; he ran his fingers over the glossy skin of an avocado and felt the roughness of a ray skin; he tasted the flesh of a Vietnamese frog and crunched locusts between his teeth. So great was the detail that the reader learned the price of travel – the uncertainties, dangers, and risk of illness (Dampier's

Daniel Defoe.

descriptions of dysentery are graphic) – as well as the elation when seabirds heralded land and local people proved friendly.

Dampier's works and their success provided a voyage format, source material, popular reference points, and a receptive market for other writers of both fiction and non-fiction. Dampier's writing undoubtedly influenced Daniel Defoe and in particular helped shape *Robinson Crusoe*. Sir Walter Scott greatly admired Dampier's writing and thought his influence on Defoe so great that the two must have known each other personally. Dampier's survival on Ascension Island, his description of unknown footsteps on supposedly uninhabited islands, his repentance for the sins of his past life on his great, storm-tossed open-boat journey to Sumatra, and his description of foreign lands all contributed. So did his involvement with Selkirk and his sensitive, sympathetic portrayal of William, the Moskito Indian so akin to Man Friday. Dampier's imprint on some of Defoe's other works is also clear. Defoe's *New Voyage Round*

Jonathan Swift.

the World by a Course Never Sailed Before had more in common with Dampier's books than mere similarity in title. The fictitious voyage's purpose was buccaneering, trade and discovery. The descriptions were strikingly similar – for example, the respective portrayals of the passage between the Moluccas and New Holland. Defoe also borrowed amply from Dampier when creating *The Life, Adventures and Piracies of the Famous Captain Singleton*.

So great was the vogue for sea voyages that they became the object of satire. Jonathan Swift owned a copy of Dampier's *New Voyage* and drew on it when constructing *Gulliver's Travels*. Lemuel Gulliver himself refers humorously and affectionately to his 'Cousin Dampier'. Gulliver's ship from Bristol to the South Seas shares a name, *Antelope*, with a ship that for some time accompanied the *Roebuck*. It also leaves England in the same year as Dampier – 1699. But more important, Swift was indebted to Dampier for a framework of realism to underpin his story. Many critics, from novelist Sir Walter Scott on, have noticed the similarities between Dampier's and Gulliver's personalities. There are also strong parallels between their simple, matter-of-fact, narrative style, which is so essential in giving a superficially credible substance to Gulliver's voyage.

John Hawkesworth, an intimate friend of Swift's who edited his works in the 1750s, pointed out more detailed parallels. For example, Swift cited the 'remote nations' of Lilliput, Brobdingnag, Laputa, and 'the country of the Houyhnhms' in Australasia. He even included maps showing Lilliput on the west coast of Australia, where Dampier landed. Dampier's description of Aborigines contributed to Swift's depiction of the Yahoos. So did Dampier's description of the chattering, dung-throwing monkeys of Campeachy. Swift's reliance on Dampier also demonstrates the enduring reputation of Dampier's works. Even when writing in the mid-1720s, Swift knew he could use Dampier as a readily identified, respected reference point around which his satirical inventions could soar.

Dampier's rational but responsive depiction of a vibrant world, stripped of myth but not of feeling, appealed to later writers keen to explore man's intellectual and emotional relationship with the universe around him. For this reason, poet Samuel Taylor Coleridge ranked Dampier among 'men of genius' and praised his 'exquisite mind'. He personified what Coleridge's friend William Wordsworth meant when he wrote:

> How exquisitely the individual mind
> . . . to the external world
> Is fitted; and how exquisitely, too –
> Theme this but little heard of among men –
> The external world is fitted to the mind.

The durability of Dampier's literary reputation is evidenced by the regard in which Coleridge and Sir Walter Scott, among others, held him. Even more impressive is the esteem with which major figures in science held him in later eras when science was evolving rapidly. Alexander von Humboldt used his works extensively into the nineteenth century. Even in 1860, when compiling the volume of the massive and authoritative *German Encyclopaedia of Physics* dealing with the weather, the author E. E. Schmid made frequent references to Dampier, often crediting him with the earliest or best available observations on meteorological phenomena. He commented that Dampier's work was so detailed and comprehensive that little could be added to it.

Another example of Dampier's lasting influence is that when Charles Darwin compiled his reading list of well over

Charles Darwin.

150 books and authors for his work on species, he included only Aristotle and four others published before 1700: Plinius, John Ray for his monumental work on plants, John Evelyn for *Sylvan* (which Darwin later dismissed as 'stupid'), and Dampier. Interestingly, he did not include Cook or Joseph Banks from the eighteenth century. The vast majority of works were contemporary.

Charles Darwin certainly valued Dampier. He believed the secret of his own success was 'patient observance'. This very quality was Dampier's greatest legacy to so many of the areas in which he worked, especially natural history. Dampier identified the importance of location to the development of animals such as turtles, birds such as boobies, and plants and trees such as the lime and nutmeg. He was the first to recognize different degrees of relationship between living things, as his use of the words *sub-species* and *species* indicate. In so doing, he was the first to foreshadow modern, systematic, worldwide biogeographic studies. He was also a leader in the understanding of migration. His detailed, accurate recording of what he saw and the comparisons he drew between his observations in different places, both familiar and exotic, provided descriptive data for others to develop.

Dampier's legacy to seamanship, discovery and hydrography has been acknowledged by his successors. Writing in the early nineteenth century, Admiral James Burney, a former lieutenant of Captain Cook and brother of writer Fanny Burney, wrote: 'It is not easy to name another voyager or traveller who has given more useful information to the world; to whom the merchant and mariner are so much indebted; or who has communicated his information in a more unembarrassed and intelligible manner'. Lord Nelson and Captain Cook praised

Dampier's 'Discourse on Winds' and recommended that their young officers read it. The next expedition to explore the Western Australian coast after Dampier in 1699 was commanded by Frenchman Thomas Baudin in 1801. His instructions referred him to Dampier, and he noted favourably in his journal that he used Dampier's detailed observations about both coast and weather to negotiate successfully a difficult night passage near Australia's Northwest Cape. To Matthew Flinders, the well-known explorer of the Australian coastline in the early nineteenth century, Dampier was England's 'celebrated navigator'. Modern hydrographers and meteorologists still acknowledge Dampier's major contributions to our understanding of how winds and currents work.

In commerce, Dampier's description of his travels and the potential he identified for trade helped stimulate not only the Scots Expedition to Darien but also the South Sea Bubble. Although both ventures were ultimately unsuccessful, by stripping away myth, uncertainty and prejudice and describing faraway lands objectively, Dampier encouraged the massive expansion of British overseas trade and influence in the eighteenth century.

Yet if Dampier's contributions were so valuable and so admired by his contemporaries and more immediate successors, why has he received so little recognition over the last century and a half, other than in western Australia as one of their first explorers? He fell victim to changing times and hardening moral attitudes. The very activity that made possible his navigational and scientific achievements – buccaneering – was seen as a taint overshadowing his attainments. His reputation was diminished by a new

Matthew Flinders.

censoriousness, and he slipped from view. A good example is the quote from 1907, that he was 'a pirate ruffian that ought to have been hung', rather than commemorated in the church of his birthplace.

Dampier's achievements were eclipsed by those who came after him and whose paths, ironically, he had helped define. James Cook is the Englishman commonly remembered for reaching Australia, not Dampier, who gave the wider world its first sight of Australian plants. In later years, greater store was set on formal education and depth of knowledge in narrow specializations. Yet the true extent of Dampier's lasting influence emerges only when, as Francis Bacon advocated, a view is taken across disciplines, both literary and scientific, both practical and intellectual.

Dampier's ability to assimilate ideas and to contribute in

so many fields shows the intelligence and curiosity central to his character. He was tolerant and open to new experiences and new influences. Although clearly a Protestant, he respected the religious beliefs of others. Edward Morgan converted to Catholicism before joining the *St George*, but for Dampier this was no bar to their continuing friendship. His description of the jewfish in his first book shows that he understood the prescriptions of Jewish dietary laws. While in the East Indies, he was careful not to offend his Muslim companions by eating or drinking items prohibited to them. He compared statues and forms of worship he found in Buddhist, Taoist and Hindu temples with insight and interest. His tolerance may have been based on a degree of agnosticism, which would have been typical of a man who found it hard to credit anything he did not see with his own eyes and scorned to attribute supernatural causes to unusual phenomena. His acute rationality may have inhibited belief in an afterlife. Dampier's logical and cautious nature, allied to a constitution both mentally and physically robust, certainly preserved his earthly life longer than a more emotional and impulsive one might have done.

Dampier's tolerance left him relatively free of racism for a man of his time. His inclination was to believe the ways of his own country were best, but he was a patriot and not a jingoistic imperialist. He did not see the white man at the apex of a triangle of humanity preordained to rule and exploit other peoples as of divine right. He saw no reason why all races could not reach comparable levels of attainment and believed each could learn from the other. He also saw some virtue in the state of nature compared with living in a more sophisticated society subject to arbitrary rule.

Dampier believed in individual liberty and that dictatorship failed both ruler and ruled. He despised Spanish colonial rule and the way it degraded the local people. He preferred free trade to imperialism and believed that every man should be free to develop his potential. (Dampier reserved some of his strongest criticisms for the 'lazy' who failed to do so.) He believed in the application of the buccaneers' democratic code and the right of everyone to have a say in the course of their lives. He even showed a touch of feminism, criticizing his colleagues for their refusal to give a female pilot a chance because she was a woman. He unhesitatingly admired the acumen of women merchants in Tonquin.

Dampier was also a humane man in a not very humane age. He despised the cruelty of some of his fellow buccaneers. When for their own protection he had to order his men to fire at native people, 'his design' was nearly always 'to frighten not to kill'. He did not slaughter animals indiscriminately, but only for the pot. When on a rare occasion he shot and wounded a monkey in sport, he immediately regretted it. Even when killing for food, he criticized his fellow countrymen for wiping out herds instead of, like the local people, culling selectively to preserve breeding stocks.

Dampier found it more difficult to apply his broad theories of tolerance and consensus to individual relationships. He did not find responsibility, either domestic or shipboard, to his taste or easy to cope with. In his day-to-day dealings with his fellow seamen and with his direct superiors or subordinates, he often thought he knew best. He was not always skilful in winning others over to his side, although he was often ultimately proved right. 'I told you so' was clearly part of his vocabulary. In his early voyages these characteristics, allied to a naturally diffident and distant manner, pushed him towards the role of a sardonic onlooker and cynical chorus to the counsels and disputes of his fellow buccaneers.

When he came to command voyages, Dampier was deprived of the refuge of detachment. Despite increasing age, he remained optimistic, undismayed by setbacks, uncomplaining of privations, and unsqueamish about what he ate, and he expected the same of others. However, he was not a natural leader, often finding no midpoint between a petulant, arbitrary dictatorship and an abdication of responsibility in response to criticism. Always self-sufficient and somewhat lacking in self-awareness, he grew increasingly intolerant of contradiction and the complaints of others. At the times of greatest stress in difficult relationships, when previously he would have retreated into himself, he seems to have resorted to drink. This had unfortunate if predictable effects, such as abusing his men as 'rogues', 'rascals' and 'sons of bitches'. Sometimes, too, Dampier's obsession with nature distracted him from his leadership responsibilities. In Bahia, on the *Roebuck* voyage, when he should have been thinking about how best to deflect Lieutenant Fisher's calumnies, he was preoccupied with pondering the relationships between waterfowls and coming up with the concept of sub-species. As a shipmate, though, he was usually faithful to his companions and his captains. His unease at his lack of loyalty to Captain Swan shines through his manuscript. In his later voyages, he chose to place old companions round him, but did not always choose well, and they showed a remarkable lack of loyalty towards him.

It is difficult fully to reconstruct Dampier's network of contacts on land, but it was clearly extensive, mutually sustaining, and covered many levels of society. He was a convincing communicator, able to subdue his didactic side to draw others out. He could empathize with them, listen and learn, irrespective of whether they were a Catholic priest in Vietnam or an English peer of the realm. He could explain cogently to others what he had seen and enthuse them with its relevance and potential. He was convincing about his own capabilities to the extent that Lord Orford, Thomas Estcourt and the Southwells trusted him to command expeditions. He could hold his own with fellows of the Royal Society, who included many prickly, cantankerous personalities. He could understand their novel thinking and apply it to his own observations. His intelligence and ability to see the bigger picture, to think laterally across it, to draw comparisons and to make connections clearly commanded their respect. He shared with some of them an occasional disputatious pedantry, challenging the extent of others' knowledge, as, for example, when he criticized the 'ingenious Mr Ringrose's' maps and depth of knowledge of cocoa production.

Dampier's intimate family relationships are harder to assess. He could have been speaking of his family when he wrote, 'Men are of diverse and contrary complexions . . . we may observe their inclinations carrying them out to various and very different undertakings . . . in a family one brother delights in a rural life', while another 'betakes himself to travel abroad'. However, he clearly remained on good terms with his own family – in particular with his farmer brother George – throughout his life.

There is, however, scant material on which to judge his relationship with his wife, Judith, interrupted as it was by

William Dampier painted at the height of his success by Thomas Murray.

his long periods at sea. She may well have been quite a formidable personality. Dampier trusted her to look after his affairs while he was away and was sufficiently wary of her reaction to prefer to communicate by letter difficult decisions about which she would not 'be pleased'. However, their marriage lasted for nearly thirty years – considerably longer than most of his day, when life spans were so short. Over that time they must have built up a mutual tolerance and affection, if not deep love.

But his attitude towards family and domesticity is not the key to Dampier. His strongest trait was a reasoned, restless, receptive curiosity, well attuned to the culture of his age, which made him hard to satisfy. He would not be denied a sight of what he called 'the vast number of objects that present themselves in the world'. Otherwise, as William Whaley, overseer of the Bybrook sugar plantation, patronizingly wrote, 'he might have been a good boiler'.

NOTES AND SOURCES

When William Dampier was writing, England still used the Julian Calendar rather than the Gregorian Calendar adopted in 1752. To avoid confusion for anyone wanting to cross-reference between this book and Dampier's texts, we have left all dates in the Julian system. To convert from the old to the new system, eleven days should be added to the dates quoted by Dampier. For example, under the Julian Calendar the *Cygnet* reached mainland Australia on 4 January 1688, but under the Gregorian Calendar it was on 15 January 1688.

To simplify the notes, we have used the following abreviations to identify some of the main archive sources:

BL   The British Library, London, U.K., which has, in addition to many printed records of the time, several important manuscript documents. Key among them are an early draft of Dampier's first book, *Voyages and Descriptions* (BL Sloane 3236), but also manuscripts relating to Cowley, Cox, Ringrose, Sharp and Wafer.

PRO The Public Record Office, Kew, U.K., which holds many relevant papers, including Dampier's correspondence with the Admiralty about the *Roebuck*, papers relating to his court-martial and to other litigation with which he was involved. *HCA* denotes papers of the High Court of Admiralty, before which much of the litigation occurred; *ADM* denotes general Admiralty files; and *C* denotes Chancery files.

RS   The Royal Society, London, U.K., which holds a considerable archive, not least of its own correspondence, *Philosophical Transactions* (*Phil. Trans.*), minutes of meetings, and other documents of the period.

SRO The Somerset Record Office, Taunton, U.K., which holds documents about William Dampier's family and, in the Helyar archive, correspondence about his time in Jamaica. All papers quoted are from the Helyar archive.

Among the many books in the bibliography, we found L. Picard's and M. Waller's very useful for providing insight into London and English society, supplementing contemporary accounts such as those of Pepys and Evelyn and the journals of the day. As well as the writings of Dampier's contemporary Edward Barlow, P. Earle's and M. Rediker's books provided background on seventeenth- and eighteenth-century seafaring. P. Cordingly, D. Mitchell and C. V. Black augmented Exquemelin's and Defoe's depictions of pirate life and the many eyewitness accounts. M. Deacon was a major source for the significance of Dampier's work on hydrology and A. Hart-Davis on the general scientific background. J. H. Baer's work is key to an understanding of the Spanish Expedition and L. R. Marchant's and A. S. George's to the geography and botany of Dampier's time in Australia.

Because this book is for the general reader, we have not given sources for each individual quote from Dampier. All quotes not otherwise sourced in the text, or in the notes that follow, are from his published books as included in the collected works edited by British poet laureate John Masefield and published in a two-volume edition in 1906. We have always shown where a quote comes from Dampier's draft of the *New Voyage* in the British Library (Sloane 3236) and does not appear in the published version because we believe this is valuable for the understanding of Dampier's editing and revision process. We have modernized spellings, punctuation and capitalization for ease of reading, where necessary, in all of Dampier's writing and that of his contemporaries.

Quotes attributed to Lionel Wafer, unless stated otherwise in this section, come from his book, *A New Voyage and Description of the Isthmus of America*. Similarly, quotes from Basil Ringrose come from his account published as part 4 of Exquemelin's *Buccaneers of America*, 1923 edition; from Sharp, from his account of his voyage, published in Captain W. Hacke's *A Collection of Original Voyages*; from Cox from BL Sloane 49 and from Cowley from BL Sloane 54.

All references to words first used in English by Dampier come from the *Oxford English Dictionary*.

PROLOGUE

17   The statement that because of Dampier, travel became the most popular form of secular literature is from the analysis in E. Arber's *Term Catalogues, 1668–1709*, vol. 3, p. viii, and is reaffirmed in N. Rennie's *Far-Fetched Facts and Fiction*, p. 59.

18   'the remarkable . . . little': quoted in J. C. Shipman, *William Dampier, Seaman-Scientist*, pp. 60–61.

18   'a mine': quoted in C. Darwin's 'Red Notebook', reproduced in *Charles Darwin's Notebooks, 1836–44*, p. 22.

18   'old Dampier': C. Darwin's diary for 4 June 1836, reproduced in *Charles Darwin's 'Beagle' Diary*.

18 'Whether or no . . . trying'; 'there . . . excellent use': quoted in A. Hart-Davis, *What the Tudors and Stuarts Did for Us*, pp. 160 and 162. Bacon himself fell victim to his enthusiasm for experiments. In April 1626, on a snowy day, he stuffed a chicken with snow to see whether it would stay fresh longer. The chicken did, but Bacon was outside for so long that he caught a chill, from which he died.

18–19 The Royal Society . . . understanding: all quotes in this paragraph come from T. Sprat, *The History of the Royal Society of London*, pp. 1, 38–40 and 124.

19 'scheme . . . wheels': M. Purver, *The Royal Society, Concept and Creation*, p. 84.

19 'human faces': RS *Phil. Trans.*, December 1699, pp. 431–34.

19 spectacles . . . dark: Purver, *The Royal Society*, p. 84.

19 'Mr Boyle . . . tobacco': RS *Journal Book*, vol. 2, p. 179.

19 The *Directions for Seamen Bound for Far Voyages* are in RS *Phil. Trans.*, January 1666, pp. 140–143.

22 'accurate': from Captain Cook's journal for 16 September 1770, reproduced in *The Journals of Captain Cook*, vol. 1, p. 417.

23 'the finest of all travel writers': quoted in H. Beck, *Alexander von Humboldt*, p. 90. The original German reads: 'der feinsinnigste Reisebeschreiber'.

23 'to read and imitate him': S. T. Coleridge, *Table Talk and Omniana*, p. 280.

24 'I dined . . . buccaneer': J. Evelyn, *Diary*, 6 August 1698.

24 'exquisite mind': Coleridge, *Table Talk and Omniana*, p. 168.

26 This draft (BL Sloane 3236) was purchased by Sir Hans Sloane and, with other manuscripts about pirates and foreign travel that he accumulated, formed part of the collections he left in his will to form the basis for the British Museum.

29 'a pirate . . . hung': quoted in A. Gill, *The Devil's Mariner*, p. 366.

I. 'A SELF-CONCEITED YOUNG MAN'

41–42 'for country . . . pound': E. Barlow, *Journal*, vol. 2, p. 342.

42 Helyar had provided . . . more brandy: the story told in these paragraphs and the quotations come from T. Hillyard's letter to W. Helyar of 11 April 1674, SRO DD/WHh/1089.

49 'hot . . . terrible': quoted in D. Pope, *Harry Morgan's Way*, p. 174.

49–50 All the favourite foods . . . 'victuals': the quotes in this paragraph come from H. Sloane, *A Voyage to the Islands . . .*, vol. 1, pp. xv, xvii, and xx.

50 'Such a crew . . . prevail': quoted in M. Pawson and D. Buisseret, *Port Royal, Jamaica*, p. 119.

50   'strumpet': Vice Admiral Vernon, *A New History of Jamaica*, p. 100.

50   'hot Amazons': quoted in Pawson, and Buisseret, *Port Royal*, p. 119.

50   'obscene . . . behaviour': quoted in M. Rediker, *Between the Devil and the Deep Blue Sea*, p. 59.

50   'A stout frigate . . . was in': quoted in C. V. Black, *Port Royal*, pp. 22–23.

50   'most debauched devils': quoted in J. H. Bennett, 'William Dampier, Buccaneer and Planter', *History Today*, July 1964, p. 470.

50   'This town . . . the world': quoted in Pope, *Harry Morgan's Way*, p. 178.

51   'critical years . . . future fortune': letter from W. Dampier to W. Helyar of 13 January 1675, SRO, DD/WHh/1090/2/60.

51–52   'The diseases . . . die': letter from G. Ellwood, 15 June 1672, RS MS.

52   'Your stomach . . . cold': 'for digestion . . . all': Sir Henry Colt's letter to his son, quoted in Pope, *Harry Morgan's Way*, p. 51.

53   'Take a hard egg . . . aforesaid': from *The Queen's Closet Opened*, quoted in M. Waller, *1700*, p. 98.

53   'needed . . . himself'; 'fair promises': letter from W. Dampier to Squire Helyar, 13 January 1675, SRO DD/WHh 1090/2/60.

54   'thought it . . . ladle': letter from W. Whaley to Squire Helyar, 27 January 1675, SRO, DD/WHh/1090.

54   'had tamed . . . shirt'; 'fast . . . mouth': Sloane, *A Voyage to the Islands*, vol. 1, p. lxiv.

54   'the nastiest . . . all': letter from W. Whaley to Squire Helyar, 27 January 1675, SRO, DD/WHh 1090, pt. 2.

54   'been some whore or other'; 'she had . . . about her'; 'great cronies' 'dirty trick': ibid.

54–55   'a good box or two'; 'returned the like'; 'could not be subject'; 'not come hither . . . would he': ibid.

55   'so diligent'; 'nipped in [his] bud'; 'like one (. . .) fatuus': letter from W. Dampier to W. Helyar, 13 January 1675, SRO, DD/WHh 1090/2/60.

55   'lofty'; 'been anything . . . boiler'; 'a self-conceited . . . nothing'; 'given to rambling . . . any place': letter from W. Whaley to W. Helyar, 27 January 1675, SRO, DD/WHh 1090, pt. 2.

III.   'TO SEEK A SUBSISTENCE'

75   'service . . . forgotten'; 'Get on . . . beach': A. O. Exquemelin, *The Buccaneers of America*, pp. 45–46.

80   'degraded clergymen': quoted in P. Ackroyd, *London, the Biography*, p. 260.

81   'the use . . . copulation': quoted in Waller, 1700, p. 36.

81   'green sickness': quoted in L. Picard, *Restoration London*, p. 96.

81–82   'an armour . . . danger': quoted in ibid., p. 97.

82   'a catalogue . . . wife': quoted in L. Stone, *The Family, Sex and Marriage*, p. 243.

IV. 'A DOOR TO THE SOUTH SEAS'

85   'fresh gale of wind': BL Sloane 2752 (an anonymous firsthand account).

89   'noisome vapours . . . climate': quoted in D. Cordingly, *Life Among the Pirates*, p. 60.

89   'as the trumpets . . . loss': quoted in *BBC History Magazine*, March 2002.

90   'cut . . . shoes': BL Sloane 2752.

90   'Ladrones!'; 'refused . . . him'; 'five or six . . . fleeing': quoted in P. T. Bradley, *The Lure of Peru*, p. 107.

90–91   The buccaneers . . . twenty men: all quotes in this paragraph are from BL Sloane 2752.

92   'crying bread . . . master': L. Wafer, *A New Voyage and Description of the Isthmus of America*, p. 2.

92   'whom . . . terrify': quoted in C. V. Black, *Pirates of the West Indies*, p. 42.

93   'The King . . . Spaniards': quoted in Bradley, *The Lure of Peru*, p. 4.

94   'sack . . . South Sea': quoted in G. Williams, *The Great South Sea*, p. 80.

95   'for three moons': B. Ringrose, BL Sloane 48.

95   The men . . . 'privy members': B. Ringrose's account, p. 298.

96   'out of sight . . . Spaniard': BL Sloane 2752.

96   'much gold': B. Ringrose's account, p. 299.

96   The buccaneers . . . 'device': all quotes in this paragraph are from ibid., pp. 299–300.

V. 'THAT SACRED HUNGER OF GOLD'

99   The sweating . . . 'adders': quotes in this paragraph are from B. Ringrose's account, p. 301.

99   'the cold . . . covering': BL Sloane 49 (John Cox's journal).

99   'Gold . . . of gold': P. Ayres, *The Voyages and Adventures of Captain Barthlomew Sharp*, p. 1.

100   'almost famished': BL Sloane 2752.

100   'the mountain . . . pass'; 'far neater . . . Jamaica'; 'bigger . . . peas':
B. Ringrose's account, p. 302.

100   'a very kind reception': BL Sloane 49.

100   'fancied much': BL Sloane 2752.

101   'which rape . . . Spaniards': B. Ringrose's account, p. 307.

101   'either . . . cassava-root'; 'count . . . twenty': ibid., p. 303.

101   'something bad': BL Sloane 46a.

103   'those . . . tired'; 'the current . . . bow': BL Sloane 2752.

103   'that fair South Sea': BL Sloane 46a (Sharp's journal).

103   'to bring . . . destruction': BL Sloane 2752.

103   'hugely glad': B. Ringrose's account, p. 304.

104   'cap . . . gold'; 'lay still': BL Sloane 46a.

104   'who . . . coming': B. Ringrose's account, p. 306.

104–6   At least . . . ripe fruit: all quotes in these two paragraphs are from
ibid., pp. 307–8.

106   'possibly could'; 'a miserable cry'; all . . . left': BL Sloane 2752.

106   'sailed . . . South Sea': B. Ringrose's account, p. 309.

106   'in an enemy's . . . seas': ibid., p. 311.

106   'stinking holes of rocks': BL Sloane 49.

107   'confined to an egg-shell': B. Ringrose's account, p. 311.

107   'perish . . . taken': BL Sloane 49.

108   'giving . . . charge': B. Ringrose's account, pp. 322–23.

108   'Sadly burnt': BL Sloane 46a.

108   'the doctors . . . soldier': BL Sloane 2752.

109   'to go home . . . Magellan': B. Ringrose's account, p. 334.

109   'we . . . ammunition': BL Sloane 46a.

109   The buccaneers . . . 'them': all quotes other than the one from Sharp
are from B. Ringrose's account, p. 331.

110   'a mutiny . . . enterprises': from an account signed 'W.D.', believed to
be William Dick, appearing in Exquemelin, *The Buccaneers of America*, p. 269.

110   'where . . . money': W. Hacke, *A Collection of Original Voyages*, Sharp's
journal, p. 38.

110   'a parcel . . . take us': Ayres, *The Voyages and Adventures of Captain
Bartholomew Sharp*, p. 24.

111   'before he was dead'; 'such cruelties': B. Ringrose's account, p. 360.

111 'and right glad . . . to get it': A. Exquemelin, *The Buccaneers of America*, p. 291.

111 'good chocolate'; 'very much . . . diseased'; 'a dish . . . liquor': B. Ringrose's account, p. 381.

112 'great plenty . . . fruit'; 'great . . . anchovies': ibid., pp. 379 and 384.

113 'Some fellow of a Spaniard': BL Sloane 2752.

113 'and good fortune': Hacke, *A Collection of Original Voyages*, p. 43.

113 'all . . . smoke': B. Ringrose's account, p. 388.

113 'We . . . clear of us': BL Sloane 2752.

114 The description of the captain's powers and of the ship's articles are given in D. Defoe, *A General History of the Pirates*, ed. M. Schonhorn, pp. 211–14.

115 'that dissembling . . . small': Hacke, *A Collection of Original Voyages*, p. 46.

115 'could not help himself': BL Sloane 2752.

115 'an old privateer'; 'stout seaman': B. Ringrose's account, p.398.

115 'This day . . . Panama': BL Sloane 3820 (Ringrose's journal).

116 'gave . . . the slip'; 'intelligence . . . affairs': B. Ringrose's account, pp. 400 and 402.

116 'daring and ferocity'; 'superhuman effort': Spanish report from Arica, quoted in Bradley, *The Lure of Peru*, p. 118.

117 'dressing . . . wounded men': BL Sloane 2752.

118 'thrust himself captain again': BL Sloane 2752.

119 'toilsome': Wafer, *A New Voyage*, p. 4.

VI. 'TWO FAT MONKEYS'

121 'found . . . anything': BL Sloane 3236.

123 'there was . . . river'; 'their stubborn nature': ibid.

125 'two fat monkeys': BL Sloane 3236.

125 'they . . . broiled': N. Uring, quoted in P. Earle, *Sailors, English Merchant Seamen, 1650–1775*, p. 89.

125–26 '[As I was] sitting . . . above it'; 'such remedies'; 'was unwilling to be left behind'; 'made hard shift to jog on': Wafer, *A New Voyage*, p. 4.

128 'not able . . . woods'; 'to terrify . . . loitering': ibid., p. 5.

133 'not only . . . observations': BL Sloane 3236.

133–36 Wafer had an extraordinary story . . . Captain Wright's ship: all the quotes in these paragraphs are from Wafer, *A New Voyage*, pp. 6–19.

137   'seats of easement': quoted in Cordingly, *Life Among the Pirates*, p. 89.

138   The story of chocolate is from S. D. Coe and M. D. Coe's *The True History of Chocolate*. The quote 'the great . . . sap' is on p. 175.

VII. The *Bachelor's Delight*

141   The quotes in the first paragraph come from J. Horn, *Adapting to a New World*, pp. 125–28.

148   'as red as blood': A. Cowley's journal, included in Hacke, *A Collection of Voyages*, p. 5.

149   'the discoursing . . . unlucky'; 'occasioned the storm': ibid., p. 6.

153   'They were . . . jewels': report to King Charles I of Spain, quoted in J. Hemming, *The Conquest of the Incas*, p. 25.

154   'enchanted islands . . . not real': BL Sloane 54 (A. Cowley's account).

155   'there was . . . twenty'; 'blind . . . sun': quoted in D. Sobel, *Longitude*, p. 43.

VIII. The Enchanted Islands

162   'I must confess . . . them'; 'our business . . . careen': BL Sloane 3236.

162   Ambrose . . . Island: the quotes in this paragraph are from BL Sloane 54. The map is BL Sloane 45.

163   'set us agog': BL Sloane 3236.

167   'Eaton's men . . . trade'; 'and would not . . . terms': BL Sloane 3236.

167   'He was . . . parted us'; 'I did . . . could not'; 'Captain Eaton . . . afterwards': BL Sloane 3236.

168   'impossible . . . boobies': ibid.

170   'This . . . condition'; 'should not long . . . consortship': ibid.

170   'would . . . mad': ibid.

170   'for the sweetest . . . tasted': ibid.

171   'men . . . molehills': ibid.

IX. 'We Ran for It'

176   'good wine'; 'made merry': BL Sloane 3236

177   'were at liberty . . . pleased': ibid.

177   'more cautious . . . abroad': ibid.

178   'by the help . . . South Seas'; 'raving'; 'the prisoners . . . dead men': BL
Sloane 3236.

178   'people . . . weakness'; 'we had . . . to do with': ibid.

179   'most desirous . . . goods'; 'those who . . . Spaniards': ibid.

179   'to be careful': ibid.

181   'The king . . . Europe over': letter from C. Swan to J. Wise, 4 March
1685, quoted in *Dampier's Voyages* (collected works), vol. 1, p. 545.

181–82   'another commander . . . temper'; 'made them quiet': BL Sloane
3236.

182   ''tis hard . . . men': ibid.

183   'ever-weary . . . uneasy': ibid.

184   'were all . . . hurt': ibid.

185   'like a company . . . appeared': ibid.

187   'inimitable wanderings': D. Defoe, *The Life and Strange, Surprising
Adventures of Robinson Crusoe*.

187   '[I believed] . . . come amiss': D. Defoe, *Farther Adventures of Robinson
Crusoe*.

187   'more to . . . wealth': BL Sloane 3236.

187   'that the doctor . . . recovery': BL Sloane 3236.

189   'how bloody-minded . . . enemy'; 'foolish women'; 'to make a trial . . .
pilot'; 'a fever . . . near his end': ibid.

190   '[On 25 December] we were forced . . . water aboard': ibid.

191   'grievous groanings'; 'their own folly ruined them': ibid.

192   'a long time before'; 'Although I was sick . . . unthinking rabble to it':
ibid.

X. 'YOU WOULD HAVE POISONED THEM'

197–98   'computation'; 'the time . . . to Guam'; 'to call . . . share'; Soon
everyone . . . 'as [the men] did': BL Sloane 3236.

200   'foulsome . . . abode': quoted in Earle, *Sailors*, p. 86.

200   'smells . . . dung etc': Sloane, *A Voyage to the Islands . . .*, vol. 1, p. xii.

200   'to poison the devil': quoted in Rediker, *Between the Devil and the Deep
Blue Sea*, p. 84.

200   'kennelling like hounds': Botting, *The Pirates*, p. 44.

201 'I reckoned . . . England': BL Sloane 3236.

202 'the obscene verses': quoted in Earle, *Sailors*, p. 94. The story of the practical joker is quoted on p. 98.

202 'Robin Hood's men': quoted in Rediker, *Between the Devil and the Deep Blue Sea*, p. 268.

203 'by God's assistance': BL Sloane 3236.

203–4 'Ah Dampier . . . mouthful': ibid.

205 'their victuals . . . peas': BL Sloane 54.

205 'many rich gifts to the Governor': BL Sloane 3236.

208 'make an experiment of it': ibid.

209 '800,000 . . . money': ibid.

XI. 'As White as Milk and as Soft as Cream'

211 'a scarlet coat . . . lace': BL Sloane 3236.

214 'tied . . . prince': ibid.

222 'occasioned . . . most of his company': ibid.

223 'deaf . . . pleasure': ibid.

223 'bought . . . Borneo': ibid.

225 'Several . . . tarried behind'; 'the liberty to leave the ship'; 'From me . . . the ship': ibid.

XII. 'This Mad Crew'

234 'the enchanted bodies of witches': quoted in Rediker, *Between the Devil and the Deep Blue Sea*, p. 182.

XIII. 'New-Gotten Liberty'

244 The identification of the landing site is made by L. R. Marchant in *An Island unto Itself*, pp. 110–22. He also discusses how long the *Cygnet* spent there and produces convincing evidence on pp. 64–72 that it was two months.

247 'a handful . . . privities': BL Sloane 3236.

248 'five people . . . men': J. Banks, quoted in Williams, *The Great South Sea*, p. 109.

248 'of good stature . . . lean'; 'want of food'; 'matted-up like a negroe's'; 'for want of combs': BL Sloane 3236

251–52 The lengthy repair work . . . behind them: the quotes in this paragraph are from Dampier's *Discourse* included in *Dampier's Voyages*, vol. 2, p. 312.

254–55 'by some that wished me well'; 'kneeled down . . . deliverance'; *matty*; 'Some beast . . . kill me': BL Sloane 3236.

XIV. 'Our Little Ark'

266 The question . . . trade: the quotes in this paragraph are from E. Yale's note of 23 April 1688 contained in the printed volume of correspondence for that year from Fort St George, in the Oriental and India Office Collection, British Library.

XVI. The Painted Prince

294 'leapt . . . fire': BL Sloane 3236.

XVII. The Rover's Return

303–4 The information about London Bridge is from P. Pierce, *Old London Bridge*.

304 'coarse and dirty'; 'the custom . . . shocked': quoted in C. de Saussure's *A Foreign View of England in the Reigns of George I and George II*, p. 94.

304–5 'Dirty and nasty . . . inhabitants': Quoted in J. Evelyn, *London Revived*, p. 37.

307 Some writers, including B. R. Burg on p. 123 of his *Sodomy and Public Perception*, have suggested that Dampier may have been gay, citing his closeness to Jeoly, of whom he was clearly fond. The buccaneer environment was relatively tolerant. Some seamen were undoubtedly homosexual, and long voyages must have proved attractive to those who were. If Dampier was gay, this may have reinforced his detachment from his ostentatiously heterosexual colleagues. There are certainly no lascivious references to the local women in his writing, as in some of his contemporaries' journals. However, unlike, for example, Robert Hooke's secret diary references to the quality and quantity of his orgasms and Pepys's coded entries cataloguing his sexual exploits, all Dampier's surviving writing was designed either for official use or for publication. He would have been unlikely to reveal sexual feats with either males or females in documents that his wife or the wider public might read. However, there is no direct evidence of a sexual relationship between Dampier and Jeoly. The greatest argument against Dampier having been a

practising homosexual, at least in his later life, is that his many antagonists on later voyages never made such claims, even though they did their utmost to discredit him at a time when such a charge would have done so.

307–8 'Jeoly's new owners . . . in Fleet Street': all quotes in this paragraph are from a handbill in the British Library, *Prince Giolo Son to King of Moangis*, no. 1198 c23.

308–9 Jeoly's owners . . . 'damning': the quotes in this paragraph are from Waller, 1700, pp. 217, 219, and 225.

309 The romanticized story of Jeoly is told in *An Account of the Famous Prince Giolo . . . Written from His Own Mouth*, printed and sold by R. Taylor in London in 1692 and held under the same British Library reference, no. 1198 c23, as the handbill quoted above.

311 'necessaries'; 'wine and fresh provisions'; 'several poor sick men': from a petition by the ship's crews, including Dampier, PRO HCA 15/16. The information about William Dampier at La Coruna was first located by Dr Joel H. Baer and reported in his article 'William Dampier at the Crossroads' in the *International Journal of Maritime History*, 8, no. 2 (December 1996), pp. 97–117, and is here supplemented by the authors' own researches in the PRO.

312 'the most horrid barbarities': quoted in Cordingly, *Life Among the Pirates*, p. 35.

313 'very conversant together': from Dampier's deposition of 25 May 1695, PRO HCA 13/81.

314 Despite being esteemed as 'a sensible man', Canby gets things wrong. Citing him as his authority, Dampier queries the conventional estimate of the distance between Guinea and Barbados of between sixty-eight and seventy-two degrees and suggests it is between sixty and sixty-two degrees. In fact, it is just over sixty-eight.

314 Dampier remained personally loyal to some of Avery's men, testifying on behalf of six at their trial in London in autumn 1696. His testimony is not recorded, but it was presumably about the abominable conditions that the crews had suffered at La Coruna and also about the individuals' characters. The men were acquitted but rearrested on closely related charges, convicted and sentenced to hang. Dampier again intervened on behalf of one, Avery's quartermaster Joseph Dawson, and contributed twenty pounds – a large sum – to the money Dawson raised for bail to allow him to plead for pardon. Despite not having cooperated with the authorities at his preliminary interrogation, and despite his senior position, Dawson was the only one of the six to escape the gallows. Indeed, he received an unconditional pardon when sentences, if commuted, were usually reduced to transportation to the colonies for a specified period.

314 Dampier meanwhile . . . back wages: all quotes in this paragraph are

from a petition by the ship's crews, including Dampier, PRO HCA 15/16.

315   'as bad as water bewitched': quoted in Rediker, *Between the Devil and the Deep Blue Sea*, p. 127.

315   'pinching the bellies': quoted in Earle, *Sailors*, p. 86.

315   'promised . . . six months': from Dampier's deposition of 25 May 1695, PRO HCA 13/81.

316   'some foul linen': quoted in T. Severin, *Seeking Robinson Crusoe*, p. 194.

317   'to be employed . . . Virginia': royal proclamation of 10 March 1693, quoted in D. G. Shomette, *Pirates on the Chesapeake*, p. 91

318–19   'The time and expense . . . . Caesar': quoted in J. Prebble, *The Darien Disaster*, p. 12.

319   The English government's attempt to associate the Scots Company with Avery's men and piracy is described in ibid., p. 94.

319   'conveniency of settlement'; 'possessed . . . Spaniards': from a document describing Dampier's appearance before the Board of Trade, sold by Sotheby's as Lot 4724 on 24 May 1946.

320   'any great service': *Calendar of States Papers, Colonies, America and the West Indies, 1697–97* (published 1904), p. 340.

XVIII. 'GOOD COPY'

322   The *Directions for Seamen Bound for Far Voyages* are in RS *Phil. Trans.*, January 1666, pp. 140–43.

323   Some men . . . 'ears': the comments in this paragraph on the effects of coffee come from *The Women's Petition Against Coffee*. The male response, cited in the footnote, is from *The Men's Answer to the Women's Petition Against Coffee*. Both are anonymous publications of 1674 and are contained in BL 1038. i. 47. In Britain's North American colonies, samples of coffee were originally given away free with purchases of tea to promote coffee drinking.

328   The information about the *Athenian Mercury* and the *Ladies Mercury* comes from J. Lindsay, *The Monster City, Defoe's London, 1688–1730*, pp. 87–89.

328   'to value good copy': J. Dunton, *The Life and Errors of John Dunton*, p. 218.

329–30   The analysis of sales for Defoe and Dampier comes from W. H. Bonner, *Captain William Dampier, Buccaneer-Author*, p. 35.

330   'diligence' and 'very intelligible and expressive': Robert Hooke's comments are in RS *Phil. Trans.*, 19 (1695–97), pp. 426–33.

331   'smatterers': quoted in M. Bragg, *On Giants' Shoulders*, p. 90.

331 'primitive purity' and 'a close . . . scholars': Sprat, *The History of the Royal Society*, p. 113.

331 'very little understood . . . reader': RS *Phil. Trans.*, 19 (1695–97), pp. 445–57.

332 'second part for the press': Sir E. M. Thompson, ed., *Correspondence of the Family of Hatton*, vol. 2, pp. 224–25.

332 'not the sort . . . back again': Dunton, *The Life and Errors of John Dunton*, p. 218.

335 The information on the importance of Dampier's findings is found in several authorities – for example, in the article 'Early Concepts and Charts of Ocean Circulation' by R. G. Petersen et al., in *Progress in Oceanography* (1996), 37, pp. 1–115 (in particular p. 38) and in M. Deacon's *Scientists and the Sea, 1650–1900*, pp. 93–174 (in particular, pp. 170–72).

XIX. 'DAMPIER'S *VOYAGE* TAKES SO WONDERFULLY'

339 The date of the *Works of the Learned* review is February 1699.

340 Dampier . . . *breeze*: the authority for this paragraph is the *Oxford English Dictionary*.

343 'large . . . sense'; 'all . . . knowledge': J. Locke, quoted in A. Sanders, *The Short Oxford History of English Literature*, pp. 264–65.

344 'the state of nature'; 'a state . . . equality': J. Locke, *Two Treatises of Government*, p. 287.

346 'witches' and 'evil spirits': Barlow, *Journal*, vol. 1, p. 55.

348 'celebrated author': quoted in Bonner, *Captain William Dampier*, p. 37.

348 'Dampier's *Voyage* . . . wonderfully': ibid., p. 33: Thompson, *Hatton Correspondence*, vol. 22, pp. 224–25.

348 'of better . . . education': Thompson, *Hatton Correspondence*, vol. 2, pp. 224–25.

348–49 'famous buccaneer'; 'a more modest man . . . consorted with'; 'the maps . . . Pacific Sea'; 'extremely tempestuous'; 'very extraordinary'; 'very profitable': J. Evelyn, *Diary*, 6 August 1698.

349 'illustrious persons': J. Evelyn, *Numismata*, p. 158.

349 'great travellers': ibid., p. 263.

349 'famous actions': ibid., p. 158.

XX. KISS MY ARSE

350 'not a fit person . . . Ships': PRO ADM 1/5262.

350–51   The expedition . . . Orford agreed: the quotes in this paragraph are from Dampier's Proposal to Orford of November 1698, PRO ADM 1/1692.

352–53   'considering the temptations . . . turn pirate'; 'and such like toys': ibid.

353   'strictly surveyed': Dampier's letter of 30 June 1698, PRO ADM 1/1692.

353   'pinching their bellies': Earle, *Sailors*, p. 86.

353   'disable': Dampier's letter of 5 September 1698, PRO ADM 1/1692.

354   'unwilling . . . voyage': Dampier's letter of 29 October 1698, PRO ADM 1/1692.

354   'very mutinously inclined': Dampier's letter of 17 November 1698, PRO ADM 1/1692.

354   'learn . . . matter': ibid.

354   'any ill affected person': Dampier's letter of 7 November 1698, PRO ADM 1/1692.

354   'he did not . . . fart': sworn evidence of gunner Philip Paine, PRO ADM 1/5262.

354   'did not understand . . . Navy': Fisher's letter of September 1699, PRO ADM 1/5262.

356   'old rogue': Fisher's evidence to court martial, PRO ADM 1/5262.

357   'much . . . Majesty's service': Dampier's letter to Lord Orford, November 1698, PRO ADM 1/1692.

357   'too far spent': ibid.

357–58   'stretch away . . . New Holland'; 'the good of the nation'; 'provided . . . to come along'; 'an exact journal': Dampier's instructions, 30 November 1698, PRO ADM 1/1692.

358   'ready . . . wind': Dampier's letter of 16 December 1698, PRO ADM 1/1692.

358   'gave . . . turd for him': Philip Paine's note of April 1699, PRO ADM 1/5262.

360   'Scots dogs' and 'a great rogue': John Rumbold's note of 10 March 1699, PRO ADM 1/5262.

360   'a pirate's life . . . best of lives'; 'for there . . . justice'; 'in strange countries'; 'he would not hurt . . . their heads'; 'all . . . pirates': Fisher's letter of September 1699, PRO ADM 1/5262.

361   'the beer was out'; 'they were a dry'; 'broke': ibid.

361   'fell to caning': ibid.

362   'old pirating dog': Dampier's letter of 22 April 1699, PRO ADM 1/1692.

362   'only got a ship . . . king and nation'; 'his scurrilous language'; 'the captain . . . as he pleased': note to Admiralty of 18 April 1699 written aboard

the *Roebuck* probably by the *Roebuck*'s master, Jacob Hughes, PRO ADM 1/5262.

362   'hot sultry . . . rain': log of *Roebuck*'s master, Jacob Hughes, PRO ADM 52/94.

362   'any disturbance'; 'brought to trial . . . offence': PRO C 9/459/62.

363   *sub-species*: this pioneering use of the term is in *Dampier's Voyages*, vol. 2, p. 395.

365   'the crew [was] healthy'; 'insolence'; 'return home . . . rid of him'; 'such infectious company': Dampier's letter of 22 April 1699, PRO ADM 1/1692.

XXI. SHARK'S BAY

378   'there was . . . darkened': log of *Roebuck*'s master, Jacob Hughes, PRO ADM 52/94.

379   'so very shy': ibid.

380   'cleaving one part': ibid.

381   'abundance of small flies . . . their ears': ibid.

381   'very shy'; 'leaping . . . on the land': ibid.

XXII. 'A FLAME OF FIRE'

390   'cut in ridges . . . their heads': log of *Roebuck*'s master, Jacob Hughes, PRO ADM 52/94.

390   'lined and . . . thronged': ibid.

392–93   'in the form . . . painted': ibid.

XXIII. 'NOT A FIT PERSON'

395   'Captain Dampier . . . search of': N. Luttrell, *A Brief Historical Relation of State Affairs*, vol. 5, p. 13.

396   'a great leak': Jacob Hughes's deposition, PRO ADM 1/5262.

396   'which I bade them do': Dampier's deposition, 29 September 1701, PRO ADM 1/5262.

396   'never . . . cut': ibid.

397   'it was impossible to save the ship': ibid.

397   'nothing now . . . lives': ibid.

398 'desolate island': ibid.

399 'a very ignorant man': letter from J. Gregson to Admiralty, 14 May 1699, PRO ADM 1/5262.

400 'renewed his petition for justice': Fisher's petition to the Earl of Pembroke, PRO ADM 1/5262.

400 'nastiness': Fisher's letter of September 1699, PRO ADM 1/5262.

400 'as soon as possible': Fisher's letter of May 1702, PRO ADM 1/5262.

400–1 Dampier's only defence . . . loggerheads with Fisher: all quotes in this paragraph are from Dampier's letter of 22 April 1699, PRO ADM 1/1692.

401 'as many . . . can be found': letter from Dampier to Burchett, 23 May 1702, in *Dampier's Voyages*, vol. 2, p. 595.

401 'two little boys'; 'a boy in the boat'; 'he did not care a fart for him': Dampier's evidence to the court martial, in ibid., p. 602.

401 'the detestable . . . sodomy': PRO ADM 1/5262.

402 'by barbarous and inhuman usage': letter from U. Norwood to Prince George of Denmark, 27 May 1702, PRO ADM 1/5262.

402 As far as can be judged . . . carpenter's adze: all quotes in this paragraph come from Barlow, *Journal*, vol. 2, pp. 451–53.

403 'as a greater terror . . . crimes': quoted in D. Botting, *The Pirates*, p. 127.

404 'it was not designedly done . . . heartily sorry': this quote is from a description of Kidd's trial in T. B. Howell, *State Trials*, vol. 14, pp. 123–234.

404 'uneasy and refractory conduct' and 'unreasonable behaviour': these quotes and the description of Edmund Halley's maritime troubles are from A. Armitage, *Edmund Halley*, pp. 139–42.

405 'frivolous': note by the court martial, PRO ADM 1/5262.

405 'very mean artist': Fisher's petition to the Earl of Pembroke, PRO ADM 1/5262.

405 'as sickly . . . confinement': evidence of P. Paine, PRO ADM 1/5262.

406 'The matter . . . to be imprisoned'; 'past dispute'; 'suppositions and surmise': note by the court martial, PRO ADM 1/5262.

406 'very hard and cruel usage': verdict of court martial printed in *Dampier's Voyages*, vol. 2, p. 604.

408 'things grown in England' and 'the most fit for English bodies': N. Culpeper, *The English Physician, or an Astrologophysical Discourse of the Vulgar Herbs of This Nation*, title page. The poppy is described on pp. 198–99.

410 'You will oblige me . . . at each': letter from J. Flamsteed to J. Woodward, 24 July 1701, British Library MS. Evelyn 3/1, no. 106.

411 'that when he came . . . mutiny': Fisher's evidence to the court martial printed in Dampier's *Voyages*, vol. 2, p. 599.

XXIV. 'BRANDY ENOUGH'

In this chapter, unless otherwise noted, words attributed to Dampier are from his *Vindication*, printed in *Dampier's Voyages*, vol. 2, pp. 579–84. Quotes from Welbe are from his *Answer to Captain Dampier's Vindication*, and quotes from Funnell are from his book *A Voyage Round the World*.

416 'the vast profits and advantages': quoted in B. M. H. Rogers, 'Dampier's Voyage of 1703', *Mariner's Mirror*, 10 (1924), pp. 366–81 from a manuscript in the possession of the Goldney family.

416 'an old ship . . . strong': A. Selkirk's deposition of 18 July 1712, PRO Chancery 24/1321.

416 The quotes about Fisher and the story of the court actions were located by Dr Joel Baer and are in PRO C 9/459 and C 33/301.

417 'I have not . . . please her': Dampier's letter to Southwell, quoted in Gill, *The Devil's Mariner*, p. 286.

418 'conceived . . . laid out': ibid, p. 285.

420 'hugger mugger . . . ship's company': A. Selkirk's deposition of 18 July 1712, PRO C 24/1321.

421 'a private consideration had changed hands': quoted in B. M. H. Rogers, 'Dampier's Voyage of 1703'.

424 'one Dampier'; 'a letter of mark ship . . . fleet'; 'with three millions of silver': Luttrell, *A Brief Historical Relation of State Affairs*, vol. 5, p. 475.

424 'I believe . . . good cargo': H. Southwell to E. Southwell, quoted in Gill, *The Devil's Mariner*, p. 281.

XXV. THE MANILA GALLEON AT LAST

In this chapter all quotes not otherwise attributed in the text or below are from Woodes Rogers's *A Cruising Voyage Round the World*. Quotes attributed to Edward Cooke are from his *Voyage to the South Sea* . . .

427 'till he had prevailed . . . advantage': Cooke, *Voyage to the South Sea* . . . , p. b3.

432 'Consult . . . satisfactory success': Quoted in C. Williams, *The Great South Sea*, p. 146.

435 'whipped and pickled': E. Cooke, *Voyage to the South Sea* . . . , p. 123.

435 'All bedding . . . provisions'; 'be allowed . . . everyone': ibid., p. 135.

438 'with much fatigue and trouble': ibid., p. 171.

443 'Captain Dampier was pilot': ibid., p. 353.

443 'violent': ibid., p. 356.

444 'great jarring among us': C. Vanbrugh's letter to owners, PRO C 104/160.

445 'a dead weight'; 'bloody noses': T. Dover's letter to owners of 11 February 1711, PRO C 104/160.

445 'the agreement . . . advantage': W. Rogers's letter to owners of 8 February 1711, PRO C 104/160.

445 'Dampier is alive': quoted in Williams, *The Great South Sea*, p. 156.

445 'For Christ sake . . . abroad': W. Rogers's letter to owners of 27 July 1711, PRO C 104/160.

445 '[Rogers is] disposing . . . death': letter from T. Dover to owners, July 1711, PRO C 104/160.

446 'incensed': Cooke, *Voyage to the South Sea* . . . , p. 455.

446 'Captain Dampier's'; '6 millions of eight': Luttrell, *A Brief Historical Relation of State Affairs*, vol 6, p. 518.

447 'diseased and weak in body': Dampier's will, PRO.

Epilogue

448 The reference to the *Tatler* is to issue no. 62 of 1 September 1709.

448 The reference to the *Spectator* is to issue no. 121 of 19 July 1711.

448 'round the globe with Dampier': From Defoe's *Compleat English Gentleman*, quoted in Williams, *The Great South Sea*, p. 175.

451 'men of genius' and 'exquisite mind': Coleridge, *The Table Talk and Omniana*, p. 168.

451–52 The lines from William Wordsworth are from the preface to his poem *The Excursion*, p. xi.

453 'It is not easy . . . manner': J. Burney, *A Chronological History of the Discoveries in the South Sea or Pacific Ocean*, vol. 4, pp. 485–86.

454 'celebrated navigator': quoted in A. S. George, *William Dampier in New Holland*, p. 20.

455   'a pirate . . . been hung': quoted in Gill, *The Devil's Mariner*, p. 366.

459   'Men are . . . rural life'; 'betakes . . . abroad': BL Sloane 3236.

461   'the vast number . . . world': ibid.

461   'he might have been a good boiler': William Whaley's letter to W. Helyar, 27 January 1675, SRO, DD/WHh/1090.

BIBLIOGRAPHY

BOOKS

Ackroyd, P. *London, the Biography*. London: Chatto and Windus, 2000.

Anon. *The Men's Answer to the Women's Petition Against Coffee*. London, 1674.

– – –. *The Women's Petition Against Coffee*. London, 1674.

Arber, E. *Term Catalogues, 1668–1709*. 3 vols. London, 1903–6.

Armitage, A. *Edmund Halley*. London: Nelson, 1966.

Ayres, P. *The Voyages and Adventures of Captain Bartholomew Sharp and Others in the South Seas*. London, 1684.

Barlow, E. *Journal*. Vols. 1 and 2. London: Hurst and Blackett, 1934.

Beck, H. *Alexander von Humboldt*. Vol. 1. Wiesbaden, Germany: Franz Steiner Verlag, 1959.

Black. C. V. *Pirates of the West Indies*. Cambridge, U.K.: Cambridge University Press, 1989.

– – –. *Port Royal*. Jamaica: Bolivar Press, Kingston, 1970.

Bligh, W. *A Voyage to the South Seas*. London, 1792.

Bohun, R. *A Discourse Concerning the Origin and Properties of Wind*. Oxford, 1671.

Bonner, W. H. *Captain William Dampier, Buccaneer-Author*. Stanford, Calif.: Stanford University Press, 1934.

Botting, D. *The Pirates*. Amsterdam, Holland: Time-Life Books, 1978.

Bradley, P. T. *The Lure of Peru*. London: Macmillan, 1989.

Bragg, M. *On Giants' Shoulders*. London: Hodder and Stoughton, 1998.

Bruce, D. A. *Economic History of Virginia in the Seventeenth Century*. 2 vols. London: Macmillan, 1896.

Burg, B. R. *Sodomy and Public Perception*. New York: New York University Press, 1983.

Burney, J. *A Chronological History of the Voyages and Discoveries in the South Seas or Pacific Ocean*. Vol. 4. London: L. Hansard and Sons, 1816.

Coe, S. D., and M. D. Coe. *The True History of Chocolate*. London: Thames and Hudson, 1993.

Coleridge, S. T. *Table Talk and Omniana*. Oxford: Oxford University Press, 1917.

Cook, J. *The Journals of Captain James Cook*. 4 vols. Edited by J. C. Beaglehole. Sydney, Australia: Boydell Press, 1999.

Cooke, E. *A Voyage to the South Sea and Round the World, Performed in the Years 1707, 1709, 1710, and 1711*. 2 vols. London, 1712.

Cordingly, D. *Life Among the Pirates*. London: Little, Brown, 1995.

Culpeper, N. *The English Physician, or an Astrologophysical Discourse of the Vulgar Herbs of This Nation*. London, 1652.

Dampier, W. *Dampier's Voyages*. Vols. 1 and 2. Edited by J. Masefield. London: E. Grant Richards, 1906 (Dampier's collected works).

– – – . *A New Voyage Round the World*; with an introduction by Sir Albert Gray. London: Argonaut Press, 1927.

– – – . *Full Works*, abridged, edited and with an introduction by G. Norris. London: Folio Society, 1994.

Darwin, C. *Charles Darwin's 'Beagle' Diary*. New York: Cambridge University Press, 1988.

– – – . *Charles Darwin's Notebooks, 1836–1844*. Edited by P. H. Barrett, P. J. Gautrey, S. Herbert, D. Kohn and S. Smith. Cambridge, U.K.: Cambridge University Press, 1987.

Deacon, M. *Scientists and the Sea, 1650–1900*. Aldershot, U.K.: Ashgate, 1997.

Defoe, D. *A General History of the Pirates*. Edited by M. Schonhorn. New York: Dover, 1999. (Originally published in 1724.)

– – – . *The Life and Strange, Surprising Adventures of Robinson Crusoe*. Oxford: Oxford University Press, 1972. (Originally published in 1719.)

– – – . *A New Voyage Round the World*. London, 1724.

– – – . *Farther Adventures of Robinson Crusoe*. London, 1719.

Dunton, J. *The Life and Errors of John Dunton*. London: J. Nichols, Son, and Bentley, 1818.

Earle, P. *Sailors, English Merchant Seamen, 1650–1775*. London: Methuen, 1998.

Edwards, H. *Shark Bay Through Four Centuries*. Shark Bay, Western Australia: Shark Bay Shire, 1999.

Evelyn, J. *Diary*. Oxford: Oxford University Press, 1959. (First published in 1818.)

– – – . *London Revived*. Oxford: Oxford University Press, 1938. (First published in 1666.)

– – – . *Numismata: A Discourse of Medals Ancient and Modern*. London, 1697.

Exquemelin, A. O. *The Buccaneers of America*. London: George Routledge and Sons, 1923.

Funnell, W. *A Voyage Round the World*. London: James Knapton, 1707.

Gage, T. *The English American*. Edited by A. P. Newton. London: Routledge, 1928.

Galvin, P. R. *Patterns of Pillage*. New York: Peter Lang, 1999.

George, A. S. *William Dampier in New Holland*. Victoria, Australia: Bloomings Books, 1999.

Gill, A. *The Devil's Mariner*. London: Michael Joseph, 1997.

Hacke, W. *A Collection of Original Voyages*. London, 1699. (Contains versions of both Cowley's and Sharp's journals.)

Harland, J. *Seamanship in the Age of Sail*. London: Conway Maritime Press, 1984.

Hart-Davis, A. *What the Tudors and Stuarts Did for Us*. London: Boxtree, 2002.

Hemming, J. *The Conquest of the Incas*. London: Penguin, 1983.

Horn, J. *Adapting to a New World – English Society in the Seventeenth Century Chesapeake*. Chapel Hill: University of North Carolina Press, 1994.

Houblon, Lady A. A. *The Houblon Family*. 2 vols. London: Archibald Constable, 1907.

Howell, T. B. *State Trials*. Vol. 14. London, 1816.

Howse, D. *Greenwich Time*. London: National Maritime Museum, 1997.

Jameson, J. F. *Privateering and Piracy in the Colonial Period*. New York: Macmillan, 1923.

Jardine, N., J. A. Secord and E. C. Spary. *Cultures of Natural History*. Cambridge, U.K.: Cambridge University Press, 1996.

Jones, S. *Almost Like a Whale*. London: Doubleday, 1999.

Kemp, P. K., and C. Lloyd. *The Brethren of the Coast*. London: Heinemann, 1960.

Lillywhite, B. *A Reference Book of London Coffee Houses*. London: Allen and Unwin, 1963.

Lindsay, J. *The Monster City, Defoe's London, 1688–1730*. London: Granada, 1978.

Lloyd, C. *William Dampier*. London: Faber and Faber, 1966.

Locke, J. *Two Treatises of Government*. London: Dent, 1975.

Lucie-Smith, E. *Outcasts of the Sea*. London: Paddington Press, 1978.

Lund, R. D., ed. *Critical Essays on Daniel Defoe*. New York: J. K. Hall, 1977.

Lussan, R. de. *Journal of a Voyage into the South Sea in 1684 with the Filibustiers*. Cleveland: Arthur H. Clark, 1930.

Luttrell, N. *A Brief Historical Relation of State Affairs*. 6 vols. Farnborough, Hants, U.K.: Gregory International Publishers, 1969.

McCarthy, M. *His Majesty's Ship 'Roebuck', 1690–1701*. Perth: Western Australia Maritime Museum, 2002.

Macintyre, D. *The Adventure of Sail*. London: P. Elek, 1975.

McConnell, A. *No Sea Too Deep*. Bristol: Adam Hilger, 1982.

McEwen, G. *The Oracle of the Coffee House*. San Marino, Calif.: Huntington Library, 1972.

McGirr, N. *Nature's Connections*. London: Natural History Museum, 2000.

McGowan, A. *Tiller and Whipstaff*. London: H.M.S.O., 1981.

Marchant. L. R. *An Island unto Itself, William Dampier and New Holland*. Carlisle, Western Australia: Hesperian Press, 1988.

Marley, D. F. *Pirates – Adventurers of the High Seas*. London: Arms and Armour Press, 1995.

Marshall, C. J., and G. Williams. *The Great Map of Mankind*. London: J. M. Dent and Son, 1982.

Masefield, J. *On the Spanish Main*. London: Methuen, 1906.

Mitchell, D. *Pirates*. London: Thames and Hudson, 1976.

Norris, G. *West Country Pirates and Buccaneers*. Wimborne, U.K.: Dovecote Press, 1998.

Pawson, M., and D. Buisseret. *Port Royal, Jamaica*. Oxford: Oxford University Press, 1975.

Pepys, S. *Diaries*. London: Dent, 1937.

Picard, L. *Restoration London*. London: Weidenfeld and Nicholson, 1997.

Pierce, P. *Old London Bridge*. London: Headline, 2001.

Pope, D. *Harry Morgan's Way*. London: House of Stratus, 1999.

Porter, R. *London, a Social History*. London: Hamish Hamilton, 1994.

Prebble, J. *The Darien Disaster*. London: Secker and Warburg, 1968.

Purver, M. *The Royal Society – Concept and Creation*. London: Routledge and Kegan Paul, 1967.

Rediker, M. *Between the Devil and the Deep Blue Sea*. Cambridge, U.K.: Cambridge University Press, 1987.

Reinhartz, D. *The Cartographer and the Literati – Herman Moll and His Intellectual Circle*. Lampeter: Edwin Mellen Press, 1997.

Rennie, N. *Far-Fetched Facts and Fiction*. Oxford: Oxford University Press, 1995.

Ringrose, B. *Journal*. Part 4 of Exquemelin's *The Buccaneers of America*. London: George Routledge and Sons, 1923.

Ritchie, R. C. *Captain Kidd and the War Against the Pirates*. Cambridge, Mass.: Harvard University Press, 1986.

Roger, N. A. M. *The Wooden World*. London: Collins, 1986.

Rogers, W. *A Cruising Voyage Round the World*. London: Cassell, 1928.

Sanders, A. *The Short Oxford History of English Literature*. Oxford: Oxford University Press, 1994.

Saussure, C. de. *A Foreign View of England in the Reigns of George I and George II*. London: John Murray, 1902.

Schilder, G., *Australia Unveiled*. Amsterdam, Netherlands: Tentrum Orbis Terranum, 1976.

Secord, A. W. *Studies in the Narrative Method of Defoe*. Urbana: University of Illinois Press, 1924.

Severin, T. *Seeking Robinson Crusoe*. London: Macmillan, 2002.

Shipman, J. C. *William Dampier, Seaman-Scientist*. Lawrence: University of Kansas Libraries, 1962.

Shomette, D. G. *Pirates on the Chesapeake*. Centreville, Md.: Tidewater, 1985.

Sloane, H. *A Voyage to the Islands Madeira, Barbados, Nieves, St Christophers and Jamaica*. 2 vols. London, 1707 and 1725.

Sobel, D. *Longitude*. New York: Walker Books, 1995.

Souhami, D. *Selkirk's Island*. London: Weidenfeld and Nicholson, 2001.

Sprat, T. *The History of the Royal Society of London*. London: 1667.

Stone, L. *The Family, Sex and Marriage*. London: Penguin, 1979.

Swift, J. *Gulliver's Travels*. London: 1726.

Thompson, Sir E. M., ed. *Correspondence of the Family of Hatton*. 2 vols. London: Camden Society Publications, 1878.

Vernon, Vice Admiral. *A New History of Jamaica*. London: J. Hodges, 1740.

Vickers, I. *Defoe and the New Sciences*. Cambridge, U.K.: Cambridge University Press, 1996.

Wafer, L. *A New Voyage and Description of the Isthmus of America*. Edited by L. E. Elliott-Joyce. Oxford: Oxford University Press for the Hakluyt Society, 1934. (First published in 1699.)

Waller, M. *1700, Scenes from London Life*. London: Hodder and Stoughton, 2000.

Ward, E. *The Wooden World Dissected*. London: J. Skirven, 1801.

Welbe, J. *An Answer to Captain Dampier's Vindication*. London, n.d. (circa 1707).

Wilkinson, C. *William Dampier*. London: John Lane, the Bodley Head, 1929.

Williams, G. *The Great South Sea*. London: Yale University Press, 1997.

Williams, G., and A. Frost, eds. *Terra Australis to Australia*. Melbourne, Australia: Oxford University Press, 1988.

Williams, L. H. *Pirates of Colonial Virginia*. Richmond, Va.: Dietz Press, 1937.

Winston, A. *No Purchase, No Pay*. London: Eyre and Spottiswoode, 1970.

Woodcock, G. *The British in the Far East*. London: Weidenfeld and Nicholson, 1969.

Wordsworth, W. *The Excursion*. London: E. Moxon, 1853.

ARCHIVES CONSULTED
(FOR MANUSCRIPT REFERENCES, SEE 'NOTES AND SOURCES')

Bodleian Library and the Fielding-Druce Herbarium, Oxford University, Oxford, U.K.

Bristol Record Office, Bristol, U.K.

British Library, London, U.K.

Cambridge University Library (Darwin Correspondence Project), Cambridge, U.K.

College of Arms, London, U.K.

Jamaica National Archive, Spanish Town, Jamaica

Mitchell Library and State Library of New South Wales, Sydney, Australia

National Maritime Museum, London, U.K.

National Portrait Gallery, London, U.K.

Peabody Essex Museum, Salem, Mass., U.S.

Public Record Office, London, U.K.

Royal Society, London, U.K.

Sedgwick Museum of Earth Sciences, Cambridge, U.K.

Somerset Record Office, Taunton, U.K.

State of Virginia Record Office, Richmond, Va., U.S.

Suffolk Record Office, Bury St. Edmunds, U.K.

Western Australia Maritime Museum, Fremantle, Australia

William and Mary College Library, Williamsburg, Va., U.S.

SEVENTEENTH- AND EIGHTEENTH-CENTURY NEWSPAPERS AND PERIODICALS

Athenian Gazette (subsequently the *Athenian Mercury*)

Ladies' Mercury

London Gazette

Spectator

Tatler

Works of the Learned

MODERN PERIODICALS

BBC History Magazine, March 2002.

Early Days (Journal of the Royal Western Australian Historical Society, 6, pt. 2, 1963, pp. 41–47, L. R. Marchant, 'William Dampier, Source Materials for his Early Years').

History Today (July 1964, pp. 469–77, J. H. Bennett, 'William Dampier, Buccaneer and Planter').

International Journal of Maritime History (8, no. 2, December 1996, pp. 97–117, J. H. Baer, 'William Dampier at the Crossroads: New Light on the "Missing Years", 1691–1697').

Journal of William and Mary College (21, 1964, pp. 53–76, J. H. Bennett, 'Cary Helyar, Merchant and Planter of Seventeenth Century Jamaica').

Mariner's Mirror (10, 1924, pp. 366–81, B. M. H. Rogers, 'Dampier's Voyage of 1703'; 19, 1933, pp. 196–211, B. M. H. Rogers, 'Woodes Rogers' Privateering Voyage of 1708–1711'; 29, 1943, pp. 54–57, J. H. Harvey,

'Some Notes on the Family of Dampier'; 33, 1947, pp. 170–78, J. Le Pelley, 'Dampier's Morgan and the Privateersmen'; 57, 1971, pp. 303–5, M. Pearson, 'A Pirate at Port Royal in 1679').

Progress in Oceanography (37, 1996, pp. 1–115, R. G. Petersen, L. Stromma and G. Kortum, 'Early Concepts and Charts of Ocean Circulation').

Terrae Incognitae (3, 1971, pp. 7–31, H. L. Burstyn, 'Theories of Wind and Ocean Currents from the Discoveries to the End of the Seventeenth Century').

U.S. Naval Institute Proceedings (August 1947, pp. 931–36, W. T. Pickering, 'Mr. Dampier Also Went to Guam – in 1686').

PICTURE CREDITS

INDEX

Aborigines, 34–37, 245–50, 247f, 297, 345–46, 379–81, 401, 451
Abrolhos Islands, 370
Acapulco, 189, 204, 209, 228, 440, 442
Achin (Banda Aceh), 253, 256, 257, 259, 260, 277, 280–85
    arriving in, 265
    Dampier left, 267, 285, 286
    Dampier's return to, 288
    factory at, 253, 265
Achinese, 257–60, 263, 264, 265, 283, 285
Addison, Joseph, 488
Admiralty, 22, 353, 354, 360, 393, 406
    Dampier letter to, 365, 400
    Dampier's orders from, 357, 362
    reporting sinking of *Roebuck* to, 399
Adventure books, 326, 343
Adventurer, Dampier as, 17, 78, 80
Age of Enlightenment, 327
Alligators, 69, 72, 190, 340–41, 364, 373
Alvarado, 78–79
Amapalla (island), 165
Ambergris, 147, 147n, 254, 254, 345
Ambrose (buccaneer), 255, 265
Andes, 88, 152
Andreas (Indian chief), 96
Animals, 21

descriptions of, 364
    location and, 453
Anne, Queen, 415
Ants, 33, 69–70
Arica, 88, 111
    attack on, 116–17
Aristotle, 453
Armadillo, 23, 69, 364
Artist on Royal Navy mission, 22, 358, 372, 378
Ascension Island, 24, 396, 398–99, 402, 449
    Dampier's rescue from, 404
Assumsion (ship), 421
Astrolabe, 155, 209
Astrologer, 179, 191, 411
Astrology, 408
Athenian Gazette, 328
Australia, 244–52, 351, 411n
    first Britons to reach, 17–18, 22, 243n, 245n, 455
    first scientific exploration of, 382
    flora and fauna, 375, 412
    Northwest Cape, 454
    scientific record of, 375
    Western, 34–37, 454
    see also New Holland
Australian coast, 374
    chart of, 370
    Western, 451, 454
Authors, 327–28
Avery, Captain John (Henry Every), 66, 311f, 312–15, 319, 352, 356, 360
    men of, in Bahia, 363, 365
Avocado pears, 23, 182–83, 183n, 448

ℬ

Bachelor's Delight (ship), 148–49, 156, 181, 182, 184, 316
  published account of, 333
Backstaff, 155
Bacon, Francis, 18, 455
Bahia, 360, 362, 363, 365, 458
  citizens of, 364
  Dampier's observations, 363–64
  Fisher and, 399, 400
Bain, William, 411*n*
Ballatt, John, 423, 425, 429
Bank of England, 174, 318, 324
Banks, Joseph, 21, 248, 453
Barbados, 399, 402
Barbon, Nicholas (If-Jesus-Christ-Had-Not-Died-For-Thee-Thou-Hadst-Been-Damned Barebones), 305–6
Bardi people, 34, 35, 247
Barlow, Edward, 41, 280, 346, 402
Bashee (island), 237
Batanes islands, 236–39
Batavia, 395, 423, 443–44
Batavia (ship), 244
Batchelor (ship), 442
Bats, 227, 389, 390*f*
Baudin, Thomas, 454
Bay of Bengal, 290
Bay of Campeachy, 56–57, 59, 65, 66, 73, 79, 84, 341
Bay of Guayaquil, 171
Bay of Honduras, 85
Bay of Panama, 102, 184
Bay of Tonquin, 280
Beagle, 21, 160, 369*n*
Beale, Alexander, 379–80, 401
Beef Island, 66, 70, 72, 73, 79
Behn, Aphra, 327
Bellomont, Lord, 355–56
Bencouli, 290, 292, 295
Benguela Current, 335
Beriberi, 189*n*
Bering, Vitus, 193
Betel nut, 212, 214, 215
Biogeographic studies, 453
Birds, 5, 70, 369, 449, 453

Brazil, 363–64
New Guinea, 388
New Holland, 245, 372
Bligh, Captain William, 207*n*, 223
Bloodletting, 52
  Kuna way, 135–36, 135*f*
Boca del Toro, 92
Boobies, 34, 61–62, 62*f*, 170, 202, 252, 398, 453
Books by Dampier, 17, 23, 26, 33, 57, 66, 73, 77, 78, 129, 143, 146, 147–48, 151, 160, 161, 187, 204, 230, 249, 313–14, 339–49, 364
  on Australia, 244
  cocoa tree in, 138
  description of Aborigines, 247–50
  drafts, 223, 225, 248–49, 317, 325–26
  first, 223, 310, 317
  first published description of New Guinea, 388
  influence of, 448–53
  influence of Royal Society work on, 324, 326
  Jeoly in, 307
  medicinal uses of plants in, 408
  revised and corrected before publication, 325–26
  second volume, 429
  sources acknowledged in, 344–45
  writings about Mindanao, 215–21
Botany, 21, 407
Bowman, William, 126–27, 132–36
Bowrey, Thomas, 267, 370*n*
Boyle, Robert, 19, 331–32, 334
Brand, James, 385
Brazil, 359, 360, 362, 363, 371, 399, 411, 418, 431
Breadfruit, 23, 206–7, 206*f*
Brief Instructions for Making Observations and Collections in All Parts of the World in Order to Promote Natural History (Woodward), 325
Bristol, 303, 427, 428, 429, 445, 450
British Library, 26, 325, 370*n*
Buccaneer Cove, 33, 158
Buccaneering, 313, 343, 454
Buccaneers, 17, 31, 33, 58, 74–77, 76*f*, 85–88

attack on Santa Maria, 99–106
code of living, 75, 114–15, 145, 214, 249, 254, 457
Dampier left, 140
in Pacific, 181
raids by, 130
scale of compensation payments, 91n
Buccaneers, Dampier voyages with, 74, 77–79, 80, 84, 85, 89–92, 93, 96, 106–19, 120–40, 227–43, 357
Australia, 244–52
East Indies, 252–56
expedition to South Seas, 145–57, 158–74, 175–93
Guam, 197–209
after leaving Cygnet, 257–67
Mindanao, 210–26
Buccaneers of America (Exquemelin), 347n
Burnaby, James, 418, 425
Burney, Admiral James, 453
Bybrook (plantation), 33, 42, 51, 53, 55, 363, 461

C

Cachao (Hanoi), 33, 268–76, 278, 279
California, 191, 440
California current, 335
Callao, 94
Campeachy, 61, 313, 330, 334, 451
Canaries, 358
Canby, John, 314, 322
Canterbury (ship), 399
Cape Blanco, 163
Cape Cormorin, 239, 252, 254
Cape Corrientes, 190, 197, 202
Cape Dampier, 393n
Cape Horn, 33, 148, 149, 191
rounding, 148n, 357, 416, 419, 432
Cape of Good Hope, 45, 294–95, 357, 368, 395
Cape St Lucas, 191, 440
Cape Town, 444
Cape Verde Islands, 15, 146, 358–59, 418
Careening, 162, 164–65, 177, 191,

250–51, 444
Roebuck, 382, 387, 395
Carib Indians, 75
Caribbean, 129, 318
buccaneering in, 74, 77
Spanish settlement in, 130
see also North Sea (Caribbean)
Carleton, Mary, 50
Carlos II, king of Spain, 311
Cartagena, 46, 92, 138–39
Cartensz, Jan, 244
Cassada, Andres Garsia, 354, 364
Cavendish, Thomas, 93, 192, 197
Cayman Islands, 50
Celebes Islands, 242–43, 290
Celebes Sea, 242
Central America, 310, 318
Chamorros, 204, 205, 207–8
Charles II, 18, 181n, 253
Restoration, 46, 138, 327
Charles II (ship), 310, 312, 354
Cheapo River, 129
Chemistry, 331
Chesapeake Bay, 141, 316
Chile, 145, 149
China, 23, 232–33, 235, 274, 275, 318
Chinese, 232–33, 235–36
Chinese Empire, 235
Chivers, Dirk, 111n
Chocolate, 111, 119, 121, 131, 138, 188, 324, 441
Chopsticks, 23, 274–75
Christian, Fletcher, 223
Christmas Island, 252
Churches
Indian, 166
Chutney, 229n
Cimarrons/maroons, 74
Cinque Ports (galley), 418, 419, 420, 421, 422n, 433, 434, 439
Circumcision, 217
Circumnavigation of world (Dampier), 17, 22, 346, 428
first first-person account of, 321
second, 424–25
third, 427–46
Clipperton, John, 422, 424
Cobre River, 33, 51
Cochinchina (Indochina), 229
Cochineal, 188

Cockles, 249, 387, 389–90

Cocoa, 137–38, 181, 324, 459

Cocoa tree, 138, 139*f*

Coconuts, 205–6, 253, 259, 363, 389

Cocos Islands, 252

Coffeehouses, 323–24, 343

Coleridge, Samuel Taylor, 23, 24, 25*f*, 451, 452

College of William and Mary, 317

Collett, Richard, 416

Columbus, Christopher, 88

Comets, 284

Commerce, 88, 454
     women in, 270, 457

Compass variations, 368, 410–11
     see also Magnetic variations

Comrade, 214

Concepcion River, 129, 136

Condoms, 81

Congo River, 123

Congreve, William, 309

Content (merchant ship), 41, 43, 44, 46

Cook, Edmund, 91–92, 96, 103, 115

Cook, James, 17, 21, 22, 207*n*, 248, 252, 352, 357, 394, 453–54, 455

Cook, John, 118
     death of, 163, 180
     expedition to South Seas, 144–45, 146–47, 148–49, 150, 158, 162

Cook, William, 115

Cooke, Edward, 427, 429*n*, 436, 438, 440, 442

Coppinger, Herman, 147, 224, 225, 231, 255, 286–87, 288

Coquimbo Bay, 112

Council(s) of war, 114, 115, 118, 420, 429

Court martial (Dampier), 24–25, 350, 400, 404–6, 415

Courtney, Stephen, 428, 431, 432, 444

Courts-martial, 400

Cowley, Ambrose, 147–48, 149, 167
     account of *Bachelor's Delight*, 333
     geographic survey of Galapagos, 162

Cowley's Enchanted Island, 162

Cox, John, 94, 107, 108, 113, 115, 118

Coxon, John, 85, 86–87, 89–90, 94, 96, 102, 103, 105, 107, 108–109, 117, 130

Crabs, 64, 132, 158, 398

Creation, 161, 188*n*
     relationship in, 364

Creatures
     characteristics of related, changed by local circumstances, 161

Crew(s)
     Cygnet, 199–202, 222–23, 224, 236, 239, 288, 341
     Duke and *Duchess*, 429–30, 431, 432, 433–39, 446
     not following Dampier's advice, 63, 123, 126
     Roebuck, 359, 360, 361–62, 371, 382, 383, 386, 392–93, 394, 401, 405
     St. George, 416–17, 418, 419–20, 422, 423, 425

Crocodiles, 253, 340, 373

Cromwell, Oliver, 46, 186

Cross-staff, 155

Cruelty, 24, 104, 111, 205, 457

Cruising Voyage Round the World, A (Rogers), 447

Cuba, 63, 64

Culpepper, Nicholas, 408, 409

Cupang, 385, 387

Curiosity, 18, 345
     culture of, 327, 408

Curiosity (Dampier), 21, 44, 74, 85, 133, 162, 187–88, 215, 239, 250, 277, 280, 290, 297, 341, 393, 456
     strongest trait, 461

Currents, 15, 252
     Dampier mapping, 17
     Dampier on, 334, 335–36, 338, 454

Curtana (ship), 267, 268, 280

Cuttlefish, 369, 411*f*

Cygnet (merchant vessel), 34–35, 150, 168, 184, 215, 258, 260, 266, 286, 287, 288, 289, 316, 383
     Aborigines on, 250
     careening, 250–51
     crew, 199–202, 220–21, 222–23, 224, 239, 288, 341
     Dampier papers on, 280

Dampier transferred to, 187
Dampier's escape from, 231, 239, 251, 252, 253, 254, 255, 256, 260–67
in East Indies, 227, 228, 229, 230, 231, 237, 242, 256
fate of, 288
former comrades from, 417
in King Sound, 371
in Mindanao, 213, 221–22, 223, 224
pets, 198, 201, 208
refitting, 230
in storm, 233–35
voyage to Guam, 197–204

ⅅ

Dampier, Anne, 44
Dampier, George (father of W. D.), 44
Dampier, George (brother of W. D.), 44n, 84, 330, 447
Dampier's relationship with, 459
Dampier, Josias, 44n
Dampier, Judith, 80–83, 84, 145, 197, 262, 293, 307, 313, 324, 399
Dampier's relationship with, 25, 459, 461
Dampier's return to, 306–7
death of, 446–47
money for, 353, 417
power of attorney, 310
Dampier, Thomasina, 44n
Dampier, William, 460f
assaulting Fisher on Roebuck, 361–62, 400, 405–6
attitude toward Aborigines, 249–50
best-selling author, 321, 339
birthplace, 27–29, 28f
business ventures, 83, 84–85, 290, 294, 307
case against, 399–401, 425
celebrity status, 17, 321, 348–49, 356–57, 428
character, 456–57
contradictions in career and character of, 16–17, 24–25
death of, 447

drinking, 418, 425, 458
early life, 44
employment, 290, 292–94, 310
employment in logwood trade, 66–72, 78–79
employment on sugar plantation, 27, 33, 51–55
engravings of portrait of, 448
failure of courage, 262
family relationships, 459, 461
financial affairs, 80, 446–47
'golden dreams', 31, 174, 318, 420
illnesses, 45–46, 189–90, 192, 193, 199, 265, 266–67, 276–77, 278, 279, 280, 284–85, 295, 395
illnesses: treatment for, 284–85
independence, 73
influence of, 17–18, 24, 455
intelligence, 456, 459
lack of recognition, 454
lack of superstition, 284
lawsuit regarding wages, 314–16
leadership, 25, 425, 445, 458–59
literary legacy, 448–53
literary success, 328–30
marriage, 80–83
memorial brass, 29
memory failing, 444, 447
papers regarding, 27
personal characteristics, 25
philosophy of, 170–71, 275
portrait, 16f, 17, 25–26, 348, 448
recognized values of his writings, 258
recording details of voyage to Guam, 204
relationships with others, 457–59
reputation, 454–55
standing with intellectual and scientific world, 406, 452
taking care of his papers, 258, 313–14
trial, 402–6
writing ability, 340
writing on board Cygnet, 200–1
writing for publication, 313–14
see also Books by Dampier; Voyages (Dampier)
Dampier Archipelago, 376
Dampier Island, 393n

Dampier Passage, 393n
Dampour (Dampier), Elinor, 143n
    and Daniel, 143
Darien, 30, 32–33, 96, 100, 168, 174,
    313, 343
    Isthmus of, 181
    Scots colony in, 318–21
    Scots Expedition to, 320, 454
    Wafer's account of, 317
Darien Indians, 109
Darwin, Charles, 21, 22, 159, 160,
    369n, 448, 452f
    Dampier's influence on, 18, 452–53
Davey, Irene, 34–35
Davis, Edward, 145, 146, 164, 165,
    166–68, 170, 172, 179–80, 183,
    184, 185, 187, 341, 405
    arrested, 316
    attempt to oust, 181–82
Davis, Jon, 155
Dead reckoning, 156, 204
Defence (ship), 294–95, 297–98, 299,
    303
Defoe, Daniel, 111n, 114, 162, 187,
    329–30, 448, 449–50, 449f
    Dampier's influence on, 17, 24, 449
Descriptive botany, 21
Descriptive zoology, 21, 69
Dick, William, 110
Dingoes, 245, 382
Directions for Seamen Bound for Far
    Voyages, 19, 322, 324, 325
Dirk Hartog Island, 36, 244
'Discourse of Trade Winds, Breezes,
    Storms, Tides and Currents'
    (Dampier), 20, 22, 102, 334–38,
    336–37f, 454
Discovery, Dampier's legacy to, 453–54
Diseases
    in Jamaica, 52–53
    in Portobello, 89
Distemper, 294, 298, 436, 437–38
Doctrine of Signatures, 408
Dolphins, 390
Don Carlos, 93–94
Dorset, estate in, 84, 85, 307
Doughty, Thomas, 365
Dove Galley (ship), 310, 312, 314, 354
Dover, Thomas, 429, 439, 443, 445
Drake, Sir Francis, 21, 89, 110n,

149n, 192, 197, 299n, 365, 406n
    Pacific voyages, 93
Driscal, Dennis, 265–66
Dropsy, 189n, 346
Dryden, John, 19, 167n, 324, 347n
Duchess (ship), 428, 429, 431, 432,
    434, 439, 440, 441, 444
Dugong (sea cow), 249, 374n
Duke (ship), 428, 429, 431, 434, 440,
    441, 442
    leaking, 443
Duke of Grafton's Isle, 237
Dunton, John, 328, 332
Durian, 219, 340
Dutch, 220, 230, 241, 243, 267, 287,
    288, 388, 415
    settlements in Timor, 383,
    385–86, 387
    trading empire, 211
Dutch East India Company, 244–45,
    296, 385
Dutch East Indiamen, 444–45
Dysentery (bloody flux), 52–53, 89,
    142, 346, 444, 449

E

Earthquakes, 310, 330
East Coker, 27–29, 44
East India Company, 211, 212, 265,
    266, 283, 288, 293, 298, 318, 446
    Avery's marauding for, 312
East Indies, 245, 267, 318
    chart of, 260
    Dampier in, 334, 456
    Dampier mission to explore, 349,
        350–69, 370–82
    map, 240–41f
    Portuguese in, 287–88
    Swan's plan to go to, 192
    voyage to, 227–43, 252–56
East Lewis Island, 376
Eaton, Captain John, 150, 152, 167,
    170, 171, 205, 207, 341
Edict of Nantes, 305
Eendracht (ship), 244
Eliot, Andrew, 29
Eliot, T. S., 29
Elizabeth, Queen, 93

Enderby (island), 376
England
  change in government, 402–3
  chocolate in, 138
  commerce, 82, 454
  Dampier's return to, 294, 299,
    303–10
  Dampier's return to, after Royal
    Navy mission, 399–401
  feared Scottish competition, 319,
    320
  and Mindanao, 211
  national debt, 318
  and South Seas, 92–94, 101
  Treaty of Madrid, 58–59
  at war, 415
English East Indiamen, 352f, 444–45
English language
  words Dampier brought into, 23,
    340
  writing in, 331
English pilot-books, 197
English privateers, 92, 179–80
Equality, Dampier's belief in, 238,
  249, 344
Equatorial currents, 20, 335
Estcourt, Elizabeth, 424
Estcourt, Thomas, 415, 424, 459
Eunuchs, 274
European rulers, 287
Evelyn, John, 19, 24, 304–5, 348–49,
  453
Experiment, 346
Exquemelin, Alexander, 75, 326,
  347n
Extinction(s), 330

ℱ

Factory(ies), 229, 230–31, 251, 266,
  290, 312
  at Achin, 256, 265
  at Bencouli, 290
Falkland Islands, 148, 419
False teeth, 238n
Fame (ship), 416
Fancy (ship), 312
Feminism, 457
Fever(s), 187, 188, 189, 266–67, 437–38

Finches, 159
Fire, making, 249
Fisher, George, 353, 354–55, 356–57,
  359–60, 458
  case against Dampier, 399–401,
    404–6
  civil claim on Dampier, 416, 425
  Dampier informed admiralty
    about, 365
  fights with Dampier, 358, 361–62
  jailed, 362–63
Flamingos, 15, 146, 359
Flamsteed, John, 410–11, 410f
Flinders, Matthew, 411n, 454, 455f
Flux/diarrhoea, 51–53
  Dampier, 266–67, 277, 278, 279,
    280, 284
  treatment for, 284–85, 433
  see also Dysentery (bloody flux)
Food
  and illness, 295
  need for, 432, 435
  sharing, 198, 249
  shortages of, 64–65, 170, 440,
    443–44
  see also Provisions
Fort Charles, 48
Fort St George, 266, 280, 288, 290,
  292
France, 415
Franklin, Sir John, 357
Freak shows, 308
Free trade, 220, 457
French
  converting Tonquinese to Roman
    Catholicism, 279
French privateers, 90, 96, 130–131,
  145, 179–80, 185
Fresh water, 148, 262
  need for 66, 158, 432
  search for, 252, 286, 375, 376, 438
  search for: Ascension Island, 398
  search for: Australia/New
    Holland, 245, 246, 378, 379,
    381, 382, 383
  search for: New Guinea, 388
  search for: Timor, 385, 386
Fruits, 182–83, 186
Funnell, William, 417n, 419, 422,
  423, 424, 425

G

Gabriel, José, 105
Gainy, George, 127
Galapagos Islands, 21, 33, 229
  buccaneers at, 154, 156–57,
    158–62
  Dampier's description of, 160–62
  map of, 159f
  privateering expedition at,
    437–38
Galen, 52
Galileo, 330
Gallo island, 175, 176–77
Ganj-i-Sawai (ship), 312, 356
General History of the Pirates (Defoe),
  114
Gentleman's Journal, 328
Geographic variation, 161
George, Prince, 415
German Encyclopaedia of Physics, 452
Ghini, Luca, 407
Glorious Revolution, 287, 355n
Goddard (chief mate), 294
Gold, 17, 96, 99, 104–105, 109, 114,
  136, 173, 174, 188, 214, 351, 391
  in Achin, 281
  amassed by Swan, 209
  Dampier's hunger for, 121, 310
  at Meangis, 291
  in Mindanao, 220
Golden Island, 96, 320
Goodlad (captain), 211, 212, 213
Gopson, Richard, 128, 132–36, 201–2
Gorgona, 120–21, 438–39
Government structures, 23
  Achin, 283, 284
  Tonquinese, 273–74
Grande (island), 431
Great Moghul of India, 283–84, 288,
  308, 312
  fleet, 312–13
Great Plague, 238n, 284
Green turtles, 21, 50, 160, 161f, 229
  migratory patterns of, 161–62,
    229
  New Holland, 373
Gregson, James, 354, 364, 399
Gret, John, 101

Grogniet, Captain, 179–80, 183, 184,
  185
Guam, 197, 440, 443, 447
  voyage to, 197–209 210, 224
Guanos (bobtail lizards), 372–73
Guavas, 186
Guayaquil, 111, 120, 152, 437, 438
  attack on, 171–73, 435–37, 446
Guinea fowl, 359
Guinea worm, 144
Gulf of Amapalla, 164
Gulf of Carpentaria, 244
Gulf of Guayaquil, 423, 435
Gulf of Mexico, 56
Gulf of San Miguel, 32, 121, 180
Gulf of Thailand, 230
Gulf Stream, 335
Gulliver's Travels (Swift), 24, 450–51
Gunpowder, 278, 292–93, 442

H

Hacke, Captain William, 332, 333,
  347
Hall, Robert, 255, 258, 259, 260, 261,
  265, 266
Halley, Edmund, 19, 20, 284, 331,
  332f, 337, 338, 406, 411
  command of *Paramore*, 404
Harris, Captain Peter (nephew), 168,
  173, 181, 183
Harris, Captain Peter (uncle), 92, 96,
  102, 108, 168
Harrison, Edward, 404
Harthop (merchant), 223, 225
Hartog, Dirk, 244
  marker plate, 375
Harvey, William, 52
Hatton, Charles, 348
Havana, 46
Havre de Grace (ship), 438
Hawkesworth, John, 451
Headhunters, 387–88
Heath, Captain, 294, 295, 298
Helyar, Cary, 53
Helyar, Colonel William, 42, 43, 44,
  46, 51, 53, 54, 55
Helyar family, 348
Herbal (Culpepper), 408

Herbaria, 407
High Court of Admiralty, 314, 315, 316
Hillyard, Thomas, 42–43
Hingson, John, 128, 132–36
Hispaniola, 74, 180
HMS *Dumbarton*, 316
HMS *Dunwich*, 354
HMS *Paramore*, 404
HMS *Royal Sovereign*, 350, 404
HMS *Sweepstakes*, 93
Hobby (trader), 84–85
Homosexuality, 67, 75, 214, 401
Honorable Council of Lords of Trade and Plantations, 319, 320, 348, 356n
Hooke, Robert, 324, 330, 334, 348
Hopiga, Edna, 36–37
Hottentots, 247, 296–97, 345–46
Houblon, Sir John, 310
Houghton, John, 327
Hudsel, Captain, 56–57, 59, 60–61, 63
Hughes, Jacob, 353, 362, 374, 378
Humboldt, Alexander von, 18, 23, 452
Hummingbird, 23, 70
Humours, theory of, 52, 407
Humpback whales, 36, 376
Hunting, 63–64, 74–75, 170, 177, 190, 219, 222, 233, 392, 434, 438
  by Indians, 77
  by logwooders, 67
Hurricanes, 71–72, 73, 334–35
Huxford, Samuel, 418, 425
Hydrographer, Dampier as, 17, 20, 336
Hydrography, Dampier's legacy to, 453–54

J

Iguanas, 34, 159, 177, 220
Ilo, 111
Inca Empire, 153
Indentured servitude, 41–43, 51, 74, 143
India, 239, 243, 266, 288, 312
Indian guides, 96, 99–106, 124–25, 127, 129–30, 133, 134, 172, 176
Indian Ocean, 253, 294, 356, 368
  monsoon currents in, 335
  piracy in, 312
Indian traders, 78
Indian women, 67
Indians, 66, 87, 94, 128
  of Cupang, 387–88
  Dampier's descriptions of, 77, 78, 132
  Dampier's views of, 73, 77–78, 132, 166–67
  enemies, 122
  musical instruments, 166
  rafts, 171
  slaves, 88
  under Spanish rule, 166–67
Individual liberty, Dampier's belief in, 457
Indrapore, 290, 294
Inquisition, 365, 400
Isabella, Duchess of Grafton, 80
Isla de Colon, 92
Isla de Plata, 110, 118, 168
Islands, naming, 237
Isle of Pines, 85, 87
Isthmus of Panama, 17, 30, 46, 94, 102, 119, 121, 130, 145, 168, 173, 258
  proposed Scottish colony on, 318–21

J

Jamaica, 46–50, 58, 64, 65, 310
  Dampier going to, 41–44, 293
  Dampier trips to, 79, 83, 84
  Dampier working on sugar plantation in, 27, 33, 51–55
  logwooding, 56–57
  Scots' appeal to, 320
  Wafer in, 91
James (ship), 310, 314
James, Captain, 56
James II, 181n, 287, 343, 355n
James River, 141
Jamestown, 141–42, 316
Japan, 318
Java, 45, 91, 395

Jeoly ('the painted prince'), 24, 288–94, 289f, 298, 299
  death of, 310
  exhibition of, 307–10
Jermyn, Henry, earl of St. Albans, 305
Jew-fish, 190, 456
John and Martha (ship), 44
Johnson, Samuel, 162
Jolly Prize (ship), 353
Journal (Dampier), 15, 33, 131, 200–1, 248, 294
  saved, 257–58, 398
  working into book, 313–14
Juan Fernandez Islands, 24, 113, 116, 150, 151f, 152, 419, 421, 432
Just society, 238, 343

Karrakatta Bay, 34–35, 250
Kent, John, 41
Kidd, William, 17, 45, 355–56, 403–4, 403f, 405n
  hanged, 404
'King Golden Cap', 103–4, 105f, 106, 108
King Sound, 34–35, 244, 247, 251, 252, 371
Kingston, 49
Kinsale, 417, 418
Kircher, Athanasius, 336
Knapton, James, 321, 328, 332–33, 347, 411, 429
Knight, John, 354
Komodo dragon, 220
Kumquats, 276
Kuna Indians, 30, 32, 95–96, 99–106, 108, 128, 173–74, 346
  Wafer with, 133–36, 317, 321

La Coruna, 310, 313, 314
La Popa (nunnery), 138–39
La Serena, 112–13
La Sounds Key, 130, 132
Lacenta (chief), 134–36

Ladies' Mercury (magazine), 328
Lagrange Bay, 36, 37, 378
Laguna, 358
Lake Titicaca, 88
Language, 215
Latitude, 155, 156
  calculating, 261
  Dampier's calculation of, 204
Lavelia, 175, 177, 185
Le Maire, Jacob, 148n
Le Maire Strait, 149
Lee, Samuel, 82n
Leeuwenhoek, Antonio van, 188n
Leon, 185–86
Lescuyer, Captain, 179
Letters (Dampier), 27
Letters of marque, 74, 109, 416, 424
Life, Adventures and Piracies of the Famous Captain Singleton, The (Defoe), 450
Lima, 94, 111, 152, 171, 176, 177, 435
  viceroy of, 152, 154
Literacy
  sailors, 201–2
Literary world, 24
Living things, relationships among, 453
Livingstone, David, 429n
Lobos de la Mar ('Seal' Island), 153
Lobos Islands, 434
Locke, John, 320, 343–44, 345f, 348
Logbook, 156, 374
Logline, 156, 208, 346
Logwood/logwooding, 23–24, 56–60, 82, 85
  Dampier and, 66–72, 73, 78–79, 84, 312–13, 334
L'Ollonois, Francois, 111n
London, 41, 303–6, 317
  Carnaby Street, 305
  Execution Dock, 17, 404
  the Fleet, 80
  Great Fire, 44, 284, 304, 306
  Piccadilly, 305
  Soho, 305–6, 317
London Bridge, 303, 303f, 306
London Gazette, 415
Longitude, 156, 227, 368, 426n
  calculating, 190, 204

Love for Love (Congreve), 309
Luttrell, Narcissus, 395, 424, 428
Lynch, Sir Thomas, 58

M

Macao, 236
Madagascar, 288, 312, 405*n*
Magazines, 328
Magellan, Ferdinand, 197
Magnetic compass, 155
Magnetic variations, 204, 322, 410–11
Malacca, 230, 285, 287
Malaria, 52, 142
Malay language, 215, 229, 290, 291, 389
Malays, 231
Mammals, 372
Manatee, 92, 123, 131
Manchu, 232
Mançanilla tree, 131–32
Mangera, 165
Mango, 228–29
Mangosteen, 280–81
Mango-Achar, 228–29
Mangrove swamps, 57, 185, 383, 435
Mangroves, 57, 68, 164, 171, 250, 374, 382, 383, 384
Manila 189, 208, 209, 222, 232, 239, 443
    'rich' ship from, 189–90, 192, 209, 228
Manila galleon, 416
    Dampier's attempt to capture, 422
    prospect of seizing, 439–42
    treasure from, 446
Man-of-war birds, 62–63, 63*f*, 71, 158, 252
Maps, 17, 162
    from *A New Voyage*, 86–87*f*, 269*f*
    for Dampier's books, 324, 338, 411
    Galapagos Islands, 162
    from *Voyages and Descriptions*, 57*f*
    of winds, 20, 336–38, 349
Marijuana, 21, 281
Marine topics, 19

Marine work, 330, 331
Mariner's Magazine, The, 278
Marquess (ship), 438–39, 440, 442, 444
Marriage, 80–82
    as financial arrangement, 82
Mary, Queen, 287, 355*n*
Matelotage, 75
Maya, 137–38
McCarthy, Mike, 398*n*
Meangis, 290, 291, 294
Medicines, 135
Mekong River, 228
Mercer, Grace, 447
Merchant seamen, 314–15
Meteorology, 296, 452
Mexican coast, 190, 192
Mexico, 93, 186–87, 189
Migration, 161–62, 453
Milton, John, 347*n*
Mindanao, 209, 229, 230, 239, 289, 290, 291
    Swan abandoned on, 224–25, 240–41, 280, 288, 341, 355
    voyage to, 210–26, 227
Mindanao (merchant ship), 288, 289
Mindanao River, 210–11, 241
Mindanaons, 210–18, 225, 346
    Dampier's description of, 215–18
Mindoro, 228
Ming dynasty, 232
Mocha, 312, 356
Mock trial(s), 202
Modyford, Sir Thomas, 58
Moll, Herman, 324, 336, 343, 411
Moluccas, 450
Monkeys, 125, 364, 431, 438, 451, 457
Monkfish, 378, 378*f*
Monsoon currents, 335
Monsoons, 20, 209, 223, 254, 257, 260, 288, 338, 383
Montague, Charles, Earl of Halifax, 326, 350, 393
Montbars of Languedoc, 111*n*
Monte Bello Islands, 245*n*
Montezuma, 138
Moody (a man), 289–91, 292, 294
Moon, eclipse of, 284, 378
Moore, William, 403–4

Moral attitudes
  in judgement of Dampier, 454
More, Henry, 212, 225, 231
Morgan, Edward, 425
  Dampier met again, 288
  mutiny by, 423, 424n
  on privateering mission, 417, 418, 420, 421
Morgan, Henry, 46–47, 47f, 66, 85, 92, 107, 168
  converted to Catholicism, 456
  expedition, 58
  in Panamanian Isthmus, 94
  raid on Portobello, 88, 89
  sinking of flagship (Oxford), 139
Moskito Indians, 85, 119, 123, 151, 253
Mowing Devil, The, 327
Murray, Thomas, 348, 448
Muslims, 209, 217, 259, 264, 281, 456
Mutiny(ies), 110, 311–12, 313, 314, 341, 362, 404, 411
  on Cygnet, 224–25
  on Duke and Duchess, 430
  on St George, 418, 422, 423, 429

N

Narborough, John, 93, 94
National Portrait Gallery, 17, 26
Native peoples, 325, 346
  Bahia, 364
  Dampier's interest in, 237–38
  New Guinea, 388–93, 392f
  Timor, 387
  see also Aborigines
Natural history, 325, 453
Natural philosophy, 18, 187
Natural selection, 21
Naturalist, Dampier as, 15, 18, 21
Nature
  Dampier's interest in, 27, 80, 131–32, 187, 250, 458
  experiences of, in Dampier's books, 340–41
  study of, 19–20, 322
Navigation, 45, 154–56
  Dampier, 368, 443, 454
Navigational instruments, 22

Navigator, Dampier as, 17, 22, 45, 192, 348, 405, 425–26, 428
Navy Articles, 67
Negril Bay, 85
Nellegree (ship), 283–84
Nelson, Lord, 453–54
New Amsterdam, 45
New Caledonia, 320–21
New Description of the Isthmus of Darien, A (Wafer), 321
New Guinea, 244, 252, 357, 376
  coast, 198f
  Dampier's description of, 429
  exploring, 383
  Royal Navy mission, 388–94
New Holland, 243, 252, 388, 450
  coast, 198f
  Dampier mission to explore, 349, 350–69, 370–82, 383, 394, 395
  landing at, 370–72
  leaving, 382
  map, 384f
  voyages to, 244–45
  see also Australia
New Spain, 162–64
New Voyage Round the World, A (Dampier), 17, 26, 321, 322, 425, 450
  amendments to, 325–26
  cultural and intellectual movements in, 343
  draft of, 340–42, 343
  money made from, 347–48
  preface and dedication, 326, 339, 342–43
  publication of, 350
  success of, 328–30
  title page, 329f
New Voyage Round the World by a Course Never Sailed Before (Defoe), 449–50
New World, 46–47, 92
New Zealand, 244, 351
Newspapers, 328
Newton, Isaac, 19, 330–31, 338
Nicholas (ship), 150
Nicobar Islands, 253–54, 258, 261, 266, 280, 286, 313
'Noble savage', 167n, 343
North Brazil Current, 335

North Sea (Caribbean), 74, 106n, 129, 169f

Northern lights, 284

Northwest passage, 191–92

Norwood, John, 386, 396, 397, 402, 405

Norwood, Ursula, 402

Notes (Dampier), 69, 77, 192, 313
    on Australia, 375

Nova Britannia (New Britain), 393

Nuestra Senora de Begona (ship), 441–42

Nuestra Senora de la Encarnacion Disengano, 441, 442

Numismata (Evelyn), 349

Nutmeg, 220, 389, 391, 453

Observance
    Dampier's greatest legacy, 453

Observations, 19
    encouraged by Royal Society, 322, 407

Observations (Dampier), 18, 20, 33, 137–38, 190, 207n, 215, 313, 346, 410, 453, 454
    Bahia, 368
    books centred on, 326
    in Brazil, 363–64
    of Hottentots, 296–97
    New Holland, 372–75, 382

O'Byrne, Admiral, 310

Ocean currents, 20, 338

One-Bush Key, 57, 72

Oort, Sarah, 355

Opium, 408, 429n

Orford, Lord, 350–51, 351f, 353, 355, 357, 402, 403, 459

Oroonoko (Behn), 327

Oxford (ship), 139

Oxford English Dictionary, 23

oysters 57, 374, 377, 387

Pacific, 92–96, 145, 349
    buccaneers in, 181
    privateering in, 427

wind map of, 20
    winds of, 337
    see also South Sea (Pacific Ocean)

Pagally(ies), 214, 215, 223, 230n

Paine, Philip, 396

Paita, 170–71

Panama, 33, 46–47, 66, 88, 96, 106n, 107, 168, 171
    defences, 183
    governor of, 109–10
    interest in, 348
    letter of threat to, 154, 178
    Morgan's attack on, 85
    proposed attack on, 105–6
    sacking of, 58
    see also Isthmus of Panama

Panama Bay, 96, 109, 119, 175, 177, 420, 421
    fruits on islands of, 182–83

Papers (Dampier), 187, 254, 294
    on *Cygnet*, 280
    lost, 398
    preserving, 33, 126, 257–58, 313

Papua, 388

Paradise Lost (Milton), 347n

Parrots, 31, 79, 201, 377, 386

Passanjan River, 264

Paterson, William, 317–21, 324

Pearl Islands, 177, 178, 179, 180

Pembroke, earl of, 412

Penguins, 153–54, 170, 201

Penn, Admiral William, 46

Penton, John, 396

Pepys, Samuel, 324, 348

Periagos, 76, 90, 184, 223, 225

Peru, 93, 145, 167, 187

Peru Current, 335

Peruvian silver, galleons with, 177

Pescadores Islands, 235–36

Petit-Goave, 180

Petrels, 369

Phenomena, unusual, 346, 456

Philippines, 209, 210, 211, 227, 239

Philosophical Transactions, 20, 327, 330, 331

Phlebotomy, 52, 136

Pickering, Captain, 418

Pieces of eight, 111, 127, 154, 185, 444
    captured by buccaneers, 109, 110

Pilot-books, 175, 197
Pinas, Don Diego de, 176, 177–78
Piracy, 74, 147, 310–12, 313, 316, 319
    Dampier and, 16, 313, 405
    Kidd guilty of, 403
Pirates, 58, 266, 359, 385, 441
    in Jamaica, 58
    pardon offered to, 316
    raids on Virginia, 143
Pirre River, 32
Pizarro, Francisco, 153
Plain sailing, 276
Plankton, 435
Plantain, 133, 218f, 219–20, 238, 346, 389
Plants, 21, 398, 453
    classification of, 409–10
    Dampier gathered, 36
    medicinal, 407–9
    specimens, 408–9
    studying, 407
Plinius, 453
Plukenet, Leonard, 410
Plunder, 312, 444
    fights about division of, 439
Poison blow dart, 23, 137
Poisons, 225–26, 230
Port Royal, 46–50, 49f, 56, 65, 82, 85, 91
    destruction of, 310
    women purchased at, 67
Portobello, 88, 89–91, 92, 177, 183
Portuguese, 147, 287–88
    settlements in Timor, 383, 386, 387
Potomac River, 141
Potosi, 88
Powhatan Indians, 142
Price, William, 416
Prickly pears, 134, 186, 346
Principia Mathematica (Newton), 330–31
Prisoners, 204, 209, 253, 256, 439
    exchange of, 178
    information from, 183
Privateering
    in Pacific, 427
Privateering expedition, 427–46
Privateering voyages
    code of conduct, 114–15
    Dampier, 415–26

Privateers, 130, 179–80, 360
    Dampier with, 73–75
Proas, 207–8, 208f, 242, 253, 265, 386, 443
Prose romances, 327
Protestant Huguenots, 305
Provisions, 168, 186, 209, 259, 444
    bartering for, 237, 245
    buying, 211, 258
    held in common, 124
    need for/lack of, 111, 129, 186, 197–98, 203–4, 205
Public Record Office, 26
Publications, new, 327–28
Publishing explosion, 327–28
Pueblo Nuevo, 110, 185
Pulling, Captain John, 416
Pulo Condore group (Con Son group), 228–29, 231, 256
Pulo Way (Weh Island), 263
Puna, 423, 424, 435, 437
Punishment, 213
    system of, 145, 281–82, 356, 435
    Tonquinese, 272–73
Purcell, Henry, 328
Puritans, 46, 48, 50

Quam, 33, 129
Quartermaster, authority of, 145
Quedah Merchant (ship), 356

R

Rafts, 171
Rain(s), 121, 122–23, 125, 128, 183, 203, 234, 235, 263, 420–21
    origin of, 338
Rainforest(s), 30, 96, 125
Rainbow (ship), 280
Raja Laut, 211–13, 217–19, 221, 222, 240, 241, 291
Raleigh, Sir Walter, 57n
Rappahannock River, 141
Rationality, 456
Rats, 50, 197, 200, 433, 444
Ray, Dr John, 409–10, 409f, 412, 453

Read, John, 224, 225, 231, 232, 241, 243, 251, 253–54, 288
  and Dampier's leaving *Cygnet*, 254–56
Realeja, 163–64, 186, 187
Red Sea, 356, 356n
Religion(s), 166, 389, 456
  Hottentots, 297
  Tonquinese, 271, 278
Reptiles, 21, 364
Responsibility, 457–8
Restoration, 46, 48, 93, 138, 327
Retes, Ynigo Ortes de, 388
Revenge (ship), 144–45
Rice Christians, 279
Ringrose, Basil, 95, 96, 103, 105, 110, 111, 118, 131, 168, 187, 347n, 459
  death of, 191
Roaring Forties, 368
Robin (Moskito Indian), 150
Robinson Crusoe (Defoe), 329–30, 449
Rock, Rex, 42–43
Roebuck (ship), 27, 36, 353, 358–63, 364–65, 368–69, 370–71, 375, 382, 384, 385, 386, 387, 389, 390, 391, 393, 394, 395, 405, 406, 409, 411n, 416, 418, 431, 450
  bell of, 397f, 398n
  book about, 429
  crossed equator, 390
  leaking, 395–97
  lessons of, 425
  loss of, 396–98, 399, 406
  map of voyage of, 366–67f
  repair of, 387
Roebuck expedition, 22, 458
Roebuck Point, 393n
Roffey, Kerrill, 355
Rogers, Woodes, 427–28, 428f, 429–32, 434, 435–46
  book by, 447
  wounded, 441, 442, 444
Romney, earl of, 355
Rooke, Sir George, 393, 404–5
Ross, James Clark, 357
Rover, The (Behn), 327
Rowe, Captain, 316
Royal Navy mission, 349, 350–69, 370–82, 383–94, 395–99
  return to England after, 399–401

Royal Navy, 45, 349
Royal Prince, 45, 393
Royal Society, 18–19, 36, 144, 324, 327, 340, 346, 368, 389, 391, 393, 399
  and Dampier, 322, 325, 326, 330–31, 459
  marine work, 330, 331
  museum of rarities, 308
  published account of work of, 327
  Woodward expelled from, 407
Ruiz, Bartolome, 153, 171
Running down the latitude, 156

Sago tree, 220
St Elmo's Fire, 23, 234, 346
St George (ship), 416–24, 427, 429, 439, 447, 456
St Helena, 45, 298–99, 395
St Jago de la Vega, 51
St Jago River, 175–76
St John's Island, 232
St Paul's Cathedral, 44, 446
Sal (island), 146
Salem witch trials, 346n
San Blas Islands, 90, 94–95, 96, 130
Santa Clara, 171
Santa Cruz, 358
Santa Maria, 31, 173, 179
  attack on, 96, 99–106, 420
  Dampier's dream of settlement at, 318
  sacking of, 168, 214
Santa Maria River, 129, 173, 180, 181
Santa Pecaque, 190–91
Santa Rosa (ship), 190
Santiago Island, 158
Santissima Trinidad, La (ship), 108, 109
Sawkins, Captain Richard, 92, 96, 107–10, 115
  death of, 110, 185
Schmid, E. E., 452
Schouten, Willem van, 148n
Science, 18
  Dampier's legacy in, 453–54

Scientific exploration, voyages of, 21, 357–58
Scotland, 318
Scots, 71
Scots Company, 318–21
Scots Expedition, 320, 454
Scott, Robert Falcon, 357
Scott, Sir Walter, 449, 450, 452
Scottish colony on isthmus (proposed), 318–21
Scurvy, 111–12, 158, 189, 193, 205, 382, 387, 412, 433
Sea (the)
  Dampier drawn to, 44, 46, 55
  movement of, 338
  work on, 330
Sea level, fluctuations in, 322, 334
Sea lion, 152, 340
Sea serpents, 112, 375, 376
Sea voyages, vogue for, 450
Seafloor, variations in, 334
Seals, 114, 152, 170, 434
Seamanship, Dampier's legacy to, 453–54
Selkirk, Alexander, 24, 419, 420, 421–22, 436, 443, 449
  found in Juan Fernandez Islands, 433–34
  statue of, 434f
Serles, Captain, 66–67
Seventh Son (ship), 310
Sex
  women and, 81
Sexual excess
  Port Royal, 50
Sexual tensions
  logwooders, 67
Shark Bay (Shark's Bay), 35f, 36, 371–75, 376, 383
Sharks, 148, 368, 371, 373–74, 388, 390, 444
Sharp, Bartholomew, 85, 86, 95, 103, 107, 108, 110, 114, 326, 347n, 405
  account of voyage of, 333
  and attack on Santa Maria, 96
  made captain again, 118–19
  deposed, 115
Shearwaters, 369
Sherard, William, 410
Sherardian Herbarium, 410

Ships
  refitting, 92
  sanitary arrangements, 137
  violence on, 402
Shipwreck, 22
  Roebuck, 27, 396–98, 399, 406
  treasure from, 310
'Short Compendium of Rules', 60
Shovell, Admiral Sir Cloudesley, 353, 354, 405, 426n
Shrewsbury, Duke of, 355
Shrubs
  Australia, 377
Silver, 114, 177, 316
  from Potosi, 88–89
Slaves, 48, 119, 126, 127, 148, 171, 173, 243, 288, 291–92, 440
  in Bahia, 364
  killing, 113
  runaway, 74
  in Virginia, 143
Sloane, Hans, 324, 348, 407
Sloths, 68, 438
Smallbone, John, 146
Smith (buccaneer), 211
Snakes, 70, 364, 373
Social practice, 23
Society
  Dampier in, 322–23, 459
  fluidity of, 327
Society of Apothecaries, 408
Sodomy, 67, 115, 401
Somers, Lord, 355, 403
Soren Larsen (brigantine), 30
Soundings, 154
  Roebuck, 369, 371, 374, 376
South America
  coast of, 152–54, 340, 420
  east coast of, 416–19
  Pacific coast, 93
South China Sea, 228
South Keys, 64–65
South Sea (Pacific Ocean), 92–96, 103, 106, 106n, 109, 169f
  expeditions to, 16, 145, 156–57, 158–74, 175–93
  maps of winds in, 349
  privateering voyage to, 430
South Sea Bubble, 454
South Sea Company, 447

Southeast Asia, 23
Southwell, Edward, 415, 417, 424
Southwell, Helen, 424
Southwell, Sir Robert, 325, 415
Southwell family, 417, 459
Sowdon, James, 290, 291, 292, 293
Soy sauce, 23, 275–76
Spain, 415
    ban on foreign trade to
        possessions, 75
    cocoa in, 138
    colonial rule, 457
    economy, 88
    and logwooders, 59–61
    Treaty of Madrid, 58–59
Spanish, 63
    and attack on Santa Maria, 104
    and Australia, 244–45
    and buccaneers, 74–75, 76–77,
        78–79, 112–13, 116–17, 120–21,
        128, 152, 153–54, 163–64,
        167–68, 170, 177, 180, 191, 228
    and buccaneers: in Guam, 204–9
    captured by buccaneers, 228
    Indians living under, 166–67
    treatment of Indians, 73
Spanish barques, 107, 107f, 108
Spanish colonists in South America,
    94
Spanish East Indiaman, 442f
Spanish Expedition, 310–13, 314,
    315
    former comrades from, 353–54,
        356, 364
Spanish fleet(s), 92
Spanish forts, 31, 78, 205
Spanish gold, 17
    Dampier in pursuit of, 427–46
Spanish Main, 17, 46
Spanish pilot-books, 175
Spanish Town, 33, 51, 54–55
Spanish treasure fleet, 88–89, 177,
    178–79, 182
    buccaneers after, 177, 182, 184
    Dampier mission to seize, 415–26
    Spanish treasure galleons/ships,
        46, 145
    Dampier's ambition of seizing,
        446
    Dampier's pursuit of, 427

Species, 409, 453
    differences within, 21
Specimens
    Australia/New Holland, 22, 372,
        375, 377, 381, 382
    bringing back, 357, 363
    loaned to Ray, 409–10
    presented to Woodward, 407, 408
    preserving, 407
    saved in sinking of Roebuck, 398,
        407
Spectator, 448
Spice Islands, 222, 318
Spice trade, 389
Spices, 189, 222, 291, 294, 304
Spider monkeys, 68
Spiders, 70
Spinifex, 375
Spragge, Sir Edward, 45
Sprat, Thomas, 331
Spratlin, Robert, 126–27, 132–36
Springer's Key, 130
Stanley, Henry, 429n
Staten Island, 149
Steele, Richard, 448
Storms, 127, 146, 149, 164, 167,
    233–35, 239, 443
    in East Indies, 261–63
    in Indian Ocean, 368
Stradling, Thomas, 418–19, 420, 421,
    422, 433
Strait of Magellan, 93, 94, 109, 148,
    149, 432
Stubbes, Henry, 138n
Sturmey, Samuel, 278
Sturt pea, 377
Sub-species, 21, 364, 409–10, 453
    concept, 458
Sumatra, 230, 251, 252–53, 256, 257,
    260, 261, 263, 266, 290
    arrival at, 263–64
    open-boat voyage to, 257–64, 343,
        449
Superstition, 284, 297
Surgeons, 91, 112, 190, 224, 267, 439
    loss of, 117
Surgeon's chest, 117n
Surgeon's Mate, The (Woodall), 112
Surgical instruments, 118f
Swallows, 162

Swan, Captain Charles, 150, 152,
168–72, 179–80, 181, 183, 184,
185, 186–87, 191, 240–41, 342, 458
abandoned on Mindanao, 225,
240–41, 280, 288, 341, 355
deposed, 224–25
illness, 187, 188–89
leadership skills, 170
in Mindanao, 211–14, 217–18,
222–25, 288
murdered, 241
plan to go to East Indies, 192
raids, 190
squabbles with Townley, 189
voyage to Guam, 197, 199, 203–5,
208, 209
Swift, Jonathan, 17, 24, 68, 248,
450–51, 450f
Sylvan (Evelyn), 453
Syphilis, 81–82

T

Taboga (island), 178, 179
Taiwan, 235
Tamarinds, 295
Tasman, Abel, 244, 252n, 351
chart by, 370, 376
Tasmania, 244
Tatler, 448
Tattoo, 289
Teat, Josiah, 197, 203, 213–14, 224,
225, 255, 288
Tenerife, 358, 363, 430
Teredo worms, 164f, 165
Terminos Lagoon, 57, 66, 79
Ternate, 443
Terra Australis, 350–52, 357
Thai fish sauce, 23
Thames, 41, 44, 303, 304, 446
Theatres, 309
Third Dutch War, 45
Thryptomene baeckeacea, 373f
Thwaite (captain), 283, 284
Tidal streams, 20, 322
Tide(s), 15, 102, 163–64, 338
cause of, 330–31
Dampier on, 334, 335
high/low, 250–51

rising and falling of, 162
Tide patterns, 251–52, 335
Tierra del Fuego, 148
Time, 227
Timor, 243, 383–88, 412
Tobacco, 142–43, 188, 212, 214
Tobasco River, 61
Tolerance, 456, 457, 461
Tonquin (Tonkin), 267, 268–76, 334
women merchants, 270, 457
Tonquin River, 268
Tonquinese, 270–76
converting to Roman
Catholicism, 279
Tonquinese language, 275
Tonquinese navy, 270–71
Tooth extraction, ritual, 250
Topography, 322, 325
Tories, 356, 403, 404
Tornadoes, 137, 148, 187, 242, 431
Tortoise, 34, 158–59, 160f
Tortuga, 74, 146
Townley, Captain, 179, 180, 183, 185,
186, 187
departed, 190
squabbles with Swan, 189
Trade, 454
British, 454
buccaneers, 237
Chinese, 236
Dampier's views of, 344
Paterson's proposals regarding,
318–19
Trade directory, first, 82n
Trade winds, 20, 199, 335, 368, 399
Travel books, 22–23, 233, 332, 347
Travel writing, 17, 339
new kind of, 448
Treaty of Madrid, 58–59
Treaty of Union, 321
Trial (ship), 245n
Trial Rocks, 245n, 395
Trinity (ship), 109, 110, 114, 116, 118
Trist Island, 66
Tropic of Cancer, 431
Tuira River, 32, 105n
Tula, 443
Tumaco, 176
Turtles, 92, 123, 229, 249, 398, 399,
431, 438, 453

Galapagos, 34
see also Green turtles
Tyler, Richard, 305
Typhoid, 142
Typhoons, 334–35
Typhus, 187

Universe, man's relationship to, 451

Valdivia, 93, 94, 149, 152, 180
Vanbrugh, Carleton, 430–31, 444
Vanbrugh, Sir John, 309
Vanilla, 131, 188
Vaughan, Lord, 324
Venables, General Robert, 46
Venereal disease, 81
Vera Cruz, 78, 79
Vindication (Dampier), 417n
Vinegar plum, 249
Virgil (Dryden), 347n
Virgin Mary, 139, 154, 166, 432
Virginia, 140, 141–44, 258, 330
    map of, 142f
    Wafer's troubles in, 316–17
Vlamingh, Willem de, 375
Volcano, 393
Volcano of Guatemala, 188
Voyage to New Holland, A (Dampier),
    17, 409–10
    first volume published, 411–12
Voyages (Dampier), 85
    accounts of, 17
    Australia, 244–52
    Dampier commanding, 458
    East Indies, 227–43, 252–56
    final, 427–46
    to Guam, 197–209
    Jamaica, 60–65
    Cygnet, 257–67, 268–85, 286–99
    Mindanao, 210–26
    New Holland, 349, 350–69,
        370–82, 383, 384, 395
        old companions on, 458
        privateering, 415–26

South Seas, 144–57
Spanish Expedition, 310–13, 314,
    315
see also Buccaneers, Dampier
    voyages with;
    Circumnavigation of world
    (Dampier)
Voyages and Descriptions (Dampier),
    17, 59, 333–38
    money made from, 347–48
    title page, 333f

Wafer, Lionel, 91–92, 95, 110, 119,
    124n, 128, 145, 167, 202, 348
    book by, 91, 92, 146, 319, 320,
        321, 332, 333, 347
    Dampier reestablished contact
        with, 316–17
    Dampier discussed writing with,
        322
    with Davis, 187
    death of, 321
    injured, 125–26, 126–27
    with Kuna Indians, 132–36, 317
    and Scots Company, 318, 319, 320
Wallis, Daniel, 231
War of the Spanish Succession, 415,
    427
Warren, Robert, 354
Water, 260, 295
    searching for: New Holland, 372,
        374
    shortages of, 45, 64, 117, 368, 438
    see also Fresh water
Waterfowls, 21, 458
Waterspouts, 242
Watling, John, 115, 116–17, 150
Weather patterns, 45
    data on, 322
Welbe, John, 417n, 418, 419, 420,
    421, 422, 423, 424, 425
Welden, Captain, 267, 268, 276, 280
Wentworth, Charles, 43–44
West Indies, 91, 310, 312, 327, 355,
    358
    naval presence in, 312
Whales, 36, 368

Whaley, William, 51, 53–55, 56, 322, 461
Whigs, 355, 355n, 402, 403, 404
Willdampia formosa, 377f
William (Moskito Indian), 24, 116, 150–52, 449
William, King, 287, 355n, 356, 393, 415
Wind(s), 232, 233–34, 261–63, 295, 330
    off Australia, 375
    Dampier on, 334, 335, 336–38, 454
    Dampier observations of, 15
    maps of, 17, 338, 349
    research on, 331
    temperature, 295–96
    types of, 20
    see also Trade winds
Wind patterns, 20, 45
    Dampier charting, 102, 137
Women, 149, 189, 239
    and buccaneers, 75
    Chinese, 232
    in commerce, 270, 457
    Indians, 67, 95–96
    and logwooders, 67
    Mindanaon, 214, 216, 219
    New Guinea, 392
    in plays, 309

Pulo Condore group, 229–30
St. Helena, 298–99
    and sex, 81
    on ships, 440, 457
    Tonquinese, 274
Women's magazine, first, 328
Woodall, John, 112
Wooders, William, 61
Woodward, John, 325, 407–10
Wordsworth, William, 451–52
Works of the Learned, The (magazine), 22, 328, 339, 412
Worms, 70–71, 144, 330
    damage to ships from, 165, 221, 444
Wren, Christopher, 44
Wright, Captain, 131, 136, 139–40
Wycherly, William, 309

Y

Yale, Elihu, 266
York River, 141

Z

Zebra, 296
Zoology, 21

WILFUL MURDER
The Sinking of the Lusitania
Diana Preston

On May 7th, 1915, the *Lusitania*, a passenger ship, was torpedoed by a German U-boat in the Atlantic. 1,200 people died. *Wilful Murder*, the first book to look at this tragedy in its full historical context, is also the first to place the human dimension at its heart. Through first-hand accounts, we relive the splendour of the liner setting sail and the horror of its final moments.

Using British, American and German research material, Diana Preston answers many of the unanswered and controversial questions surrounding the *Lusitania*: why didn't Cunard heed warnings that the ship was a German target? Had Cunard's offices been infiltrated by German agents? What was really in the *Lusitania*'s hold, and was she armed? Did international outrage change the outcome of the First World War?

And perhaps most importantly, was the *Lusitania* sacrificed to bring America into the war? Engrossing and brilliantly researched, *Wilful Murder* casts dramatic new light on one of the world's most famous maritime disasters.

'A complex story of heroism and great courage . . . compulsively readable' *Independent on Sunday*

'It is not easy, nowadays, to write an original book on the First World War . . . but Preston has succeeded' Norman Stone, *Sunday Times*

'Very good . . . Preston has done an extraordinary amount of work, particularly in tracing the memories of survivors' *Sunday Times*

'Sets a standard which other books have not achieved' *Irish Independent*

'Clear and effective . . . benefits from exhaustive research' *TLS*

0 552 99886 9

CORGI BOOKS

Fabulous magazine

'The book is the perfect read for anyone with a passion for love, life and travel.' *Love it!* magazine